Wout Van Praet
**Specificational and Predicative Clauses**

# Topics in English Linguistics

Editors
Susan M. Fitzmaurice
Bernd Kortmann

## Volume 112

Wout Van Praet

# Specificational and Predicative Clauses

A Functional-Cognitive Account

ISBN 978-3-11-153446-6
e-ISBN (PDF) 978-3-11-077199-2
e-ISBN (EPUB) 978-3-11-077205-0
ISSN 1434-3452

**Library of Congress Control Number: 2022934831**

**Bibliographic information published by the Deutsche Nationalbibliothek**
The Deutsche Nationalbibliothek lists this publication in the Deutsche Nationalbibliografie; detailed bibliographic data are available on the Internet at http://dnb.dnb.de.

© 2024 Walter de Gruyter GmbH, Berlin/Boston
This volume is text- and page-identical with the hardback published in 2022.
Cover image: Brian Stablyk/Photographer's Choice RF/Getty Images
Typesetting: Integra Software Services Pvt.

www.degruyter.com

# Acknowledgements

Before we delve into the study of copular clauses, I would like to take the time to thank the people who have given me the intellectual, moral and emotional support to write this book.

First and foremost, I would like to thank my former supervisors, Kristin Davidse and Lieven Vandelanotte. They have been wonderful mentors, who put a great deal of energy, effort and commitment into the project that has led to this book. The final product would not be what it is without their feedback and contributions. I am very grateful for everything they have taught me and for their generous and continuing support.

Many thanks further go out to Elwys de Stefani, Francisco Gonzálvez-García, Karen Lahousse, Laurence Meurant and Jeroen Darquennes, who, as part of my doctoral committee, commented on earlier versions of this book. I would also like to thank Bill McGregor and Eirian Davies, who have been very kind and helpful in giving feedback on my research.

During my research stays in Cardiff and Manchester, Gerard O'Grady and Tine Breban have also been very generous with their time and help. Their willingness to exchange ideas with me has greatly benefited this project. I am particularly grateful to Gerard for introducing me to theories of information structure and prosody.

At the Universities of Namur and Leuven, I had the pleasure of working with great colleagues, many of whom have become more friends than colleagues. Noémie, Caroline, Ngum, Ditte, Myriam, Simon, Ruth, Nathalie, Maria, Vera, Sophie, Florence, Maud, Margaux, Christian, Laurence, Dirk, Elisabeth, Jeroen, Valérie, Norbert, Leonie, Sophie, Alysson, Nadine, An, and Lut. Thank you for all the uplifting advice, distractions and encouragement.

I also owe an enormous amount of gratitude to my friends and family. To my parents, to my sisters Elke and Joke, and to my friends Jolien, Maria Clara, Carolle, Astrid, Michelle, Tobias, Joke, Eveline, Stella, Bram, Lieven, Ellie, Michael, Sven. Thank you for your love and friendship and for reminding me time and again that there are other things in life than copular clauses. Very warm thanks go to Ward, in particular, for being a great best friend. And, of course, I would especially like to thank Gaetano for being as supportive as you have been and for putting up with all the late nights of work and the kitchen-table monologues about linguistic puzzles.

Finally, I would like to thank the editorial team at De Gruyter Mouton and particularly the anonymous reviewer whose comments and feedback pointed my attention to unresolved issues. Their help has improved the book a great deal.

# Abstract

As one of the basic clause types, copular clauses have been discussed in many linguistic studies. Still, they continue to spark much debate, particularly when it comes to distinguishing different subtypes. This book explores two of the more common subtypes, namely predicative and specificational clauses. While most studies agree on the analysis of the first type, the second – specificational clauses – remains a contentious issue. A particular concern is how specificational clauses with indefinite 'variable' NP (e.g. *one of my favourite authors is Virginia Woolf*) compare to, and contrast with, other copular clauses, especially specificational clauses with definite 'variable' NP (e.g. *My favourite author is Virginia Woolf*) and predicative clauses with indefinite predicate nominative (e.g. *Woolf is a great writer*). This book addresses this question by making specificational clauses with indefinite variable the centre of attention, comparing them to the other two clause types. The book consists of two main parts. The first offers a general descriptive analysis of specificational and predicative clauses, in response to the existing literature (Chapter 3). The second part examines the implications of the general functional-structural analysis in the first part for the contextualised use of the different clause types. The book investigates these aspects of use – including lexicogrammatical realization (Chapter 4), the use of aspect and modality (Chapter 5), information structure (Chapter 6), and discourse-embedding (Chapter 7) – by taking a corpus-based approach, examining both written and spoken data. In doing so, it offers an empirical basis for testing some of the widespread assumptions that exist about predicative and specificational clauses.

https://doi.org/10.1515/9783110771992-203

# Contents

**Acknowledgements** —— V

**Abstract** —— VII

**Key to Transcription Conventions** —— XIII

**Chapter 1**
**Introduction** —— 1
1.1 A concise overview of the English copular clause system —— 4
1.2 Theoretical framework —— 13
1.3 Goals of the research and structure of the book —— 18

**Chapter 2**
**Corpus compilation and methodology** —— 21
2.1 Describing the corpora: Wordbanks *Online* and the London-Lund Corpus —— 21
2.1.1 WordbanksOnline: The 'Times' and 'British Spoken' subcorpora —— 22
2.1.2 The London-Lund Corpus of Spoken English —— 22
2.2 Data compilation and coding —— 25
2.2.1 Exhaustive extraction of data from the 'Times' and 'British Spoken' sections of WB —— 25
2.2.2 Non-exhaustive extraction from LLC —— 29
2.3 Frequencies of copular clause types —— 31
2.3.1 Exhaustive extractions of data in the WB subcorpora —— 31
2.3.2 Non-exhaustive extractions of prosodic evidence from the LLC —— 34
2.4 Conclusion: What's in a number? —— 36

**Chapter 3**
**A functional-structural analysis of predicative and specificational clauses** —— 38
3.1 Predicative clauses —— 42
3.1.1 State of the art —— 42
3.1.2 The multi-layered organisation of predicative constructions with an indefinite NP —— 47
3.1.3 The referential status of the indefinite predicate nominative —— 60
3.2 Specificational clauses —— 69
3.2.1 State of the art —— 69
3.2.2 The multi-layered structure of specificational constructions —— 81
3.2.3 The referential status of the variable NP —— 98

3.3 Revisiting the discourse function and information structure of predicative and specificational clauses —— 105
3.3.1 Semantic-pragmatic accounts of information structure —— 106
3.3.2 A functional account of discourse organisation and information structure —— 111
3.4 Conclusion —— 116

**Chapter 4**
**The indefinite NP in predicative and specificational copular clauses —— 119**
4.1 A cognitive-functional model of the English NP —— 122
4.1.1 The head of the NP —— 123
4.1.2 Premodifiers —— 125
4.1.3 Post-head dependents —— 126
4.1.4 Determiners and focus markers —— 128
4.2 Method —— 132
4.2.1 Questions and hypotheses —— 132
4.2.2 Data collection —— 134
4.2.3 Data analysis —— 135
4.3 Results —— 136
4.3.1 The head noun and classifiers —— 136
4.3.2 Pre- and postnominal dependents: Modification and complementation —— 148
4.3.3 Determination —— 160
4.4 Conclusion —— 171

**Chapter 5**
**Aspect and modality in the copular clause —— 173**
5.1 Background —— 175
5.1.1 Aspect —— 175
5.1.2 Modality —— 179
5.2 Case study —— 182
5.2.1 Hypotheses —— 183
5.2.2 Data collection and coding —— 184
5.2.3 Quantitative and qualitative case study —— 186
5.3 Conclusion —— 202

## Chapter 6
**The prosodically coded information structure of specificational and predicative copular clauses —— 205**
- 6.1 Background —— 208
- 6.2 A usage-based study of focus marking —— 216
- 6.2.1 Data collection and data analysis —— 216
- 6.2.2 Results —— 222
- 6.3 The prosodic marking of information focus —— 240
- 6.3.1 Focus marking in predicative and non-reversed specificational clauses of one TU or less —— 240
- 6.3.2 Beyond focus marking: prosodic prominence and discursive organisation —— 247
- 6.3.3 The intonation of reversed specification —— 259
- 6.4 Conclusion —— 264

## Chapter 7
**The discourse embedding of predicative and specificational clauses —— 266**
- 7.1 Background —— 267
- 7.1.1 The discourse status of NPs in specificational and predicative clauses —— 267
- 7.1.2 A multifactorial investigation of discourse status: Identifiability and discourse-familiarity —— 270
- 7.2 Methodology of the corpus studies —— 287
- 7.3 A corpus-based investigation of the discourse-embedding of predicative and specificational clauses —— 287
- 7.3.1 The embedding of predicative vs non-reversed specificational clauses —— 287
- 7.3.2 The embedding of indefinite vs definite variable subjects —— 291
- 7.3.3 The embedding of non-reversed vs reversed specificationals with in definite variable —— 294
- 7.4 Conclusion —— 301

**Conclusion —— 303**

**References —— 311**

**Index —— 325**

# Key to transcription conventions

## Common prosodic marking

| | |
|---|---|
| # | tone unit boundary |
| \ | fall |
| / | rise |
| \/ | fall-rise |
| /\ | rise-fall |
| = | level |

## Additional prosodic annotation in LLC

| | |
|---|---|
| ^ | onset |
| . | brief pause |
| - | unit pause |
| ' | normal stress |
| " | heavy stress |
| : | higher pitch than preceding syllable |
| ! | booster higher than the preceding pitch prominent syllable |
| [ ] | partial words or phonetic symbols |
| * | simultaneous talk |
| (( )) | incomprehensible words |

# Chapter 1
# Introduction

The verb *be* is one of the most functionally diverse words in the English language. This study focuses on one of those functions, namely the use of *be* as a copular verb in 'NP *be* NP' structures.

As Halliday (1985: 123–124) observes, the copular clause system forms a particularly interesting topic for linguistic research, since copular clauses not only "tend to be the most frequent [but also] perhaps the most informative of the primary clause types" (*ib.*). In its use as a copula, the verb *be* shows a great deal of "rather subtle multivalence" (Halliday 1985: 123–24) in that it figures in various copular clause types, each with its own distinct meaning.

Many studies of copular clauses distinguish between two main subtypes, most commonly referred to as 'specificational' and 'predicative' clauses. SPECIFICATIONAL[1] clauses are defined by their semantic function of specifying a VALUE for a VARIABLE (e.g. Higgins 1979; Declerck 1988; Huddleston & Pullum 2002): for instance, in (1) the NP *the most famous Belgian painter* sets up a variable, for which the NP *Rubens* specifies a value that conforms to that variable.

(1) The most famous Belgian painter is Rubens. (Visit Flanders, *The Flemish Masters*, 2016)

PREDICATIVE clauses, on the other hand, have a different meaning: rather than specifying a value for a variable, they DESCRIBE an entity as being an instance of a certain type. Thus, in (2), the entity *Rubens* is described as *a superstar* and *a rich and famous man who ran a successful workshop*. In this book, I will refer to the two semantic roles in the predicative clause as the DESCRIBEE (i.e. the entity being described, e.g. *Rubens*) and the DESCRIPTION that is given of the describee.

---

[1] Throughout this book, I will use small caps to emphasise important concepts for the descriptive analyses. Italics will be used (i) to discuss examples in the text and (ii) to indicate, within an example, which clause is the copular clause if extra context is given (e.g. "He started smoking *when he was a student*"). If the discussion of the copular clause centres on one specific part of the copular clause, that part will be underlined for clarity, e.g. the premodifier in "Rubens was . . . a rich and famous man"). Finally, boldface will be used to give emphasis to part(s) of an example (for instance to mark information focus, e.g. "Rubens was **a superstar**"). When examples from other studies are given, I will cite them as they were presented there. For instance, in example (6b) below, Patten (2016: 81) does not use boldface but small caps to indicate information focus, which I then copied to stick as closely as possible to Patten's own interpretation of the example.

(2) At the time of his death in 1640, Rubens was a superstar, a rich and famous man who ran a successful workshop. (www.visitantwerpen.be/en/wie_was_peter_paul_rubens)

There is general agreement in the literature that the description in the predicative clause is realised by a non-referential expression, in the sense that it does not 'pick out' a person or a thing (e.g. Kuno 1970; Declerck 1988: 56–62, 65–68; Mikkelsen 2005: 65–67). Instead, this non-referential expression is assumed to designate a property, regardless of whether the non-referential expression is an NP, as in (2), an adjective (e.g. *Rubens was successful and proud of it*) or a PP (e.g. *By the end of his life, he was in a bad way because of his chronic gout*). In the first case, this non-referential NP is commonly referred to as the 'predicate nominative', which captures the idea that the NP "predicate[s] some property (characteristic, attribute, quality) of the referent of the subject NP" (Declerck 1988: 3). As Declerck (1988: *ib.*) observes, the same 'property NP' analysis also underlies the use of other terms to refer to predicative clauses, such as *attributive* (Lyons 1968; Halliday 1970a; Gundel 1977), *characterisational* (Kuno & Wongkhomthong 1981), *qualifying* (Mathesius 1975; Quirk et al. 1985), *property-assigning* (Dik 1980) and *ascriptive* (Kahn 1973).

A more contentious issue is the analysis of specificational clause structure, which remains a topic of ongoing debate in both formal and more functional descriptions of copular clauses. Some have argued that specificational clauses are like predicative ones in that they involve one referential NP (i.e. the value) and one non-referential 'property' NP (the variable). Others view specificational and predicative clauses as categorically distinct: on this account, the variable NP is not viewed as denoting a property but, instead, as a referential expression that designates a person or a thing. The disagreement, in other words, is mainly over what is expressed by the variable NP and how this affects the meaning of the specificational clause as a whole. This issue goes to the heart of the question about the symbolic relation between grammar and semantics: does the 'NP *be* NP' sequence have the same meaning in specificational and predicative clauses? If it does, at what level of linguistic analysis (e.g. grammar, pragmatics, information structure, discourse structure) can a difference between the two clause types be discerned? If the clauses do not have the same semantics, how are their different meanings coded by their grammatical structure, and how is this reflected in their formal behaviour?

The focus in existing descriptions of specificational clauses has mainly been on the ones with a definite variable,[2] illustrated in (1). The ones with an indefinite

---

**2** Throughout this book, I will use the terms 'variable' and 'value' to refer both to the semantic functions in the specificational clause and to the expressions that realise these functions. Hence,

variable, e.g. *a real famous Belgian* in (3), have often been overlooked and sometimes even dismissed as impossible (e.g. Geach 1968: 35; Higgins 1976: 138, 1979).

(3) A real famous Belgian was the old master Peter Paul Reubens [sic]. (Wordbanks *Online*, henceforth WB)

Authors who have acknowledged the possibility of indefinite variable NPs have often struggled to accommodate them in their analysis of specificational clauses (e.g. Declerck 1988; Keizer 1992; Mikkelsen 2005; Patten 2012). This has led to attempts to 'explain away' indefinite variable NPs by stressing how they are similar to definite ones or how indefinite NPs can be *coerced* into a 'variable NP' interpretation (e.g. Declerck 1988: 19–21; Mikkelsen 2005: 154; Patten 2012: 37). As I will argue throughout the book, such a perspective on indefinite variables not only ignores the differences in the semantics and pragmatics between definite and indefinite NPs, but it also misses out on the opportunity to make valuable generalisations about the distinct meaning options offered by the specificational clause type.

This book will, therefore, provide an in-depth description of specificational clauses with an indefinite variable, which I will compare and contrast both to the ones with a definite variable and to predicative clauses with an indefinite predicate nominative. This will lead to a better understanding of what exactly the variable NP expresses, what that tells us about the meaning of specificational clauses, and how this meaning compares to the meaning of predicative clauses.

In the remainder of this chapter, I will briefly introduce the topic of specificational clauses with an indefinite variable by giving a concise overview of the copular clause system of which they are part (Section 1.1). Here, I will also pinpoint specific shortcomings of existing descriptions of specificational clauses with indefinite variable in other studies. In Section 1.2, I will then set out the general tenets of the cognitive-functional framework that is applied to the descriptive analyses of the copular clauses in this study. The approach I will take combines elements from Halliday's (1967a,b, 1968, 1985) functional grammar, Langacker's (1987a, 1991) cognitive grammar and McGregor's (1997) semiotic grammar. These approaches endorse the view that language is primarily a system of meanings and that the abstract meanings by which we interpret our experi-

---

while strictly speaking the variable as a semantic function is not itself definite or indefinite, I will use the term as a shorthand for 'the expression realising the variable'. Therefore, what is meant by an '(in)definite variable' is, more accurately, 'an (in)definite NP that functions as a variable'.

ence are represented by the system (i.e., the grammar) in a natural, symbolic way. The notion of a 'natural' grammar implies that language is 'usage-based' (a term coined by Langacker 1987a: 46): linguistic units are abstracted from usage events, i.e. actual instances of language use (e.g. Langacker 2001: 143), so that it is the uses of language that have shaped the system (e.g. Halliday 1994: xiii). From this perspective, this book is committed to describing the grammar of English copular clauses by reference to how they are used. Finally, in the last part of this chapter, I will wrap up the introduction by stating the goals of the research and presenting an outline of the structure of the book (Section 1.3).

## 1.1 A concise overview of the English copular clause system

While specificational clauses with an indefinite variable have received relatively little attention in studies of copular clauses, the 'prototypical' specificational clauses with a definite variable have been a topic of long-standing debate that remains lively to this day (e.g. Higgins 1976, 1979; Akmajian 1979; Declerck 1988; Mikkelsen 2005; den Dikken 2006; Patten 2012, 2016). Most, if not all, authors agree on the general definition of specificational clauses as specifying a value for a variable, e.g. the value *John Thomas* for the variable *the bank robber* in (4). Higgins (1976: 155) further describes the function of specification as similar to enumerating the items on a list: the meaning of the variable can be thought as the heading of a list and the value(s) as listing the items that can be subsumed under this heading (*ib.*).

(4)   The bank robber is John Thomas. (Declerck 1988: 5)

Declerck (1988) paraphrases Higgins' (1976) idea of 'listing' as meaning that every specificational clause can be glossed as "The following values satisfy the variable: value$_1$, value$_2$, etc.", e.g. "The bank robber is: John Thomas" (*ib.*: 5).

As noted in the introductory section, specificational clauses and their relation to predicative ones have been analysed roughly from two perspectives. The first, so-called 'inverse', approach views specificational and predicative clauses as sharing the same "core predicative structure" involving one referential and one non-referential NP (Mikkelsen 2005: 2; see also Williams 1983; Partee 1986a,b; Moro 1997; Adger & Ramchand 2003; den Dikken 2006; Patten 2012). On this account, specificational clauses are analysed as 'inverted' predicative clauses. For some (e.g. Moro 1997; Mikkelsen 2005: 2), this inversion operates on the grammatical level: the non-referential NP serves as complement in predicative clauses but as subject in specificational ones. For instance, when the non-referential 'predicative' NP *the lead actress in that movie* switches its complement function in (5a) for the subject function in (5b), the erstwhile predicative sentence in (5a) becomes a specificational sentence in (5b).

(5) a. Ingrid Bergman is the lead actress in that movie. (Mikkelsen 2005: 1)
    b. The lead actress in that movie is Ingrid Bergman. (*ib.*)

A major problem with this view is that it ignores the fact that specificational clauses can have either the variable – i.e. the so-called 'non-referential' NP – or the value – the 'referential' NP – as subject (Huddleston 1984: 457–58; Halliday 1985: 123). Hence, in answer to the question *Who is the lead actress in that movie?*, both (5a) and (5b) can specify that the value *Ingrid Bergman* satisfies the variable *the lead actress in that movie*. If the difference between predicative and specificational clauses is attributed to the complement vs subject function of the 'non-referential' NP, then such an account fails to acknowledge that (5a) can have both a predicative and a specificational reading.

Another interpretation of the 'inverse' account (e.g. Patten 2012, 2016) is that the difference between predicative and specificational clauses lies not in their 'inverse' subject/complement assignment but in their 'inverse' focus-marking. This analysis has the advantage that it does take into account the fact that specificational clauses allow for a 'subject-complement switch' (Huddleston 1984: 457–458). (To avoid confusion with the term 'inversion', I will hereafter refer to the possibility of a subject-complement switch as 'reversibility'.) On the 'inverse focus' account, the recognition criterion for specificational clauses is not the grammatical function of the 'non-referential' NP. Instead, what matters is that the "specificational reading is brought about if the referent [NP] is focused" (Patten 2012: 35, 2016). Patten (2016: 81) adds that the 'referent' NP (i.e. the NP denoting the value) is always focal when it serves as complement, e.g. *Diane and Carla* in (6a). When the 'referent' NP is subject, however, the clause is ambiguous between a predicative and a specificational reading. In that case, the clause only "acquires a specificational reading", if "the subject is placed in focus" (*ib.*: 80), which she indicates with small caps in (6b).

(6) (Who were the waitresses?)
    a. The waitresses were Diane and Carla. (Patten 2016: 79)
    b. DIANE and CARLA were the waitresses. (*ib.*: 80)

An issue for Patten's 'inverse focus' account, however, is that, while specificational clauses are claimed to inherently focus on the referential (value) NP, predicative clauses can either have (neutral) focus on the non-referential 'property' NP, as in (7a), or (contrastive) focus on the referential NP, as in (7b).

(7) a. John is a surgeon. (Patten 2012: 34)
    b. JOHN is a surgeon. (*ib.*: 35)

If the meaning difference between specification and predication hinges on their information structure, then the question becomes how 'reversed' specificational clauses with a focal value subject, like (6b), can be distinguished from predicative clauses with contrastive focus on the describee, like (7b).

Moreover, both versions of the 'inverse' account have grappled with the occurrence of indefinite variables. While the interpretation of the variable as a non-referential expression naturally allows for indefinite NPs, the problem that the inverse account faces is that some indefinite NPs appear not to be acceptable as a variable (see, for instance, Heycock 2012: 226), e.g. *???A surgeon is John*. Both Mikkelsen (2005: 154) and Patten (2012: 37) suggest that only those indefinite NPs that show certain similarities with definite NPs can be used as a variable in specificational clauses. For Mikkelsen (2005), those similarities have to do with the discourse conditions imposed on the variable. For Patten (2012), the explanation is that the semantics of the variable require an implicature of contextual uniqueness (i.e. only one instance corresponds to the description given by the variable). While such an implicature naturally attaches to definite NPs, indefinite NPs need to be *coerced* into such a reading, which only some indefinite NPs allow for (*ib.*: 37). However, as will be demonstrated in this book, neither analysis succeeds in capturing the full meaning potential and formal behaviour of specificational clauses with an indefinite variable.

The other position in the debate addresses the objections to both versions of the 'inverse' account by viewing specificational and predicative clauses as categorically distinct (e.g. Zaring 1996; Heycock & Kroch 1999; Han & Hedberg 2008; Hedberg & Potter 2010; Heycock 2012). On this so-called 'equative' account, the specificational relation holds between two referential NPs: in other words, the variable NP does not denote a property but picks out a person or thing. This analysis is part of a long tradition treating specificational clauses as providing IDENTIFYING information (e.g. Kuno 1970: 351; Harries-Delisle 1978: 422; Atlas & Levinson 1981; Kuno & Wongkhomthong 1981: 76; Halliday 1982: 68; Huddleston 1984: 187; Declerck 1988: 10; Huddleston & Pullum 2002: 266–269). Huddleston & Pullum (2002: 266), for instance, argue that a specificational clause like *The chief culprit was Kim* "serves to specify, or identify, who the chief culprit was". The idea of specification as a form of identification goes back to Halliday (1967b, 1985: 114–117, 1994: 122–123), who interprets specification as a process with "two functions, resembling the two terms in an equation, where the one serves to identify the other, as in *x* = *2*" (Halliday 1970a: 155).³ This approach is motivated by the observation that specificational clauses can 'reverse', i.e. they allow for either the variable/identified or the value/identifier to become subject of the clause (Huddleston 1984: 457–458; Halliday 1985: 123; Huddleston & Pullum 2002: 268; Heycock 2012: 221).⁴ This is illustrated by the felicity of using (4') as an alternate for (4).

(4')   (Who is the bank robber?) John Thomas / he is the bank robber.

Such a 'subject-complement switch' is not acceptable for predicative clauses (Huddleston 1984: 457; Halliday 1994: 133), in which the NP providing the description always serves as complement of the clause: in predicative clauses, it is only the word order of the clause that can be altered, not the subject-complement assignment. In the two verses from the nursery rhyme in (8a,b), for instance, the pronoun *he* referring back to *Old King Cole* takes the nominative in both predicative clauses, signalling that the subject is constant.⁵

(8)   a.   Old King Cole $_{(subject)}$ was a merry old soul $_{(complement)}$,
       b.   And a merry old soul $_{(complement)}$ was he $_{(subject)}$ / *him.

Declerck (1988) explicitly links the reversibility of specificational clauses, contrasting with the non-reversibility of predicative clauses, to the semantics of identification: "since the referents of the two expressions [in the first type] are identified with each other, it does not really matter which expression is placed first" (*ib.*: 40).

The analysis of specificational clauses as inherently identifying or 'equative' is, however, problematic for a number of reasons. First, if we start from the basic

---

**3** The same interpretation of specification as a form of identification, or equation, is also found in the use of the terms 'equative' (Huddleston 1971; Kahn 1973) or 'equational' (Bolinger 1972b; Harries-Delisle 1978), as Declerck (1988: 2) observes.
**4** Halliday (1967a,b) actually applied the terms 'value' and 'variable' exactly the other way round from how they have come to be used in the literature and how I also present them here. The semantic model that motivated his use of the terms 'value' and 'variable' was semiotics. He therefore called the more abstract term 'value', as in Saussure's 'valeur', and the more concrete entities that can realise it 'variables'. By contrast, the standard use of 'variable' and 'value' is taken from mathematical logic (see, for instance, Akmajian 1970 and Higgins 1979). In this book, I will follow the standard use of the term 'variable' and 'value' to refer respectively to the more abstract vs more concrete entities.
**5** Example (8b) is a predicative clause with fronted complement, which has to be strictly distinguished from a specificational clause (Heycock 2012: 220).

premise that identification is concerned with the identity of the two referents in the clause, an identifying clause can be characterised as expressing that the two referents that are being related in some way "coincide in the same entity" (Dik 1980: 32). This implies that the relation between the two referents must be one of one-to-one correspondence: such a relation can be coded only be a structure in which the copular verb links two definite expressions, to which an implicature of uniqueness attaches (Hawkins 1978: 161, 1991). Specificational clauses with an indefinite variable, by contrast, cannot be interpreted as setting up a one-to-one correspondence. Indefinite NPs do not exclude that there are other instances of the relevant type specifications in the context besides the one denoted by the NP (Hawkins 1978: 184–186). In other words, they do not imply reference to a contextually unique instance. Therefore, specificational clauses with indefinite variable cannot set up a one-to-one correspondence and, in that sense, cannot be identifying (contra Huddleston 1984: 187; Declerck 1988: 21; Halliday & Matthiessen 2004: 235). Since specificational clauses with indefinite variable are also reversible, reversibility cannot be a recognition criterion of identifying semantics, e.g. (9a,b).

(9) a. Nia gazed out toward the field, hoping to catch a glimpse of Cephan. There were some dark-haired young mermyds [sic] at the far end of the field, but she couldn't be sure *one of them was him*. (WB)
   b. ... but she couldn't be sure *he was one of them*.

In fact, the awkwardness of interpreting specificational clauses with indefinite variable as identifying is reflected in Huddleston's (1984: 187) own analysis. He claims, for instance, that the sentence *One thing we don't want is more taxes* "identifies the one thing we don't want" (*ib.*). By reformulating the indefinite NP *one thing we don't want* explicitly as a definite NP, he appears to gloss over the non-uniqueness implicature that attaches to indefinite NPs. The NP *one thing we don't want* quantifies 'one' instance of 'things we don't want', but it does not identify this instance as contextually unique (i.e. as the 'only' instance of its type in the current discourse context). This leaves open the possibility that other items than *more taxes* may correspond as values for the same variable. The NP *more taxes*, therefore, specifies 'one' value for that variable, but it does not identify '*the* one (and only) thing we don't want'. To appreciate the full meaning potential of specificational clauses, the actually coded meaning of the indefinite variable NP cannot be disregarded and needs to be taken seriously for the description of specificational structure and semantics.

Second, the analysis of specification as a form of 'equation' ignores the meaning difference between specificational clauses and so-called (TRUE) 'EQUATIVE' clauses, or 'IDENTITY STATEMENTS' (e.g. Wiggins 1965: 42; Kripke 1971;

Higgins 1976: 166; Declerck 1988: 110–112; Mikkelsen 2005; Heycock 2012), e.g. the well-known example in (10) and the contextualised one in (11).

(10) The Morning Star is the Evening Star.[6]

(11) *Australia is not America*. The nation that calls itself 'the lucky country' might have shared with the USA a relative sense of peacetime security, with no history of the London Blitz or the IRA, but it does not share America's economic stature, political clout or military might. (WB)

Identity statements, or equatives, are taken to express 'true' identity, in that the expressions that are equated identify their referent independently of each other (Wiggins 1965: 42; Declerck 1988: 111). By equating these referents – e.g. 'the Morning Star' and 'the Evening Star' – identity statements express that the descriptions that are being equated refer to one and the same individual – e.g. the planet Venus in (10). This can be paraphrased as follows: the object referred to as *a* is 'the same as' (or 'identical with') the object referred to as *b* (Declerck 1988: 110). The identity statement can be glossed as '$a = b$' or '$b = a$'. Alternatively, a negative equative can express that two referents cannot be equated as being the same individual, e.g. (11).

Such a relation of 'true identity' is not found in specificational clauses. As will be argued in this book (specifically in Chapter 3), the referents of the variable and the value are not of the same degree of abstraction and, hence, cannot be equated with each other in the way that the referents of an identity statement can be equated. The same argument underlies Higgins' (1976, 1979) 'list' analogy, in which the variable is interpreted as the heading of a list that "delimits a domain" and the value picks out "a particular member of that domain" (1976: 132). However, the value does not thereby identify the variable: "the heading of a list [i.e. the variable] does not refer to any item at all, nor does the set of items in the list itself say anything about the heading of the list" (*ib.*). For this reason, "the specificational reading of a copular sentence is not the expression of some kind of identity" (*ib.*: 133). In (12), the variable *the essential issue* establishes reference to an issue, not to the actual individuals (*the people of Haiti*) referred to by the value NP, nor to something metonymically associated with them (e.g. 'their plight', 'their well-being'). As Halliday (1994: 228) argues, the entities referred to by the variable and value NPs are of a different order of abstract; while the former

---

[6] The example in (10) is one of the 'puzzles' presented by Frege (1892) and is translated from the German example *Der Morgenstern ist der Abendstern*.

(e.g. *the essential issue*) is realised by the latter (e.g. *the people of Haiti*), they do not refer to the same entity. This is evidenced, for instance, by the fact that asking 'who or what the essential issue is' is different from asking 'who or what the people of Haiti are' or 'what their plight is'. This argument will be developed in further detail in Chapter 3.

(12)   Kofi Annan appealed Tuesday for a long-term international commitment to Haiti, saying the effort to stabilize the country could take years. [. . .] *The essential issue is the people of Haiti.* (WB)

Declerck (1988: 3) makes a similar case when he draws a distinction between identification by equation and identification by specification: only the first type "state[s] a relation of identity between two entities", while the second type "reveals the identity of some entity" (*ib.*). In other words, to use Higgins' (1976: 132) list analogy, the value is taken to 'identify' an item that can be listed under the variable rather than the variable itself. However, the meaning proposed by Declerck for SPECIFICATIONALLY-IDENTIFYING clauses does not cover all examples of specificational clauses. In (13), the value *somebody who knows the victim* specifies what (sort of) person is likely to satisfy the variable, but it by no means identifies a specific instance.

(13)   It's a fact with homicide that most often *the murderer is somebody who knows the victim.* (WB)

While I agree with Higgins and Declerck that specification cannot be conflated with identification, I also note that neither offers a fully-fledged semantics-pragmatics of specificational clauses covering all subtypes.

Third, and finally, while the reversibility of specificational clauses and of equative clauses has been advanced as a central argument for both having identifying semantics (e.g. Heycock 2012: 226), not all clauses with identifying semantics are reversible. Higgins (1976), for instance, distinguishes 'IDENTIFICATIONAL' clauses like (14a)-(16a) from both specificational and equative clauses and shows that these clauses cannot reverse, as shown by the infelicity of (14b)-(16b).

(14)   a.   That is Boston. (Higgins 1976: 148)
       b.   *Boston is that. (*ib.*: 149)

(15)   a.   This is the house I mentioned. (*ib.*: 148)
       b.   *The house I mentioned is this. (*ib.*: 149)

(16) a. That man is Joe Smith. (*ib.*: 148)
 b. *Joe Smith is that man. (*ib.*: 149)

Identificational clauses have 'deictic' subjects – either a demonstrative pronoun, as in (14a) and (15a), or an NP determined by a demonstrative, as in (16a) – which establish exophoric reference to an entity in the situational context (Halliday & Hasan 1976: 33). Higgins (1976: 137) takes this to imply that the hearer has minimal acquaintance with the referent of the deictic expression: s/he does not have any knowledge about the entity "but merely a hic et nunc confrontation". The purpose of identificational clauses is, then, to 'identify' the entity by linking it to a name – e.g. *Boston, Joe Smith* – or a description – e.g. *the house I mentioned* – which the hearer is fully, or at least more, acquainted with.

Declerck (1988: 95) subsumes Higgins' identificational clauses into a more broadly conceived non-reversible copular clause type, which he calls 'DESCRIPTIONALLY-IDENTIFYING'. These clauses seem to differ only from Higgins's (1976) 'identificational' type in that the subject of a 'descriptionally-identifying' clause need not be realised by a deictic phrase but can also be a name or a personal pronoun, e.g. (17a,b).

(17) a. Mike? Who's Mike? – Mike is my brother. (Declerck 1988: 95)
 b. Mike? Who's Mike? – He is my brother.

Like Higgins (1976), Declerck (1988: 105) interprets the referring expressions used as subject in terms of the "hic et nunc acquaintance" that the speaker and hearer have with the entity being referred to: "the hearer can pick out the person in question from a group that is being shown to him but he may [be] unable to recognize the person as somebody he knows, i.e. of whom he has a 'backing of descriptions'[7]" (Declerck 1988: 96). The NP that provides such a 'backing of descriptions' and thereby 'identifies' the referent of the name or personal pronoun (e.g. *my brother*) can only be complement (18) but not subject (18') of the descriptionally-identifying clause.

---

[7] Declerck (1988: 95–96) borrows the term 'backing of descriptions' from Strawson (1959: 20), who claims that "it is no good using a name for a particular unless one knows who or what is referred to by the use of the name. A name is worthless without a backing of descriptions which can be produced on demand to explain the application".

(18)   **A.** Hello Jean. – **B.** Hello. – **A.** Yes Jean. – **B.** Er you want erm. You were going to ask me about Sidney. – **A.** Sidney? Who is Sidney? – **B.** *Sidney is my male cat.* (WB)[8]

(18')   Sidney? Who is Sidney – *My male cat is Sidney/him.

Importantly, Declerck (1988: 106) stresses that descriptionally-identifying clauses differ from predicative clauses with a definite predicate nominative, e.g. (19).

(19)   The USA is no longer the all-out supporter of Israel it once was. (WB)

In (19), the subject referent is fully identifiable and familiar to the speaker and hearer. The description given by the predicate nominative, therefore, does not serve to identify the referent but merely to characterise it in some way. While there is merit in the distinction that Declerck (1988) draws between descriptionally-identifying clauses and predicative clauses with definite predicate nominative, the distinction is sometimes hard to make and has been criticised by other authors (e.g. Keizer 1990). Descriptionally-identifying clauses will not be looked at in this book, nor will I include predicative clauses with definite predicate nominative in the case studies. This book focuses on the neglected specificational clause type with indefinite variable and contrasts it with its closest alternate options in the copular clause system, predicative clauses with indefinite predicate nominative and specificational clauses with definite variable NP.

Finally, Declerck (1988: 113–115) observes that there is one other clause type that does not fit the traditional distinction between predicative and specificational clauses, namely DEFINITIONS, e.g. (20).

(20)   A motor car is a vehicle that has four wheels and is propelled by an internal combustion engine. (Declerck 1988: 113)

Definitions share features both with predicative and with specificational clauses. Like predicative clauses, they are not reversible and do not alternate with clefts. That is to say, reversing the sentence in (20) or turning it into a cleft sentence no longer results in a sentence with a definitional meaning (Declerck 1988: 113), e.g. (20') and (20'').

---

[8] The clause in (18) is an attested example from a phone-in conversation on a radioshow, taken from the Wordbanks*Online* (WB) corpus. In the example, Speaker A is the host of the radioshow and Speaker B is a caller, who was probably told by the producers of the show that the host would talk to her about her cat Sidney.

(20')   A vehicle that has four wheels and is propelled by an internal combustion engine is a motor car.

(20'')   ?It is a four-wheeled vehicle with an internal combustion engine that is a motor car. (Declerck 1988: 113)

At the same time, definitions differ from predicative clauses in that they answer an implied question (e.g. *What is a motor car?*), which specificational clauses seem to do as well (Declerck 1988: 114; see also Ross 1972, 2000; Schlenker 2003). However, the question is, in this case, not one that asks for specificational information but for defining information. For that reason, Declerck (1988: 114–115) proposes to treat definitions as a distinct clause type in their own right.

In conclusion to this section, the brief overview of existing descriptions of copular clauses demonstrates that specificational clauses with indefinite variable remain a weak spot in the typology of copular clauses. Accounts that have denied the acceptability of indefinite variables altogether overlook valuable generalisations both for specificational clauses and for the larger copular clause system of which they are part. Analyses that have attempted to explain the meaning and behaviour of indefinite variables have so far not been able to present a fully adequate characterisation of specificational clauses with indefinite variable, as acknowledged by some of the authors themselves (e.g. Mikkelsen 2005: 159). The study in this book will therefore focus on specificational clauses with an indefinite variable, and their place in the copular clause system, to come to a better understanding of these clauses as a meaningful construction in its own right.

## 1.2 Theoretical framework

This study approaches the topic of specificational copular clauses from a cognitive-functional perspective. More specifically, this study inserts itself in the cognitive-functional approaches that assume a natural relation between semantics and lexicogrammar (Hjelmslev 1961; Bolinger 1968: 196; Halliday 1985, 1994; Langacker 1987a, 1991; Wierzbicka 1988; McGregor 1997; Davidse 1999). The lexicogrammar is understood here as the structured system of regular patterns in language, in which form and function are inseparably connected as aspects of the 'sign' or symbolic unit (McGregor 1997: 1; see also Langacker 1987a: 57, 2017a). The idea of a 'natural', non-arbitrary grammar is opposed to the formal approach in which syntax, or grammar, is seen as autonomous from semantics and concerned only with form, not with meaning. Against this, cognitive and functional approaches view language as essentially a tool for expressing meaning (Wierzbicka 1988: 1): the lexicogrammar exists to code semantic functions and, hence, bears a symbolic relation to semantics (Langacker 1995: 2–3).

This type of cognitive-functional analysis can be underpinned by Hjelmslev's (1961[1943]) semiotics. Hjelmslev (1961) elaborated the Saussurian view of the linguistic sign as a pairing of expression and content by analysing both the expression-side and the content-side as consisting of three strata, *viz.* form – substance – purport. The essence of the linguistic sign is the interaction between expression-form (phonological organisation) and content-form (lexicogrammatical organisation), which together form the abstract, or *schematic*, linguistic system, specific to each language. Substance, secondly, can be defined, in contrast with the form's schematic nature, as specific *usage*. Content-substance consists of the contextually grounded instances of use of lexicogrammatical schemata, while entities of expression-substance are viewed by Hjelmslev as the *hic-et-nunc* manifestation of schematic expression-form. For instance, a unique pronunciation [r] is a manifestation of the phoneme /r/ in a specific context of use and is classified under /r/ with various "other possible pronunciations, by other persons or on other occasions, of the same sign" (Hjelmslev 1961: 57). Purport, finally, lies outside the sign function. It is characterised, on the content plane, as "amorphous [unformed] thought-mass" (Taverniers 2008: 376) and, on the expression plane, as an "amorphous, unanalysed sequence of sounds" (*ib.*: 378). Content-purport, in other words, is non-linguistic experience that is *formed* into 'content-substance' (i.e. 'usage-based semantics', or contextual meaning) specific to each language by that language's 'content-form' (i.e. its lexicogrammatical system). Expression-purport results from the infinity of phonetico-physiological possibilities (Davidse & Ghesquière 2016: 87), within which each language lays down its phonemes and phonotactics (expression-form), as derived via abstraction from actual phonetic usage (expression-substance). Because of the interactions between purport, substance and form, the linguistic system (form) cannot be considered autonomous or self-contained, as it is fundamentally usage-based (McGregor 1997: 3). Accordingly, descriptive analyses of linguistic phenomena must be grounded in observations from empirical data, which are to be characterised as accurately as possible based on the evidence from usage.

The interaction between the abstract system ('form') and usage ('substance') plays a fundamental role in both cognitive and functional approaches – notably in Halliday's Systemic Functional Grammar (SFG) and Langacker's Cognitive Grammar (CG). On the one hand, the lexicogrammatical system is derived through a process of abstraction (schematisation) and categorisation from specific 'usage events' (Langacker 1987a: 66) or actual 'instantiations' of language (Halliday 1992: 20; Langacker 1999: 99). The grammar is, therefore, shaped by usage. On the other hand, the system sanctions usage. The grammar allows speakers to verbalise experience into meaning. At the same time, the grammar, as the meaning potential of a language, "circumscribes in terms of objective possibilities and restrictions the semantics of that language" (Davidse 1999: 4). The lexicogrammatical choices that a speaker makes always impose a certain 'construal' on our experience (Langacker 1991: 294; Halliday & Matthiessen 1999: 1). This is because each difference in lexicogrammatical form involves a difference in meaning (Wierzbicka 1987: 24). Hence, while examples like *he's a teacher* and *he teaches* capture a generally similar idea, the different grammatical structures that they instantiate construe the experience in different ways. This is also reflected in the notion of the 'coding gap' (Davidse 1999: 3–4). If two languages differ with regard to a certain lexicogrammatical pattern, then the meanings coded by those patterns are also different. For instance, in Dutch, one could say *ik ben jarig*, which would translate to *it's my birthday* in English or *ich habe Geburtstag* in German. All three expressions capture the same 'thought', or purport, but the ways in which the purport is 'worded' in the three languages do not 'mean' exactly the same.

The term 'lexicogrammar', used in SFG and CG, captures the idea that there is no sharp distinction between lexis and grammar. Instead, lexis and grammar, but also morphology, form part of a continuum, or cline, consisting in flexible assemblies of symbolic units (or form-meaning pairings) that are schematised to varying degrees (Langacker 1986: 2, 2015; Halliday 1961: 267). The lexis is located at the 'more delicate', or 'less schematic', end of the cline, while grammatical patterns range from less to more schematic. Therefore, though lexis and grammar differ along certain parameters (e.g. the level of precision and detail and the degree of complexity of the structures they attend to), it would be arbitrary to divide them into separate components (Langacker 1987a: 3, 2001: 8–9; Wierzbicka 1988: 1–2). Moreover, since the lexicogrammar is usage-based, CG and SFG also deny a rigid distinction between 'semantics' and 'pragmatics' (Langacker 1987a: 154, 1997: 234–235; Halliday & Matthiessen 1999: 12). While meaning at the system level involves decontextualisation by virtue of being abstracted from usage events, at least some pragmatic, contextual meanings are retained in the system. In this book, I will use the term 'semantics' to refer to meanings that are explicitly coded by the grammar; the term 'pragmatics' will be used to talk about linguistically triggered but non-coded meanings, e.g. conversational implicatures. In making this difference, I do not mean to say that the distinction between semantics and pragmatics is absolute or of an entirely different nature. Evidence for this is the fact that 'pragmatic' (i.e. linguistically triggered but non-coded) meanings can become 'semantic' (i.e. actually coded) when they occur sufficiently frequently with an expression that they become conventionalised.

There are, of course, also areas where CG and SFG differ, for instance in their perspectives on 'meaning'. CG interprets meaning as conceptualisation, that is, as a cognitive process.⁹ More specifically, meaning, or semantic structure, is conceptual structure that is shaped for symbolic purposes according to the options and restrictions of the grammatical system (Langacker 1987a: 98). In Hallidayan SFL, on the other hand, meaning is understood essentially as "a social, intersubjective process" (Halliday & Matthiessen 1999: 2), placing the emphasis outside the mind of individual language users. From the social perspective, meaning "becomes an act of collaboration, sometimes of conflict, and always of negotiation" (Halliday & Matthiessen 1999: 2). But despite the different emphases that the two approaches place, their accounts of language and meaning are, to a very large extent, compatible and often complementary.¹⁰ Halliday (1978: 38–39) himself does not rule out a cognitive perspective towards language and meaning, but he simply states "that it is not a necessary one for the exploration of language". Langacker (1997) takes a stronger position and states that both the cognitive and the cultural perspectives are necessary to account for language: hence, "despite its mental focus, cognitive linguistics can also be described as social, cultural, and contextual linguistics" (*ib.*: 240). This goes back to the usage-based stance, adopted in CG: the mental processing "constitutive of language has to be studied and described with reference to the social and contextual interaction of actual language use" (*ib.*: 248). It is this position that is also advocated by the kind of cognitive-functional approach that I assume here.

But what is more, the two approaches do not only differ in their perspectives on meaning; they also give different interpretations to the place of 'semantics' in the linguistic system. In Langacker's CG, the term 'semantics' is used to refer to what Hjelmslev (1961) describes as the content-side of the linguistic sign (which excludes 'purport'), either at the system level or at the usage level. Likewise, Halliday's SFG also recognises a 'formal' semantics (in the Hjelmslevian sense) and a 'contextual' one. But whereas CG takes it that symbolic units at the system level (i.e. in the grammar) consists of a semantic pole and a phonological one, SFG does not consider semantics and phonology to be *components* of grammatical units (i.e. categories or items). Instead, the lexicogrammar is interpreted as a 'stratum' of the linguistic system that is in between the semantic stratum and the phonologi-

---

**9** Langacker's (e.g. 1986: 2) statement that Cognitive Grammar "equat[es] meaning with conceptualization (or cognitive processing" cannot be taken to mean that he draws no distinction between linguistic and non-linguistic meaning. Instead, Langacker (1987a: 97–98) uses the term 'conceptual structure' as covering both non-linguistic and linguistic conceptualisation, but he reserves the term 'semantic structure' for the latter, i.e. "conceptual structure that functions as the semantic pole of a linguistic expression" (*ib.*: 98).
**10** This is recognised by an increasing number of authors (e.g. Davidse 1999; Nuyts 2008; Gonzálvez García & Butler 2006; Butler 2013).

cal one. The different strata are linked via the semiotic process of realisation: the semantic stratum is realised by the grammatical stratum, which in turn is realised by the phonological stratum. In that sense, semantics relates to grammar as a more abstract level of content that is encoded, or symbolised, by the grammar (or, rather, by the realisation of the grammar by phonology).[11] Hence, as Davidse (1999) points out, "the grammatical category 'means' the semantic category, because the former stands in a realization relation to the latter" (*ib.*: 2), not because the former 'includes' the latter. Hence, as Halliday (1994: xxvi) notes, "the only way of referring to the category is by the category itself: *the* means 'the'." The grammar, in other words, is purely abstract code, which can be looked at either through the semantic meaning it realises or through the phonological form by which it is realised (Davidse 1999: 6). Ultimately, however, both CG and SFG agree that the lexicogrammar forms the symbolic association between semantics and phonology, even if they explain the workings of the symbolic association differently.

On Halliday's interpretation of language as usage-based, the 'external' functions for which language is put to use are reflected in the meta-functional diversification of the linguistic system (see also Davidse 1999: 7). The three meta-functions that Halliday (e.g. 1970b, 1985) distinguishes are the 'ideational', the 'interpersonal' and the 'textual'.[12] The *ideational* dimension "provides a conceptual framework for the encoding of experience in terms of processes, objects, persons, qualities, states, abstractions and relations" (Halliday 1968b: 209).[13] The ideational dimension can therefore be referred to alternatively as the *representational* dimension. The *interpersonal* dimension is concerned with the speaker assuming a role in the speech event, in relation to the representation as well as to the hearer with whom s/he interacts. Finally, the *textual*, or discursive, dimension has to do with how what is said is structured as a piece of communication, and how it is made relevant in the co- and context (Halliday 1968: 210).

---

**11** A detailed description of the conception of 'semantics', which has been interpreted in multiple ways in SFG, would be beyond the scope of this study. For a very good, insightful overview I refer the reader to Taverniers (2011, 2019), who provides an overview of the different kinds of 'semantics' that are distinguished in SFG and how they relate to Hjelmslev's (1961) semiotic model of language.
**12** Strictly speaking, only the 'ideational' and the 'interpersonal' meta-functions reflect the external functions of language, since the 'textual' meta-function is a purely linguistic dimension.
**13** Following Laffut & Davidse (2002), I approach process-participant relations with a cognitive-functional model indebted to both Halliday (1970b, 1985) and Langacker (1987a, 2015). I model process-participant relations as involving dependency, viz. complementation structures (Langacker 1987a), thus obliterating Halliday's (1985) distinction between particular 'experiential' constituent structures and logical 'dependency' structures.

It is with these general theoretical tenets that I will approach the study of specificational clauses with indefinite vs definite variable and of predicative clauses. In the title of the book, I describe this approach as 'functional-cognitive': this reflects the fact that, in many aspects, the study takes Halliday's (e.g. 1967b, 1994) account of copular (or 'relational') clauses as a starting point but develops it further by combining insights from both functional and cognitive linguistics. I take it that, despite their differences, these two approaches are generally compatible, thereby subscribing to the position taking by a growing group of 'functional-cognitive', or 'cognitive-functional', scholars (e.g. Davidse e.g. 1999; Heyvaert 2003; Taverniers 2005; Nuyts 2008; Butler 2013; Davidse & Breban 2019).

Given its usage-based focus, the research will be grounded in examinations of actually attested patterns of use, as found in evidence from corpus examples as well as from 'diathesis alternations' (e.g. Levin 1993; Davidse 1998a, 2011; Perek 2012, 2016). Such alternations "probe for linguistically pertinent [. . .] meaning" (Levin 1993: 1) and allow us to draw up linguistically-based, rather than intuition-based, descriptions and generalisations. Based on the evidence from attested examples, a functional-structural analysis of copular clause types will be presented by abstracting schematic coding structures from their instantiating expressions: for instance, the structural alternations that the clause types allow for in usage can serve as evidence for the process-participant configurations of these clause types, implying different valency relations (Davidse 1998a). The structural description of the copular clause types will be further elucidated in a number of corpus studies, by looking at the specific realisations of the copular constructions and their substructures (e.g. the lexicogrammatical realisation of the NPs and the VP, the prosodic realisation of the copular clauses, the discourse-familiarity of the NPs).

The theoretical principles formulated in this section feed into the research questions that this book will address. These will be laid out in the final section of this chapter (Section 1.3), in which I formulate the goals of the research and describe the structure of the book.

## 1.3 Goals of the research and structure of the book

The aim of this book is to provide a comprehensive account of English specificational copular clauses with an indefinite variable that accurately describes their semantics and pragmatics. By focusing on these clauses in particular, this study addresses specific issues in studies of copular clauses, which have struggled with the acceptability of indefinite NPs as a variable. Not only does the failure to take into account indefinite variables leave a gap in the literature, but it also points to descriptive inaccuracies in the existing characterisations of other related clause types, notably specificational clauses with a definite variable and predicative clauses with an indefinite NP complement. It is necessary, therefore, to compare and contrast these three clause types, both in terms of their lexicogrammatically coded semantics and their implementation in specific contexts of use (including their discourse-embedding, their intonation, etc.).

Based on the discussions in previous studies (see Section 1.1) and on the theoretical tenets of the cognitive-functional framework (Section 1.2), I formulate the following research questions. First, do specificational clauses have the same process-participant configurations (i.e. the same schematic representational meaning) as predicative clauses, and how are these similarities or differences coded structurally? Secondly, what is the referential status of the variable, especially when realised by an indefinite NP? Thirdly, how are specificational and predicative clauses realised prosodically and what does this tell us about the information structure of the two clause types? Following from that question: is information structure a defining aspect of the meaning of specificational clauses (e.g. Lambrecht 2001; Lehmann 2008; Patten 2012, 2016)? Finally, is it essential to the meaning of specificational clauses that the variable expresses 'given' or familiar information in specific contexts of use (e.g. Declerck 1988; Mikkelsen 2005)? Are there differences between indefinite and definite variables in terms of discourse-familiarity?

The structure of the book will follow the order of these research questions. In CHAPTER 2, I will first present an overview of how the sets of corpus data on which the analyses in this book are based were compiled. By also reporting on the distribution of the copular clause types in the datasets, I will provide an initial indication of how specificational clauses with an indefinite variable compare quantitatively to the other clause types.

In CHAPTER 3, I will then set out the functional-structural analysis, which forms the cornerstone of the book. The account developed counters those approaches that view specification as the 'inverse' of the predication relation. I come in on this debate from a well-defined angle by focusing on predicative clauses with indefinite predicate nominative and specificational clauses with indefinite variable. Predicative clauses with indefinite predicate nominative are viewed as prototypically "exhibiting a relation of class inclusion" (Patten 2016: 77), which makes them the logical starting point to consider the question whether their inversion yields a specificational interpretation. The analysis will focus on the lexicogrammatically coded semantics of the two clause types, which I discuss in terms of their different process-participant configurations and the possible grammatical (subject-complement) relations that these configurations allow for. The different *participant* statuses of the NPs in these lexicogrammatical structures will be argued to correlate with different *referential* statuses. Finally, I will show that discursive functions that have been attributed in existing studies to predicative and specificational clauses, relating mainly to information focus, have to be kept separate from the process-participant and subject-complement patterns described in this chapter. The descriptive analyses set out in Chapter 3 form the basis for the dedicated corpus studies in the rest of the book.

CHAPTER 4 continues the focus of Chapter 3 on the contrast between predicative clauses with indefinite predicate nominative and specificational clauses with indefinite variable NP. It will home in on the NPs realising the indefinite predicate nominative and indefinite variable. By studying differences in (i) head nouns, (ii) pre- and postmodifiers and (iii) determiners and quantifiers of these two NPs, the corpus study in this chapter will demonstrate that the different semantic roles of the NPs influence the lexicogrammatical realisation of these NPs. This will be advanced as evidence for the semantic contrast between predicative and specificational clauses and for the meaningfulness of the indefinite variable NP as a contrastive option to the definite variable NP, motivated by the non-uniqueness implicature of the indefinite NP. CHAPTER 5 will then examine how the semantics of the specificational and predicative processes, and the discursive functions that these clauses can serve, correlate with the use of aspect and modality in specific contexts of use.

CHAPTER 6 will concentrate on the prosodically coded information structure of specificational and predicative clauses. As noted in Chapter 3, many pre-empirical assumptions have been made about the nature and the importance of focus marking to distinguish between these two clause types. By looking closely at the specific prosodic realisations of the specificational and predicative structures, I will examine to what extent these assumptions hold up and how the role of intonation, specifically focus, in the copular clauses is to be interpreted. Closely related to this is the discourse-embedding of the clauses, which forms the topic of CHAPTER 7: here, the focus will be on the discourse-familiarity of the variable and the value in specificational clauses, and the 'describee' (the entity being described) and the description given of it in predicative clauses. The aim here is to examine the hypothesis formulated in previous studies (e.g. Declerck 1988; Mikkelsen 2005) that it is a necessary condition for the variable to express 'given' information. The failure to do so has been put forward as a motivation for why (certain) indefinite NPs cannot serve as variable. The validity of these claims will be tested by looking at specific corpus examples. This will offer a better understanding of the role of discourse status for the acceptability of indefinite variables.

The book will close with some concluding remarks and suggested avenues to be explored in future research.

# Chapter 2
# Corpus compilation and methodology

In accordance with the usage-based focus of the cognitive-functional approach, the analyses in this study are grounded in a detailed investigation of corpus data of specificational clauses with an indefinite variable, specificational clauses with a definite variable, as well as predicative clauses with an indefinite predicate nominative. In this chapter, I will describe how these data were gathered and give an overview of the frequencies of the different clause types in the datasets. This will give a general indication of how the typical and atypical patterns of the copular clause types that will be discussed in the following chapters are to be interpreted in the larger picture of (a part of) the English copular clause system.

In Section 2.1, I will first introduce the two corpora from which the data are taken and provide background information about each. Section 2.2 will be devoted to describing the method of extracting the relevant data from the corpora and the criteria for judging whether extracted examples were relevant for the purpose of this study. Next, Section 2.3 offers a summary of the frequencies of different copular clause types in the different corpora. The chapter will be rounded off with a conclusion in Section 2.4.

## 2.1 Describing the corpora: Wordbanks*Online* and the London-Lund Corpus

To keep the comparison between the datasets consistent, the corpora, or at least the relevant subsections, that were consulted for the corpus studies focus on British English. This is important primarily for the data in studies of prosody in Chapter 6, for which the London-Lund Corpus of Spoken English (LLC) was used: it is known, for instance, that not only pronunciation of individual words but also broader intonation patterns can differ between regional varieties of English. Because the LLC focuses on British English (mostly from well-educated Londoners), the choice was made to also focus the data collected from the other corpus, Wordbanks*Online*, on British English. In the following subsections (2.1.1 and 2.1.2), I will first provide a general introduction to the two corpora, to then explain how the data from each corpus were extracted in Section 2.2.

## 2.1.1 Wordbanks*Online*: The 'Times' and 'British Spoken' subcorpora

Wordbanks*Online* (WB) is an online corpus of English that contains approximately 550 million words, from a wide range of texts from various sources (e.g. newspapers, books, magazines, transcribed spoken data). The corpus compilation spans the period between 1972 and 2005, but the majority of the data (i.e. 70.48%) range between 2001 and 2005. WB covers eight varieties of English: British, American, Australian, Canadian, Indian, South African, Irish and New Zealand English. British and American English, however, represent the bulk of the data, accounting for 46.91% and 34.93% of the corpus respectively.

For the studies in this book, I focused solely on British English to ensure consistency in the variety of English between the different corpus studies: as the prosodic analyses were based on the London-Lund Corpus of Spoken English – which looks at British English spoken by educated Londoners – the decision was made to also examine examples of British English from WB.

To arrive at representative datasets of the different copular types that are studied in the book, I worked with specific subsections of the WB corpus. The first was the 'Times' subcorpus, which focuses on formal written English collected from the newspaper 'The Times' (and its Sunday issue 'The Sunday Times'). The Times corpus comprises a total of roughly 46.7 million words from 240 different documents. The other subcorpus was the 'British Spoken' subsection of WB, which brings together data from the 'British Spoken Corpus: Cobuild' (21.5 million words from 2,661 documents) and the data from 'BBC World Service' (approximately 20 million words from 143 documents). While no added information is given about how the first set of data were compiled, the data from the BBC World Service focus on television and radio programmes, though it is not mentioned whether these spoken data were spontaneous or scripted.

Extracting data from the specific subsections allowed me to collect an – initially large – number of hits necessary to arrive at samples in which the total number of specificational clauses with indefinite variable was sufficiently large to enable reliable statistical analyses in the corpus studies.

## 2.1.2 The London-Lund Corpus of Spoken English

For the prosodic analyses of focus assignment and prominence marking, the study of information structure in Chapter 6 of this book examined datasets extracted from the London-Lund Corpus of Spoken English (LLC). The LLC was compiled as part of two projects: (i) the Survey of English Usage (SEU) at University College London, where it was first launched by Randolph Quirk and further developed by Sydney Greenbaum, and (ii) the Survey of Spoken English (SSE), initiated by Jan Svartvik at Lund University as a sister project of the SEU (see Svartvik 1990).

The original SEU project aimed to assemble and analyse a corpus comprising samples, or 'texts', from both written and spoken British English. This yielded a total of 200 texts, half of which were prosodically transcribed spoken data, including both dialogues (e.g. face-to-face conversations, phone calls) and monologues (e.g. lectures). The written texts comprised not only printed and manuscript material but also examples of English read aloud (e.g. broadcast news and scripted speeches): the latter were, hence, not included as 'spoken data', since they originated in written rather than in spoken English. In the follow-up SSE project, the aim was to make available the spoken material from the SEU project in computerised form. The first version of the SSE project included 87 prosodically transcribed texts (435,000) from the original SEU project; the remaining 13 texts from the original spoken data were later included in a second version, totalling 100 texts (roughly 500,000 words).

The London-Lund Corpus presents itself as the end result of the SSE project, hence focusing only on data from spoken English. It consists mostly of conversations between educated speakers from London, recorded between 1953 and 1987. The data include both sound files and their transcriptions, prosodically annotated by the compilers in the British 'nuclear tone approach' (e.g. Crystal [1969], which was heavily influenced by Halliday [1967b,c]). The transcriptions are therefore marked for tone unit (TU) boundaries (#), the onset (i.e. the first prominent syllable in the TU), the location of the nuclear accent, the direction of the tone movement (falls \, rises /, fall-rises \/, rise-falls /\, and level tones =), boosters (i.e. relative pitch levels), two degrees of pause (short pauses and unit pauses (*viz.* of one stress unit or foot)), and, finally, two degrees of stress (normal and heavy). An excerpt from the LLC is given in Figure 1.

As shown by the visualisation in Figure 1, the transcriptions in LLC code one TU per line. The first two rows indicate from which sample, or text, the data are transcribed (e.g. samples 1.1 and 1.2 in Figure 1). Because most of the samples in LLC are data from conversations, the identity of the speaker is given as 'A' and 'B' and sometimes 'C' or even 'D' (depending on the number of participants). Most recordings were made without prior knowledge of the participants. In some cases, however, one or more participants were informed about the recording and typically had the task of keeping the conversation going. Their identity is coded in lower case, e.g. 'a' in Figure 2. The description of the corpus by the annotators states that the contributions of these 'non-surreptitious' speakers to the conversation were not prosodically annotated (as shown in Figure 2), even though at some points in the corpus they are. In the data I collected, I therefore included all examples that were prosodically annotated, regardless of whether the speaker was aware of being recorded or not.

```
1 1   7912010 1 1 B    11   .* I must ^watch the t\ime _Reynard#           /
1 1   7912020 1 1 A    11   *((^qu=ite#))                                   /
1 1   7912030 1 1 A    11   ^[=m]#*                                         /
1 1   7912040 1 1(B    11   *((or I ^may miss the b\ank#))*                 /
1 1   7912050 1 1 A    11   *^y\es#                                         /
1 1   7912060 1 1 A    11   ^y\es#*                                         /
1 1   7912070 1 1 A    11   ^y\es#                                          /
1 1   7912080 1 1 A    11   you ^m\ust# -                                   /
1 1   7912090 1 2 B    11   ^now [@] I shall see you :ten o`clock on .      /
1 1   7912090 1 1 B    11   Wednesday m\orning#                             /
1 1   7912100 1 1 A    11   ^on Wednesday m\orning# .                       /
1 1   7912110 1 1 A    11   ^thank you for dropping /in _Sam#               /
1 2    1   10 1 1 A    11   1it went off ^very very !sm\oothly#             /
1 2    1   20 2 1 A    21   1*((at))*                                       /
1 2    1   30 1 1 B    11   1*^ah\a#*                                       /
1 2    1   20 1 1(A    11   1that ^meeting of the executive com:m\ittee#    /
1 2    1   40 1 1 A    11   1((3 to 4 sylls)) *-* and I ^r\ang you# **-**   /
1 2    1   50 1 1 A    11   1on the ^way to the /air_port# -                /
1 2    1   60 1 1 A    11   1and +[@:m]+ ^you were /out#                    /
1 2    1   70 1 1 B    11   1*^y\es#*                                       /
```

**Figure 1:** Visualisation of the transcriptions in LLC.

```
1 7   19 1570 1 1 A    11   "^m\/y dread#                                   /
1 7   19 1580 1 1 A    11   is ^always :{h\earing} 'what you`ve !s\aid#     /
1 7   19 1590 1 1 A    11   because I ^think your "!\/own 'voice#           /
1 7   19 1600 1 1 A    11   ^sounds !h\orrible# .                           /
1 7   19 1610 2 2 a    20   oh yes I can`t play it back to you actually because/
1 7   19 1610 2 1 a    20   it`s [@:m] . it it it - ruins the *[@:m]        /
1 7   20 1620 1 1 A    11   *^y\eah# .                                      /
1 7   20 1630 1 1 A    11   ((the ^matching it \up))#*                      /
1 7   20 1610 1 1(a    20   the effect a bit* .                             /
```

**Figure 2:** Visualisation from LLC.

To facilitate the coding of the data, the extraction of the copular examples in my own data was not done in the original text files from the LLC (as visualised in Figures 1 and 2). Instead, I used a file in which the transcriptions were not presented with one TU per line, but with one conversational turn per line. The text file in which the data were presented in this way was kindly offered to me by a colleague, Ditte Kimps (see Kimps [2016] for more information), who re-arranged the lines by means of a Perl script (Wall et al. 2000). In doing so, she also excluded superfluous metatextual tags (viz. between the text source indication in the first two rows and the speaker identity tags A, B, etc.). The visualisation in Figure 3 shows how this improves the readability considerably. The prosodic annotation remained the same in the line-per-speaker file as in the original text. Prosodically annotated examples cited throughout this book will be presented as in Figure 3, rather than in the original one-TU-per-line style.

```
<1 2b B> ^you`re on th\at#
<1 2b A> "^n/\o _no _no# . ^D\ave is# .
<1 2b B> "^D\ave is _on _that# . ^\ah#
<1 2b A> and ^that`s [dhi] ^that`s [dhi] *(( . ^wh\at do you [m] 'call it#))*
<1 2b B> *^that`s the "g\auleiters#* ^y\es#
<1 2b A> ^well "!that`s [dhi dhi: dhi: @] . "!!s\yllabus _gauleiters#
<1 2b B> ^[\mhm]# - and ^what are !y\ou _then#
<1 2b A> ^I`m on the :academic :c\ouncil#
<1 2b B> ^\ah# *((^v\ery nice po_sition#))*
<1 2b A> *((to ^wh=om#))* [dhi] ^board of the faculty re"!p\ort# - -
<1 2b B> ((^g=ood#))
```

**Figure 3:** Presentation of the LLC transcriptions with one line per speaker.

## 2.2 Data compilation and coding

This section describes how the datasets of copular clauses that served as the basis for the descriptive analyses in this book were compiled and categorised into the specific relevant subtypes. The data were gathered from the corpora introduced in Section 2.1. Given the different nature of the data in the two corpora, the extraction of data from WB and from LLC called for different methods, which will be set out in Sections 2.2.1 and 2.2.2 respectively. An overview of the distribution of the copular clause types in the resulting datasets will be given in Section 2.3.

### 2.2.1 Exhaustive extraction of data from the 'Times' and 'British Spoken' sections of WB

The data from WB were collected with the aim of extracting an initially large dataset of 100,000 examples containing a form of the verb *be* from the Times subcorpus and another set of 100,000 examples from the British Spoken subcorpus. Given the smaller size of the latter corpus, only the extraction from the Times totalled 100,000, while the extraction from British Spoken yielded a total of 65,540 hits for *be*. The aim for both samples was to select all examples of predicative clauses with an indefinite NP complement, and all examples of specificational copular clauses with either a definite or an indefinite variable. This was partly done automatically by searching the sample for specific patterns (e.g. "be a(n)|one|another"). The annotation of relevant vs irrelevant examples was, however, double-checked manually so as not to leave out relevant examples that could have been overlooked by focusing on specific patterns (such as predicative clauses in which the verb *be* is not immediately followed by an indefinite article, e.g. *they are definitely pawns in a game*).

The query to arrive at these datasets was fairly broad and, hence, produced a large number of irrelevant hits. These included auxiliary uses of *be* (e.g. *Mother and baby are doing well*; *The viura grape is used for white rioja*), but also certain 'copular' uses of *be*, such as in clefts (e.g. *It will not be the millionaires who suffer most*), pseudoclefts (e.g. *What we want is Watneys*), equatives or identity statements (e.g. *one country's terrorist is another's freedom fighter*), tautologies (e.g. *The facts are the facts*), and what Higgins (1979: 221) calls 'identificational' clauses (e.g. *We're not in Los Angeles. This is Florence, Montana, for crying out loud*). In addition, to allow for a systematic comparison between specificational clauses with indefinite variable and predicative clauses with an indefinite NP complement and specificationals with definite variable, I did not include predicative clauses with complements other than the ones realised by indefinite nominals. In other words, I did not take into account predicative clauses with adjectival complements (e.g. *That argument was **unwinnable***), prepositional complement (e.g. *you're not **in the team***), adverbial complements (e.g. *the options are **there***), bare noun complements (e.g. *Lloyd George was **MP for Caernarfon***), and definite NP complements (e.g. *Who's Paul Martin? Paul Martin is **the Prime Minister of Canada***).

The data that were included were, therefore, (i) predicative clauses with an indefinite NP complement, e.g. (1), and (ii) specificational clauses, both with a definite variable, e.g. (2), and, of course, (iii) specificationals with an indefinite variable, e.g. (3).

(1) She's a shy person. (WB)

(2) The virtue of the British system is that general elections generate a clear result and an equally stark notion of responsibility. (WB)

(3) One virtue of a gasoline engine over a diesel is the faster response to the throttle, which simplifies running in big seas. (WB)

For both kinds of specificational clauses, I did not only consider the ones in which the variable functioned as subject – i.e. so-called 'non-reversed' clauses, as in (2) and (3) – but also the ones in which the value was subject – i.e. 'reversed' clauses, e.g. (4) and (5).

(4) If there's money to be made from selling caravans to the Chinese, *Michael Heseltine is the man to do it*. (WB)

(5) Many former prisoners of war struggled with memories of experiences that shaped the rest of their lives. *Graham Lait was one of them.* (WB)

The inclusion of reversed specificational clauses, especially the ones with an indefinite variable complement, raises an important question that is ignored if specificational clauses are only considered in their non-reversed form. By having the referentially more specific entity serve as subject (e.g. *Graham Lait* in [5]), reversed specificational clauses come to resemble predicative clauses, in which the subject is exclusively realised by the more specific entity, e.g. *she* in (1). As will be described in more detail in Chapter 3, the two clause types differ, however, in a number of essential ways, which feed into the following probes.

First, as is illustrated by examples (2)-(5), specificational clauses allow for either the variable or the value to be construed as subject, so that a specificational clause construed in either way is expected to also allow for the alternate construal. This is evidenced by the felicity of having the indefinite variable subject in (2) become the complement in (2'), and vice versa for (5) and (5').

(2') The faster response to the throttle, which simplifies running in big seas, is one virtue of the British system.

(5') ... One of them was Graham Lait.

Predicative clauses, by contrast, do not allow for such a subject-complement switch (Huddleston 1984: 187–88; Halliday 1994: 119–20), as shown by the infelicity of a predicative interpretation for (1').

(1') *A shy person is her.

Second, predicative and specificational clauses allow for different coordination patterns (Davidse 1999: 202ff): while it is possible for predicative clauses to coordinate patterns of *be* + complement, e.g. (6), specificational clauses do not allow for this option, neither in their non-reversed nor in their reversed form, e.g. (7a) and (7b) respectively.

(6) Arsenic is a weed-killer and was a favourite poison of murderers. (WB)

(7) a. ... *One of them is Graham Lait and is John Smith.
 b. ... *Graham Lait was one of them and was one of the most well-known victims of shell-shock.

An explanation as to why predicative clauses do allow for such coordination, while specificational clauses do not, will be presented in Chapter 3.

Third, because of their specificational semantics, specificational copular clauses alternate with clefts, which also set up a specificational variable-value relation (e.g. Davidse 2000; Davidse & Kimps 2016). In cleft constructions, however, the variable is coded by a cleft relative clause, while the value is invariably construed as the complement in the main clause. Moreover, the difference in the (in)definiteness of the variable NP is reflected, in cleft constructions, by the distinction between *it-* and *there-*clefts. Specificational copular clauses with definite variable alternate with *it-*clefts, with which they share an implicature of exhaustiveness (i.e. the implication that only one value can be specified for the variable), e.g. (8). Specificational copulars with an indefinite variable, on the other hand, alternate with *there-*clefts, since both imply that multiple values can (potentially) correspond to the same variable, e.g. (9).

(8) If there's money to be made from selling caravans to the Chinese, *it's Michael Heseltine who's the man to do it.*

(9) ... There's Graham Lait who's one of them.

While predicative clauses can also be moulded into a cleft construction, the fact that they do not set up a variable-value relation allows, in principle, for either the 'describee' or the 'description' to become the value of the cleft, e.g. (10a,b). The resulting cleft, however, is no longer predicative but specificational.

(10) a. It's Anne who's been a Francophile all her life.
 b. It's a Francophile, not an anglophile, that Anne's been all her life.

The three recognition criteria mentioned here lend themselves as general tests to probe for the specificational vs predicative distinction. The descriptive analysis of these criteria will be set out in Chapter 3.

Finally, while the study in this book focuses on declarative clauses, interrogative and imperative clauses were also coded for. For imperatives, only predicative clauses were observed, since it is logically impossible for a specificational clauses to be imperative: specificational clauses assert, or probe for, facts; they do not give commands. For interrogatives, both predicative (e.g. *So what sort of a man is he?*) and specificational clauses (e.g. *What's the alternative?*) were attested.

## 2.2.2 Non-exhaustive extraction from LLC

Because the analysis of information structure figures prominently in the description of specificational and predicative clauses (see, for instance, Declerck 1988; Mikkelsen 2005; Lahousse 2009; Patten 2012, 2016), part of the aim of the book is to provide an empirical investigation of information structure, notably focus marking, in the different copular clause types. To do so, it is necessary to look at examples of spoken data, for which I consulted the LLC, as described in Section 2.1.2. Since the focus for the study of intonation was on a detailed qualitative analysis, the data extraction from LLC was not exhaustive.

To identify the relevant examples, i.e. of specificational clauses with indefinite variable, the ones with definite variable and predicative clauses with an indefinite NP complement, I used the same recognition criteria as for the coding of the data in WB (Section 2.2.1), *viz.* reversibility, coordination patterns, cleft alternates. Since the focus of this book is on specificational clauses with indefinite variable, the aim was to collect a total of at least 100 examples of this clause type, but an exhaustive extraction of all specificational clauses with indefinite variable in the corpus would have been too time-consuming. Because the LLC is not part-of-speech-tagged, the collection of the data was carried out manually: this was done by reading through the transcriptions and annotating all examples of specificational clauses with indefinite variable until a total of at least 100 examples was reached. In the process, I also coded all specificational clauses with a definite variable and all predicative clauses with an indefinite NP complement up to the point in the corpus where the set goal of 100 specificationals with indefinite variable was met. (Coincidentally, the 100th specificational example with an indefinite variable was immediately followed by another example with indefinite variable: this last example was included as well, leading to a final total of 101 examples of specificational clauses with indefinite variable.) This method ultimately led to a total of 354 specificational clauses with definite variable and 545 predicative clauses. Because the intonation of interrogative clauses differs significantly from the intonation of declarative ones, the focus was kept on declarative clauses only, since the aim of the prosodic analyses was to investigate information structure rather than mood structure.

After identifying the examples in the transcriptions, the original soundbites for these examples were looked for in the audio recordings. The samples, or texts, in LLC (Section 2.1.2) are each stored as (a) separate (set of) sound file(s): while the transcriptions give an indication of which text the data represent – as shown by the first two rows in the visualisation in Figure 1, *viz.* texts 1.1 and 1.2 – extracting the soundbites had to be done by listening to the recordings. Because of the time-consuming nature of the extraction task, I did not gather the soundbites for all the examples from the transcribed data: while I did include all of the 101 specificational clauses with indefinite variable, the decision was made to only collect 300 soundbites for the specificational clauses with definite variable and another 300 for the predicative clauses. The remaining examples for which no soundbites were extracted – i.e. 54 specificational clauses with definite variable and 245 predicative clauses – were only examined based on their original prosodic annotation in LLC, but not on any additional instrumental analyses in Praat.

The analyses in Praat, a software package for speech analysis (Boersma & Weenink 2016), allowed for the annotated intonational features in LLC (e.g. tone, tonality and tonicity) to be supplemented with information from acoustic speech signals such as waveforms (i.e. a visible representation of sound) and spectrograms (i.e. a representation of the number of high and low frequencies in the signal) (Boersma & van Heuven 2001: 341). Of particular interest to the study in this book is the possibility of drawing pitch and intensity lines in Praat (cf. the black and the grey line in Figure 4). Both pitch and intensity (i.e. perceived as loudness) will be examined in the prosodic analyses in Chapter 6 as factors potentially influencing the prosodic prominence of information conveyed in an utterance.

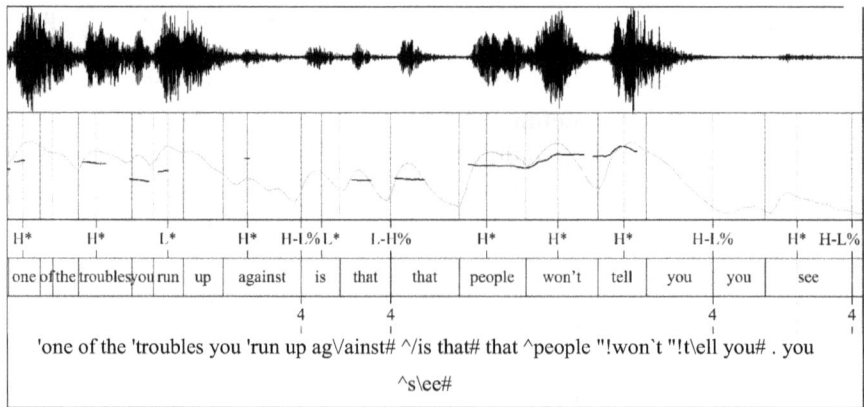

**Figure 4:** Praat picture with the pitch contour (in bold) and the intensity contour (in grey).

The results from the data compilation – notably the frequencies of the different clause types– will be presented in Section 2.3.

## 2.3 Frequencies of copular clause types

This section will give a broad overview of the distribution of the copular clause types in the extracted data samples. Because of the different nature of Wordbanks*Online* and the LLC – notably the absence of lemmatisation and part-of-speech tagging in the latter – only the coding of the clause types in the sample from WB was done exhaustively. This means that, while the distribution of the clauses in the samples from WB (in Section 2.3.1) provides a good indication of how frequent the types are in relation to each other, caution is warranted in interpreting the frequencies of the types in the LLC (Section 2.3.2), even if they roughly reflect the same proportions as in WB.

### 2.3.1 Exhaustive extractions of data in the WB subcorpora

The extraction of predicative and specificational copular clauses yielded a total of 11,285 declarative examples from the 'Times' subcorpus and 7,898 declarative examples from 'British Spoken'. The interrogatives were much less frequent in both datasets, totalling only 217 examples and 190 respectively. Imperative clauses were extremely rare, attested only 4 times in the 'Times' sample (all of which were predicative clauses) and not at all in 'British Spoken'.

The frequencies of the specific copular clause types were roughly the same in both samples. For declaratives, predicative clauses were, by far, the most frequent, accounting for 66% and 61% of the two datasets. For specificational clauses, the ones with definite variable subjects were much more common than all other specificational types, representing respectively 22% and 29% of the data. Indefinite variable subjects, by contrast, were much less frequent, occurring in only 4% of both sets. It is interesting to note that, while reversed specificational clauses (with the value as subject) are overall not frequent, the ones with an indefinite variable were not as rare as would be expected given the ratio of non-reversed vs reversed specificational clauses with a definite variable. Specificational clauses with indefinite variable complements occurred in 2% of the 'Times' and 'British Spoken' sets; whereas the ones with definite variable complements occurred in respectively 6% and 4% of the sets. A potential explanation for these frequencies could be that reversed specificational clauses promote the implication of a comparison between the value subject vis-à-vis potential other values (see Chapters 6 and 7). As will be discussed in later chapters, such a comparison between potential values is particularly prominent in specificational clauses with indefinite variable, as they imply that multiple values can correspond to the same variable.

Interrogative clauses, on the other hand, were more likely to be specificational than predicative, i.e. respectively 70% and 30% in the 'Times' corpus and 72% and

28% in 'British Spoken'. Moreover, in the Times corpus, 82% of the predicative interrogatives were polar interrogatives (i.e. 54 examples), e.g. (11), while only 18% were WH-interrogatives (i.e. 12 examples), e.g. (12). In the British Spoken set, polar interrogatives were attested in 91% of the predicative interrogatives (i.e. 48 examples), while WH-interrogatives were found in only 9% of the data (i.e. 5 examples).

(11)   Are you a beach bunny or an ice maiden? (WB)

(12)   I knew Amanda, but what sort of person was Maureen? (WB)

With WH-interrogatives, the WH-pronoun could either probe for the describee, e.g. (13), or for the description, e.g. (14). In the latter case, however, the interrogative was often used not to ask a genuine but a rhetorical question (e.g. *What is risotto?*), to which the answer is provided in the predicative interrogative itself (e.g. *a warm, savoury rice pudding*).

(13)   Who wants to be an engineer? (WB)

(14)   What is risotto, after all, but a warm, savoury rice pudding? (WB)

For specificational interrogatives, the proportions of polar and WH-interrogatives are markedly different. In the Times corpus, only 3% of all the specificational clauses were polar interrogatives (i.e. 5 examples), while the other 97% (i.e. 146 examples) were WH-interrogatives. In British Spoken, only 2 polar interrogatives were found (2%), while all 131 other examples were WH-interrogatives (98%). It should, furthermore, be pointed out that the distinction between non-reversed and reversed clauses is only evident with polar interrogatives, e.g. (15) and (16).

(15)   Isn't the bag of the moment that one with the dog on it? (WB)

(16)   Isn't that the problem? (WB)

In specificational WH-interrogatives, on the other hand, it is always the value that is probed by the WH-pronoun. The interrogative pronoun always occurs in initial position, but, as the plural subject-verb agreement in (17) suggests, its initial position does not mean that the pronoun necessarily serves as subject of the specificational clause.

(17)   *What are the main types of water systems?* There are two main types of water system in the UK: low- and high-pressure. (WB)

Finally, while rare, it is also possible to find specificational interrogatives with an indefinite variable (i.e. 1% in British Spoken, but no examples in the Times corpus). This is evidenced by the example in (18).

(18) *What are some of the bad things about living in Resolute?* Bill asks. A lack of education, and comuniction [sic], I guess. The lack of possibilities to do anything but survive. (WB)

A summary of the absolute numbers and relative distributions of the different copular clause types is given for the Times corpus in Table 1 and for the British Spoken sample in Table 2. The data taken from the two corpora will form the basis for the descriptive analysis of predicative and specificational clauses in Chapter 3 as well as for the corpus studies in Chapters 4, 5 and 7.

Table 1: The distribution of copular clause types in the Times subcorpus of WB.[14]

| declarative | | | | |
|---|---|---|---|---|
| predicative | | | 7,504 | (66%) |
| specificational | indefinite variable | non-reversed | 438 | (4%) |
| | | reversed | 182 | (2%) |
| | definite variable | non-reversed | 2,494 | (22%) |
| | | reversed | 667 | (6%) |
| **interrogative** | | | | |
| predicative | | | 66 | (30%) |
| specificational | indefinite variable | non-reversed | 0 | |
| | | reversed | 0 | |
| | definite variable | non-reversed | 149 | (69%) |
| | | reversed | 2 | (1%) |

---

14 To ensure reliability of the comparison between clause types in the corpus studies and the descriptive analyses, ambiguous examples were excluded from the datasets. Ambiguity mostly arose between predicative clauses and reversed specificational clauses with indefinite variable: 38 examples were coded as ambiguous. With reversed specificational clauses with definite variable, some ambiguity between a specificational reading and a predicative or descriptionally-identifying reading was found as well, *viz.* in 17 examples. Non-reversed specificational clauses are generally more straightforward to interpret. Only 8 ambiguous examples were found for non-reversed clauses with indefinite variable and 12 for the ones with definite variable. The ambiguity in both cases arose typically due to the difficulty to interpret the subject NP and the complement NP as referential or non-referential (e.g. *Here, the boss in question is an American who runs a fleet of 12 cruise ships*, in which the complement NP could point to a specific individual that specifies the variable *the boss in question*, or the subject NP could point to an individual of whom the complement gives a description in the form of a non-referential complement NP).

**Table 1** (continued)

| imperative | | | | |
|---|---|---|---|---|
| predicative | | | 4 | (100%) |
| specificational | indefinite variable | non-reversed | 0 | |
| | | reversed | 0 | |
| | definite variable | non-reversed | 0 | |
| | | reversed | 0 | |

**Table 2:** The distribution of copular clause types in the 'British Spoken' subcorpus of WB.[15]

| declarative | | | | |
|---|---|---|---|---|
| predicative | | | 4,843 | (61%) |
| specificational | indefinite variable | non-reversed | 317 | (4%) |
| | | reversed | 149 | (2%) |
| | definite variable | non-reversed | 2,280 | (29%) |
| | | reversed | 309 | (4%) |
| **interrogative** | | | | |
| predicative | | | 53 | (28%) |
| specificational | indefinite variable | non-reversed | 2 | (1%) |
| | | reversed | 0 | |
| | definite variable | non-reversed | 128 | (69%) |
| | | reversed | 3 | (2%) |
| **imperative** | | | | |
| predicative | | | 0 | |
| specificational | indefinite variable | non-reversed | 0 | |
| | | reversed | 0 | |
| | definite variable | non-reversed | 0 | |
| | | reversed | 0 | |

### 2.3.2 Non-exhaustive extractions of prosodic evidence from the LLC

Since the extraction of data from LLC focused primarily on finding sufficient data for specificational clauses with an indefinite variable – for which the aim was to

---

[15] As for the extraction from the *Times* subcorpus, the extraction from the *British Spoken* subcorpus included some ambiguous examples, which were excluded from the datasets for the corpus studies. 35 examples with an indefinite NP complement were ambiguous between a predicative reading or a reversed specificational reading. 34 examples with a definite NP complement were ambiguous between a predicative or descriptionally-identifying reading and a reversed specificational reading. As in the *Times* subcorpus, fewer ambiguity arose for the non-reversed specificational clauses in the *British Spoken* subcorpus as well. 12 examples were found for non-reversed specificational clauses with indefinite variable and 14 examples for the ones with definite variable. Here too, the ambiguity mostly arose, in both cases, due to the interpretation of the complement NP as referential or non-referential.

## 2.3 Frequencies of copular clause types — 35

find at least 100 examples – the proportion of these examples are slightly higher in the set from LLC than in the samples from WB (see Table 3). In the extraction from LLC, 'non-reversed' specificational clauses with indefinite variable subjects accounted for 8% of the copular clauses, e.g. (19), while the 'reversed' ones with indefinite variable complements represented 2%, e.g. (20).

(19) ^one of the !s\/implest# and ^least de!m\/anding prepa'rations# . ^is the :in'tact pro'fused :r\at 'heart# (LLC)

(20) you ^can't !r\eally do en/ough# for ^those who :really "!\are in _need# . *and ^housing :subsidies is a :classical example :\of_that#* (LLC)

Their counterparts with a definite variable made up 31% and 4% of the data respectively, e.g. (21) and (22).

(21) *^well my !v\ague* am'bition# **is to ^get** ^y\es#* is to ^get an :[ae] an [ae] an ad:ministrative 'post **h\ere#** (LLC)

(22) A. ^y\eah# ^\I like tr/avelling# -
B. ^y\eah# . it's ^((qu/ite fun))# – ^widens one's . v/iew of the 'world# . ((^qu/ite good#))
A. well I ^think I'll 'take . !things a :step at a t/\ime# ((for ^n/ow#)) -
B. ^w=ell# . *^y\outh hostelling's# the ^ideal 'way of d\oing it#* (LLC)

Finally, while predicative clauses were slightly less frequent in the extraction from LLC, they still remain the most frequent copular clause type (55%), e.g. (23).

(23) ^he's !not a rel\/axed 'lecturer# but ^he's . a "!dr\iving 'lecturer# ^you kn\/ow# (LLC)

**Table 3:** The distribution of copular clause types the LLC sample.

| | | | | |
|---|---|---|---|---|
| predicative | | | 545 | (55%) |
| specificational | indefinite variable | non-reversed | 81 | (8%) |
| | | reversed | 20 | (2%) |
| | definite variable | non-reversed | 312 | (31%) |
| | | reversed | 42 | (4%) |

## 2.4 Conclusion: What's in a number?

This chapter described how the data that will form the basis for the analyses in the following chapters were collected and coded. The distribution of the copular clause types in the datasets gives a first general indication of how frequent each type is in relation to the others. While the analyses in the following chapters will focus on declarative copular clauses, it was interesting to note, for instance, that predicative clauses were, by far, the most frequent of the declarative clauses, but that, for interrogatives, specificational clauses – at least the ones with definite variable – were much more common. This would seem to go to the observation made by Declerck (1988: 6) and Keizer (1992: 91–96) that specificational clauses are often used to answer an explicit or implicit question, while predicative clauses are not felt to answer a question (even though they can) (Declerck 1988: 55).

Specificational clauses with indefinite variable, by contrast, rarely occur in interrogative form. As I will explain throughout this book, indefinite variables trigger an implicature of non-exhaustiveness: they imply the speaker's assessment that multiple values may satisfy the criteria set up by the variable. This can be either because the speaker knows that multiple values do in fact correspond to the variable's criteria, or because s/he is not certain that the specified value is the only possible specification of the variable. The indefiniteness of the variable is, therefore, a meaningful choice, whereby the speaker assumes a position with respect to the specificational relation. This interpersonal meaning, potentially involving tentativity or reticence, would seem more likely to arise in declarative contexts, in which the speaker her- or himself is required to assume responsibility for an assertion, rather than conferring it to the hearer, as is the case in interrogatives.

In the declarative data, specificational clauses with indefinite variable were more frequent: even if they remain the least frequent of the three 'major' clause types, they are by no means negligible. In fact, if we zoom in on specificational clauses only, it turns out that the ones with indefinite variable represent about 15 to 16% of all specificational clauses in the samples from WB and up to 28% of the specificational data in the sample from the LLC. (As explained above, the percentages for the LLC sample should be treated with caution because of the data design.)

For this reason, the premise that indefinite variables are only marginally acceptable – if they are believed to be acceptable at all – cannot be maintained (contra, for instance, Geach 1962: 35; Higgins 1979: 138; Heycock & Kroch 1999: 379). To fully understand what defines and characterises specificational clauses as a general clause type, it is therefore necessary to revisit, refine and potentially reject existing assumptions by looking at the functional meaning and formal behaviour of specificationals with indefinite variables as a research topic in its own right. Not only will this lead to a better description of specification, but it will also provide insight into the intricate relationships between lower-level coded meanings, such as indefiniteness, and the clause-level meaning of the copular relation to which the former contributes.

# Chapter 3
# A functional-structural analysis of predicative and specificational clauses

In this chapter[16] I aim to give a functional-structural analysis of specificational clauses with an indefinite variable NP, which I contrast, for descriptive purposes, with predicative clauses with an indefinite predicate nominative. In the literature on copular clauses, the semantic contrast between these two clause types is traditionally formulated in terms indebted to logic.[17] Predicative clauses, like (1), are said to "predicate some property (characteristic, attribute, quality) of the referent of the subject NP" (Declerck 1988: 3): in (1), for instance, the property of being *an Irish hero* is ascribed to *Mary Robinson*.

(1) A known fighter for women's rights, human rights and forward-thinking climate change policy, *Mary Robinson is an Irish hero*. (Google)

Specificational clauses, on the other hand, are described as setting up a 'presupposed' variable, e.g. *my personal Irish hero* in (2), which is specified by a value, e.g. *Michael Collins* (e.g. Akmajian 1979; Higgins 1979; Declerck 1988; Keizer 1992).

(2) For the record *my personal Irish hero is #MichaelCollins* without whom the Republic of Ireland would not be here today. (https://twitter.com/hashtag/michaelcollins)

In both functional and more formally oriented accounts of English copulars, the finer points of description of the two clause types have been a topic of long-standing debate. The main unresolved question is how predicative and specificational clauses relate to each other: are specificational clauses the 'inverse' of predicative clauses (e.g. Williams 1983; Partee 1986a,b; Heggie 1988; Moro 1997; Mikkelsen 2005; Patten 2012, 2016) or are they categorically different (Halliday 1967b; Declerck 1988; Keizer 1992; Heycock & Kroch 1999; Heycock 2012). The former account analyses the two copular types as sharing the same 'predicative structure' in which copula *be* links a referential NP with a non-referential 'property' NP.

---

**16** Substantial parts of this chapter are an elaborated version of sections in Davidse & Van Praet (2019).

**17** In this chapter, I will develop an account that hews closer to the lexicogrammatically coded meaning particularly of the predicative clause.

https://doi.org/10.1515/9783110771992-003

The specificational reading has been argued to be brought about by the 'inverse' realisation of the non-referential NP as subject rather than complement (e.g. Mikkelsen 2005: 61): here, inversion is viewed as a matter of grammatical function in the copular clause. Alternatively, the inversion has been explained in terms of focus assignment (Patten 2012: 35): the specificational meaning comes about by assigning information focus to the referential (value) NP, e.g. *Michael Collins* in (2), whereas predicative clauses typically have the focus on the non-referential NP, like *an Irish hero* in (1).[18] (Authors like Higgins [1979: 234–236], Partee [2000: 199] and Mikkelsen [2005: 133] also argue for a 'fixed' specificational information structure with focus on the referential value NP, but they do not necessarily make it the distinguishing criterion between specificational and predicative copulars.) In attributing the difference between predication and specification to information structure, Patten (2012), unlike Mikkelsen (2005), allows for the 'non-referential' variable NP to serve either as subject (3a) or as complement (3b) of the specificational clause. (Examples [3a] and [3b] also appeared in Chapter 1 as [6a] and [6b].)

(3) a. The waitresses were Diane and Carla. (Patten 2016: 79)
    b. DIANE and CARLA were the waitresses. (Patten 2016: 80)

The other position in the debate argues against the idea that specificational copulars are derived from a core predicative structure; instead, it stresses that the two clause types are functionally and structurally different. A common objection to the 'inverse' account is that the specificational variable NP "exhibits properties that are associated with arguments, rather than with predicates" (Heycock 2012: 224; Heycock & Kroch 1999). Moreover, not all predicative NPs can be used felicitously as subject of a specificational clause, e.g. $^{??}$*A doctor is John* (Heycock 2012: 220). Heycock (2012: 226) concludes that "genuinely predicative copular constructions cannot invert." Instead, Heycock & Kroch (1999) and Heycock (2012) propose that specificational clauses involve two arguments (rather than one argument and a predicate), which are coded by two referential NPs: specificational clauses are a sort of equative clause, in which "the copula is flanked by two expressions of the same semantic type" (Heycock 2012: 209), as illustrated in (4) and (5). However, Heycock & Kroch (1999: 381) note themselves that this classification "runs afoul of the intuition that the former are asymmetric in interpretation in a way that 'true equative' are not" (Heycock & Kroch 1999: 381).

---

**18** Patten (2012: 34–35) recognises that in predicative clauses, the focus is typically on the complement, *John is a* SURGEON (Patten 2012: 34), but can also be on the subject, *JOHN is a surgeon* (Patten 2012: 35).

(4) The Morning Star is the Evening Star.

(5) Recent events in Northern Ireland demonstrat[e] how *yesterday's terrorist is today's respected politician*. (WB)

In view of the arguments adduced by both sides, some authors have consequently revised their position. Partee (2010), for instance, retracts her own previous 'inverse' account (Partee 1986a), acknowledging for specificational clauses that "both NPs are of type e [i.e. referential], but with [the variable] NP$_1$ less referential than [the value] NP$_2$, perhaps 'attributive'" (2010: 25). A similar view is proposed by Declerck (1988: 14ff) and Keizer (1992: 178–180), who follow Higgins (1979: 264) in viewing the specificational variable as neither non-referential (or 'predicative') nor (fully) referential. Instead, they describe the variable NP as weakly-referential (Declerck 1988) or 'superscriptional' (Higgins 1979; Keizer 1992).

This chapter will focus on the issues addressed in the 'inverse', the 'equative' and the 'superscriptional' position, which will be examined in specificational clauses with an indefinite variable NP, e.g. *a real hero* in (6).

(6) Who is your favourite fictional hero? – I don't really have a pretend one, *but a real hero would be British Paralympic swimmer Ellie Simmonds*. She won loads of medals at London 2012.
(UCL People, June 2013: 13, https://issuu.com/uclcomms/docs/people_2013/31)

This allows me to tackle the main issues in the debate from a well-defined angle. The general consensus is that the indefinite predicate nominative is 'non-referential'. Thus, to consider the question whether or not specification arises by inversion of predication, we need to systematically compare predicative clauses with an indefinite complement NP with specificational clauses with an indefinite variable NP. Only by comparing the two clause types can we tackle the issue of the analysis of specificational clauses with indefinite variable and pinpoint the similarities and differences between the functions of predication and specification.

The account proposed in this chapter takes a functional-cognitive approach to linguistic analysis and is committed to the tenet that the lexicogrammar exists to symbolise semantic structure (e.g. Bolinger 1968; Langacker 1991; Halliday 1992; McGregor 1997). This entails adhering to Bolinger's (1968) adage that all formal elements are meaningful and that "a difference in form spells a difference in meaning" (Bolinger 1968: 27). The overt form of constructions has to be respected when we analyse their structural assemblies and the semantic functions coded by them (Langacker 2017a: 10). Langacker (1999: 152) holds that grammatical constructions have composite structures, some of whose components are transparently assembled, whilst others may be "only partially discernible (or even indiscernible) within the composite whole". This view of structural assembly (Langacker 1987a, 1999, 2017a) requires the analyst to identify not only which precise units are involved in structural relations, but also in what order these relations are put together. Structural analysis is concerned with "the order in which component structures are successively combined to form progressively more elaborate composite structures" (Langacker 1987a: 310). The order of assembly that analysts have to identify is the one that accounts best for the composite semantics of the structure, as conceptual dependencies between elements are "largely responsible, in the final analysis, for their combinatory behaviour" (Langacker 1987a: 305). The relation between the lexicogrammar and semantics of a specific language is a natural, largely compositional relation.

In the proposed analysis, I will address two crucial issues of the current debate. First, do specificational clauses share with predicative clauses a core predicative structure, onto which they map either a different subject-complement assignment (cf. Mikkelsen 2005) or a different focus structure (cf. Patten 2012)? Or do specificational and predicative clauses have different verb-argument structures? Second, what is the referential status of the indefinite variable NP and does it differ from the status of the indefinite predicate nominative?

To answer these questions, I will first provide a functional-structural account of the predicative clause type, which elucidates its verb-argument structure, or in Langacker's (1991) terms, its process-participant configuration (Section 3.1.2.1). I will take the position that predicative clauses have a 'one-place predicate' in which '*be* + predicate nominative' jointly express a process and that the describee is the only participant in that process. Next, I examine how the process-participant configuration interacts with grammatical subject-complement assignment (i.e. the 'mood structure', in Section 3.1.2.2). Since the describee is the only participant in the predicative process, predicative clauses have a 'fixed' mood structure: only the describee can be subject of the clause. Furthermore, I will assume, in accordance with the general consensus, that the predicate nominative is 'non-referential', though I propose some refinements to what this means (Section 3.1.3). For specificational clauses, I will likewise describe their process-participant configuration (Sections 3.2.2.1 and 3.2.2.2) and their mood structure (Section 3.2.2.3). Unlike predicative clauses, specificational clauses will be described as 'two-place predicates', i.e. transitive clauses with a two-participant configuration. Both the variable and the value are participants in the specificational process; both can, therefore, be subject. In Section 3.2.3, I will discuss the referential status of the (indefinite) variable NP, which I will argue is not non-referential but establishes 'generalised reference' (Langacker 1999; Breban & Davidse 2003). Finally, in

Section 3.3, I will describe the variation in information structure (more specifically, the distribution of focal versus non-focal information) found in predicative and specificational clauses. Despite information structure forming the crux of many accounts of specificational clauses, I will argue that they are in much need of evidence-based revision. Information focus is not inherent in the meaning of the value in specificational clauses (Van Praet & O'Grady 2018; Van Praet 2019a): not only is it possible for the value to be non-focal, but there can also be multiple foci in one clause, so that both the variable and the value can have focus. The discussion in Section 3.3 will provide the basis for a more in-depth investigation of information structure in Chapter 6 and of discourse-embedding of the clause in Chapter 7.

## 3.1 Predicative clauses

### 3.1.1 State of the art

If the question of copular clause types has been heavily debated in the literature, the topic of predicative clauses has caused uncharacteristically little disagreement: both in functional and more formally oriented frameworks, most authors agree on the semantics of predicative clauses as involving attribution, class-membership or class-inclusion[19] (e.g. Halliday 1985; Declerck 1988; Keizer 1992; Patten 2012). On closer inspection, however, underlying discrepancies between the different accounts need to be resolved. In this section I survey existing accounts of predicative clauses with an indefinite NP complement, focusing on the latter's referential status and on how the NP is integrated into the larger predicative clause structure.

The predicate nominative is generally viewed as a non-referential NP, in the sense that it does not 'pick out' an entity in the universe of discourse (e.g. Kuno 1970; Declerck 1988: 56–62, 65–68; Keizer 1992; Mikkelsen 2005: 65–67). A key

---

[19] The relations of class-membership and class-inclusion express similar yet distinct concepts. The former is characterised as the relation between a class and an instance, or member, of that class (e.g. *Skippy is a kangaroo*), while class-inclusion refers to the relation between a class and a subclass of that class (e.g. *A kangaroo is a marsupial*). Like Declerck (1988: 1) and Lyons (1968: 389), I do not take the distinction to warrant separate explanations of the semantics coded by the predicative clause structure. More specifically, while class-membership and class-inclusion are logically distinct, the difference between them is concerned with the referential status of the subject referent (i.e. an individual vs a generic instance) rather than with the linguistically coded meaning of the predicative clause itself.

argument is that the predicate nominative cannot be referred back to by a definite anaphoric nominal with the same values for animacy, gender and number as the predicate nominative. This is illustrated by (7a) and its discursive rejoinders in (7b).

(7) a. Shirin Ebadi is a lawyer. (Mikkelsen 2005: 54)
    b. *Yes, Shirin Ebadi is her/that lawyer.

Instead, predicate nominatives, e.g. (8), can use the same proform, *so*, for anaphoric retrieval as adjectival and participial predicates, as shown in (9) and (10) respectively (Keizer 1992: 88–89).

(8) Gold is a precious thing and *so* are you! (WB)

(9) The kids were happy and *so* were we. (WB)

(10) At the end he was still standing and *so* was his spirit. (WB)

This observation has led to the assumption that, like adjectives (e.g. *happy* in [9]), predicate nominatives designate properties (Partee 1986b; Mikkelsen 2004, 2005). In formal semantic accounts of noun phrase interpretation (e.g. Partee 1986b, 2004), such property NPs are interpreted as sets of individuals. In (7a), the predicate nominative *a lawyer* is then explained as "denot[ing] the set of all lawyers" and what the predicative clause asserts is that the subject *Shirin Ebadi* is a member of that set (Mikkelsen 2005: 53–54).

The idea of the predicate nominative as expressing a property or a set features in other less formal accounts as well (Halliday 1985: 128; Declerck 1988; Keizer 1992; Leech & Li 1995: 185–186; Francis 1999; Huddleston & Pullum 2002: 217, 252–254; Patten 2012, 2016). Declerck (1988), for instance, holds that predicative clauses express a relation of class-membership or class-inclusion (*ib.*: 1) or can be glossed as "predicat[ing] some property (characteristic, attribute, quality) of the referent of the subject NP" (*ib.*: 3). Halliday (1985: 114–115, 124) explicitly connects the notions of attribution and class-membership, stating that if "some entity is being said to have an attribute, this means it is being assigned to a class" (*ib.*: 124). He therefore views predicative clauses like *Sarah is wise* and *John is a poet* as conveying the same meaning that '*x* is a member of the class *a*', with the class either being 'the class of wise ones' or 'the class of poets' respectively (*ib.*: 114–115). To capture the similarity between predicative clauses with adjectival and nominal complements, Lyons (1977: 472) claims that the property-denoting semantics of the latter requires them to be interpreted as nouns rather than full NPs (see also Partee 1986b: 365). In a sentence like *John is a writer*, Lyons views the use of a noun phrase complement as "a purely automatic consequence of the fact that the subject NP is singular and 'writer' a count noun" *(ib.)*. Keizer (1992: 163–164) objects to this view, arguing that "it cannot be denied that there is an important difference between adjectival and bare nominal non-verbal predicates on the one hand, and nominal non-verbal predicates on the other." The latter, for instance, "can take any kind of modification possible for terms [i.e. referring expressions] in general", but although "they appear to have term structure" (that is, to have the structure of a referential expression), "they do not fulfil all the requirements of full terms" (*ib.*: 162). To capture both the commonalities and differences between predicative clauses with adjectival, bare noun and full NP complements, Keizer (1992: 163–167) therefore proposes, within a Functional Grammar approach, that they must all "be converted into one-place predicates by means of a Non-verbal Predicate Formation rule" (*ib.*: 166). Such a conversion rule, she claims, accounts for the non-argument status and non-referentiality of the predicative complement (*ib.*: 163).

Within a cognitive grammar framework, Langacker (1991, 2015) proposes a different analysis of indefinite predicate nominatives, which is a critique of the property NP analysis that has come to be the mainstream view. Langacker (1991) stresses that indefinite predicate nominatives do not express relations but entities. The fact that predicate nominatives have the form of a full NP, rather than a noun, entails that they do "not represent a type specification but rather an instance of that type" (Langacker 1991: 67). In the analysis Langacker (1991) proposes, he goes on to draw a distinction between the semantics of the indefinite predicate NP – as coded by its lexicogrammatical form – and the general function it serves in the predicative construction.

The functional equivalence of adjectival, prepositional and nominal predicative complements consists, for Langacker (1991: 205), in their integration with the clausal head *be* to form a COMPOSITE PREDICATE.[20] In this composite predicate, *be* merely profiles[21] "the continuation through time of a stable situation characterized only as a stative relation" (*ib.*: 65). In the maximally schematic process thus expressed, the stative relation "has no specific content" which therefore needs to be 'supplied' by a stative predication (*ib.*: 205). Adjectival and prepositional phrases express, by default, atemporal, stative relations, as they do when used as nominal modifiers, e.g. *the tall girl*, *the picture on your desk* (Langacker 2015: 3). Because they express relations, they can be "straightforwardly" (Langacker 1991: 205) integrated

---

[20] As mentioned in Chapter 1, small caps are used to highlight important concepts for the descriptive analysis.
[21] Langacker (1991: 551) uses "profile" as a technical term for the designatum of a linguistic expression.

with *be*, since *be* and the adjective or prepositional phrase make "complementary semantic contributions" (Langacker 1991: 205): the schematic relation expressed by *be* is naturally elaborated by the specific relations expressed by adjectives or prepositional phrases. The only change effected by the integration is the "temporalization" of the "stative relation" (Langacker 1991: 65), e.g. (11) and (12).

(11)   Alice is hungry. (Langacker 1991: 64)

(12)   Alice is on the counter. (*ib.*)

Less straightforward is the combination of a copular verb and a NP, as in (13), since a NP designates an instance, not a relation.

(13)   Alice is a mouser. (Langacker 1991: 64)

An analysis that treats (13) as being functionally equivalent with (11) and (12) "is possible, however, only if the predicate nominative is treated as a stative relation" (Langacker 1991: 65). Therefore, Langacker (1991: 65) proposes that "a nominal such as 'a mouser', when it occurs in certain constructions, is *construed as* a stative relation" (italics mine). A similar position is taken by Croft (1991: 71), who argues that "a noun, which in reference is zero valency, must be coerced into an inherently relational concept", so that it is "forced to behave as if [it] ha[s] a valency of one" (*ib.*: 69). That is, *be* combines with a NP like *a mouser* to form an intransitive composite predicate (Langacker 1991: 64), whose sole participant is an intransitive subject. At the same time, Langacker (1991: 66) notes that "the entity [i.e. the instance] profiled by the nominal is retained as the relational landmark". In making this argument, Langacker (1991) reiterates the view that the overt form of a construction, in this case the full nominal form of the predicate nominative, needs to be respected when we analyse its meaning (i.e. as designating an instance, not a property or a type).

Picking up on the claim that the predicate nominative is coerced into a relational reading, Patten (2012: 19) analyses the semantics of predicate NPs in terms of a *content mismatch*, involving incongruous form-meaning mappings (Francis & Michaelis 2003: 5). Following Francis & Michaelis (*ib.*), Patten (2012: 19–20) views the predicate nominative as involving a category mismatch, in which the formal properties of a NP are not associated with the congruous meaning of a referring expression but with the semantic properties of a relational category, namely a predicate. She follows Langacker's (1987a, 1991) approach to process-participant relations: the verbal predicate designates the process (a temporal relation) and contains schematic semantic components that are elaborated by the participants.

She starts, however, from a descriptive claim, which Langacker (1991: 65–66) explicitly rejects, *viz.* that "the copula *be* serves *only* to 'temporalize' the stative predication" (Patten 2012: 46, italics mine). This leads her to claim that "it must be the predicate nominatives themselves that are relational" (*ibid.*). Patten (2012) thus describes the predicate nominative as designating "an instantiation *relation* between the landmark[22] [i.e. the predicative complement], which is semantically specified, and the trajector [i.e. the subject referent], which is specified only schematically (to be elaborated by the subject nominal)" (*ib.*: 46, italics and additions between square brackets mine). As a result, the predicate nominative is argued to designate type specifications with a valency of one, like adjectives. Patten (2012: 46) refers in this context to Taylor (2002: 362), who holds that, "despite the presence of the indefinite article", which he deems "an idiosyncratic feature of English", predicative nominatives "tak[e] on adjective-like characteristics." Hence, both Patten (2012) and Taylor (2002) subscribe to the view of the predicate nominative as a property NP and attempt to explain this notion within a cognitive framework. However, the treatment of predicate nominatives as expressing a relational property glosses over the important differences they have with adjectival and bare noun predicates, as argued by Langacker (1991), and which a functional-structural analysis of grammatically coded meaning must account for (see Section 3.1.2.1).

In the following sections, I will develop the analysis of predicative clauses with indefinite predicate nominatives in line with Langacker's (1991: 67–68) point that the indefinite NP integrates with *be* to form a composite predicate. I will further outline the processes of derivation and reclassification by which an NP can become part of a predicate expressing a stative relation at a higher level of conceptual organisation. I will also spell out the functionality of using an NP, rather than for instance an adjective, as predicative complement in terms of its being able to carry *both* entity-type specifications and qualities that are ascribed to the subject (Section 3.1.2.1). The consequences of this analysis will then be spelt out in terms of the predicative clause's grammatical relations, i.e. its subject-complement assignment (Section 3.1.2.2), and the referential status of the predicate nominative (Section 3.1.3). The information structure of predicative clauses will be discussed later in Section 3.3, where I revisit the existing accounts of information structure, specifically information focus, and challenge the assumption that predicative and specificational clauses can be distinguished straightforwardly based on the assignment of information focus.

---

**22** Within Langacker's (1987a, 1991) cognitive semantics, *trajector* and *landmark* refer to the 'figure' and 'ground' of a represented relation.

## 3.1.2 The multi-layered organisation of predicative constructions with an indefinite NP

To analyse the semantics of predicative clauses with an indefinite NP, I will examine their functional-structural organisation in respect of two layers of coded meaning. These two layers are referred to in functional theories as the *representational* and *interpersonal* layers of organisation (Halliday 1970b, 1994, Hengeveld 1989). The representational layer is concerned with *representing* experienced processes in the world as well as processes within our consciousness, and involves the construal of process-participant configurations, the area traditionally referred to as verb-argument structure.[23] The interpersonal layer moulds these representations into *interacts* (e.g. an assertion, question, command) by constructing the speaker and hearer's roles in the exchange. This layer is construed by the grammatical relations of subject and complement, i.e. the mood structure (Halliday 1967a,b, 1968, 1970b, 1985, 1994). I take it that predicative clauses represent intransitive relations between a describee (participant) and a description (non-participant). This relation is coded by a one-place composite predicate in which the main conceptual import is provided by the complement (Section 3.1.2.1). Predicative clauses will be explained as having a fixed 'mood structure' as a result of their intransitivity: the semantic function of 'describee' is invariably associated with the grammatical function of subject (Section 3.1.2.2). The consequences and implications of this multi-layered analysis will be spelt out in the relevant sections.

### 3.1.2.1 Process-participant configurations

The central argument made here about the representational structure of predicative and specificational clauses is that they differ in the types of relational processes they express, in other words that they are semantically non-equivalent (contra the so-called 'inverse' approach, see Section 3.2.1.1). Whereas predicative clauses are intransitive, I will analyse specificational clauses as transitive process-participant configurations in an account indebted to Halliday (1967a,b, 1968) (see Section 3.2.2.1). To elucidate the intransitive analysis of predicative clauses, I will look more closely into two claims made by Langacker (1991, 2015). Firstly, as indicated in Section 3.1.1, I follow Langacker (1991, 2015) in viewing predicative clauses with an NP complement as *functionally* analogous to predicative clauses with an adjectival or prepositional complement. Nominal predicates are, just like

---

[23] To talk about the semantics of this layer of organisation, I follow Halliday (1985, 1994) and Langacker (1991, 2015), who use the terms "process" and "participants".

adjectival or prepositional predicates, integrated with *be*, forming an INTRANSITIVE COMPOSITE PREDICATE.[24] Since the interpretation of predicative clauses as involving a composite predicate is not generally accepted, I will provide further support for this claim from the distinctive coordination pattern that predicative clauses allow for. Secondly, by being integrated with *be*, the nominal predicate is reclassified, at a higher level of conceptual organisation, as being "relational despite its nominal form" (Langacker 1991: 66). At the same time, "the entity [i.e. an instance] profiled by the nominal is retained as the relational landmark" (*ib.*, additional comment between brackets mine): in other words, while the complement NP is reconstrued as part of a composite relational predicate, that does not undo its nominal function of designating an instance. In the second part of this section, I will, therefore, argue, following Langacker (1991), against the idea that the meaning of predicative NPs is 'adjective-like' by contrasting the functional-structural potential of full NPs with that of adjectives and bare nouns.

### The composite predicate analysis of be + predicate nominative

Firstly, I maintain, with Halliday (1985, 1994), Langacker (1991) and Davidse (1999), that predicative clauses express intransitive processes. For instance, in (14), *an alert listener* forms together with the verb *be* a composite predicate, in which *he* is the only participant. I characterise the semantics of this participant role as the 'describee' – i.e. the entity of which a description is given – and that of the intransitive process as the 'description'.

(14) He is an alert listener. (WB)

In support of the analysis of *be* + predicate nominative as forming a *composite predicate*, an alternate can be adduced to demonstrate the 'unithood' of *be* + predicate nominative, namely the possibility of coordinating units of *be* + predicate nominative (Davidse 1999: 202ff). This coordination pattern is not possible with the complement of specificational clauses, as shown by the pseudocleft example (15a), cited by Declerck (1988: 75). Out of context, this example is ambiguous between a predicative and specificational interpretation.

(15) a. What I need is a car and a boat. (Declerck 1988: 75)
 b. What I need is a car and is a boat.

---

[24] A similar analysis of *be* + predicate nominative forming an intransitive composite predicate was also argued for from a functional perspective, with reference to Halliday (1985), by Davidse (1999: 202ff)

On the specificational reading, the speaker claims to need two things, one being a car and the other a boat. On the predicative reading, however, the referent of *what I need* can be characterised as 'being both a car and a boat', i.e. an amphibian. Now, only on the predicative reading is it possible to coordinate both the two indefinite predicate nominatives, as in (15a), and the two composite predicates consisting of *be* + complement, as in (15b). The semantics coded by (15a) differ (slightly) from those in (15b), in that the former expresses the single process of ascribing a coordinated attribute, while the latter expresses the coordination of two ascriptive processes, each of one attribute. An attested example[25] of the coordination of two ascriptive processes is given in (16).

(16) Saddam Hussein's regime was a threat and was a danger. (WB)

Of course, (15b) and (16) could also be interpreted as examples of coordinated clauses with ellipsis of the subject in the second clause. This does not change the fact that (15b) and (16) can only be interpreted as predicative clauses. Specificational clauses do not allow for either the coordination of *be* + complement or the coordination of two specificational clauses in which the second subject is elided (e.g. *The richest teens are Prince William and Prince Harry* (WB) :: \**The richest teen is Prince William and is Prince Harry*) (see Section 3.2.2.3). This reveals that it is precisely the unithood of *be* + predicative complement that sanctions these coordination patterns, thus offering support for their analysis as a composite predicate.

If the integration of *be* + predicative NP forms an intransitive composite predicate, then it should share essential features with what are uncontroversially accepted to be composite predicates. Light verbs such as *have*, *make* and *take* plus a nominalisation, like *take a very long breath* in (17), have been shown to be proportionate to intransitive predicates (e.g. *breathe very deeply*) (Langacker 1991: 24–25; Halliday 1994; Davidse & Rymen 2008).

(17) She... took a very long breath. (WB)

In both types of composite predicate (i.e. with copula or light verb), the verb, e.g. *be* or *take*, specifies the temporal and aspectual dimensions of the predicate and the nominal complement provides its specific semantics. The nominal comple-

---

**25** Examples of predicative clauses with coordination of *be* + predicative complement are not frequent. In the *Times* and *British Spoken* subcorpora of Wordbanks*Online* combined, only eight such examples were found.

ment is 'non-referential' in both cases, in that it does not pick out an individual, even though it does designate an instance. On Langacker's (1991: 25) account, *a very long breath* in (17) is an episodic nominalisation, that is, an NP representing the component states of an 'entitised' or reified instance of breathing. Its integration with the verb *take* results in an intransitive composite predicate, depicting a single bounded episode, tracked through time. The profiled temporal relation has a valency of one, i.e. the participant taking a breath. Similarly, in predicative clauses, the predicate nominative specifies the particular content of the *being* relation. The composite predicate, of *be* + predicate nominative, makes schematic reference to one participant or 'be-er', the entity predicated on (i.e. the 'describee'). The analysis of '*be* + predicate nominative' as a composite predicate is perhaps demonstrated most clearly when it can be reformulated by means of an intransitive predicate (e.g. *You could be a winner today in our great £120,000 Bingo game*[26] versus *You could win today in our great £120,000 Bingo game*).

### The construal possibilities of full predicative NPs in contrast with predicative adjectives and bare nouns

In this section it will be argued that the point that "the entity profiled by the nominal is retained" (Langacker 1991: 66) in the predication relation is essential to understanding the construal possibilities of the predicate nominative construction. This requires us to look at the semantic functions that can be served by the elements of indefinite predicative NPs. I will demonstrate that the functional-structural potential of a full NP predicative complement combines type specification, which is the only function of bare noun complements, and quality-attribution, which is the sole function of adjectival complements.

In full NPs, the head noun designates the general type of entity, of which the whole NP depicts an instance (Langacker 1991: 144): the type "specifies the basis for identifying various entities as being representatives of the same class but is not tied to any particular instance of that class" (*ib.*: 53). Therefore, the semantics of type-attribution, class-membership or categorisation, in terms of which predicative clauses have typically been discussed (see, for instance, Halliday 1985: 114–115; Declerck 1988: 1; Keizer 1992: 91; Patten 2012: 42), are, on a Langackerian cognitive grammar analysis, only coded by predicative clauses with bare noun complements. In (18), for instance, a correspondence relation (Langacker 1991: 69) is set up between the instances *Anne Boleyn* and *Katherine Howard*, on the one hand, and the (sub)type *queen of England*, on the other.

---

26 The example with predicate nominative was taken from Wordbanks*Online*.

(18) Anne Boleyn and Katherine Howard were both queen of England at the time of their death.

The claim that the predicate nominative likewise denotes a type, class or property is typically motivated by its 'non-referentiality' (see e.g. Kuno 1970: 356–357; Declerck 1988: 56). However, as Langacker (1987a: 187, 1991: 96) points out, what is designated by a NP, *viz.* an instance, is distinct from nominal reference, in traditional terms (cf. Kuno 1970): the latter is not concerned with what kind of 'entity' is expressed (i.e. a relation, state, type, instance, etc.) but with the epistemic status of this entity in the discourse context. I will return to the epistemic, or referential, status of the instance designated by the predicative NP in Section 3.1.3.

An important consequence of acknowledging that predicative NPs designate instances is that it allows for a better appreciation of the semantic functions that are realised by the various elements in NP structure and that contribute to the designation of an instance. The NP and its head "represent the same entity at contrasting levels of specificity: the [type] is a coarse-grained representation showing only gross organizational features, whereas its instantiation delineates the entity in precise, fine-grained detail" (Langacker 1987a: 191). According to Langacker (1987a: 235–236, 309–310; 1991: 142–148), all representational modifiers (realised by elements such as adjectives, prepositional phrases and restrictive relative clauses) serve to narrow down the general type into a more delicate (sub)type. Davidse & Breban (2019) propose a crucial modification to this analytical model. They argue that only some representational modifiers, *viz.* subclassifying ones, apply to the type, whereas others apply to the instance.

SUBCLASSIFYING modifiers restrict the semantic scope of the type denoted by the head noun (Adamson 2000: 57). Subclassifying modifiers express semantic components that contribute to the conception of a *subtype* of the entity designated by the head, e.g. *steam/electric train* 'type of train powered by steam/electricity'. Whether realised by nouns like *steam* or adjectives like *electric*, subclassifying modifiers are semantically 'nominal': they are part of a composite structure representing an entity-type (Davidse & Breban 2019: 335).

Modifiers applying to the instance, on the other hand, describe QUALITIES. Following Halliday (1985, 1994), Davidse & Breban (2019: 339) label such modifiers 'epithets', which are typically realised by adjectives. Since qualities apply to instances and instances can manifest those qualities differently, it is possible to comment on the degree or extent to which a quality applies to an instance. Here, the semantic distinction between bounded and unbounded qualities comes into play (Bolinger 1967, 1972a; Paradis 1997, 2000, 2001). Unbounded adjective meanings invoke regions on a scale that do not involve a boundary, e.g. *red* in *red sauce*. Such qualities can be graded relative to an implied standard, with submodifiers like *very* heightening the degree, as in (19). Bounded adjective meanings construe properties defined by a boundary that has to be reached for the quality to be present, e.g. *empty* in (20). They take submodifiers that assess to what extent the boundary is reached, e.g. *almost/completely empty*.

(19)  Sambal Oelek is a <u>very red</u>, spicy sauce. (Google)

(20)  Imagine that *your torso – the area between your shoulders and your pelvis – is a <u>completely empty</u> chamber*. No muscles, no bones, no internal organs… (Google)

By contrast, if modifiers serve a subclassifying rather than a qualitative function, (un)boundedness is not semantically at issue: neither degree modifiers nor approximating modifiers can then be used, e.g. *?a very red wine, \*an almost dry run*.

The distinction between subclassifying and qualitative modifiers is central to the construal possibilities offered by full NP predicates in contrast with adjectival and noun predicates. Adjectives can only express qualities, as in (21). Nouns can be used predicatively in English with certain meanings such as one-member roles (Langacker 1991: 69, 71) or 'institutional' roles (e.g. *queen, president, treasurer*) (Huddleston 1984: 186). Because bare nouns express pure types (Langacker 1991: 67), they only allow for subclassifying modifiers as in (22), but they cannot take qualitative modifiers, which apply to instances only, as illustrated by the infelicity of (23b). Full NP complements, by contrast, can take both subclassifying and qualitative modifiers, e.g. (23a).

(21)  Mary Stuart was very controversial.

(22)  a.  Mary Stuart was queen of Scotland.
      b.  Mary Stuart was incumbent queen of Scotland and dowager queen of France.

(23)  a.  Mary Stuart was a very controversial queen of Scotland but a wholly legitimate dowager queen of France.
      b.  *Mary Stuart was very controversial queen of Scotland.

It is because – and only because – the indefinite predicate nominative designates an instance that the predicate can be used to attribute to the subject referent not only type specifications, but also instance-oriented qualities, which can be further submodified in either a scalar way, e.g. *very controversial*, or in a proportional way, *wholly legitimate*.

Because of the different functional-structural potential of a full NP in contrast with adjectives and nouns, it is important to recognise the distinct relation that is set up by predicative clauses with NP complements. Predicative clauses with adjectival complements, like (21), express a correspondence relation between an instance, e.g. *Mary Stuart*, and a quality, e.g. *very controversial*: the function of such clauses is one of QUALITY-ATTRIBUTION in a strict sense and their meaning can be glossed as the subject referent being 'ascribed the quality' denoted by the complement. Predicative clauses with noun complements, like (22a,b), set up a correspondence relation of an instance to a type or class: only these clauses serve a function of pure TYPE-ATTRIBUTION or CLASSIFICATION. Their meaning can be glossed as follows: the subject referent 'is classified as' the type denoted by the complement. Predicative clauses with full NP complements, like (23a), then, designate an instance of a type, which can 'carry' *both* entity-type specifications and qualities that are ascribed to the subject referent. In other words, a predicative complement NP can implement *both* the classifying and the qualifying functions, so that the subject referent is described not simply as corresponding to a type or as exhibiting certain qualities, but as an instance – with individual (gradable) qualities – of a type. I will further elaborate on this point in Chapter 4, where I will present a quantitative and qualitative corpus study of the lexical realisation of head nouns and modifiers in indefinite predicative NPs.

The idea that predicative clauses with indefinite NP complement set up a correspondence relation between two instances has led Langacker (1991) to the following claim: while predicative clauses with an indefinite NP complement *imply* a relation of class-membership, or class-inclusion, they actually "*profile* [i.e. designate] a relationship of identity" (*ib.*: 68, original italics). In a sentence like *Alice is a thief*, Langacker (1991) thus claims that the "inclusion of Alice in the *thief* class is therefore specified indirectly, via her identification with an arbitrary member" (*ib.*: 68). The use of the term 'identification' to capture the semantics of predicative clauses has drawn criticism, for instance from Taylor (2002: 362) and Davidse (1999: 215), who rightly point out that it obscures the difference between predicative and what are traditionally understood as identifying clauses, e.g. (24).

(24) Remember Matthew Simmons? *He was the Crystal Palace supporter who was famously attacked by Eric Cantona.* (WB)

Indeed, by arguing that predicative clauses like (23a) and identifying clauses like (24) both specify "the identity of two instances", Langacker (1991: 67) holds that they "are equivalent in all essential respects." However, while there is value in acknowledging the similar meanings coded by the NP-*be*-NP structures of these clauses, it is equally important to recognise the *semantic-pragmatic* difference between them. Declerck (1988: 95–109) and Keizer (1992: 90–105) argue that the difference between sentences like (23a) and (24) resides, roughly speaking, in the referential status of the complement NP (and not in its respective (in)definiteness, as Langacker [1991: 67–68] would appear to claim). The complement NP in predicative clauses is argued to be non-referential, in the sense that it does not pick out an individual. In identifying clauses like (24), on the other hand, the semantic-pragmatic function of identification implies that the complement NP is referential, i.e. that it does refer to an individual that is, in principle, identifiable by both the speaker and the hearer. Such 'descriptionally-identifying' clauses are used, Declerck (1988: 105) argues, when the hearer only has 'hic-et-nunc acquaintance' with the subject referent: the complement NP "links up [the subject referent] with an individual or set that [the hearer] knows in the sense that he has a 'backing of descriptions' of it" (*ib.*). Since predicative clauses like (23a) ascribe type specifications and qualities to the subject (as discussed above) rather than identifying the subject (in the specific sense outlined here), it is best to reserve the term 'identification' for sentences like (24).

Summing up, in this section, I defended the position that predicative clauses construe *be* + predicate nominative as a composite, intransitive process. This was argued to involve the reclassification of the predicate nominative as a *relational* substructure of the clause predicate: its function is to provide the specific content of the stative relation schematically expressed by *be*. At the level of the predicate nominative's own internal structure, an *instance of an entity-type* is profiled, which allows the speaker to attribute to the subject referent both entity-type specifications (via the predicate nominative's head and any subclassifying modifiers it may have) and qualities (via qualitative modifiers it may contain). In this respect, the functional-structural potential of predicative clauses with NP complements is different from predicative clauses with noun or adjectival complements. In the light of the argumentation offered within a cognitive grammar framework in this section, I reject the claims that "predicate nominals designate types" (Patten 2012: 46) or have "adjective-like characteristics" (Taylor 2002: 362). In Chapter 4, I will further elaborate on this claim, citing evidence from the lexical realisation of indefinite predicative NPs in attested corpus examples.

### 3.1.2.2 Mood structure

This section describes how the construal of an intransitive composite predicate circumscribes the 'mood structural' configurations available to predicative clauses. Mood structure pertains to the structuring of the conceptual content of the predicative process into interacts, such as imperatives, declaratives, and interrogatives (Halliday 1970a,b, 1994). It consists generally of two parts, i.e. the 'mood element', formed by subject and finite, and the 'residue', which contains a predicator and potentially complements and adjuncts (Halliday 1994: 68–92). In this section, I discuss the fact that the predicate nominative cannot become subject and, therefore, cannot figure in the mood element of the predicative clause. I attribute this to the notion of a complex predicate which fuses 'predicator' *be* and predicate nominative, as discussed in Section 3.1.2.1. In addition, I will spell out what the implications are of this fixed subject-complement assignment for the interpersonal functions of the predicative clause.

According to Halliday (1967b: 199, 1994: Chapter 4), the system of 'mood' is concerned with the meaning of the clause as an exchange. The realisation of different mood structures (e.g. imperative, declarative, interrogative) depends on the mood element, i.e. the configuration of subject and finite (Halliday 1970b: 360, 1994). The presence or absence of the mood element provides the basic choice between an indicative and an imperative clause respectively (Halliday & Matthiessen 2004: 114): these two moods code the two basic types of 'exchange', namely exchange of 'information' (i.e. via a proposition) and exchange of 'goods and services' (i.e. via a proposal). Predicative clauses are normally indicative, but imperative predicative clauses do occur in small numbers. In the remainder of this section, I will therefore focus firstly and mostly on indicative predicative clauses and briefly address imperative clauses at the end of the section.

Indicative clauses can be further divided into declaratives and interrogatives, as coded by the relative order of subject and finite. These formal elements, combined with prosody in speech, allow the speaker to enact a speech role. For instance, with a congruently used declarative, the speaker assumes the role of declarer, which at the same time assigns to the hearer the role of receiver of information. In this sense, Halliday (1994: 68) notes, utterances are intrinsically speech '*inter*-acts'. As is assumed in many functional theories (e.g. Halliday 1970b, 1985; Hengeveld 1989; McGregor 1997), such interacts involve speaker-assessment of the propositional material being exchanged in relation to a given speech context. According to Halliday (1985, 1994; Halliday & Matthiessen 2004) and Davies (2001), this speaker-assessment is construed by polarity and modality, which scope over a proposition, defined by Halliday (1970b, 1994) as a state-of-affairs (henceforth, SoA) located in time. By making specific choices of a polar and/or modal value, the speaker assesses whether or not the temporally located SoA is the case or is likely to be the case. In English, both polarity and modality are structurally associated with the subject-finite relation. Propositions are accepted or rejected, or assessed as (un)likely, in terms of the subject-finite relation. The function of the finite in the clause is to "relate the proposition to its context in the speech event" (Halliday 1985: 75), which Langacker (1991: Chapter 6) refers to as 'clausal grounding'. The systems of tense and modality represent the two ways of grounding a proposition in the discourse: one does so by reference to the time of speaking; the other by reference to the judgement of the speaker (Halliday 1985: 75; Langacker 1991: 240).

The subject also has a specific interpersonal function: it is not understood as a mere syntactic category, but it functions semantically as the element "by reference to which the proposition can be affirmed or denied" (Halliday 1985: 76).[27] It is, in other words, the function that "specifies the entity in respect of which the assertion is claimed to have validity" and "in whom is vested the success or failure of the proposition" (*ib.*). Halliday (1994: 73) uses the semantic shorthand 'element with modal responsibility' for this interpersonal function of the subject, where *modal* is derived from 'mood', not 'modality'. In Langacker's Cognitive Grammar, the subject is not interpreted as serving an interpersonal function; nonetheless, Langacker (1987a: 231, 2017b: 192) does attribute to the subject a special kind of prominence that is compatible with the role Halliday sees for the subject. The subject (or 'trajector') is described as the primary reference point that "anchors the entire process" (Langacker 2017b: 192): it "stands out as the entity being assessed", and this assessment takes the form of its relationship to the rest of the process (Langacker 1987a: 231). The fact that the subject functions as the entity in terms of which the proposition is assessed is illustrated in (25), where the validity of the original proposition is being negotiated in the back-and-forth between speaker and hearer: while the finite's polar and/or modal values change from one exchange to the other, the subject, in terms of which the proposition's validity is assessed, remains constant.

(25) Duncan will be a big plus for us. – Will he? – Yes, he will. – No, he won't. – Well, he might be.

---

**27** Systemic Functional Linguistics is quite unique in assigning an interpersonal function to the subject of a clause. In that respect, it differs, for instance, from Cognitive Linguistics, in which the entity construed as subject is one of the participants, which are responsible for turning the type specification of the VP into an instance of that type (Langacker 1991: 33). Davidse (1997: 422, 1998b), who combines a systemic-functional with a cognitive approach, argues that it is specifically the subject and not the object(s) that functions as the 'Instantiator' of the process; the non-subject participants merely elaborate the process-type of the VP into a subtype. Moreover, the subject does not only contribute to the instantiating function but also to the grounding function of the clause (the latter being an interpersonal function): Davidse (1997: 422) proposes that clausal grounding (i.e. linking the process-instance to the speech event) does not only concern tense and modality but also person deixis, which is coded by both subject and finite. This is consistent with Langacker's (1991: 247) claim that 'subject-finite' agreement is part of the grounding predication. Davidse (1997, 1998b) thereby shows that the SFG account of the subject function is compatible with a CG account (and see also Taverniers [2005] for a similar argument).

The observation that the describee is invariably construed as subject of the predicative clause is therefore not only of structural importance, but it also has semantic significance. Regardless of its position in the clause, the describee is always the modally responsible element. Hence, the validity of the assertion always rests on the describee. Therefore, it is always the describee in terms of which the predication is made. (Note that the very concept of a 'predicative' clause, in its original core meaning, captures the idea of a fixed mood structure: something is 'predicated' of the subject and the predicate describes what that is.)

The remainder of the mood structure is what Halliday (1994: 78–81) calls the 'residue'. Within the residue, the 'predicator', or the non-finite VP of the clause, is responsible for coding so-called 'secondary' temporal relations relative to the primary tense marking of the finite (e.g. anteriority vis-à-vis the future tense of the finite in *Next year he will <u>have been</u> a student for seven years*). It also specifies voice and, importantly, the process that is predicated of the subject (Halliday 1994: 79). The residue can also contain complements[28] and adjuncts: complements are the elements in the residue that have the potential to become subject; adjuncts lack this potential because, unlike complements, they do not correspond to participants in the transitivity structure but to circumstances. Since arguments can only be constructed around participants (Halliday & Matthiessen 2004: 123), participanthood is a necessary precondition for potential subjecthood. As argued in Section 3.1.2.1, the experiential role of the predicate nominative is to elaborate the process schematically profiled by *be*. Modally, the predicate nominative therefore does not function like an ordinary complement; instead, its structural integration with *be* means that it joins with the predicator element in the mood structure. As a result, in predicative clauses, it is the combination of predicator *be* and predicate nominative that jointly specifies not just the clausal process and the 'voice' of the clause but also the 'secondary temporal relations' that can be expressed. This is evidenced, for instance, by the fact that only some predicate nominatives allow for the predicative process to be construed progressively (e.g. *you're being a jerk*), while other do not (e.g. \**you're being a student*). I will come back to this point in Chapter 5, in which the use of aspect and modality in predicative and specificational clauses will be studied in more detail.

Despite its fixed mood structure, declarative predicative clauses do allow for different orders in which the clausal elements can occur. Beside the default subject-VP-complement (SVO) order (26a), both less frequent complement-subject-VP (OSV) (26b) and complement-VP-subject (OVS) patterns (26c) are possible with

---

**28** Halliday (1985, 1994) uses the term 'complement' both for complements in copular clauses and for objects in non-copular clauses.

predicative clauses. The substitution of the nominative pronoun *he* for *Shaun* shows that the reordering of the clausal constituents does not involve a switch in grammatical function.

(26) a. Shaun/he is a delightful man. (WB)
　　 b. A delightful man Shaun/he is.
　　 c. A delightful man is Shaun/he.

The variants express different contextualisations of the predicative process. They are used as different resources for structuring the predicative clause into an operationally relevant text that is coherent within itself and with the discourse context (Halliday & Hasan 1976: 27). In the unmarked order for declarative predicative clauses, the subject and finite, in that order, precede the complement, as in (26a): the describee serves here as 'point of departure' for the predicative proposition and what is predicated of it is subsequently added as elaboration. The typically new information of the predicate nominative is thereby presented in final position, where – as Bolinger (1952) and Poutsma (1928: 387) point out – it may be given special prominence, as it typically provides a conclusion to the message communicated in the clause.[29]

The default SVO order may be overridden, however, for special rhetorical purposes. In (27), which provides an attested example of the OSV word order in (26b), the complement *tender mercies* is placed in initial position, thereby preceding the subject and finite. As a result, not the describee but the description is selected as point of departure for the exchange of information, so that the description provides the 'joint' between the prior context and the new proposition. By contrast,

---

**29** Bolinger (1952) considers two distinctions relevant for word order: (i) before and after, and (ii) initial and final. The first distinction, relevant to the sequential processing of information, is determined by various factors, such as the combinatorial possibilities allowed for by the lexicogrammar (for instance, by constituency), scopal and framing relations, etc. The second distinction is reminiscent of Halliday's (1967b, 1985) notion of 'thematic structure'. Like Halliday (1967b), Bolinger (1952) attributes special prominence to the initial position in the clause, as it sets the point of departure from which the clausal message is developed. (Unlike Halliday [1967b: 112], however, Bolinger [1952] does not equate the initial element with 'what the sentence is about'.) In line with Poutsma (1928: 387), Bolinger (1952: 1122) further considers final position as potentially lending prominence to information presented there: as (temporary) end-point, it serves as conclusion to the message. Therefore, Bolinger's (1952: 1125) functional analysis of word order focuses on the cognitive reality of the encoding and decoding of the message as a linear sequence and the potential manipulation of this sequence. While the distinctions he proposes are binary, they are neither explicitly dichotomous nor absolute: "gradation of position creates gradation in meaning when there are no other intervening factors" (Bolinger 1952: 1125).

the finite's final position lends prominence to its positive polarity and non-modal value: the speaker thereby emphasises the affirmative function of the clause. The rhetorical effect is one of insisting on the validity of the proposition. The fronting of the complement, which repeats the earlier mentioned *mercies*, *signals* the link of the description to the prior discourse.

(27)  Mercy is defined as kindness in excess of what might be expected. And for the multitude of your sins, God has a multitude of mercies. *Tender mercies they are*, compassionate kindness far in excess of what you deserve. (WB)

In the OVS pattern, illustrated in (26c) and in the attested examples (28) and (29), the rhetorical effect is different. Declarative OVS patterns are marginal in Present-Day English (Los 2009): going back to Middle English (Halliday 1967a: 70), their use is now archaic and found mostly in literary writing, as is the case in both (28) and (29). Hence, its effect would appear to be mostly poetic, as in (29), or to create a bombastic, slightly dramatic impression, as in (28).

(28)  To my amusement, I have discovered that I am greatly more suited to the life of a hired man than I am to the role of overseer, my once-soft hands more fitted to the pickaxe than the pen. *A university man am I*, younger son of a tycoon, who should be growing a belly behind a desk and conversing with Cabots and Lodges, yet here I stand with a mason's trowel in my hand, speaking only to God. (WB, from "Folly: A Novel" by Laurie R. King, 2001)

(29)  Lord Malibor prepared his ship, *A gallant sight was she*, With sails all of beaten gold, And masts of ivory. (WB, from "Valentine Pontifex" by Robert K. Silverberg, 1983)

Finally, while predicative clauses are normally indicative, imperative predicative clauses can be found in small numbers (i.e. in 4 out of 7,574 predicative examples in the datasets from Wordbanks*Online*, see Chapter 2, Section 2.3). As mentioned earlier, unmarked imperative clauses lack a mood element, which means that the role of describee in such clauses is not encoded. The implied subject, however, is taken to be the addressee (Halliday 1994: 76; Langacker 1991: 504). This is made explicit when the imperative is followed by a tag question, which takes pronoun *you* as its subject, e.g. (30).

(30)  Don't be a rotten beast, will you? (WB)

In the marked construal, the imperative can take an overt subject, in which case it receives special emphasis (Langacker 1991: 504), e.g. (31).

(31) Now you be a good boy! (WB)

The subject in such cases also counts as the modally responsible element in the clause. However, it is not the validity, or factuality, of the clause that is at stake here, but the realisation of the predicative process (Halliday & Matthiessen 2004: 117). In other words, the success of the proposal is vested in the addressee, whether s/he is implied or coded explicitly.

In sum, the functions of subject and complement in the predicative clause cannot be shifted across the two NPs. Halliday (1994: 119–120) refers to this feature of predicative clauses as non-reversibility and Huddleston (1984: 187–188) as the impossibility of a subject-complement switch. The fixed construal of the predicate nominative as complement is motivated by its integration in the composite relational predicate: it does not express a participant but provides the specific content of the process expressed by the predicate. The only possible subject is, therefore, the describee, in which is vested the validity of the proposition of indicative clauses or the success of the proposal in imperative clauses.

### 3.1.3 The referential status of the indefinite predicate nominative

The referential status of the indefinite predicate nominative has sparked little debate in existing accounts of copular typology. Most authors agree that, in the predicative construction, the indefinite predicative NP is non-referential (e.g. Kuno 1970; Akmajian 1973; Higgins 1979; Declerck 1988; Keizer 1992; Heycock & Kroch 1999; Partee 2000; Mikkelsen 2005; Heycock 2012; Patten 2012, 2016). However, as discussed in Section 3.1.2, that does not mean that the NP denotes a property or a type: on the tenet that to differences in lexicogrammatical form correspond differences in meaning (e.g. Bolinger 1968; Wierzbicka 1988), it is essential to recognise that predicative NPs differ from adjectival and noun complements, in that they denote instances, which carry type specifications and can carry qualities as well. The question to be answered in this section is then not whether predicative NPs denote instances or not, but how the designated instance is characterised in relation to the discourse context, i.e. what status it has in the context. To answer this question, I will first consider Langacker's view of 'predicative' reference as a special kind of non-specific reference (Section 3.1.3.1), to which I will then propose a refinement (Section 3.1.3.2), *viz*. that predicative NPs differ from indefinite NPs with non-specific reference in terms of one feature: individuality. This is correlated with the fact that the predicate nominative does not express a participant in the predicative process.

### 3.1.3.1 Langacker's view on predicative reference as non-specific reference

About the referential status of the predicate nominative, Langacker (1991) makes two (not uncontroversial) claims. First, he characterises the reference of indefinite predicate nominatives as involving a *virtual* instance "conjured up solely for purposes of making a type attribution", without "any status outside the confines of this predicate nominative construction" (Langacker 1991: 68). For that reason, Langacker (1991: 67–68) proposes, secondly, that predicate nominatives designate non-specific instances, analogous to the generally recognised non-specific reference of indefinite NPs in sentences like *John is looking for a job*. He holds that, in both types of context, an ARBITRARY member of the class denoted by the common head noun is referred to. While I agree with Langacker's (1991) first point, I will propose an alternative to his second claim that captures the referential status of the predicate nominative more precisely.

The notion of indefinite NPs with non-specific reference has been associated in the literature with contexts of use like (32). Their meaning is characterised in contrast to indefinite NPs with specific reference, as in (33): Langacker (1999: 167–168) describes SPECIFIC instances as introducing an instance into the discourse that is not yet accessible as a unique instance to the hearer but that, on a following mention, can be marked as a unique instance. Langacker (1999: 275–276) describes such instances as located in the ACTUAL domain of instantiation: that is, they have a status in actuality. For physical entities, the actual domain is primarily spatial (Langacker 1991: 18).

(32) *non-specific:* Grace wants a cat, preferably a Persian.

(33) *specific:* Last night, I was woken by a cat meowing outside my door.

Like Prince (1981a: 231), Langacker (1991: 103–107, 1999: 273–278) takes specific indefinite reference as a default, against which all other kinds of indefinite reference are characterised as *non*-specific. They are all "cases of non-specificity in which a conceived instance $t_i$ of [a type] T is invoked for a particular limited purpose and has no standing except in that context" (Langacker 1991: 106). These instances are located in what Langacker (1999: 276) refers to as the STRUCTURAL domain, in which generalisations are made about an "aspect of the world's structure". Instances located in the structural domain are *virtual*, since they have no status outside the 'mental space' created for their particular immediate purpose (*ib.*, see also Fauconnier 1985, 1994), e.g. the mental space of Grace's desire in (32). Therefore, in contrast with specific instances, non-specific instances are known solely by virtue of the speaker and hearer's knowledge of the type to which the instance corresponds, e.g. 'cat', and any qualitative features that may be explicitly ascribed to that instance, e.g. *Grace wants a well-behaved cat*. For this reason, Langacker (1991: 104) interprets such instances as ARBITRARY.

For NON-SPECIFIC indefinite NPs in the narrow traditional sense of (32), the concept of an arbitrary member of a class is readily accepted (e.g. Bache 2000: 179). Langacker (1999), however, extends this analysis to the instances designated by GENERIC indefinite NPs as well, e.g. *a cat* in (34).

(34)  generic:  A cat can see in the dark.

Generic NPs, Langacker (1991: 106) holds, are used to describe "REPRESENTATIVE instances of the category" (small caps mine). Their representativeness "derives from the notion of random selection", in that a random (or arbitrary) member of a class is bound to have the properties of all the members of that class (Langacker 1999: 274). For Langacker (1991, 1999), the two kinds of non-specific reference therefore do not differ in the kind of instance they invoke but solely in the *particular purpose* for which they are invoked. For generic NPs, the purpose is to make a statement about *all* instances of the category: what is attributed to a representative instance can be assumed to hold of roughly all other instances of the category too (e.g. *A cat is a mammal*).

Finally, indefinite PREDICATIVE NPs, such as *Alice is a thief* in (35), are also characterised by Langacker (1991: 67–68) as designating "an arbitrary member of the *thief* class (just as the object of *find* is an arbitrary member of the *job* class in *Jason would like to find a job*)" (Langacker 1991: 67). The difference between *a thief* in (35) and *a job* in the example Langacker cites is, therefore, essentially reduced to the immediate purpose of the 'non-specific' indefinite NP, which for predicative clauses is "making a type attribution" (Langacker 1991: 68).

(35)  predicative:  Alice is a thief. (Langacker 1991: 67)

Figure 5[30] represents Langacker's (1991, 1999) characterisation of instances located in the actual plane and those located in the structural plane: the type T

---

**30** This figure narrows down Langacker's (1999: 275) figure, which visualises the structural and actual planes of both entities and processes, to a visualisation of the instances designated by

projects down (as visualised by the arrows in Figure 5) into both actual and arbitrary instances, but while actual instances are characterised as having a status in actual space (depicted by the line *s*), the conception of an arbitrary instance is presented, by Langacker, as holding in the structural plane, which generalises away from actuality. Instances that hold in the structural plane are not characterised in relation to concrete space (which is represented by the absence of a link to the spatial line *s*): in other words, instances that hold in the structural plane are virtual.

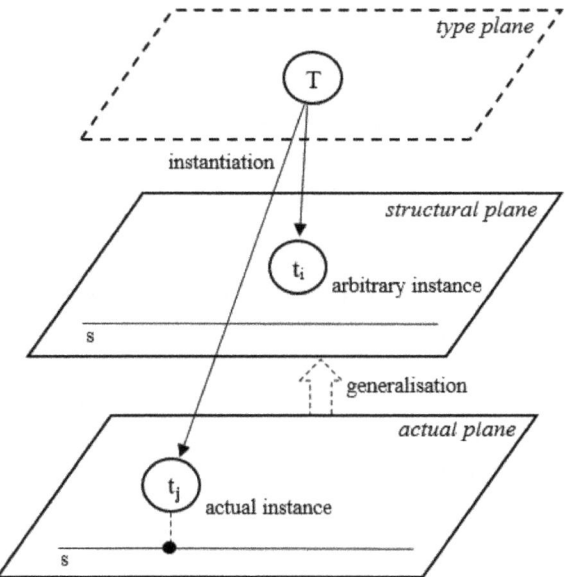

**Figure 5:** The representation of instances as pertaining to actuality vs structural knowledge (adapted from Langacker 1999: 275).

While I agree that all three 'non-specific' instances can be contrasted with specific ones by their being virtual rather than actual, a more fine-grained analysis of their differences is needed to come to a positive characterisation of the three instances. I will attempt to present such an analysis in Section 3.1.3.2.

---

indefinite NPs only. The original time lines *t* are adapted here as spatial configurations *s*, onto which instances can be located. Thus, instances in the actual plane are characterised in relation to concrete space, while 'non-specific' instances are not.

### 3.1.3.2 Predicative reference as a distinct kind of reference

To account for the conceptual differences between (narrowly defined) non-specific, generic and predicative indefinite NPs, I argue that they can be characterised with regard to their different values for the following parameters (Davidse & Van Praet 2019): inferred identifiability, presupposition of existence, individuality, and domain of instantiation. From these differences, I will further describe the conceptual meaning of each instance by explaining in what relation it stands to actuality. In doing so, I will put forth that predicative indefinite reference has to be recognised as a fourth distinct type of reference.

As Davidse & Van Praet (2019: 11) argue, indefinite NPs with GENERIC reference, as in (34) *A cat can see in the dark*, differ most from the other types of indefinite reference, because they are the only ones whose referent is *identifiable*: these NPs enable mental contact by the hearer with the class as such. Davidse (2004: 518) has argued that the identifiability of the class is, as suggested by Carlson (1978: 33, 196), probably best thought of as a pragmatic implicature triggered by generic contexts. The type specification provided by the head noun feeds into reference to '*that* kind of entity with the type characteristics designated by the head noun'. The designatum of an indefinite singular NP with generic reference thus has INFERRED IDENTIFIABILITY. This inferred identifiability is evidenced by the fact that the referent of an indefinite singular generic NP can further be tracked in the discourse by overtly definite NPs, as in (36). In such cases, the definite NP does not mark the identifiability of an individual instance but rather of the (sub)-class itself, as evoked in the prior sentence: in (36), the demonstrative *this* codes the identifiability of the subclass of the class *animal* with the name *cat*, not the identifiability of an individual cat (cf. \**This cat can't see in fine detail or colour*). If a representative instance is referred back to by means of another full NP with the same head noun *cat*, then that NP will likewise take the form of an indefinite NP to express the same generic meaning, as illustrated in (37).[31]

(36) A cat can see in the dark. / But this (kind of) animal can't see in fine detail or colour.

(37) A cat can see in the dark. But a cat can't see in fine detail or colour. That's because a cat has a high number of rods in its retina.

---

**31** Both (36) and (37) are made up.

Indefinite NPs with SPECIFIC reference mark the instance as 'not presumed identifiable' at the current stage of the discourse to the hearer, as in (38), and possibly to the speaker, as in (39), cited by von Heusinger (2002: 245).

(38) A student in Syntax 1 cheated on the exam. I caught him in the act and took away his copy immediately.

(39) A student in Syntax 1 cheated on the exam. We are all trying to figure out who it was. (von Heusinger 2002: 245)

In both cases, however, the designatum is a specific individual whose identity is in principle 'knowable'. Such NPs thus have the feature 'INDIVIDUALISED', i.e. they refer to one individual (von Heusinger 2002: 272). They also carry a PRESUPPOSITION OF EXISTENCE, which Langacker incorporates by locating them in the actual plane of instantiation. For physical entities, their representation in actuality is primarily spatial, but also involves the temporal dimension, as creatures and things do not exist for all eternity. All these features are shown to be present by the fact that, in examples like (38) and (39), *A student in Syntax 1 cheated on the exam* can be continued with statements such as *I caught him in the act* or *As soon as s/he is found, that student will be expelled*, which are both about events in the actual plane, and designate the student as an existing individual who can in principle be known.

Indefinite NPs with NON-SPECIFIC reference in the narrow sense, as in (32) *Grace wants a cat, preferably a Persian*, do not mark the virtual instance as identifiable and carry no presupposition of existence. Many authors have treated non-specific indefinite reference as analogous to what Donnellan (1966) termed 'attributive' reference (e.g. Heringer 1969: 94; Taglicht 1972: 12; Rivero 1975: 39; Palacas 1977: 202; Klein 1980: 153; Prince 1981a: 231; Declerck 1988: 50): non-specific indefinite NPs are thus interpreted as allowing speaker and hearer to conceive of (or 'conjure up') an individual that fits the type specifications of the NP, but without the presupposition that such an individual exists (Keizer 1992: 179). With Prince (1981a: 231) and von Heusinger (2002: 252), I hold that the instance referred to is nevertheless 'individualised': in (32), for instance, Grace is depicted as harbouring the desire for an individual cat (i.e. a 'cat-token' rather than a 'cat-type'). To account for this ambiguity, I propose to make two points: (i) what the non-specific indefinite NP actually designates in examples like (32) *Grace wants a cat, preferably a Persian*, is an INTENSIONAL instance in the structural plane (Rigter 1982: 96; Davidse & Vandelanotte 2011: 241), i.e. an instance that is the complement of so-called intensional verbs like *want, need, seek*, etc.; (ii) this intensional instance implies the *potentiality* of an individual in the actual plane. With regard to the first point, it can be pointed out that verbs like *want, need, seek*, etc., create, as Rigter (1982: 96) and Abbott (2010: 58–59) point out, 'intensional contexts': within such contexts, individuals can be talked about without presupposing their existence. Their 'actualisation' is merely potential. Therefore, it is possible, on the one hand, to continue a sentence with a non-specific indefinite NP by asserting that, in fact, an actual instance corresponds to its 'intension' (e.g. *Grace has always wanted a cat and, yesterday, she finally bought one*). On the other hand, it is also possible that no actual instance corresponds to the non-specific NP's designatum, e.g. *John was looking for a job but he ended up not finding any*. Furthermore, the observation that the instance of a non-specific indefinite is individualised but potential is evidenced by example (40), about which two points can be made. On the one hand, the non-specific indefinite NP, e.g. *a cat* in (40), can be referred back to via a personal pronoun and it can be ascribed qualities that apply to an individual. On the other hand, such anaphoric reference and quality-attribution are only possible as part of a proposition that expresses a *potential* SoA: this is illustrated by the use of the modal *should* in (40).

(40)   Grace wants a cat. It should be sleek, proud, but still affectionate.

Finally, following Davidse & Van Praet (2019: 12), I argue that it is the 'individuality' parameter that distinguishes predicative reference, as in *Alice is a cat*, from non-specific indefinite reference. As is generally recognised, a predicative NP does not establish a discourse referent (Kuno 1970: 356–57; Declerck 1988: 56; Keizer 1992): this observation has led to its interpretation as 'non-referential'. However, on a cognitive grammar account, nominal reference is understood as the process by which NPs denote instances (Langacker 1991: 67). In this particular framework, the question is not whether indefinite predicate nominatives denote instances, but what *type of instance* they denote. I follow Langacker (1991: 67–68, 1999) in viewing the predicate nominative as denoting a virtual instance; I do not, however, agree with Langacker's interpretation of it as a non-specific 'arbitrary' instance. The virtual instance designated by the predicate nominative does not only lack a presupposition of existence, but it is also devoid of all individuality. This is evidenced by the impossibility of referring back to an indefinite predicative NP with a definite NP or with a gendered pronoun within another predicative construction: *Alice is a cat. *Yes, Alice is that cat/her*. Because the instance denoted by the predicate nominative bears no relation whatsoever to actuality, it can be considered a 'DESCRIPTIONAL' entity, i.e. an entity 'conjured up' solely in terms of the 'internal content' of the nominal description but without the implication that the description applies to an individual (person or object).[32] This descriptional instance serves as a purely virtual entity for conceptualising type specifications and qualities. It does not imply that any actual instance corresponds to the description. This is evidenced by the fact that it is possible for *no* individual at all to correspond to the instance denoted by the predicate nominative, e.g. (41).

(41)  No one is a bottomless pit of adrenaline. (WB)

On a final note, it is important to discuss the commonly made observation that the predicate nominative is semantically 'more general' than the instance referred to by the subject. This has often been correlated with the semantics of class membership (42) and class inclusion (43) (Declerck 1988: 1; Halliday 1985: 114–115).

(42)  Skippy is a kangaroo.

(43)  A kangaroo is a marsupial.

In line with the description developed here, I suggest that the 'semantic generality' of the predicative NP has to be related to its being part of a composite predicate (Section 3.1.2.1). We have seen that, within the composite predicate, it is the predicate nominative that provides the specific conceptual content of the stative relation. But the instances referred to by the subject always have greater semantic specificity than the instance designated by the complement. In examples implying class membership, like (42), the subject instance has more semantic specifications than the complement instance. A proper name like *Skippy* involves a more elaborate conception, as its meaning is not limited to its being a particular instance of *kangaroo* but also includes more precise specifications relating to the animal's individual characteristics in the well-known Australian children's series (cf. Langacker 1991: 61). With predicative clauses like (43), in which the indefinite subject NP *a kangaroo* has generic reference, the concept *kangaroo* has more specific semantic content than the concept *marsupial*, to which it stands in a relation of hyponymy. On Langacker's (1991, 1999: 275–276) account, the virtual instance designated by the predicative NP is located in the structural plane, i.e. it is an abstract entity without a relation to actuality, and it is as such that it is incorpo-

---

**32** The difference between the 'internal content' of a nominal description and its application to an individual boils down to the distinction between the logical notions of 'intension' and 'extension', or Frege's 'Sense' and 'Reference'. Other authors have discussed the reference to a 'descriptional instance' in similar terms, such as 'qualitative' reference (Chen 2009: 1661) or 'predicative' reference (Prince 1981a).

rated into the composite predicate. The entity semantics of this 'descriptional' virtual instance allows the speaker to ascribe relevant type specifications to the subject entity as well as – degree modifiable – qualities. The subject entity itself can be an actual instance (42), a representative one (43), an intensional instance (44), or no instance at all, as we saw in (41). In all cases, the predicate nominative itself expresses a virtual instance that is semantically less specific than the subject instance.

(44) Grace wants a cat and it should be a Persian.

In sum, I conclude that the descriptional instance designated by the predicate nominative should be recognised as a fourth type besides the three explicitly distinguished by Langacker (1991: 102–105, 1999) – *viz.* specific, non-specific and generic reference. The distinct sets of values for the three parameters discussed above allow us to set apart the predicate nominative's reference from the reference of specific and non-specific indefinite NPs (cf. Table 4). Indefinite NPs with generic reference, which express representative instances, differ from the other three types listed in Table 4 by the fact that they have inferred identifiability as a representative of an identifiable type: the questions of presupposition of existence and individuality are, hence, not relevant to generic reference. Hence, indefinite NPs with generic reference are not included in Table 4.

**Table 4:** Summary of the distinct values of different types of indefinite reference.

|  | existential presupposition | individuality | type of instance |
|---|---|---|---|
| specific | + | + | actual |
| non-specific | – | + | intensional |
| predicative | – | – | descriptional |

The distinctness of predicative reference can thus be established on the basis of generally applicable referential parameters and tests. The reason why it lacks 'individuality' can, as argued in Davidse & Van Praet (2019: 13), be explained by the fact that the predicative NP does not designate an entity separate from, and participating in, the process of predicative ascription. Rather, it semantically specifies that predicative process. The instance it designates is merely 'got up', so to speak, to carry entity-type specifications and instance-oriented qualities, which are ascribed to the subject referent. By contrast, NPs with non-specific reference to an arbitrary instance do designate instances participating in processes. In (32) *a cat* is the object of Grace's desire. Because this is an entity participating in a process, its individuality is entailed. In our analysis, the 'non-referential' status of the predicate nominative is thus inextricably linked to its being part of the composite predicative process.

## 3.2 Specificational clauses

In the literature, specificational copular clauses have often been treated as the main counterpart to predicative ones, with which they have been compared and contrasted in various ways. The focus has been on the functions of the two NPs in specificational clauses and the referential status that correlates with those functions. Roughly three positions have been taken with regard to this question. One position treats specificational clauses as the 'inverse' of predicative ones. The idea is that they likewise involve one referential and one non-referential NP, but differ in terms of their 'inverse' subject-complement assignment (e.g. Mikkelsen 2005) or their 'inverse' focus-marking (Patten 2012). In contrast to the 'inverse' approach, others have argued that both NPs in the specificational clause are referential, so that the specificational clause forms a subtype of 'equative' copular clauses (e.g. Heycock & Kroch 1999; Heycock 2012). A third position acknowledges the referential asymmetry between what is termed the 'variable' and the 'value', but it does not conclude that the variable NP is therefore non-referential. Instead, it argues that the referential status of the variable NP should be characterised in its own terms, for which concepts such as 'superscription' (e.g. Higgins 1979) or 'weak referentiality' (e.g. Declerck 1988; Keizer 1992) have been proposed. In Section 3.2.1, I survey and assess the three positions. I then go on to develop my own position with regard to the semantic import of variable and value as participant roles (Section 3.2.2) and the referential status of the indefinite variable NP (Section 3.2.3). The information structure of specificational clauses will be discussed in Section 3.3, in contrast with the information structure of predicative clauses.

### 3.2.1 State of the art

In this section I survey existing accounts of specificational copular clauses, paying particular attention to the analyses of the (indefinite) variable NP that have been proposed in the literature. I will discuss three main views on specificational clauses, *viz.* the so-called 'inverse' approach (e.g. Williams 1983; Partee 1986a,b; Mikkelsen 2005; Patten 2012, 2016), the 'equative' approach (e.g. Heycock & Kroch 1999; Rothstein 1999; Heycock 2012), and, finally, an approach that brings together a diverse group of linguists (Higgins 1979; Declerck 1988; Keizer 1992;

Huddleston & Pullum 2002) focusing on the variable and value semantics of the arguments in the specificational clause, with the variable typically being interpreted as a 'superscription'.

### 3.2.1.1 Specificational clauses as inverse predicative clauses

A prominent line of thinking, going back to Williams (1983), is to treat specificational clauses as inverted predicative structures (e.g. Partee 1986a,b; Heggie 1988; Moro 1997; Mikkelsen 2005). Mikkelsen (2005), for instance, posits that "specificational and predicational clauses share a core predicational structure" (*ib.*: 2), which "involve[s] one referential and one predicative [i.e. non-referential] element" (*ib.*: 49). On this formal-semantic account, the two clause types "differ only in which of the two [NPs] is realized in subject position" (*ib.*: 2). Specificational clauses are thus taken to be derived from predicative ones, with the non-referential predicate being thought of as "rais[ing] to subject position" (*ib.* 61, see also Moro 1997): what characterises specificational clauses is that their subject is non-referential and the complement referential, which sets them apart from predicative clauses, with referential subjects and non-referential complements. Mikkelsen (2005: 62) adds that, on the inverse analysis, "indefinite specificational subjects are expected under the predicate raising analysis proposed [by her], since (at least some kinds of) indefinites can clearly function as predicates."

Patten (2012, 2016) proposes to reframe the formal-semantic analysis of specification as 'inverted' predication within a cognitive construction grammar account. She holds that specificational meaning "derives from the same nominal predication relation of class inclusion" between one non-referential 'property' NP and one referential NP (Patten 2012: 57).[33] In both specificational and predicative constructions, this non-referential 'property' NP is "analysed as designating a type and as profiling a relation between that type and the schematic instance of that type, which is then elaborated by an argument expression" (Patten 2012: 57).[34] The specificational reading, however, "involves interpreting this relation from the opposite perspective, as listing the membership of a set rather than attributing a property to a referent" (Patten 2012: 57). Patten (2012: 34) contests, however, the idea that "specificational clauses are derived via movement operations" like

---

**33** Patten (2012, 2016) appears to use the term 'class-inclusion' as synonymous with 'class-membership' or at least as a cover term for both concepts: on her account, predicative and specificational clauses have one NP denoting a 'type' (or class) and one NP denoting an instance of that type (i.e. a member of that class).
**34** Note that, if the theoretical tenet is assumed that semantics are coded by lexicogrammatical structure, then the claim that a full NP designates a type or a relation is not tenable, neither for predicative clauses as argued in Section 3.1.2 nor for specificational clauses.

predicate-raising (*ib.*: 34); she argues instead for "a monostratal model of language" in which specificational and predicative clauses make up two separate constructions. On Patten's (2012, 2016) account, the distinction between them lies not in the different grammatical functions of the non-referential and referential NPs (contra Mikkelsen 2005), but in their different information foci. The specificational reading "relies on a particular information structure, in which the referring expression is in focus" (Patten 2012: 57).[35] As a result, Patten's (2012) account diverges from formal inversion accounts, in that she acknowledges the possibility that the referential NP, i.e. the value, can be either subject or complement, as in (3a,b) restated here as (45a,b), so long as the referential NP, e.g. *Diane and Carla*, is focal.

(45) a. The waitresses were Diane and Carla. (Patten 2016: 79)[36]
 b. DIANE and CARLA were the waitresses. (Patten 2016: 80)

While Patten (2012, 2016) considers both (45a) and (45b) as specificational, she views the two clauses as different constructions, *viz.* a 'specificational inversion construction', like (43a) *The waitresses were Diane and Carla*, and a 'specificational non-inversion construction', like (45b) *DIANE AND CARLA were the waitresses*. In her constructional taxonomy (cf. Figure 6), Patten (2012: 58) makes the somewhat surprising claim that the latter construction is a direct subtype of the predicate nominal construction (i.e. of the predicative clause type).[37] The specificational inversion construction, by contrast, is said to form its own separate construction, involving a "mismatch" between the abstract predicate nominal semantics and its grammatical coding of the predicate as subject (Patten 2012: 59). Hence, the only thing that specificational inversion and non-inversion constructions share is their fixed information structure, with focus on the value (*ib.*: 58).

---

**35** Patten (2012, 2016) offers no explicit definition of the notion of information focus and seems to assume the notion is self-explanatory. She does not explicitly link the notion of focus to prosody, but her use of small caps in examples like (45b) suggests that she views focus as being marked by prosodic prominence. In Section 3.3, I will discuss the functional definition of information focus I work with and the prosodic means by which it is marked.
**36** Patten (2016: 79–80) only capitalises Diane and Carla when they occur as subject of the specificational clause in (45b), not as complement in (45a). Though she does not comment on this, it suggests that either she considers the focus on Diane and Carla in (45b) as a marked option, or that she thinks the focus on Diane and Carla is obvious in (45a) but not in (45b) (and, hence, needs to be made explicit).
**37** I will take issue with Patten's claim that non-inversion specificational clauses are a direct subtype of predicate nominal clauses below in Section 3.2.2.

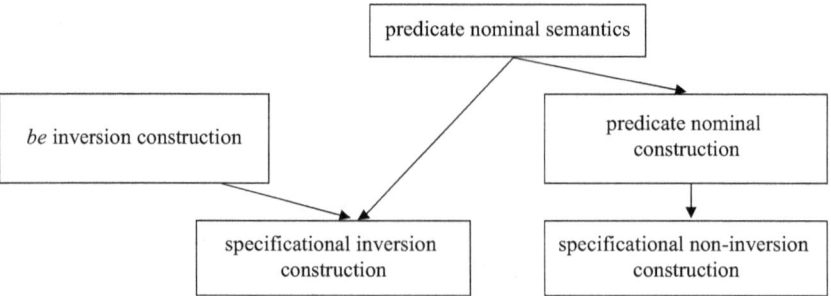

**Figure 6:** Patten's constructional taxonomy (Patten 2012: 60).

By vesting the felicity of a specificational reading in the clause's information structure, Patten (2012, 2016) is confronted with the problem that predicative clauses can focus not only on the non-referential predicative NP (e.g. *at home she's ^very much the little w\oman#*), but also on the subject referent (e.g. *^th\/at was a 'silly 'question#*), on both the subject and the complement (e.g. *I thought the :epic and the !n\ovel# - were a ^similar sort of [@m] - - th\ing#*) or even some other clausal element like the copula (e.g. *^well well !w\ell# . so ^you still !\are a member of 'A'C#*) or an adverb (e.g. *I ^don't 'think he's a :strong 'runner :\/anyway#*). Patten (2012: 35) partly acknowledges the issue that focus cannot provide a clear distinguishing criterion. She argues that, in sentences with a definite 'property' NP like (46a), focus on the referential NP always results in a specificational interpretation. By contrast, sentences with an indefinite property NP like (46b) (cited also in Chapter 1 as [7b]), she holds, do "not invite this interpretation; even when the referent *John* is focused [. . .] there is still the sense that we are ascribing a property to *John*" (*ib.*).

(46) a. JOHN is the best surgeon. (Patten 2012: 35)
 b. JOHN is a surgeon. (*ib.*)
 c. A philosopher who seems to share the Kiparskys' intuitions on some factive predicates is Unger [. . .] (1972). (Delacruz 1976: 195 [Mikkelsen 2005: 151], quoted in Patten 2016: 91)

Patten (2012: 37) attempts to resolve the issue by claiming that the specificational reading is "facilitated if the predicative NP denotes a *restricted* set (for which it is possible to list all its members) and if the individuals referred to can be taken as an *exhaustive* list of members within the described set" (Patten 2012: 37; original italics). Therefore, "the kinds of indefinite NP predicate to occur in the specificational inversion construction would be those that share most in common with definite NPs" (Patten 2012: 49). More specifically, they must be "anchored to the discourse in some way" and "contain modifying information which specifies the type to such a degree that exclusiveness[38] is not implied" (Patten 2012: 57–58), as in (46c). About this example, Patten (2012: 54) claims that "there is no implication that there is [. . .] more than one such philosopher". In sum, Patten claims that indefinite variable NPs obligatorily contain modifiers like the restrictive relative clause in (46c), which cancel the conversational implicature of 'exclusive', or 'non-unique' reference which indefinite NPs typically have (Hawkins 1978: 186, 1991).

In Section 3.2.2, I will argue for an alternative analysis, which correlates the semantics of the specificational clause and its two NPs with their grammatical form, i.e. their structure and their grammatical behaviour. In Section 3.2.3, I will specifically focus on the referential status of the indefinite variable NP, arguing that it is neither predicative nor non-referential (as claimed by Mikkelsen 2005). I will also argue against the idea that an indefinite variable NP can be used felicitously only if it approximates a definite variable NP and is non-committal with regard to 'exclusive', or 'non-unique', reference.

### 3.2.1.2 Specificational clauses as equative clauses

In the formal tradition, the analysis of specificational clauses as inverted predicative clauses has been argued against by, amongst others, Heycock & Kroch (1999: 379) and Heycock (2012). Heycock & Kroch's (1999) main counterargument was that not all predicative clauses have an 'inverted' specificational counterpart. Heycock (2012) takes the stronger position that "the only kind of predicates that seem to be able to invert are those that can be interpreted as being equative with their subject" (Heycock 2012: 224). In equative clauses "the copula is flanked by two expressions of the same semantic type" (Heycock 2012: 209). She illustrates this point with (47) and (48).

(47) a. John is the one thing that I want a man to be, i.e. honest.
 b. *The one thing that I want a man to be, i.e. honest, is John.

(48) a. The one thing I want a man to be is honest.
 b. Honest is the one thing I want a man to be.

---

[38] Patten refers here to Hawkins' (1978: 186–187) implicature of 'exclusive', i.e. 'non-inclusive', reference, which, he holds, is typically associated with NPs with an indefinite article. For instance, in an example like *She swatted a fly*, *a fly* does not carry an implicature that there is only one instance of 'fly' in the context; rather, there may be other flies besides the swatted one in the context. By contrast, if a definite NP, e.g. *She swatted the fly*, is used, this definite NP has an implicature of 'inclusive' reference, i.e. there is only one instance of 'fly' in the context.

Both (47) and (48) contain NPs with a restrictive relative clause with a gap in the predicative position. This is the reason, Heycock (2012: 225) argues, why such an NP can function either as a predicate ascribed to a subject, as in (47), or be "equated with another predicate", as in (48). Only the latter, where there is an equative relation, inverses. But, as Heycock points out, (48a) is not a predicative clause. On her analysis, both (48a) and (48b) are equative. Heycock (2012: 226) concludes that "the real generalization is that genuinely predicative sentences *cannot* invert". Predicative and specificational clauses are categorically different, and the latter cannot in principle be derived from the former. Heycock also argues against the non-referential status ascribed to the subject NP in examples like (48a), which "exhibits properties that are associated with arguments, rather than predicates" (Heycock 1992: 224).

Therefore, Heycock & Kroch (1999) and Heycock (2012) propose to analyse specificational copular clauses as equatives with two referential NPs, parallel to what are viewed as canonical equatives such as (49) in the formal tradition. The same position is taken by Rothstein (2001: 240–241), who argues that specificational (and equative) clauses have a structure that looks just like the structure of ordinary transitive clauses.

(49)  The Morning Star is the Evening Star.

However, Heycock & Kroch (1999) acknowledge that specificational clauses differ from 'true' equatives, in that, in the former, "there is one noun phrase that is clearly 'less referential' than the other" (Heycock & Kroch 1999: 343). They concede, therefore, that their equative account of specificationals "runs afoul of the intuition that [they] are asymmetric in interpretation in a way that 'true equatives' are not". Heycock (2012), then, follows Romero (2005) in proposing that this less referential NP, e.g. *the winner* in (50), is an intensional entity of the same type as occurs in concealed questions such as (51). Romero (2005) argues that the verb *be* in specificational copulars is an intensional verb, like *know* and *guess*, "requiring an intensional object as its semantic argument" (Romero 2005: 690). An intensional entity occurs in an intensional or opaque context such as created by verbs of propositional attitude like *know* and *guess*, whose objects can involve the intension of the NP. In (51) *they* want to guess 'who *the winner* is', whoever that may be (Romero 2005: 697).

(50)  The winner was Julia. (Heycock 2012: 228)

(51)  They guessed the winner. (Heycock 2012: 228, see also Romero 2005: 721)

Despite the intuitive appeal of the argument for intensionality, problems arise when we take into account specificational clauses with an indefinite NP as subject, e.g. (52).

(52) Who around here is a doctor? – One doctor is Bill; another is John. (Heycock 2012: 220)

Heycock (2012: 220) notes – correctly, in my opinion – that indefinite NPs can only function as subject of a specificational clause if they are 'strong' indefinites, that is, if they carry a presupposition of existence. This is, however, in contradiction with the idea that specificational subjects denote intensional objects. As Moltmann (1997: 1) describes, indefinite NPs that are used as the complement of a verb like *look for* allow for both an 'extensional' (i.e. specific) and an 'intensional' (i.e. non-specific) reading, e.g. (53). However, only on the extensional reading does the indefinite NP carry a presupposition of existence, which Moltmann (1997: 1) glosses as follows: "There is a horse $x$ and John is looking for $x$". The intensional reading of the indefinite NP contrasts with the extensional reading exactly in that it does not carry an existential presupposition (e.g. 'John is looking for a horse; any horse will do') (see also Section 3.1.3).

(53) John is looking for a horse.

This, of course, problematises the account that Romero (2005) proposes for (definite) specificational subjects: either we allow for two separate analyses for definite and indefinite specificational subjects – with the former denoting intensional objects (i.e. non-specific instances) and the latter extensional objects (i.e. specific instances) – or we provide an alternative analysis that captures the commonalities of all specificational subjects but that can also accommodate the differences between definite and indefinite ones. I believe that the second option is to be preferred.

In Section 3.2.3, I will present an analysis that shares the view of specificational clauses as categorically different from predicative clauses and that explains the intuitions that the variable NP has features of a participant (e.g. Rothstein 2001). However, viewing specification as equative has all the problems recognised, and not adequately solved, by Heycock & Kroch (1999) and Heycock (2012). While it recognises that specificational clauses involve two referential NPs, it does not provide a compelling analysis for the referential asymmetry that exists between the two NPs. Especially for the analysis of indefinite variable NPs, as in (52), I hold that the analysis of specificational clauses as equatives is untenable.

### 3.2.1.3 Specificational clauses as variable-value clauses

The third tradition I survey stresses that specificational clauses are distinct from both predicative clauses and 'true' equatives like (49) above. This position goes back to Higgins (1979: 133), who contends that "the specificational reading of a copular sentence is not the expression of some kind of identity." Rather, a specificational subject serves a 'superscriptional' function, resembling "the heading of a list [. . .], to which the items on the list conform as 'values' of that variable" (*ib.*: 155). The specificational subject does not pick out an individual, but designates a *variable*, which "delimits a domain and the [value] [picks out] a particular member of that domain" (*ib.*: 132). When a value is assigned to a variable, "it in some way gives the content of the constitution of what is referred to by [the variable]" (Higgins 1970: 152). Higgins' notion of "variable" and "value" seems to be taken from mathematical logic, where the variable is the 'x' element in a mathematical equation, for which the actual mathematical value is sought. However, while the notion of a variable avoids the issues that the equative approach faces for indefinite variable NPs, Higgins (1979: 138) maintains that "except under rather special circumstances, indefinite noun phrases cannot be used superscriptionally [i.e. as variable]."

Declerck (1988), who is strongly influenced by Higgins (1979), likewise interprets the semantics of specificational clauses in terms of a variable-value relation. Following Halliday (1967b: 230; Halliday 1985) and Huddleston (1984: 457), Declerck (1988: 9) stresses that a crucial characteristic of specificational clauses is the possibility of a subject-complement switch,[39] which sets them apart from predicative clauses, e.g. *Bill Gates is a philanthropist*, and, what he calls, 'descriptionally-identifying' clauses, like *Bill Gates is the principal founder of Microsoft Corporation*. While Declerck (1988: 13), like Patten (2012), holds that specificational clauses typically have focal values, his account does not distinguish specificational from predicative clauses based on their different information structures. Instead, he follows Higgins (1979) in arguing that predicative clauses have non-referential complements but that the variable NP in specificational clauses is neither non-referential nor referential. Declerck (1988: 47f) proposes that definite variable NPs constitute what Donnellan (1966) referred to as the 'attributive' use of definite NPs, as in *Smith's murderer must be insane* (Declerck 1988: 47), which

---

**39** Higgins (1973: 57) follows Halliday (1967a: 67), where he "points out an important distinguishing mark of specificational copular sentences, the fact that the subject and predicate complement can change places". However, Higgins (1973) himself works with the notion of 'deep subject', which leads him to characterise the variable as the specificational (deep) subject: "the Subject in some way delimits a domain and the specificational predicate determines a member of that domain" (Higgins 1973:132)

may be uttered by someone hearing the atrocious details of Smith's murder, without having any idea who actually did it.

However, as Donnellan's attributive NPs are inherently definite, the notion does not fully fit specificational clauses, which may have either definite or indefinite variable NPs. To cover both, Declerck (1988: 47) introduces the concept of "weakly referring" NPs, which, he holds, in the case of definite NPs are attributive, and in the case of indefinite variable NPs have non-specific reference (Declerck 1988: 50).

Keizer (1992: 179) partly counters Declerck's (1988) claim and argues that "what are traditionally regarded as non-specifics are not weakly referential". Non-specific indefinites, as in *Grace wants a cat*, lack the presupposition of existence that attaches to both definite and indefinite variable NPs, where "we know that someone or something answering the description exists, but we are not able to identify this person or thing" (Keizer 1992: 179). Therefore, Keizer (1992: 179) contends that the "conclusion must be that weakly referential terms form a subclass of attributive expressions: they are attributive expressions occurring in specificational sentences." "For the sake of convenience", she takes the term 'weakly referential' to be synonymous with Higgins's (1979) concept of 'superscription' (*ib.*: 180). However, the redundancy that comes from explaining the variable as an 'attributive NP in specificational contexts' does not clarify how the variable's referential status differs from other attributive NPs, nor does it provide an explanation for the status of indefinite variable NPs. The question of how variable NPs, especially indefinite ones, refer is in much need of further investigation.

Halliday's (1967a,b, 1968, 1994) functional account of specificational clauses as variable-value relations does not explicitly discuss referential status. His analysis is one of the earliest expositions of the position that English specificational clauses are transitive two-participant configurations. Halliday's (1967a,b, 1994) argument for the transitivity of specificational clauses is inextricably linked to the subject-complement re-assignment they allow for. According to Halliday (1967a: 67; 1967b: 230), the clearest recognition criterion distinguishing specificational from predicative clauses in English is found at the level of subject-complement relations. In specificational clauses, the subject and complement functions can be re-assigned to the two NPs (Huddleston, 1984: 457, Huddleston & Pullum 2002: 266), as illustrated by (54a) and (54b) below, which can be contextualised as the two possible responses to the question 'which is the ugly one?', for instance, on a photo. The switch from subject *I* (54a) to complement *me* (54b) is marked by the change from nominative to accusative case. This switch is also signalled by the person marking on the VP, which agrees with the first person subject in (54a) and the third person subject in (54b). Halliday (1967a: 67) argues that the fact that either NP in specificational clauses can be construed as subject entails that the verb *be* is used as "a 'transitive' verb".

(54) (a) I                          am   the ugly one.
        subject                          complement
        identifier/value                 identified/variable
    (b) The ugly one                is   me (complement).
        subject                          complement
        identified/variable              identifier/value

Halliday (1967b: 230) characterises the representational semantics of transitive copular clauses like (54) as 'identification by specification'. He argues that two semantic dimensions are needed to characterise the way in which the NP referents participate in specificational-identifying *be*. The first dimension is that of identification. One participant is the 'element to be identified', the 'identified', e.g. *the ugly one* in (54); the other participant is the one that brings about identification, the 'identifier', *I/me* in (54). The identified is like the 'x' in an equation: an abstract element whose identity is being looked for. The identifier, Halliday (1967b: 224) says, is the participant that corresponds to the WH-item of the WH-question presupposed by the copular clause: *Which is the ugly one?*. While the identifier typically carries the information focus signalled by tonic prominence, this is not "true in a hundred per cent of all instances" (Halliday 1994: 117). Both in terms of distribution and functional load, identifier and information focus are distinct categories: identifier/identified is a dimension of the representational semantics, while focal/non-focal information are categories of information structure.

The second semantic dimension of specification is interpreted by Halliday (1967b: 222ff) as a symbolic relation in which a more abstract entity is 'realised' by a more concrete one. The semantic model he invokes is taken from semiotics.[40] For Halliday (1967b), the roles of value and variable invoke the two sides of a symbolic relation, such as found in semioticians' view of the linguistic sign. In a

---

[40] Halliday (1967a,b) in fact applied the terms value and variable exactly the other way round from how they have come to be used in the literature. The semantic model that motivated his use of the terms "value" and "variable" was semiotics. He therefore called the more abstract term "value", as in Saussure's 'valeur', and the more concrete entities that can realise it "variables". By contrast, the standard use of "variable" and "value" is taken from mathematical logic (see, for instance, Akmajian 1970 and Higgins 1979). While Halliday's opposite use of the terms value and variable is at first sight startling, the semantic notions involved are not wholly unrelated. The variable in mathematical logic is a place-holder, a 'symbol', which thus conceptually somewhat resembles Halliday's (1967a,b) notion of 'value' as the more abstract term in the symbolic relation. To avoid terminological confusion I adhere to the standard use of value and variable, also when I discuss Halliday's (1967a,b) semantic model.

specificational relation like (55), the variable describes the abstract function or meaning of an entity, i.e. *one of my weaknesses*, while the value refers to the more concrete entity realising the variable, i.e. *puddings and creamy pastries*. In specificational copulars, the variable is always the element to be identified and the value the element bringing about identification.

(55) a. One of my weaknesses is puddings and creamy pastries. (Google)
b. Puddings and creamy pastries are one of my weaknesses.

The notion of 'symbolic representation', however, does not bring out that the variable has, in a crucial way, a CRITERIAL function in the selection of the value, which Higgins' (1976) semantic definition of the variable as 'delimiting a domain' does bring out. I will return to this issue in Section 3.2.2.2 below. Moreover, Halliday (1967b: 227–228) reified the suggested 'realise' glosses into THE meaning of specificational clauses. This led him to claim that specificational clauses with the variable as subject, as in (55a), are 'passive' clauses because they can be glossed as 'one of my weaknesses is realised by puddings and creamy pastries'. (55b) is glossed as 'pudding and creamy pastries realise one of my weaknesses'. However, if we assume the theoretical principle that the overt form of expressions has to be respected, this analysis is untenable in view of the fact that the verb *be* has no means of expressing a passive relation in either (55a) or (55b).

According to Halliday (1967b: 229, 231, 236, 237), the crucial alternate to identify the value in a specificational copular is the corresponding cleft: this is because specificational configurations only allow the value as the clefted element. To specificational clauses with a definite variable NP, e.g. (56a,b), corresponds, irrespectively of which NP is subject, an *it*-cleft, which invariably construes the value as the clefted element, e.g. *the Hotel Boomerang* in (56c). In this respect, the possibility of construing the corresponding *it*-cleft is a recognition criterion of specificational copulars as such, as also pointed out by Declerck (1988: 10).

(56) a. Where to stay: the Parador El Hierro . . . has doubles from £80 a night, B&B. Or in Valverde, *the best option is the Hotel Boomerang*. (WB)
b. [. . .] The Hotel Boomerang is the best option.
c. It's the Hotel Boomerang that is the best option.

Specificational copular clauses with an indefinite variable NP have tended to be overlooked and so has the type of specificational cleft corresponding to them (but see, for instance, Davidse & Kimps 2016). The cleft alternate for indefinite specificational copulars is the *there*-cleft, as pointed out in Van Praet & Davidse (2015). Thus, to the specificational clauses with an indefinite variable *a good option* in

(57a,b) corresponds a specificational *there*-cleft, as in (57c). Unlike *it*-clefts, specificational *there*-clefts do not carry an implicature of exhaustiveness but one of non-exhaustiveness. I will describe, in Section 3.2.3.2, that specificational copular clauses with indefinite variable NP likewise trigger an implicature of non-exhaustiveness, and contrast in this respect with specificational copulars with definite variable NP (see Section 3.2.3.2).

(57) a. You should also look for a tablet with a CPU that's tuned for both performance and battery life. . . *A good option is the Asus Transformer Book T100*. (COCA)
 b. [. . .] The Asus Transformer Book T100 is a good option.
 c. There's **the Asus Transformer Book T100** that's a good option.

Predicative clauses do not express a variable-value relation and, hence, do not alternate with only one type of cleft sentence in which one element is consistently construed as the clefted element. Either the predicative subject or complement can occur in the post-copular 'value' slot of the cleft. For instance, corresponding to a sentence like *John is a surgeon* in (46b), we can get both *it's a surgeon that John is* and *it's John who's a surgeon*. Thus, the fact that specificational clauses alternate only with clefts that have the value as clefted element is a criterion to distinguish specificational from predicative copulars.

In Section 3.2.2, I propose an account of specificational clauses that is strongly indebted to the tradition of viewing specificational clauses as involving variable-value relations. I will describe both the transitivity structure and the variation in subject-complement assignment of specificational clauses (Section 3.2.2) as well as the referential status of the indefinite variable NP (Section 3.2.3) within a cognitive-functional approach. I will elaborate on observations that specificational clauses resemble 'ordinary transitive structures' (Rothstein 2001: 240–241) in terms of their distinct process-participant configuration. With regard to this point, I will examine both the actually coded meanings of specificational clauses (Section 3.2.2.1) and the pragmatic inferences that the coded meanings trigger (Section 3.2.2.2). I will then relate these semantics-pragmatics to the mood structure variants that specificational clauses allow for (Section 3.2.2.3), in contrast to those of predicative clauses as described in Section 3.1.2.2. Finally, I will propose an in-depth analysis of a crucial moot point in the literature on specificational clauses, namely the referential status of the variable NP: by focusing on the indefinite variable NP, I attempt to overcome the fixation in the literature on definite variable NPs. I will argue that both kinds of variable can be explained in terms of Langacker's (1999, 2005) notion of reference to a 'generalised' instance (Section 3.2.3).

## 3.2.2 The multi-layered structure of specificational constructions

In this section I analyse specificational clauses, in contrast with predicative ones, as coding transitive relations, of which the 'variable' and the 'value' form the two participants. I will elucidate how precisely the conceptual import of the variable and value as *lexicogrammatically coded* participant roles is to be understood (Section 3.2.2.1), and which pragmatic mechanisms are triggered by this linguistic coding (Section 3.2.2.2). I further demonstrate that the transitivity of the specificational configuration is evidenced by the possibility of either the variable or the value functioning as subject of the clause (Section 3.2.2.3).

### 3.2.2.1 Process-participant relations: Coded meanings

The transitivity of specificational relations, involving two participants, was first argued for by Halliday (1967a,b, 1985). A central argument is the recognition criterion that the functions of subject and complement can be re-assigned over the specificational clause's two NPs: Halliday made the case about clauses with definite variable NP. It is important to stress that these grammatical arguments also apply to specificational clauses with indefinite variable NP, as in (58): the variable can be felicitously construed as either subject, e.g. (58a,b), or as complement, (58c). The fact that the reversing of the constituent order involves a real subject-complement switch is shown if we substitute *Queen Elizabeth the Queen Mother* for a pronoun, which is realised in the accusative case as complement (58b) but in the nominative as subject (58c). (I will return to the implications of reversibility in Section 3.2.2.3 on mood structure.)

(58)    a.    One member of the Royal Family who continued to be on good terms with Blunt was **Queen Elizabeth the Queen Mother**. (WB)
        b.    One member of the Royal Family who continued to be on good terms with Blunt was **her**.
        c.    **She** was one member of the Royal Family who continued to be on good terms with Blunt.

Halliday (1985: 76) holds, firstly, that it is a characteristic of Present-Day English that only entities that participate directly in the process and "have a direct line to the process" (*ib.*) can be selected as the subject. Potential subjecthood is a corollary of participanthood. Hence, the fact that both the variable and the value can be construed as subject is evidence of the transitivity of the specificational clause (Halliday 1967a: 67). Secondly, it is also significant that the complement designating the value is coded in the accusative if it is a pronoun manifesting case, like *her* in (58b). This contrasts with the absence of accusatives in predicative clauses. As Halliday (1967a: 70) notes, "A clause such as *it is me* can only be extensive [i.e. transitive], because of the pronoun complement – there is no intensive [i.e. intransitive] form such as *it seems me, it became me*". The very use of the accusative for the complement is strongly associated with transitive clauses in English, which suggests that specificational clauses have a degree of transitivity.

On Halliday's (1967a,b, 1985) account, the transitivity of the specificational relation in contrast with the intransitive predicative one is interpreted to mean that (at least) two verbs *be* have to be distinguished, or that *be* should be attributed two (or more) meanings. Alternatively, it can also be argued that the same verb *be* figures in both predicative and specificational clauses and that the semantic difference(s) between the two clause types can be attributed not to the polysemy of *be* but to the structural assembly of the two constructions. For the analysis of structural-functional relations, it is crucial to look at "the order in which component structures are successively combined to form progressively more elaborate composite structures" (Langacker 1987a: 310). The order of assembly of a composite structure is taken as accounting for the composite semantics of the structure, as conceptual dependencies between elements are "largely responsible, in the final analysis, for their combinatory behaviour" (Langacker 1987a: 305).

Thus, the different composite semantics of predicative and specificational clauses can be accounted for by how the clauses are structurally assembled, specifically the order in which their two NPs are integrated with *be*. In Section 3.1.2.1, predicative clauses were analysed as involving a composite predicate, derived by the integration of *be* + predicate nominative: the intransitive composite predicate designates a more elaborate "stative relation at a higher level of conceptual organisation" (Langacker 1991: 66). It is this composite predicate rather than *be* itself that assigns a participant role to the subject referent. In specificational clauses, by contrast, no composite predicate is involved: only *be* is part of the relational predicate, which makes schematic reference to two participants, viz. two 'be-ers'. Structurally, the two NPs integrate directly with the VP: the VP is a two-place predicate coding a transitive relation.[41]

In further support of the transitivity of specificational clauses, I return to the coordination pattern of *be* + complement discussed in Section 3.1.2.1. The felicity of this coordination pattern with predicative clauses, e.g. *Saddam Hussein's regime was a threat and was a danger*, confirms the idea that *be* + complement are

---

[41] It is, of course, possible for specificational clauses to have values that are realised by other grammatical categories than NPs. In such cases, however, I take it that the 'XP' realising the value is reclassified as a nominal, analogously to, for instance, the use of the adjective *red* in *red is a beautiful colour*, in which 'red' is used to denote a concept rather than a quality per se.

integrated into a composite predicate and thereby come to form one unit. Specificational clauses, by contrast, resist the coordination of two instances of *be* + complement, both when the value is the complement and when the variable is the complement, e.g. (59) and (60) respectively.

(59) (What helps to soothe pain?) *A good remedy for pain is vitamin C and is fish oil.

(60) (What helps to soothe pain?) *Vitamin C is a good remedy for pain and is also a strong antioxidant.

Example (60) shows that it is not possible to coordinate two instances of *be* + variable complement NP and retain a specificational reading: the sentence can only be read as a predicative clause, possibly with (narrow) focus on the subject (see also Section 3.1.2.1). The only coordination pattern that specificational clauses allow for is when the value and/or the variable is realised as a coordinated NP, e.g. (61) and (62), or when two specificational clauses are coordinated, e.g. (63).

(61) (What helps to soothe pain?) A good remedy for pain and a strong antioxidant is vitamin C.

(62) (What does an infection control doctor do?) An increasing role for an infection control doctor is surveillance and collecting data on hospital acquired infections. (WB)

(63) For the last two months I've been sleeping with four other men. *One is my daughter's father and another is my boyfriend's brother*, as well as two others. (WB)

As befits a transitive relational process, there is a clear asymmetry between the two participants in the specificational clause (Halliday 1985: 103, 114–17). As set out in Section 3.2.1.3, Halliday (1967a,b) interprets this asymmetry in terms of a symbolic relation, mapped onto an identification relation, in which a more abstract term is 'realised' by a more concrete entity, e.g. 'the rules realise the problem' or 'the problem is realised by the rules' in (64).

(64) The rules are the problem, not the people dealing with them. (WB)

Importantly, the asymmetry between these participant roles is *not* intrinsic to the meaning of *be* itself: instead, it is a semantic specification brought about by the elaboration of the process of 'being' into a process of specification. The fact that the 'being' relation is semantically neutral to the (a)symmetry of the instances it relates is manifested by the possibility of 'identity statements' or 'true equatives', in which the 'being' relation is construed as symmetrical, as in (65) and (66). In (66), the symmetry between the equated instances is manifested in the possibility of recursive equation. This type of recursiveness is not possible in asymmetrical 'being' relations, as shown by the infelicity of (67). As a result, the asymmetry that Halliday (1967a,b, 1985, 1994) notes for the identifying relation, and that is also attested in the specificational relation, has to be considered a consequence of the clausal construal of the process of 'being' into a process of specification. Hence, the glosses in terms of 'symbolic realisation' that Halliday (1967a,b) suggests cannot be reified into the meaning of *be* (contra Halliday 1967a,b).

(65) The Morning Star is the Evening Star.

(66) Brussels is Bruxelles is Brussel. (https://deskgram.net/belgiansolutions)

(67) *The winner is my brother is John.

I suggest instead that the two participants of the specificational relation can be thought of as the element to be specified (the 'specified') and the element doing the specifying (the 'specifier'). (These terms are inspired by Halliday's (1985, 1994) explanation of the identifying relation in terms of an 'identified' and an 'identifier'. However, as Higgins (1979) points out, the function of specification is distinct from identification, as I also argued in Chapter 1. This is evidenced by the possibility of indefinite variable NPs, which do not denote uniquely identifiable instances and which therefore cannot be used for the expression of a one-to-one correspondence or identification.) It is in the sense of a 'specified' and a 'specifier' that the terms variable and value for the two participants in the specificational relation expressed by *be* should be understood: the variable is the element that defines the 'x' to be specified, while the value is the element that specifies the 'x', i.e. specifies elements that fit the bill of the specifier. As is typical of participant roles, they generalise over variation at the level of mood structure, where they can map onto subject and complement as an independent choice (see Section 3.2.2.2).

Halliday's semantic model of the variable and the value as an abstract function and the (more) concrete form by which it is realised has the advantage that it can also be applied to more marked specificational examples like (68) and (69), which do not identify any actual entity corresponding to the variable. In (68), *the winner* 'is realised by' *nobody*; in (69), *a great first date* 'would have to be realised by' *something different*.⁴²

(68) And the winner is. . . nobody. (https://foreignpolicy.com/2009/09/01/and-the-winner-isnobody/)

(69) I think *a great first date would be something different*. . . not like movies or going to dinner. . . going rock climbing together. . . doing an activity and then going to dinner, so that you guys share an experience, and then you have something to talk about, and it's not the same old thing. (https://marriedbiography.com/madeline-zima-biography/)

As touched upon in Section 3.2.1.3, what the notion of 'symbolic realisation' fails to capture, however, is the way in which the variable NP stipulates criteria that delimit the concrete forms by which it is – and is not – realised.

The idea that the variable 'delimits' its corresponding value(s) is present in both Akmajian (1970: 19) and Higgins (1973: 157). Akmajian (1970: 19), for instance, states that the value "must belong to the appropriate semantic class, i.e. the class represented by the variable." For Higgins (1973: 156–157), the analogy of a list – with the variable describing the heading of the list and the value the item(s) on that list – implies that there are "well-formedness conditions" to which the items *conform* as values for the variable. Patten (2016) has later drawn inspiration from both Akmajian (1970) and Higgins (1973): she interprets their analyses as getting "very close to the concept of class-inclusion" (Patten 2016: 84), which she views as the semantic relation expressed in specification clauses (cf. Section 3.2.1.1). However, apart from the already explained issues with Patten's treating the variable NP as designating a type (see Section 3.2.1), Higgins' (1973) notion that the value 'lists' the items that figure under the 'heading' of the variable does not really work for examples like (68) and (69), where *nobody* and *something different* cannot be said to figure on the lists of *the winner* and *a great first date* respectively. *Nobody* denies the existence of a qualifying value and, hence, specifies that the list of 'winners' is empty. *Something different* is an indefinite NP with

---

42 Evidence for the interpretation of (69) as a specificational clause is found in the following text, where the speaker contrasts non-qualifying examples of 'a great first date' (e.g. 'movies', 'going to dinner') with a qualifying example (e.g. 'rock-climbing'). The speaker in (69) specifies what would be 'a great first date' by spelling out the more specific criteria (i.e. being 'different') to which a 'first date' needs to conform to qualify as 'great'. The specificational reading can be brought out more clearly by glossing the clause as 'a great first date would be anything that is even slightly different'.

non-specific reference, lacking a presupposition of existence: here too, the value does not 'list' items corresponding to the variable; rather, it specifies what qualities a value needs to have to meet the criteria stipulated by the variable. Finally, even in more typical cases, the 'list' analogy does accurately gloss the meaning of the specificational process. In specificational clauses with definite variable, which carry an exhaustiveness implicature, there is only one value that conforms to the variable. That means that for the majority of specificational clauses – the ones with definite variable account for 85% of them, see Chapter 2 – the 'list' of values consists of only one item, which seems at odds with the whole notion of a list.

In view of the problems with these models, Davidse & Van Praet (2019: 21) developed an alternative model: they propose that, in the specificational relation, the variable NP sets up a CRITERIAL abstract entity.[43] The notion of a criterial entity is inspired by Davidse & Kimps's (2016: 121) explanation of the variable constituent in specificational clefts as "a criterial characterization set up by the speaker to which the value(s) must correspond": in clefts, the variable, coded by a cleft relative clause, has the meaning of an 'x' with a particular role in a SoA. This semantic model can be extended to specificational copulars. Unlike the cleft relative clause, however, the variable NP, such as *the problem* in (64), does not express an 'open' proposition but an entity (Delahunty 1984). For this abstract entity, a more concrete one is sought based on the criteria expressed in the variable NP: these criteria are formed by the semantic type specifications contained in the variable NP itself, plus any relevant additional specifications retrieved from the context. For instance, in (70), the variable NP itself contains the type specifications *good account*. As an account is always an account of something, the contextual type specifications *on cattle ranching on the plains* are naturally added, leading to an inferred set containing all 'good accounts on cattle ranching on the plains'.

(70) On cattle ranching on the plains, a good account is Lewis Atherton, *The Cattle Kings* (1961), but see also Don Worcester *The Chisholm Trail* (1980). (WB)

---

[43] The notion of a 'variable', to an extent, implies its criterial function. What is important in Davidse & Van Praet's (2019) account is that the variable NP in specificational copulars realises its criterial function by reference to an instance (or entity). This account allows us to describe more carefully how different kinds of 'variable', in copulars and clefts, stipulate criteria in different ways (e.g. via type specifications and/or qualities with variable NPs vs via a semantic role in a process with cleft or fused relative clauses). This distinction is missing from the account based on the 'list' analogy.

The criteria set up by the variable in a given context thus determine which instances correspond as values for the variable and which do not. Because of its criterial function, the variable has a logical priority in the specificational relation. Setting up the criteria that have to be met is inherently "in some way 'prior' to the actual assigning of the value" (Davidse & Kimps 2016: 135).

As pointed out by Halliday (1967a,b), Declerck (1988), Romero (2005) and Heycock (2012), the variable relates to a presupposed WH-question, which is answered by the value. As we saw in Section 3.2.1, Halliday (1967a,b) proposed to capture this semantic dimension by a second set of roles, which are mapped onto variable and value in a fixed way in specificational clauses. The variable is the element to be identified', the 'identified', and the value is the one that brings about identification, the 'identifier'. I do not think that this semantic dimension has to be captured by a distinct set of roles. Moreover, the roles of identified and identifier do not fit the semantics of specificational copulars with an indefinite variable NP, as such a variable NP typically generalises over more concrete instances than are actually referred to by the value NP. However, it is essential to the semantics of the variable that it designates an abstract entity whose corresponding concrete values are being looked for. As noted in Section 3.2.1, the very notion of 'variable' as taken from mathematical logic includes the idea that it is an 'x' whose actual value is being looked for. Hence, the semantics of the definite variable NP *the problem* in (64) can be glossed as 'the x that are the problem = ?' and those of the indefinite variable NP *a good account* in (70) as 'an x that is a good account on cattle ranching on the plains = ?'. Likewise, it is an intrinsic element of the value role that it indicates the more concrete values meeting the criteria of the variable.

In the unmarked case, the value NP indicates the concrete entity or entities that fit the criteria of the variable, e.g. *Queen Elizabeth the Queen Mother* in (58) above, and/or which entities do not fit these criteria, e.g. *the people* in *the rules are the problem, not the people dealing with them* in (64). But occasionally the value NP may also negate the existence of a more concrete entity corresponding to the criterial abstract entity, e.g. *the winner is nobody* in (68). Another marked option is for the value NP to designate a non-specific instance, which lacks a presupposition of existence (see Section 3.1.3), e.g. *someone – qualitatively – different* from ordinary dates in (69). Note that the semantics of the participant role of the variable NPs in such marked cases still involves the notion of 'meeting the variable's criteria'. In view of all the above considerations, the function of specificational copular clauses is essentially one of setting up and meeting criteria. Rather than a relation of class-inclusion (contra Patten 2012, 2016) or one of identification (contra, for instance, Huddleston & Pullum 2002: 266), the specificational clause is therefore best understood as a MATCHING relation between a criterial abstract entity and a more concrete one satisfying those criteria (or not).⁴⁴

#### 3.2.2.2 Process-participant relations: Inferred meanings

In Section 3.2.2.1, I proposed, following Davidse & Van Praet (2019), that the variable NP conveys criterial semantic specifications, some of which are explicitly expressed by the lexical material of the variable NP, while others are derived contextually.

The starting point in this section is that, from these criterial semantic specifications of the variable NP, the notion of a SET of QUALIFYING INSTANCES can be inferred. Contra Patten (2012: 37), this does not mean that the variable NP as such "denotes" a set of instances.⁴⁵ The set is delimited by the lexical material and added contextual specifications, which the variable NP represents as an abstract entity. From these criterial specifications, speaker and hearer infer a set that contains all the more concrete entities that correspond to the variable's criterial specifications. In principle, this set can be empty, as is the case with examples like *the winner is nobody*. The inferring of this set is independent of whether the variable NP is definite or indefinite. The choice between construing the variable NP as definite or indefinite is motivated by the contrasting implicatures of exhaustiveness and non-exhaustiveness they trigger at the clause level. When the variable NP is definite, as in *The problem is Macron*, the implicature is that the specificational clause will specify all the entities in the inferred set with its value NP. When the variable NP is indefinite, as in *a good remedy for pain is vitamin C*, the implicature is that the specificational clause will not provide all qualifying entities with its value NP.⁴⁶

---

**44** The semantic model of criteria-meeting has been proposed earlier, as pointed out in Davies (2018), by Austin (1970), who referred to it as 'bill-filling'. Austin discusses various readings of the copular clause *That's a daphnia*, one of which is a specificational reading: "we speak of 'identifying a daphnia' (or 'identifying the daphnia') when you hand me a slide and ask me if I can identify a daphnia (or the daphnia) in it. [...] we are trying to find an object to fill a given bill: hence the name of [...] 'bill-filling'." (Austin 1970: 143–143). Davies (2018: 4) points out that we can challenge such a specificational assertion by asking "Does the item referred to by the subject qualify as covered by the complement?/ does it come up to scratch?/ does it fit the bill?".
**45** Recall that Patten's (2012, 2016) idea that a definite variable NP directly *denotes* a restricted set leads her to posit that indefinite variable NPs somehow also denote a restricted set, typically of one member. This then requires her to argue that the implicature of 'exclusive', non-unique, reference typically associated with indefinite NPs is cancelled with indefinite variable NPs.
**46** I return to the issue of (non-)exhaustive specification below.

## 3.2 Specificational clauses — 89

The very notion of a set of qualifying entities implies that there are also potential candidates that do NOT satisfy the criteria. That is, a second, different type of set is inferred: a more nebulous set of potential candidates that in some way fail to meet the criteria. This set of POTENTIAL BUT FAILED CANDIDATES contrasts with the first set of the qualifying entities. While the first set is necessarily bounded when the variable NP is definite and potentially bounded when it is indefinite,[47] the second set has undefined boundaries: it is hard – if possible at all – to draw a boundary around all the entities that potentially might – but ultimately do not – meet the variable's criteria.

This, in turn, means that the act of specification implies the selection of qualifying entities from the larger set that contains both the qualifying entities and potential but failed candidates, which – prior to the specification – jointly form the SET of POTENTIAL INSTANCES. This is visualised in Figure 7.

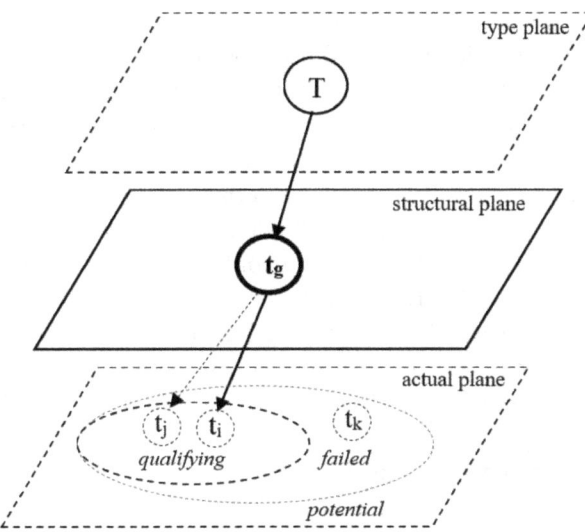

**Figure 7:** Inference of a set of potential instances, including qualifying and failed ones.

This idea can be contrasted with Higgins' (1979: 132) claim that the variable NP "delimits a domain" from which "the value picks out a particular member". It is not made clear how precisely the variable NP delimits a domain, and the relation

---

**47** Unlike definite determiners, indefinite determiners do not single out an instance in relation to the set of all contextually relevant instances of the type (Davidse 2004): therefore, it cannot be determined from the indefinite NP itself how many other instances of the same type obtain in the local discourse context, so that the boundaries of such a set are unclear.

between that domain and the members referred to by the value NP is represented as a straightforward relation between set and members (which is, indeed, how Patten represents the semantics of specificational copulars). Defining for the specificational relation, however, are the criterial specifications which the speaker chooses to convey with the variable NP: it is these criteria that form the standard against which the accuracy of the qualifying relation is assessed. In other words, the distinction between qualifying entities from potential candidates that do not qualify is made by assessing whether an instance *conforms to* the criterial specifications (or 'satisfies' them, in Declerck's [1988: e.g. 5] terms), not by picking out members from the set the variable NP is alleged to denote. Specificational constructions are always used in contexts where qualifying entities have to be distinguished from non-qualifying ones (with some of the latter sometimes being mentioned explicitly).

A central concern in the literature is the issue of the exhaustiveness or non-exhaustiveness of the specificational acts expressed by various types of specificational constructions, including clefts and pseudoclefts.[48] For specificational copulars, it is generally accepted that the ones with a definite variable NPs carry a CONVERSATIONAL IMPLICATURE of EXHAUSTIVENESS (cf. Declerck 1988: 28–35). That is, on their default interpretation, they list all the qualifying entities in the set defined by the criterial specifications of the variable NP. The exhaustiveness implicature stems from the use of a definite determiner, typically the definite article, in the variable NP: "the implicature can only arise if the variable is uniquely defined" (Declerck 1988: 31). To NPs with definite article attaches an implicature of 'inclusive' reference, which entails that reference is made to all the instances of the relevant type specifications in the discourse context (Hawkins 1978: 161, 1991). On hearing (71), the hearer will therefore conclude in good faith that the set inferred from the specifications 'black sheep of the family' contains only *Bishop's wild daughter and wife,* and no one else.

(71)   The black sheep of the family are Bishop's wild daughter and wife. (http://www.angelfire.com/mb/jmorris/fallout/ffamilies.html)

As is well-known, general conversational implicatures can be cancelled (e.g. Mosegaard Hansen 2008: 1396). If the exhaustiveness implicature of (71) proves to

---

**48** In specificational clefts the implicatures of exhaustiveness and non-exhaustiveness stem from respectively the choice of subject *it* or *there*. As pointed out by Halliday (1967b: 238), an *it*-cleft like *It was John who painted the shed* uniquely specifies who painted the shed ("John and no others"), while a *there*-cleft like *There was John who painted the shed* conveys that "John, possibly among others" painted the shed.

be unfounded, the utterance will not be said to have been false. Rather, "although technically true", it "is deceiving because it is not as informative as it should be, and therefore violates one of Grice's (1975) principles of conversation" (Declerck 1988: 30). Hence, it is possible to continue (71) as follows: *and, come to think of it, Bishop's youngest son has also been a bit of a scapegoat lately.*

The distinct function of specificational copulars with an indefinite variable NP, on the other hand, is to implicate that the specified value may not – and, in fact, most commonly does not – exhaust the set of qualifying entities for the variable NP. The implicated NON-EXHAUSTIVENESS stems from the indefinite NP's 'exclusive' reference (Hawkins 1978: 186, 1991). The indefinite determiner signals that reference is not made to a contextually unique instance (Langacker 1991: 102–103): it is therefore not excluded that there are other instances of the relevant type specifications in the context. This exclusive implicature forms the basis for Patten's (2012, 2016) explanation of how indefinite variable NPs fit, as a marked option (2012: 42, 2016: 94), into her account of specificational clauses. She takes it, firstly, that it is the inclusiveness of definite NPs that makes them "well-suited to the specifying [variable] function" (2012: 47) and that the "specificational meaning is at odds with an indefiniteness interpretation" (2016: 94). Following Higgins (1979), she interprets specification as an act of 'listing', which she views as informative only if "the number of possible members (or *instances*) [of the set denoted by the variable] is small enough to be usefully listed" (Patten 2012: 48). Therefore, the kind of indefinite NPs that felicitously occur as specificational variable "would be those that share most in common with definite NPs" (Patten 2012: 49). More specifically, she suggests "that the fundamental property of these particular indefinite NPs is that they do not rule out an inclusiveness interpretation" (*ib.*: 54). Hence, for Patten (2012: 54), the indefinite NPs that can function as variable are the ones that enable the reading that the value "can be taken as representing the set's (potentially complete) membership." Therefore, on Patten's (2012, 2016) account, the notion of a non-exhaustiveness implicature does not accord with the very function of specification.

The fact that the set of qualifying instances is *inferred* from the type specifications of the variable NP rather than being denoted by it – as Patten (2012: 47) claims – pinpoints the flaw in Patten's (2012, 2016) argument. As stated earlier, the variable NP – whether definite or indefinite – designates an abstract entity, not a set. The type specifications associated with this abstract entity, irrespective of whether the variable NP is definite or indefinite, determine the inference of a set of qualifying entities, e.g. all *black sheep of the family* in (71), and all the books meeting the criterial type specifications *good account on cattle ranching on the plains* in (70) above. The choice of using a definite or indefinite determiner in the variable NP is motivated by the implicatures of exhaustive versus non-exhaustive specification which they trigger. With a definite variable NP, e.g. *The black sheep in the family*, the implicature is that the value NP specifies all the entities in the inferred set, viz. *Bishop's wild daughter and wife*. With an indefinite variable NP, e.g. *a good account (on cattle ranching on the plains)*, the implicature is that the value NP does not specify all the entities in the inferred set. This is what we see in the specificational clause in (70), where the value refers to the book "Lewis Atherton, *The Cattle Kings* (1961)", after which is added "but see also Don Worcester *The Chisholm Trail* (1980)". Many text examples of specificational copulars with indefinite variable NP involve discursive schemata of enumeration in one form or other, as in (70) and (72), whereby several values are enumerated, either in the same sentence (70) or in different sentences (72). Mostly an implicature of non-exhaustiveness applies to the enumerated values. In (72) the existence of multiple qualifying entities is, in fact, asserted in the first (non-copular) sentence by the statement that *there are many reasons for reaching out to meet the needs of people around you*. Three concrete values are enumerated in three successive specificational clauses with an indefinite variable NP containing the type specification *reason* (which implies *for reaching out*, etc.). This enumeration hence triggers the implicature that the three values given do *not* exhaust the set of *all* reasons.

(72) There are many reasons for reaching out to meet the needs of people around you. One reason may be to simply lend a helping hand. Another may be to put your gifts and talents to use. But a valid reason could be that you must take action against the nonchalance and indifference others have toward the needs at hand. (WB)

Like the exhaustiveness implicature, the implicature of non-exhaustiveness can be cancelled. If we continue, for instance, the specificational clause in (73) with *And, in fact, that seems to be the only option at this point*, there would be no contradiction, only a sense that the preceding indefinite specificational is unnecessarily vague.

(73) The losses incurred by ITV Digital cannot continue. *One option is to close the business altogether*. (WB)

To the extent that the exclusiveness implicature of indefinite NPs is weaker than the inclusiveness implicature of definite NPs (Lyons 1999: 261), it is not surprising that it may, with some indefinite variable NPs, be weakened, as in examples (74) (cited earlier as [46c]) and (75). In both examples, the restrictive relative clauses ascribe to the designated instance involvement in a state-of-affairs that is so specific that it narrows down the inferred set of qualifying instances to such an extent that the criterial specifications can be interpreted as singling out one particular instance. Yet, it is significant that the speaker specifically does not commit to such an interpretation, opting nevertheless for an indefinite determiner. As will be discussed in Chapter 4, such examples are rare, however, in attested corpus data: hence, to centre the analysis of specificational clauses with indefinite variable around such examples – as is largely the case in both Mikkelsen (2005) and Patten (2012, 2016) – is to interpret the atypical as the default.

(74) A philosopher who seems to share the Kiparskys' intuitions on some factive predicates is Unger. (Delacruz 1976: 195, as quoted in Mikkelsen [2005: 117] and Patten [2016: 91])

(75) A Telegraph veteran who faces a particularly uncertain future is David Twiston Davies, widely known as Twist'n'Shout, who was told yesterday that he was being relieved of his post as letters editor. (WB)

The indefinite variable NP often contains evaluative adjectives, as with *a good alternative* in (76) and *a classic instance* in (77).

(76) Bacon and sausage have far too much fat and contain a walloping amount of sodium as well. *A good alternative is turkey breakfast sausage.* (WB)

(77) I think we should pare down the number of buyers we do business with from the existing 60 to a more reasonable 10 or 12. That will yield us higher sales and bigger profits. *Hexagon Denim is a classic instance.* Over 80 per cent of its sales is routed to just 8 buyers worldwide. (WB)

The effect of such evaluative modifiers is to delineate within the set of entities that qualify in terms of mere representational specifications, a SUBSET of qualifying entities satisfying EXTRA QUALITATIVE criteria. It is then from this reduced subset that the entity designated by the value NP is selected. I do not agree with Patten (2012) that lexical modifiers as a rule "lexically imply uniqueness" (Patten 2012: 55) and that such implied uniqueness is necessary to make indefinite variable NPs acceptable. Specificational copulars provide speakers with the option of non-exhaustive specification, which may be chosen for various reasons such as the speaker's inability to identify all qualifying entities, or to distinguish qualifying from non-qualifying entities. In this context, Van Praet & O'Grady (2018: 87) associate the implicature of non-exhaustiveness with a "lack of epistemic certainty", which they find reflected, for instance, in the high frequency of rising tones on which specificational clauses with indefinite variable NP are uttered, as in (78). I will come back to this in Chapter 6.

(78) I **bel/ieve** // that one of [dhi:] major difficulties of this **c/ountry** // is the growing **imb\alance** // of the **bur\/eaucracy** // and **st\ate interf/erence** // (LLC)[49]

Finally, the notion of a set of potential entities – comprising the set of qualifying entities and the set of potential but failed candidates – explains why specificational clauses with definite variable imply contrastiveness[50] (Declerck 1988: 24) and why the ones with indefinite variable do not. From the implicature that the set of qualifying entities inferred from a definite variable are specified exhaustively by the value, it follows that the value contrasts with the rest of the set of potential entities: since the latter are not part of the exhaustively specified set of qualifying entities, they are, by inference, relegated to the set of potential but failed candidates. Sometimes, a potential but failed candidate, e.g. *the millions he has in the bank* in (79), is made explicit by means of a negative specificational clause, which is then typically accompanied by the specification of the actual qualifying entity, e.g. *in what he's done on the pitch*.

(79) The legacy of a footballer is not the millions he has in the bank but in what he's done on the pitch. (WB)

Specificational clauses with indefinite variable do not, by default, carry a meaning of contrastiveness. The implicature that the actually specified value does not exhaust the set of qualifying entities means that the relation of the value vis-à-vis the rest of the set of potential entities cannot be taken to align with the contrast between qualifying vs failed candidate values. While the latter contrast therefore does not figure prominently in specificational clauses with indefinite variable, the inferred set of potential but failed candidate values is nevertheless part of their backgrounded meaning. This is shown by the negative specificational clause in (80), in which an entity is specified as explicitly *not* qualifying

---

**49** The examples from the London-Lund Corpus of Spoken English (henceforth LLC) are reproduced in simplified prosodic annotation, which indicates only the tone unit boundaries by double slashes, the information focus by small caps and rising and falling pitch movement by \ and boldface.
**50** The implication of contrast has also been noted for clefts by e.g. Gundel (1977: 550), Harries-Delisle (1978), Laeven (1983: 140), and for clefts and non-cleft specificational clauses by Chafe (1976: 33–37) and Kuno (1972: 269).

for the variable. In such rare negative specificational clauses with indefinite variable, the meaning of contrastiveness is given salience by the explicit mention of a non-qualifying, i.e. failed, candidate value.

(80)   Private presses become established for a variety of reasons (*of which making a fortune isn't one*). (WB)

In examples where the indefinite variable NP contains lexical modifiers that comment on the validity of the value-variable relation, e.g. *a real sensation would be. . .* in (81), the contrast between qualifying (e.g. *any celebrity couple actually staying together*) vs non-qualifying candidate values (e.g. *the split between Kate Winslet and her husband Jim*) is also brought out.

(81)   The split between Kate Winslet and her husband Jim was described in some quarters as a "showbiz sensation". *A real sensation would be any celebrity couple actually staying together.* (WB)

To sum up the discussion about the process-participant relations in specificational clauses, I have set out, in Section 3.2.2.1, how the meaning of the variable and value as two participants in the specification relation can be defined, and which pragmatic inferences and implicatures are triggered by their lexico-grammatical coding (Section 3.2.2.2). In the following section I discuss how the different mappings of the process-participant relation onto the clausal subject-finite-predicator-complement structure yields different perspectives onto the specificational relation.

### 3.2.2.3 Mood structure

In the discussion of predicative clauses (Section 3.1.2.2), I showed that while the order of the NPs in the predicative clause can be modified (in the form of SVO, OSV, and even OVS alternations), the roles of 'describee' and 'description' are invariably fixed to the respective grammatical functions of subject and complement. Specificational clauses, by contrast, do not have a fixed mood structure: not only is it possible to change the clauses' constituent order, but the NPs fulfilling the semantic roles of 'variable' and 'value' can also felicitously switch grammatical functions (Huddleston & Pullum 2002: 268). For instance, if we change the constituent order of the specificational clause in (82a,b), then the erstwhile complement *Ellie Simmonds* becomes subject in (83a,b). The fact that this type of reversibility is not a mere re-ordering of the variable and value but a true subject-complement switch is evidenced if we replace the proper name

*Ellie Simmonds* by a pronoun. When the value occurs in postcopular position, the accusative form *her* is used, as in (82b); the nominative form *she* is not possible here, as shown in (82c). As accusative marking of the postverbal NP is a crucial point, an attested example is given in (84), in which the postverbal NP includes the accusative pronoun *me*. In precopular position, on the other hand, the value takes the nominative form, as illustrated by *she* in (83b); the accusative form *her* is not acceptable in precopular position, e.g. (83c).

(82)  a.  Who is your favourite fictional hero? I don't really have a pretend one, but *a real hero would be British Paralympic swimmer* **Ellie Simmonds**. (UCL Alumni Magazine, 4 June 2013, p. 29, < https://issuu.com/ uclcomms/docs/people_2013/31>)
 b.  A real hero would be **her**.
 c.  *A real hero would be **she**.

(83)  a.  **Ellie Simmonds** would be a real hero.
 b.  **She** would be a real hero.
 c.  ***Her** would be a real hero.

(84)  "There were only three people at that stage who would say no to Liam," he [Ian Robertson] says. "One of them was Noel, one of them was Marcus and *one of them was me*." (WB)

In contrast with predicative clauses, it has been argued that an OSV order is not a possible alternate of specificational clauses (Declerck 1988: 63), neither with the value as subject (83) nor with the variable as subject (82). An example like (85) can only have a predicative reading, which can be contextualised, for instance, as a rejoinder for a proposition in which heroic features are attributed to Ellie Simmonds: A. *Ellie Simmonds is a real hero / really heroic*. – B. *Oh yes, a real hero / really heroic she is*. The sentence in (86), by contrast, cannot be grammatical at all: on a specificational reading, the OSV pattern is excluded altogether; on a predicative reading, the predicate nominative cannot be subject.

(85)  A real hero Ellie Simmonds / she is.

(86)  *Ellie Simmonds / her a real hero is.

Importantly, the choice to construe the value or the variable as subject implies two different perspectives on the specificational relation. In view of Halliday's (1994: 76) point that the subject is the element "on which the validity of the information is made to rest" and in which "is vested the success or failure of the proposition", the specificational clause allows for two types of proposition and can make two types of claim. Moreover, different rhetorical pressures are put on the complement.

If the subject is the value, as in (83a,b) above, then the validity of the proposition is made to rest on the criteria-meeting meaning of the value, ELLIE SIMONDS *is a real hero*. The perspective construed is that of the subject/value QUALIFYING for the variable. The rhetorical pressures on the complement are to correctly formulate the criteria of the variable that the subject/value qualifies for. Example (87), cited by Halliday (1967b: 226), illustrates this point.

(87) Which is the leader? John is the **leader**, but Bill's the one who does the work. (Halliday 1967b: 226)

The complement/variable *the leader* is taken to carry a marked information focus, assigned to it in order to emphasise the contrast with the variable in the following clause, *the one who does all the work*. The validity of *John is the* LEADER is vested in the subject/value *John*, but he is implied to meet the criteria of *leader* only nominally. The next proposition states that subject/value *Bill* qualifies properly for the criteria that would normally be specified in regard to genuine 'leadership'.

If the subject is the variable, as in (82a,b) above or (88) (which re-states the previously used example in [70]), the validity of the proposition is vested in the criteria-stipulating meaning of the variable.

(88) On cattle ranching on the plains, a good account is Lewis Atherton, *The Cattle Kings* (1961), but see also Don Worcester *The Chisholm Trail* (1980). (WB)

This 'CRITERIAL' perspective on the proposition can be glossed as the subject/variable stipulating criteria for proper exemplification by the value/complement, e.g. *a good account* 'exemplifies as' the book by *Lewis Atherton, The Cattle Kings*. The proposition in (69) above – *a great first date would be something different* – is clearly made to rest on the criteria of the variable *a great first date* and the rhetorical pressures on the complement are to handle the exemplification, or embodiment, of those criteria correctly. The complement does not specify an actual entity meeting the criteria but indicates that proper exemplification of the criteria of the variable requires something out of the ordinary (i.e. 'something different' from your typical date).

The point that specificational copulars can be construed as two different types of proposition contrasts them with predicative copulars, to which only one proposition corresponds, whose validity is vested in 'the entity predicated on', its only possible subject. Irrespective of whether the information focus in an example like

*John is a surgeon* in (46b) is on *John* or *a surgeon*, the pressures on the complement are always to attribute a correct characterisation, e.g. *a surgeon*, to *John*.

In sum, from the possible and impossible variants of declarative specificational clauses in (82) to (84), the following three features of their mood structure can be derived, in terms of which they contrast with predicative clauses (see Section 3.1.2.2). Firstly, subject and complement can be re-assigned over the two NPs of specificational clauses. Secondly, the complement of specificational clauses is coded by the accusative. Thirdly, the subject and complement functions are tied to preverbal and postverbal position respectively: OSV-order is not possible, whereas this is a central structural possibility for predicative clauses. These morphosyntactic differences strongly suggest that a specificational clause is neither grammatically nor semantically "quite literally the inverse of predication" (Patten 2012: 56), if we view semantic functions as inherent in grammatical structure (Langacker 2017a).

### 3.2.3 The referential status of the variable NP

In this section, I address the question of the referential status of the variable NP. As pointed out in the state of the art (Section 3.2.1), much of the debate on specificational clauses has focused on whether the variable is non-referential (Williams 1983; Partee 1986b; Mikkelsen 2005; Patten 2012), referential (Heycock & Kroch 1999; Heycock 2012), or if it should be characterised in different terms (Higgins 1979; Declerck 1988; Keizer 1992). As with the discussion of the referential status of the indefinite predicate nominative (Section 3.1.3), this will require explaining what kind of instance the variable NP denotes and the domain of instantiation in which it holds. In a nutshell, I argue that the crucial characteristic of the variable NP is that it refers to what Langacker (1999, 2002) calls a GENERALISED instance, whose domain of instantiation is not concrete space, but the more abstract structural plane. But unlike with other instances in the structural plane, this generalised instance triggers a presupposition of existence. This is true both when the generalised instance is introduced by a definite or by an indefinite NP. However, as pointed out by examples such as *the winner is nobody*, the typical inference of existence can be cancelled. Following Stalnaker (1973, 1974), I therefore treat existence as a PRAGMATIC, i.e. cancellable, presupposition. I explain this presupposition in relation to the way in which reference to a generalised instance is established: following Breban & Davidse (2003) and Breban (2011), I hold that generalised instances imply 'dual reference' (Ward & Birner 1995: 732). That is, while the designatum of the NP with generalised reference is a more abstract (criterial) entity, there is always the implication of more concrete instances corresponding to the abstract entity. These more concrete instances hold in the *actual* domain of instantiation – hence, the presupposition of existence – even if this pragmatic presupposition may be cancelled in special cases like *the winner is nobody*. I will first explain how reference to a generalised instance is established, before discussing how generalised reference triggers a pragmatic presupposition of existence, both with definite and with indefinite variable NPs.

### 3.2.3.1 The variable NP has generalised reference

Langacker (1999, 2002) illustrates the concept of 'generalised' instantiation with example (89). He explains that, on the reading that *a student* refers to three different individuals, the NP does not pick out an actual instance that can be characterised in relation to concrete space and time. Instead, it captures an observed commonality by invoking an imagined instance of a type that generalises over three actual occurrences (Langacker 2005: 172). Hence, generalised reference comes about through local abstraction over more concrete instances, which are typically located in the spatio-temporal domain of instantiation. The generalised instance itself does not hold in the spatio-temporal (actual) domain of instantiation, but in the more abstract structural domain.

(89)   Three times during the class, a student complained. (Langacker 2005: 172)

Breban & Davidse (2003), Davidse, Breban & Van linden (2008) and Breban (2011) have drawn attention to the role that secondary determiners – which assist in the primary determiner's identifying function by adding more specific referential information, as with *identical*, *similar* and *comparable* – can play in the construal of generalised instances, as in (90). The NP *an identical punishment* generalises over, and by using *identical* explicitly indexes the commonalities between, the punishments inflicted by the parents and the daughter. It is a local text-bound generalisation, construed by the speaker at the time of utterance. The reference is to a fictive entity, abstracted from the spatio-temporal coordinates of the actual punishments it generalises over.

(90)   This mother was merely repeating an identical punishment inflicted on her by her own parents when she was a child. (WB, quoted by Breban 2011: 522)

At the same time, the generalised instance is not disconnected from actuality (as is the case with non-specific and predicative reference, cf. Section 3.1.3): while the designatum of an NP like *an identical punishment* in (90) is a generalised instance, the generalisation implies more concrete – typically actual – instances corresponding to it. While these specific instances are not actually 'linguistically predicated' (in Langacker's [1987a, 1991] terminology), they are construed as part of the 'base' for expressing a generalised instance. Breban (2011: 519) explains this in terms of the notion of 'dual reference'. This concept was introduced by Ward & Birner (1995: 732), who use it to describe the referential status of definite NPs in postverbal position in existentials like *the usual ceremony associated with such an occasion* in (91). Ward & Birner (1995: 732) interpret such NPs as establishing reference to an identifiable (hearer-old) 'type' and to a hearer-new token of that type. Breban (2011: 518), however, explains that it is not just a 'type' that is identifiable but a generalised instance: the generalised instance is identifiable on the basis of its previous manifestations. At the same time, this generalised instance also pragmatically introduces a *new* attestation of the generalisation into the discourse, namely the specific ceremony held for the occasion of President Mubarak's state visit in (91) or one specific occurrence of *the president's weekly radio address at 10:06 am* in (92), where the specification that it is *on improving health care* applies to the specific rather than the generalised instance.

(91) President Mubarak of Egypt is due in London in a few hours at the start of a state visit. He and his wife will be staying at Buckingham Palace as the guests of the Queen, and there'll be the usual ceremony associated with such an occasion. (WB)

(92) The president's weekly radio address at 10:06 am is on improving health care. (WB)

I propose that the same mechanism of generalised reference can account for the referential status of the (indefinite) variable NP in specificational copular clauses (see also Davidse & Van Praet 2019: 29). As illustrated in (93), the variable NP *another triumph* instructs us to conjure up a fictive instance abstracted from actual time and space, into which feeds the mention of Hemingway's 'rising reputation' associated with *"For Whom the Bell Tolls"* in the preceding clause, but which, at the same time, introduces a new instance with the same type specifications. These type specifications are provided both in the variable NP and the preceding discourse, *viz. triumph (for Hemingway as a writer)*.

(93) His reputation as a writer fluctuated wildly; he was praised in the 1920s but flopped in the 1930s. It rose again in 1940 with "For Whom the Bell Tolls"; another triumph was the Pulitzer Prize for "The Old Man and the Sea". (WB)

These explicit and contextual type specifications of the variable NP designate the abstract criterial entity in the structural domain of instantiation. The secondary determiner *other* situates this new generalised instance relative to the previously mentioned successes for Hemingway as a writer (*viz. in the 1920s* and *in 1940 with "For Whom the Bell Tolls"*). At the same time, *another triumph* pragmatically introduces a new instance in the actual domain of instantiation. This implied instance has the feature individuality – it is a particular instance of Hemingway's literary triumphs – but it is not a specific IDENTIFIABLE individual: it is not the instance identified by the value NP, *the Pulitzer Prize for "The Old Man and the Sea"*. This point is clearly evidenced by examples such as *One easier solution is the new suck-able varieties from Gambia* in (94), in which the variable NP *one easier solution* implies reference to an actual solution, but not to the individual instances (*the new suck-able varieties from the Gambia,* etc.) referred to in the value NP.

(94) A good mango has a neon-orange flesh, oozes juice and should not be stringy or fibrous. By necessity it will be messy to eat or to carve ... *One easier solution is the new suck-able varieties from the Gambia, arriving in July and August.* (WB)

Because generalised reference is characterised as an abstraction over instances in the actual spatio-temporal plane, Langacker (1999, 2005) likens it to generic reference. However, as Breban (2011: 511) points out, the two are accessed in discourse in very different ways. While generic instances make "GLOBAL generalizations that pertain to the world's inherent structure" and hence project "an open-ended set of potential actual occurrences", generalised instances like *another triumph* or *one easier solution* "are concerned with LOCAL generalizations, i.e., they capture what is common to a few occurrences only" (Breban 2011: 513, emphasis mine). In other words, the purpose of the generic use of an indefinite NP is to denote an entity that represents the type and features associated with a whole class (e.g. *a cat* hunts for mice). These semantic specifications are not tied directly to any actual individual but are accessible as the ready-made concept of the class as such (see Section 3.1.3). By contrast, generalised reference is local and text-bound: the semantic specifications that feed into the conception of the abstract generalised instance are interpreted with reference to the local discourse context (e.g. 'triumph for Hemingway as a writer' in [93]). The purpose is not to represent a familiar class, but to denote a generalised instance that implies more concrete instances, e.g. *an added benefit is...* , *the only/real problem is...*) (cf. Section 3.2.2.2). Unlike with generic reference, the implication of corresponding more concrete instances is central to the process of generalised reference.

Based on Langacker's conventions of visual representation (see Figure 5 in Section 3.1.3), generalised reference, and its referential duality, can be illustrated as in Figure 8. The type specifications project down into the explicit designatum of the indefinite variable NP, *viz.* a generalised instance $t_g$ in the structural plane (bolded).

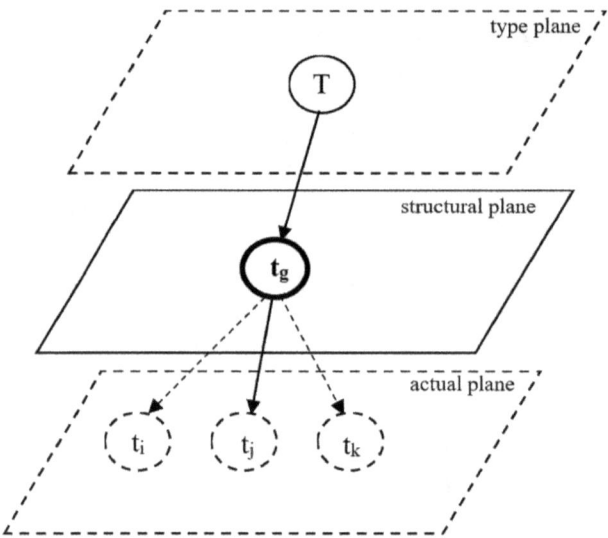

**Figure 8:** The dual reference of the indefinite variable NP, which designates a generalised instance $t_g$ and implies more concrete instances.

By the mechanism of dual reference, a more concrete, instance is implied: the implication of a corresponding more concrete instance – typically in the actual domain of instantiation – is an essential part of the meaning of the generalised instantiation (as indicated by the solid arrow pointed down to an instance in the actual plane). The implied actual instance itself is not, however, designated by the variable NP (and, hence, indicated in dashed lines in Figure 8). In the case of an indefinite variable NP, the use of the indefinite determiner activates an exclusiveness implicature so that the possibility of other potentially qualifying instances is not ruled out (as represented by the dotted lines to other instances in the actual domain).

### 3.2.3.2 The existential presupposition and exclusiveness implicature of the indefinite variable NP

In this section, I argue that both the presupposition of existence and the implicatures of inclusive versus exclusive reference do not attach to the generalised instance of the variable NP but to the more concrete instances it implies. As argued in Section 3.2.3.1, these implied instances are not part of the variable's designation.

First, however, I want to point out, against Langacker (1999, 2005) and Breban (2011: 529) that generalised reference does not only generalise over spatio-temporal (i.e. actual) instances. That is certainly true for examples like *a student* in (89) or *an identical punishment* in (90). In the context of the variable NP, however, examples like (95) show that a generalisation can also be made over generic instances. The meaning of the variable NP in (95) is to introduce 'a similar but more colourful and even smaller *class of* (British garden) bird', rather than an individual bird. The generalisation made by the variable is, nevertheless, ad-hoc and text-bound (Breban 2011: 530): in (95) the generic NP *the wren* feeds into the generalisation *A similar but more colourful and even smaller bird*.

(95) [In an online article about the UK's most common garden birds] The wren's one of the UK's smallest birds. [. . .] A similar but more colourful and even smaller bird is the goldcrest, although this little bird is less often seen in gardens. (https://www.saga.co.uk/magazine/home-garden/gardening/wildlife/birds/common-garden-birds)

Therefore, I propose that the essential meaning of generalised reference is the process of generalisation itself – which is ad-hoc and text-bound – not the kind of instances over which it generalises.

Let us now turn to the presupposition of existence which has been associated with variable NP in the literature. In example (96), the coded designatum of the indefinite variable NP *another version* is the generalised instance, which, as marked by the indefinite determiner, is being introduced into the discourse. Its type specifications are provided in the variable NP and the preceding discourse, e.g. *version [of YHVH]*. These semantic specifications set up the abstract criterial entity designated by the variable in the structural domain of instantiation. The secondary determiner *other* situates this new generalised instance relative to the previously mentioned *many variations of the name*. At the same time, *another version* pragmatically introduces a new instance in the actual domain of instantiation. It is to the implied concrete instance, a particular version of JHVH, that the presupposition of existence applies.

(96) This was Yahweh or Jehovah, the name of God artificially constructed [. . .] with the Hebrew consonants YHVH [. . .] There were, in fact, many variations of the name in several Semitic dialects – Yahu, Jah, Jeud, Ieu, Yahweh, Jahveh, Yaho and Iao, while another version was Yeshua or Jeshua (Latin: Jesus, Joshua or Jeud). (WB)

As is characteristic of pragmatic presupposition, the presupposition of existence may also be contextually suspended (Stalnaker 1973, 1974), as is the case in (97). Here, the use of the hypothetical modal *would*, in combination with the specification of the non-specific instance *anything with driving*, results in the absence of an existential presupposition: the speaker neither implies nor rejects that an actual individual corresponds to the criterial entity of *a dream job*.

(97) A dream job would be anything with driving... (Google)

If the value NP itself expresses that there is no entity that satisfies the criteria of the variable, as in *The winner is nobody*, then the pragmatic presupposition of existence is explicitly cancelled, rather than merely suspended. Note that such cases of explicitly negated existence are possible when the variable NP is definite – as with *The winner is nobody* – but not when it is indefinite – e.g. *\*One of the winners is nobody*; *\*A good solution is nothing*. This is because negating the existence of qualifying values is at odds with the exclusiveness implicature that attaches to the indefinite variable NP.

Finally, I consider this exclusiveness implicature in more detail. Like the presupposition of existence, the exclusiveness implicature operates at the level of the implied instance. Thus, in (98), the indefinite variable *a good example* (of messages issued by computer devices) implies reference to only one such message but carries an exclusiveness implicature that there may be other instances. This is why it is possible – though not frequent – that the value NP in (98) lists three such messages and indicates by 'etc.' that this list is incomplete. The same possibility of coordinating values, specified for the same variable, is also shown in *another version was Yeshua or Jeshua (Latin: Jesus, Joshua or Jeud)* in (96).

(98) A good example would be: "SEQUENCER: does not play notes", "SYNCHRONISATION: Spectralis does not send clock", "USB: Spectralis not recognized" etc. (Google)

Note that the use of conjunction *or* to coordinate *Yeshua* and *Jeshua* in (96) suggests that the speaker presents these items as alternatives that individually exemplify the variable. Conjunction *and*, on the other hand, has an additive function (Quirk et al. 1985: 636). It is used either when the variable NP is plural and the coordinated items list values that individually qualify for the variable, e.g. (99), or when the variable NP is singular but the coordinated items jointly specify one value for the variable, e.g. (100).

(99) [Libra moons] are creative and often artistic, *good examples being <u>Marcel Duchamp and Edouard Manet</u>*. (WB)

(100) Another of Dale's favourite soap plots was <u>the murder and back-garden burial of Trevor Jordache by his wife Mandy and daughter Beth in Brookside</u>. (WB)

The additive function of *and* is why it is not possible to coordinate separate values when the variable NP is singular: it would mean that the one instance denoted by the variable NP is realised cumulatively by multiple instances listed by the coordinated values. But that does not mean that the use of *or* to coordinate these values undermines the point that they each may satisfy the variable. *Or* is used here, e.g. in (96), to present the values as *non-contrasting* alternatives: the speaker does not present the values as a choice between one or the other, but s/he presents them as different options each of which meeting the criteria stipulated by the variable.

Importantly, the exclusiveness implicature is reflected in the nominal structure of the variable NP. For instance, in *a similar but more colourful and even smaller bird* in (95) above, the qualitative modifiers explicitly comment on how the implied (generic) instance compares to other qualifying instances (e.g. *the wren*). The nominal structure of the indefinite variable NP, in particular the use of modification, will be discussed at length in Chapter 4.

By way of conclusion, we can now compare the referential status of the indefinite predicative NP and the indefinite variable NP in terms of the parameters of referentiality, identifiability, individuality, existence, and domain of instantiation, as discussed in more detail in Section 3.1.3. Both designate instances in the structural domain of instantiation, but on the other parameters they differ. Indefinite predicative NPs, which are traditionally called 'non-referential', designate instances *only* in the structural domain of instantiation, without individuality, and they have no presupposition of existence. Indefinite variable NPs have generalised reference: they designate an abstract criterial entity in the structural domain of instantiation. By the mechanism of dual reference, however, they imply reference to a more concrete instance corresponding to the abstract criterial entity. It is to this (implied) more concrete instance that the pragmatic presupposition of existence and the implicature of exclusive reference applies. In sum, I have proposed that the suggestion, raised in the literature (e.g. Declerck 1988; Keizer 1992), that the specificational variable has 'weak reference' or that it is referential but more abstract than the value (Section 3.2.1) can be captured more accurately in terms of the notion of generalised reference.

## 3.3 Revisiting the discourse function and information structure of predicative and specificational clauses

In this section, I survey existing accounts of information structure in copular clauses. A question that needs to be addressed is whether predicative and specificational clauses can be distinguished in terms of their contrasting 'information structures' (as is assumed by many authors, e.g. Moro 1997; Mikkelsen 2005: 51, 162–163; Patten 2012). If so, in what *way* can they be contrasted? To answer this question, it is necessary to first revisit what is meant by information structure in English, and particularly by the concept of 'focus', which has been subject to "terminological profusion and confusion" (Matić & Wedgwood 2013: 128). Information structure, in broad terms, is concerned with the clause as a message. It deals with the status of clausal elements as components of that message and the way they are organised into an act of communication (Halliday 1967b: 199). Since Gundel (1988: 211–213), two dimensions of information structure are commonly recognised: a REFERENTIAL dimension and a RELATIONAL one. The referential dimension is concerned with the question whether or not the referent of a linguistic expression is marked as assumed known by the hearer, which includes the IDENTIFIABILITY of referents (Halliday & Hasan 1976; Martin 1992; Langacker 1991; Gundel et al. 1993) and their DISCOURSE-GIVENNESS (Prince 1992; Birner 1994; Kaltenböck 2005). The 'relational' dimension, on the other hand, is concerned with the difference between backgrounded and focal information in the information unit. It is the latter dimension in particular that has been the focus of much debate. The interpretation of information focus that has been adopted in many studies of copular clauses is the semantic-pragmatic one, which goes back to Chomsky (1969) and Akmajian (1970, 1973) and was later adapted by Lambrecht (1994). In Section 3.3.1, I will first review these accounts and discuss how they have been adopted specifically for the analysis of copular clauses. In Section 3.3.2, I will then present the functional account of information structure which follows, amongst others, Halliday (1967) and Tench (1996). It is this second account of information structure that I adhere to and that will be used later in this book to discuss the information structure patterns of specificational and predicative clauses in Chapter 6.

### 3.3.1 Semantic-pragmatic accounts of information structure

The influential semantic-pragmatic interpretation of information focus dates back to Akmajian (1970, 1973). He views focus as a *semantic* component representing new information "not because the [focus] constituent is necessarily novel, but rather because the semantic relation which the constituent enters into is novel with respect to a given universe of discourse" (1973: 218). This semantic relation is interpreted as one between a focus and a presupposition, which "reflects the intuitive feeling that non-focal information is generally indeed presupposed by the speaker to be known to the hearer" (1970: 192). To the semantic explanation of information structure, Akmajian (1970) adds that the "semantic prominence [of the focus] is correlated with prosodic prominence" (*ib.*: 192) and characterises the focus as the constituent that "contains the intonation center, i.e. the position of highest pitch and stress" (*ib.*: 190). This goes back to Chomsky's (1969: 26) point that "the focus is the phrase containing the intonation center, and the presupposition is determined by replacing the focus with a variable (we overlook, for the moment, a fundamental equivocation in the latter formulation)."

Lambrecht (1994, 2001) holds a similar view of focus as the "semantic component in a pragmatically structured proposition whereby the assertion differs from the presupposition" (1994: 213). Like Akmajian (1970, 1973), he explains the presupposition part as "the set of propositions lexicogrammatically evoked in the sentence" which the speaker assumes to be predictable to the hearer (Lambrecht 1994: 52). According to Lambrecht (1994), the elements that can be in focus "are either predicates or arguments (including adjuncts), or else complete propositions" (*ib.*: 215). These different options represent three general types of 'focus structure', i.e. 'predicate-focus', 'argument-focus' and 'sentence-focus' (Lambrecht 1994: 223, 2001: 485). These focus categories correspond to "three basic communicative functions" (Lambrecht 2001: 485): predicating a property of a given topic ('predicate focus'), specifying an argument in a presupposed open proposition ('argument focus') and introducing a new discourse referent or expressing an event involving such a referent ('sentence focus') (*ib.*). While Lambrecht (1994: 213) stresses that focus-marking must be "sharply distinguished from its grammatical realization in the sentence", the definitions he gives for the first two types of focus are basically co-extensive with the semantics of predicative and specificational clauses respectively. It is significant, in that respect, that he glosses predicate-focus as having a "categorical" function, while argument-focus is "also called 'specificational', 'identificational', or 'contrastive'" (2001: 485). This means that while not all sentences with argument-focus necessarily take the form of a specificational clause, all specificational clauses (including copulars as well as clefts) are expected to have argument-focus.[51] For instance, in the non-copular clause in (101), Lambrecht (1994: 212), like Akmajian (1973: 218), interprets *Mitchell* as focal because it specifies the argument in the presupposed open proposition [*x* urged Nixon to appoint Carswell], resulting in the novel assertion that [*x* = Mitchell].

(101) MITCHELL urged Nixon to appoint Carswell. (Akmajian 1973: 218, as cited in Lambrecht 1994: 212).

But since non-copular clauses are ambiguous when it comes to focus structure (Lambrecht 2001: 489), a way to ensure that the sentence in (101) is not interpreted as having predicate-focus would be to turn the clause into a specificational copular one, where the ambiguity is resolved (*ib.*).

---

51 Lambrecht (2001: 489) explicitly commits to this position for cleft constructions.

(101') The one who urged Nixon to appoint Carswell is MITCHELL.

Moreover, Lambrecht (1994: 225, 2001) "insist[s] on the fundamental importance of prosody for the marking of focus structure", though he sees focus marking and prosodic prominence (or 'sentence accentuation') as autonomous but interrelated factors. Prosodic "sentence accentuation is not a focus-marking device per se but a general device for the marking of semantic portions within a pragmatically structured proposition, whether focal or not" (1994: 214). Like focus, prosodic accentuation is thus defined as a *semantic-pragmatic* category but one that marks the "degree of communicative importance of the prosodically highlighted element" (1994: 242) rather than its 'unpredictability' per se (as focus does). While Lambrecht (1994, 2001: 482) considers it possible to have multiple prosodic accents in one sentence, the "focus constituent necessarily requires an accent since the relation between the focus denotatum and the proposition is by definition unpredictable" and, hence, communicatively important (Lambrecht 2001: 479). What is more, though Lambrecht (1994: 225) does not claim that the relationship between focus and prosody is universal, he does insist that, at least in English, prosody is of fundamental importance in the marking of focus structure (*ib.*: 224–225).

Akmajian's (1970, 1973) and Lambrecht's (1994, 2001) accounts of information structure are adopted in many studies of copular clauses, in which the idea of a focus relation has been used to define or characterise the distinction between specificational and predicative clauses (e.g. Declerck 1988; Mikkelsen 2005; den Dikken 2006; Patten 2012, 2016). Declerck (1988), for instance, claims that "in any specificational sentence the value part represents 'new' information while the variable part expresses 'old' information", so that "the value part is the 'focus' and the variable part is the 'presupposition' of the sentence" (*ib.*: 11–12). Like Akmajian (1970, 1973) and, later, Lambrecht (1994, 2001), Declerck (1988: 14) interprets the presupposition both pragmatically and semantically: not only does it "represent old information" but it also "refers to something that is logically presupposed." To the semantic-pragmatic definition of the presupposition-focus relation, he also adds a prosodic dimension, in that "the focus of a specificational sentence in the sense that it expresses new information (value) is also intonationally the focus" (*ib.*: 13). It is significant that, in contrast to the lengthy discussion of information structure in specificational sentences, Declerck (1988) barely mentions the information-structural properties of predicative clauses. He does observe that, in predicative clauses, the subject typically represents old information and the complement new information (*ib.*: 61); he only does so, however, to make the case that the subject referent is typically identifiable and, hence, coded by a definite description. Moreover, in examples that are ambiguous between a specificational and a predicative interpretation (e.g. when the more specific NP is the subject), Declerck (1988: 69) suggests that the interpretation is signalled by the intonation pattern of the sentence: "if the sentence has a neutral intonation pattern (rather than an intonation with contrastive accent on a particular constituent), the sentence will be interpreted as predicational" (*ib.*). Patten (2012, 2016) proposes a similar argument but attributes much more significance to it. On her account of specification as the inverse of predication (see Section 3.1.1), the specificational interpretation of a copular clause "relies on a particular information structure, in which the referring expression is in focus" (Patten 2012: 57). In examples like (102), stated earlier in (3b) and (45b), "if the subject is placed in focus (marked by intonation in [102]), the sentence acquires a specificational reading" (Patten 2016: 80).

(102)  DIANE and CARLA were the waitresses. (Patten 2016: 80)

Following Mikkelsen (2005), Patten (2012) adds that the information structure of specificational clauses is conditioned by the "discourse requirement" that "the precopular element is not newer to the discourse than the postcopular element" (*ib.*: 57). For Mikkelsen (2005), who unlike Patten (2012, 2016) only recognises specificational clauses with variable ('non-referential') subjects, the idea that "specificational subjects must be discourse-old" (*ib.*: 134) even holds the promise of explaining why "specificational clauses exist at all" (*ib.*: 135).

In many accounts (also Lambrecht 1994: 52, 2001: 485), the focus is equated with the role of the value as a constituent in the specificational clause, and the presupposition with the variable (sometimes even explicitly so, e.g. Akmajian [1970: 190]). This does not only obscure the function of the information focus in its own right, but it also proves particularly problematic when used as a distinguishing criterion between predication and specification. Because of the conflation of the information-structural meaning of focus with the lexicogrammatically coded 'value' role, it becomes logically circular to characterise the value in a specificational copular clause as 'in focus'. An account in which the distinction between specification and predication hinges on the marking of 'focus' therefore loses its explanatory power.

Furthermore, in some accounts, notions of discourse-familiarity (given-newness or (un)predictability) are added to the definition of focus and presupposition. The implication is then that the specificational variable represents, by definition, 'old' information (as, for instance, Declerck [1988: 12] claims). This is contradicted by attested examples of specificational clauses used 'out of the blue', for instance as a newspaper headline in (103), and for which it is therefore not possible to claim that the variable is given or at least more familiar than the value.

(103) Two eminent political scientists: *The problem with democracy is voters.* (https://www.vox.com/policy-and-politics/2017/6/1/15515820/donald-trump-democracy-brexit-2016-election-europe)

Lambrecht (1994: 210, 222–223) views 'all-new' sentences as expressing 'sentence-focus': in cases like (103) where no distinction between presupposed/old vs focal/new information obtains, "the focus element coincides with the entire proposition" (*ib.*: 210). The function of focus is then "to indicate the absence of a focus-presupposition contrast" (*ib.*). While the idea of a 'broad focus' scoping over an entire proposition is not problematic per se, its occurrence with specificational clauses does pose a challenge to Lambrecht's (1994, 2001) other category of 'argument focus'. Since he defines argument-focus in terms of a "specificational" function (2001: 485), specificational clauses, in principle, preclude any other focus pattern. The fact that specificational clauses actually can have so-called 'sentence-focus' means either that they lack specificational semantics, which is logically impossible, or that the definition of 'focus', specifically argument-focus, in terms of a specificational variable-value relation is problematic.

Finally, the assumed correlation of focus, as marked by a prosodic accent, with the value constituent is refuted by examples of specificational clauses with non-focal values, not only in specificational copulars, e.g. (104), but also in specificational clefts, e.g. (105).

(104) I'm keeping very well in with l/ittle S\ally# bec\ause# <u>she's the one who's going to do my sh\opping# when I'm \old#</u> (LLC)

(105) it was them that kicked down the w\alls# (COLT[52])

Against such conflations, I propose to distinguish: (i) the semantics of the constituents and structural relations coded at lexicogrammatical level (as set out in Section 3.2.2.1); (ii) pragmatic presuppositions and implicatures triggered, in specificational clauses, by linguistic signals at level (i) (as explained in Section 3.2.2.2); (iii) the information structural meanings, both relational and referential. In the remainder of this section, I will first briefly describe the discourse functions that the semantic relations of predication and specification can serve in specific contexts of use (Section 3.3.2.1). I will then home in on the prosodically coded patterns of information focus in both clause types (Section 3.3.2.2).

---

**52** The Bergen Corpus of London Teenage Language, henceforth COLT.

### 3.3.2 A functional account of discourse organisation and information structure

#### 3.3.2.1 The general discourse functions of predicative and specificational clauses

As argued in Section 3.2.2.1, the meaning of the specificational relation implies a logical order, in which the variable's criterial function makes it in some way logically prior to the specificational value (Davidse & Kimps 2016: 135). Regardless of which item occurs as subject, the discourse-pragmatic function of specificational clauses is always to find a value for a variable. The meaning of the predicative clause, by contrast, does not imply such a logical order. The act of description can serve two main discourse functions, which can be summarised as follows: (i) ascribing type-representational and/or qualitative features to the describee, or (ii) indicating of an entity whether it falls under the description given by the predicate nominative (see Davidse & Van Praet 2018).[53] This is illustrated in (106) and (107) respectively: the interrogatives in (106a) and (107a) explicitly probe for the clauses' specific discursive functions; in the declarative clauses in (106b) and (107b) the elements towards which the informational completion of the clauses is oriented is indicated in bold. (Other attested examples of the more marked discourse use of the predicative clause are given by the interrogative predicative clause [108] and the declarative one in [109].)

(106) a. What (race) was his grandfather?
b. His grandfather may have been **a Jew/Jewish**.

(107) a. Who is a Jew/Jewish?
b. The halakhic view is that any child born to a Jewish mother is Jewish... As an example, ***the children of Madeleine Albright*** *(who was raised Catholic and was unaware of her Jewish ancestry) would all be Jews.* (religion.wikia.org/wiki/Who_is_a_Jew%3F)

(108) Aha and so we've got a mixture here mm. Erm but are all of you teachers? How many teach? How many people do other things? **Who are teachers?** How many of you teach young learners. (WB)

---

[53] This distinction was noted in Davidse & Van Praet (2019), where it was discussed in terms of two different types of informational completion.

(109)  Who's an American? Well, if you are born here. [...] *I'm an American.* I was born in this country. (David Halle, *America's Working Man*, p. 233)

Two recognition criteria can show that predicative clauses like (107b) and (109) cannot be mistaken for reversed specificational clauses with value/subject: first, it is possible to substitute the predicate nominative by an adjectival complement with a similar meaning, e.g. ... *would all be Jewish* in (107b) or ... *am American* in (109). Second, neither of the two clauses allows for a subject-complement switch, as illustrated by the infelicity of (107b') and (109').

(107b')  *Jews would be the children of Madeleine Albright.

(109')  *An American is me.

To account for these differences, I borrow Austin's (1953: 233–234) notion of a 'direction of fit': Austin (1953: 234) argues that there is "a difference in direction of fit between fitting a name to an item (or an item with the name) and fitting an item to a name (or a name with the item)." I interpret these two directions of fit in semantic-pragmatic terms: how are the coded relations of predication or specification used in a specific context?[54] The notion of the direction of fit can then be used to capture certain intuitions formulated in the literature about predicative versus specificational clauses, whereby specificational clauses have been claimed to have a fixed information structure in contrast with predicative clauses (e.g. Patten 2012: 35). Rather than putting this contrast in terms of information structure, I argue that specificational clauses have a 'fixed' direction of fit, whereas predicative clauses are "not fixed in the same way" (Mikkelsen 2005: 51).

---

54 Austin (1953: 234) also distinguishes a second relation, which he interprets in terms of *matching* X to Y or Y to X: in the former, the 'onus of match' is on the X-element; in the latter, the onus is on the Y-element. Austin (1953: 236) states that the element "on which lies the onus of match is put as subject" and that different matching relations can be distinguished depending on whether the sense or the type of the subject element – which can be a name or an item – is assessed as matching the type or sense of the complement element (1953: *ib.*). For present purposes I will not consider the question of different matching relations as relevant to the discussion of predicative and specificational clauses. Austin's (1953) idea that the onus of match is always on the subject element, regardless of its interpretation, does fit, however, with the descriptive analyses in Sections 3.1.2.2 and 3.2.2.3 that the subject is the element in terms of which the validity of a proposition is assessed.

### 3.3.2.2 Prosodically coded patterns of information structure

The directions of fit discussed in Section 3.3.2.1 correlate with different implementations of the predicative and specificational relations in specific contexts of use. These directions of fit do not equate with different patterns of focus marking in information structure. Following Halliday (1967b: 204–207), but also e.g. Tench (1996), Verstraete (2007: Chapter 3), I assume that the information unit is demarcated, in spoken discourse, by the tone unit (TU). The domain of the focus in the information unit is prosodically marked by the placement of the tonic or nuclear accent, i.e. the most prominent syllable carrying the pitch movement in a tone unit (TU), e.g. f\or(est) in (110) and \Edgton in (111). (The tonic accent is indicated, in prosodic transcriptions like (110) and (111), by the placement of tones – e.g. rises /, falls \ – within a tone unit, the boundaries of which are indicated by the symbol #.)

(110)  he was ^only a :f\orest worker# (LLC)

(111)  my ^name _is - 'Doctor :M _P \Edgton# (LLC)

I take it that the function of focus is to signal NOTEWORTHINESS[55]: this meaning is relational in the sense that, within one tone unit, the nuclear accent marks an item as noteworthy vis-à-vis unaccented and hence less noteworthy information. Importantly, as Halliday (1967b: 203) points out, the tone unit is not

---

[55] The term 'noteworthiness' is chosen to emphasise that while focus marking interacts with newness of information, it is not determined by it. I believe it is, in that respect, a better term than 'unpredictability' (e.g. Halliday 1967b: 205; Lambrecht 1994: e.g. 6) or even 'newsworthiness' (McGregor 1990: e.g. 366), which imply a close link with given-newness of information, even if the authors themselves are careful to distinguish between focus marking and discourse-familiarity. The concept of 'salience', which for instance Dik (1997: 326) proposes to describe the function of the focus, is even more confusing. While the term 'salience' has been interpreted in a variety of ways in the literature, it is most commonly used to refer to the degree of accessibility of referents, or their activation status in the discourse (e.g. Prince 1981b: 228; Gundel et al. 1993: 275–279; Lambrecht 1994: 100): information is 'salient' if it is highly accessible from the prior text or context. In this context, it should also be pointed out that Gundel *et al* (1993: 275–279) do explicitly link 'focus' to 'salience' (or activation status), but what they mean by information being 'in focus' is entirely different from the way in which 'focus' is used here and in most other studies of information structure. For Gundel et al. (1993), being 'in focus' has to do with the referential dimension of information structure, not with the relational one: information is 'in focus' if it has already been 'activated' (i.e. evoked in the prior co- or context) and is "at the center of current attention" (*ib.*: 279). Their use of the term 'focus' is, therefore, equivalent to a referent being highly accessible. This use of the term is, in other words, exactly the opposite of how it is used in the relational dimension of information structure.

necessarily co-extensive with the sentence or the clause, so that one clause can consist of multiple tone units and, hence, can have more than one focus, as in (112) and (113).

(112)  (^Pete B/askerdon# ^is a !s\ad 'man# (LLC)

(113)  ^one of the !b\/ig 'problems in 'medicine# is ^leading qu\estions# (LLC)

The segmentation of an utterance into a sequence of tone units, i.e. the utterance's tonality, therefore reflects the speaker's choice to signal *how many* parts of the utterance express a unit of information that s/he wants the hearer to attend to. Halliday (1967b: 204) argues that this is motivated by the 'recoverability' of information: for him, "what is focal is 'new' information" (*ib.*: 204), though this "does not necessarily imply factually new information" (*ib.*: 205). Instead, Halliday (1967b: 207) views the concepts of 'given' and 'new' as *functions* assigned to a piece of information by focus marking, i.e. the placement of the tonic accent. Often, but not necessarily, what is *presented as* new is also *actually* new (Halliday 1967b: 204): alternatively, "the newness may also lie in the speech function, or it may be a matter of contrast with what has been said or what might be expected" (Halliday 1967b: 206). The former is illustrated in (114), in which the focus is on the finite, resulting in emphasis on the affirmative function of the clause; the latter case is shown in (115), in which the given (non-qualifying) value *th\/at* is marked as focal in contrast to the actually qualifying value in the following clause, *viz. that you've got "!m\asses# of cr\iticism# to ^r\ead.*

(114)  the ^world is "!f\ull of 'people# who "^l\ove {to ^pl\ay these *war#}# "^war g\/ames# [. . .]- you ^kn/ow# - it ^\is a 'game to them# (LLC)

(115)  I sup^pose it's :reasonable to ex:p\ect# ^y\/ou 'know# ^every ^every . :person :reading :\English# to have "^b\ought 'or# ^somehow to have been :given their :own 'copies of :Sh\akespeare# . ^but [@:] "!th\/at isn't the 'point# the ^point 'is that you've got "!m\asses# of cr\iticism# to ^r\ead# (LLC)

Since focus marking correlates only typically with actual discourse-givenness, the function of focus is better described in terms of its core meaning, *viz.* "that which he [the speaker] wishes to be interpreted as informative" or, in other words, noteworthiness (Halliday 1967b: 204). It will be in terms of this definition that I will use the notion of 'focus' throughout the rest of the book.

As argued in Van Praet & O'Grady (2018) and Van Praet (2019a), the definition of information focus as signalling noteworthiness, rather than one in terms of a variable-value relation, reveals a more complex information structure than is assumed, for instance, by Akmajian (1970) and Lambrecht (1994, 2001). On the one hand, the principle that the value carries information focus holds up as a default (*viz.* in 85.9% of the dataset in Van Praet & O'Grady [2018]). This confirms that the value, which logically forms the point of completion in the specificational 'fitting' relation, naturally attracts information focus. The main – motivated – exception is formed by examples with non-contrastive anaphoric non-focal value, e.g. *that* in (116).

(116) A. all sorts of things go into port don't they I mean it's not just - wine
  B. ^I !can't re'member 'what :p\ort is then# ^sherry 'is - - :just "w\/ine# . that is ma"^t\ured# . ^in the {c\asks} of . br\andy#
  A. that's right
  B. or ^maybe the p\ort's {^br\andy#}# I ^can't re:m\ember# - but ^anyway ma!tured in 'spirit :c\asks# and <u>^that's the 'only [w@] 'reason that 'they're called :f\ortified 'wines#</u> ^rather than w/\ines# (LLC)

On the other hand, the possibility of predicative and specificational clauses being segmented into multiple tone units, as illustrated in (112) and (113), means that both clause types can take multiple information foci in specific contexts of use. For predicative clauses, the pattern with a non-focal describee and a focal description is attested in most of the examples studied in Van Praet (2019a) (see also Chapter 6), e.g. (110). For specificational clauses, on the other hand, the pattern with non-focal variables and focal values, e.g. (111), is found in only a minority of cases (i.e. 18.66% of the whole dataset examined in Van Praet & O'Grady [2018]). In the light of these observations, it clearly cannot be maintained that this pattern is the default (Lambrecht 1994) or the obligatory information structure of specificational clauses (Patten 2012, 2016). Instead, I will explain that the variable's function of stipulating the criteria in the specificational relation can also motivate informational prominence. As I will set out in more detail in Chapter 6, the main information structural difference between predicative and specificational clauses is, therefore, not in terms of their contrasting information foci, but rather in how different degrees of noteworthiness make the components of the clause stand out, or fit in, with the surrounding discourse context.

To sum up, I have argued, in this section, against the idea that predicative and specificational clauses can be distinguished in terms of their contrasting 'information structures' (e.g. Moro 1997; Mikkelsen 2005: 51, 162–163; Patten 2012). Instead, I distinguish between (i) the lexicogrammatically coded semantic relations of predicative and specificational clauses, (ii) the pragmatic inferences and implicatures triggered by the coded meaning at level (i), and (iii) information focus as the presentation of information as *noteworthiness*, which is coded, in spoken discourse, by prosodic prominence, notably the assignment of the nuclear accent.

I have, moreover, argued that the semantic relations at level (i) differ in that specificational clauses imply one direction of fit – in which the variable's criterial function makes it logically prior to the value – while predicative clauses allow for two directions of fit. I have shown that the functions of description and specification can be realised in spoken discourse by various specific intonation patterns. Even if the marking of information focus correlates with the discourse-pragmatic functions, there is no one-to-one correspondence between the two: focus marking is far more intricate than is commonly assumed and typically does not reduce to a binary sentential contrast between describee/non-focal vs description/focal in predicative clauses or between variable/non-focal vs value/focal in specificational ones. In Chapter 6, I will explore the topic of information structure in more detail, focusing specifically on prosodic focus marking in the two clause types. In Chapter 7, I will consider the discourse-embedding of information in predicative and specificational copulars.

## 3.4 Conclusion

In this chapter I have set out a functional-structural analysis of predicative clauses with an indefinite predicate nominative in contrast with specificational clauses with an indefinite variable NP. The two constructions were analysed as involving different process-participant configurations, which I characterised as intransitive and transitive respectively. I defended the claim that the intransitive predicative process was coded grammatically by a composite predicate derived from *be* + predicate nominative. By being integrated with this composite predicate, the predicate nominative is construed as relational despite its nominal form, allowing it to specify the content of the processual relation (Langacker 1991: 66). The integration of the predicate nominative in the composite predicate was evidenced by the impossibility to construe it as subject: the predicate nominative does not express a participant in the predicate process. Nevertheless, while contributing to the expression of a stative relation at a higher level of conceptual organisation, the predicative NP was argued to denote an instance rather than a type, class or property (as is commonly argued): it is because of its nominal structure and the fact that it denotes an instance that the predicate nominative can attribute a fine-grained characterisation combining type specifications and qualitative features to the subject referent. The argument that the predicate nominative denotes an instance raised an additional question: how can this be reconciled with its generally assumed non-referentiality? Following Langacker (1991, 1999), I assumed the position that the predicative NP denotes a virtual instance that "has no status outside this predicate nominative construction" (1991: 68): I further characterised this instance as purely 'descriptional', i.e. characterised solely by virtue of its representational and qualitative features and devoid of all individuality or existential presupposition. This descriptional instance, therefore, is expressed purely for the purpose of giving a characterisation of the describee with which it corresponds.

A similar functional-structural analysis was proposed for specificational clauses, focusing specifically on the ones with an indefinite variable NP. I explained that the specificational process differs from the predicative one, in that both of the specificational clause's NPs express participants in the transitive specificational relation. These participants were characterised as having the roles of variable and value. The transitivity of the specificational relation is coded by a two-place predicate, i.e. a relational predicate that makes schematic reference to two participants (i.e. two 'be-ers'). The variable and the value NPs integrate directly with this relational predicate and thereby elaborate the schematic 'being'-relation into a specificational relation between variable and value. As evidence for the transitivity of the specificational relation I illustrated the clause's potential to construe either the variable or the value as subject: as Halliday (1967a: 67) argued, only entities that participate in the relational process can function as subject. In correlation with the participanthood of the variable and value, the NPs that realise the two functions were explained as being 'referential' (in the sense of establishing a discourse referent). I proposed, however, to analyse the referential status of the variable NP in terms of Langacker's (1999, 2005) notion of 'generalised instance'. As Breban & Davidse (2003) and Breban (2011) observed, generalised instances imply 'dual reference' (a concept introduced by Ward & Birner [1995]): while the variable NP denotes a generalised entity at a higher level of abstraction, it simultaneously makes implicit reference to a more concrete instance it abstracts away from. I argued that it is because of the implication of a more concrete instance qualifying for the abstract generalised entity that both definite and indefinite variables can give rise to a presupposition of existence: this presupposition is a pragmatic, hence cancellable, inference that attaches to an implied instance in the actual domain of instantiation. Furthermore, to this implied more concrete instance also attaches an implicature of exhaustiveness, when the variable NP is definite, but an implicature of non-exhaustiveness, when the variable NP is indefinite. These implicatures are likewise pragmatic and, even though they arise by default, they can in principle be cancelled.

Finally, I revisited the explanation of the distinction between predication and specification in terms of their supposedly different information structures. I discussed the common conflation of various layers of meaning – syntactic, semantic and discourse-pragmatic – to explain the notion of 'focus'. Against such conflations, I proposed to distinguish between the lexicogrammatically coded meanings of predicative and specificational clauses, the pragmatic inferences they give rise to, and, finally, the prosodically coded marking of information focus. In characterising focus in terms of its prosodic coding, I cited evidence that a binary clause-level distinction between non-focal and focal information is not the default for specificational clauses: instead, the information structures of predicative and specificational clauses are better explained in terms of their *typical* behaviour, for instance with regard to the number of information units and hence the number of foci that each clause contains. In specificational clauses, the typical assignment of focus to both the variable and the value indicates that both participants contribute noteworthy information to the discourse, so that neither tends to be informationally backgrounded. I will return to the analysis of information focus versus non-focal information and the discourse familiarity of the constituents of copular clauses in Chapters 6 and 7.

In the following chapters, I will elaborate on the analysis set out in this chapter, by conducting contrastive corpus studies of the constituents of predicative and specificational clauses. In Chapter 4, I will focus on the lexical realisation of the indefinite NP in the two constructions, analysing how their different functional meanings motivate their different formal realisations, specifically their different choices of head nouns, pre- and postmodifiers and indefinite determiners. In Chapter 5, I will study which kinds of aspectual and modal meanings can be expressed in the two clause types: the observations made in this chapter will be explained in terms of the meaning potential of predicative and specificational clauses, which I relate to the semantics of their relational predicates.

# Chapter 4
# The indefinite NP in predicative and specificational copular clauses

Chapter 3 developed an account of the semantics and pragmatics of predicative clauses with indefinite predicate nominative and specificational clauses with an indefinite variable NP. Central to this account is the rejection of the idea that "specificational meaning is quite literally the *inverse* of predication" (Patten 2012: 243). The interpretation of specificational clauses as inverted predicative ones suggests that the semantics of both clause types have to be understood in terms of a relation between one referential NP and one non-referential 'property' NP (e.g. Williams 1983; Partee 1986b; Mikkelsen 2005; Patten 2012, 2016). Patten (2012: 35) takes this to mean that both clauses express a set-membership relation, in which the referential NP is classified as a member of the class denoted by the property NP. On her account, the difference between the two clause types is that predicative clauses classify an instance as a member of a class "with many members", whereas in specificational clauses the class denoted by the variable NP needs to be "small enough" for its members to be "usefully listed" (Patten 2012: 48). The validity of the interpretation of a clause as specificational depends on whether the variable can be understood as expressing a sufficiently restricted set that can be specified exhaustively. Specificational clauses with indefinite variable NP are therefore only acceptable if the NP is "specified [...] to the extent that it does not rule out a uniqueness (or inclusiveness) interpretation" (Patten 2012: 55).

I argued against the idea that either the predicate nominative or the variable NP denotes a class or a property. The fact that both have a full NP structure entails that they do "not represent a type specification but rather an instance of that type" (Langacker 1991: 67). Hence, while an NP and its head noun "represent the same entity", they do so "at different levels of specificity" (Langacker 1987a, 1991): the noun specifies the type that gives gross categorising features of an entity, while the NP denotes an instance that "delineates the entity in precise, fine-grained detail" (*ib.*). Following Langacker (1987a, 1991), I therefore drew a distinction between what the predicate nominative and the variable NP designate – i.e. an instance – and the referential status of the instance in the speech context. The PREDICATE NOMINATIVE was described as a non-referential NP: it expresses a 'virtual' instance with no status in concrete space and time (Langacker 1991: 67–68). This instance is 'conjured up' to attribute entity-type specifications to the subject, often also adding qualities (e.g. *he's a smart man*). The VARIABLE NP, by contrast, is a referential expression. It designates a generalised instance, whose semantics includes two central components. First, the generalised instance is an abstract 'criterial' entity: the variable gives a "criterial characterization" of an entity in a more abstract domain (Davidse & Kimps 2016: 121). Secondly, the variable implies that (a) more concrete instance(s) correspond(s) to this abstract criterial characterisation. The meaning of the variable can therefore be glossed as 'variable = $x$', in which $x$ is an implied more concrete instance that needs to be specified (Austin 1970: 134–143; Halliday 1967a,b; Huddleston 1984).[56] For Halliday (1967b: 224), the variable is "that element which corresponds to the WH-item in the WH-question presupposed by that clause."[57] The '$x$ to be specified' must correspond to the type specification (TS) of the variable, which is given by the explicit representational material in the variable NP but often supplemented with relevant TS from the preceding discourse. This meaning is in some form or other present in studies like Higgins (1979), Declerck (1988) and Huddleston & Pullum (2002), but I add the idea that the variable stipulates CRITERIA TO BE MET by the value (Austin 1970; Davidse & Kimps 2016). More specifically, these criteria are the representational TS found in the variable NP, to which TS retrieved from the preceding text often have to be added.

The semantics of the predicate nominative and variable NP trigger different pragmatic implicatures. While to specificational clauses attaches an implicature of exhaustiveness (with definite variable NPs) or non-exhaustiveness (with indefinite variable NPs), no such implicature is found in predicative clauses (Declerck 1988: 28–35). The implicature of (non-)exhaustiveness arises from the fact that the variable's criterial semantic specifications trigger the inference of a set of qualifying entities (Davidse & Van Praet 2019: 24). Since definite determiners imply that reference is made to all the instances of the relevant TS in the discourse context (Hawkins 1978: 160–161, 1991), the inferred set of qualifying entities is taken to be specified exhaustively when the variable NP is definite. By contrast, when the

---

**56** Like Higgins (1979) and Declerck (1988), Austin (1970: 134–143), Halliday (1967a,b) and Huddleston (1984) described the $x$ in the 'variable = $x$' relation as the 'element to be IDENTIFIED'. They point out that the identifying meaning is that the value satisfying $x$ serves to identify this $x$-element but not the variable itself (e.g. Higgins 1976: 132). In other words, on their account, the value identifies the more concrete instance implied by the variable, but not the actually designated abstract criterial entity. Hence, the specificational clause cannot be seen as identifying in the strict sense: such a meaning is not possible, for instance, when the variable NP is indefinite (see Chapter 1). Therefore, it is better to describe the $x$ as an 'element to be SPECIFIED', which sticks more closely to the actual meaning of the specificational clause.

**57** The same idea is also found in Declerck (1988: 11) and in more formal approaches which view the variable, or pre-copular element, as an implied question and the value, or post-copular element, as its partly elided answer (den Dikken, Meinunger & Wilder 2000; Ross 2000; Schlenker 2003).

variable NP is indefinite, the inferred set of qualifying instances is not specified exhaustively, since indefinite determiners do not exclude that there are other instances of the relevant TS in the context (Hawkins 1978: 186, 1991).

The account of the semantics and pragmatics of the variable outlined in Chapter 3 underlines, contra (some) existing views (e.g. Geach 1968: 35; Higgins 1976: 138; Mikkelsen 2005: 154; Patten 2012: 37), that the indefinite variable is not something marginal for which conditions making it acceptable have to be specified. Instead, specificational clauses with indefinite variable are a positive option motivated by the implicature of NON-EXHAUSTIVENESS, which is based precisely on the implicature of the indefinite NP that there is no inclusive reference to all instances with the relevant TS (i.e. Hawkins' [1991] 'exclusiveness' implicature).

This chapter continues the description of specificational clauses with indefinite variable – both variable subjects and variable complements – and how they differ from predicative clauses with indefinite predicate nominative. More specifically, it focuses on the CONTRAST between the indefinite variable NP and the indefinite predicate nominative in a quantitative and qualitative corpus study. This study examines how the functions of the NPs in the whole clause impact on the various internal functions of the NPs, coded by the head, modifiers and determiners. To my knowledge no such study has ever been carried out, even though authors like Declerck (1988), Mikkelsen (2005: 154–157) and Patten (2012: 55) have commented on the importance of premodifiers in indefinite variable NPs. So far, however, claims about the lexicogrammatical realisation of the variable have been based on simple concocted examples and some ad hoc text examples.

The study of the construal of the indefinite NP seeks to answer the following general research questions. First, are there statistically significant differences in distribution of structural elements (e.g. different functional types of modifiers) and their lexical realisation (e.g. abstract or concrete nouns as head) in predicative and specificational clauses? Second, are the same functions (e.g. epithet) associated with comparable lexical sets (in terms of lexical types and lexical subclasses), or is for instance the lexical set of the same function more restricted in the one copular type than in the other? Third, if there are differences, do they support the posited semantic contrast between predicative and specificational clauses? Can these differences plausibly be related to the posited semantics of the two clause types, and do they put more semantic flesh on the account proposed in Chapter 3? Finally, does this systematic study lead to greater insight to interpret contextualised data? Can we, for instance, elucidate different semantic functions of what at first sight might seem similar elements (e.g. the adjective 'good' in *He's a good man* vs *A good example is . . .*, in which *good* ties in with the 'criterial' component of the variable)?

In the following section (4.1) I set out the cognitive-functional model of the NP that I have applied in the case study. The research design of the case study and information about the data compilation and the data analysis will be described in Section 4.2. The results of the case study will be analysed in depth in Section 4.3, where I will discuss the specific choices of head noun (Section 4.3.1), premodifiers and post-head dependents (Section 4.3.2), and indefinite determiners (Section 4.3.3) for the NPs in predicative clauses and (non-)reversed specificational clauses. A concluding discussion in Section 4.4 will summarise the findings.

## 4.1 A cognitive-functional model of the English NP

The study in this chapter is indebted to a long tradition of functional-structural analyses of the English NP (e.g. Halliday 1985, 1994; Langacker 1991, 2016, 2017a; Bache 2000; Breban & Davidse 2003; Ghesquière 2014; Davidse & Breban 2019). It shares with these accounts the view that nominal structure, like all lexicogrammatical structure, symbolises semantic functions: these functions are coded by distinct modification and complementation relations between elements in the English NP (including modifier-head and submodifier-modifier relations). Its internal organisation is functionally motivated: the (canonical) noun phrase is a layered (hierarchical) structure, the component structures of which are progressively combined to form more elaborate composite structures (Langacker 1987a: 310). The order of assembly in which those component structures are integrated with each other is motivated by their conceptual dependencies (*ib.*: 305).

The English NP can roughly consist of four structural zones, as summarised in Table 5. In the rest of this section, I will discuss each zone and the elements it subsumes individually. I will start with the head in Section 4.1.1, after which I will discuss premodifiers (Section 4.1.2) and post-head dependents (i.e. modifiers and complements) (Section 4.1.3). Finally, I will conclude the discussion of the English NP with a discussion of determination (Section 4.1.4).

**Table 5:** The functional structure of the English NP (based on Ghesquière 2014: 24).

| determination | | | premodifiers | | | | type specification | | post-head |
|---|---|---|---|---|---|---|---|---|---|
| focus marker | primary | secondary | meta-designative | intensifier | epithet | classifier | | head noun | |
| just | the | same | former | rather | dull | cabinet | | members | no one likes |

## 4.1.1 The head of the NP

The HEAD of the NP is typically a common noun (e.g. *a flower*) but can also be a member of another class, for instance an adjective coerced into a common noun reading (e.g. *the young*) or substitute *one* (e.g. *a young one*). The head specifies the type of entity, of which the whole NP designates an instance (Langacker 1991: 144ff): this type specification (TS) makes an initial delimitation among potential referents by "specif[ying] the basis for identifying various entities as being representatives of the same class" (Langacker 1991: 53).

The TS provided by the head can be objective or subjective. In the first case, the recognition of an entity as an instance of a certain type is based on objective criteria, e.g. *a nurse*. In the second case, the criteria for the classification are subjective: this is the case, for instance, with degree nouns like *idiot*, for which the instance-type correspondence can be graded (Bolinger 1972a: 303) e.g. *quite an idiot* or *what an idiot*.

The head can also be given by the substitute noun *one* (Halliday & Hasan 1976: 92ff), e.g. *a young one*. Substitute *one* can be recognised by the fact that, like common nouns, it can take modifiers (as with *a young one*), that it can be marked for plurality (e.g. *the young ones*), and that it can be immediately preceded by definite and indefinite determiners, as illustrated in (1).

(1) On an average of about twice or more during a century there arises within the Tory Party a movement of young men, decried by their elders as revolutionary, who preach reform in the name of Conservatism. *Such a one was Disraeli*. (WB)

The meaning of substitute noun *one* is that the TS of the NP in which it is used has to be retrieved from the preceding text (Halliday & Hasan 1976: 92). Substitute *one*, hence, 'carries over' the head of some previously given NP, potentially but not necessarily accompanied by modifying or complementational elements found in that NP (*ib.*: 94). In (2), for instance, *one* in *a major one* does not just retrieve the TS 'problem', but also what is expressed by the complement 'with the deterrence argument (in favour of the death penalty)'.

(2) Such is the tainted image of retribution that supporters of the death penalty, publicly at least, appeal to arguments with a more utilitarian flavour. Hence the appeal to deterrence. A minor problem with the deterrence argument is that there is no convincing evidence that the death penalty significantly deters. *A major one is that the appeal to deterrence alone is morally flawed*. (WB)

Halliday & Hasan (1976: 101) observe that substitute *one* does not occur without a modifier (e.g. *a classic one* or *ones I like*), except if it combines with a determiner (e.g. *that one*) or a quantifier (e.g. *several ones*). As will be discussed in Section 4.1.4, substitute *one* has to be distinguished[58] from quantifier *one*, which can function as a secondary determiner (e.g. *the one thing you can't do*) or as a primary determiner when no other primary determiner is present (e.g. *one thing you can't do*) (Davidse 2004). Unlike the substitute, quantifier *one* can stand on its own if the rest of the NP is elided (e.g. *If you want a cup of coffee, make yourself one*) (Halliday & Hasan 1976: 101). In that case, *one* will establish a cohesive link to the preceding text, though not via substitution but via ellipsis of the head (*ib.*: 105). In making a case for ellipsis, Halliday & Hasan (1976) are not claiming that the function of the head is realised by some zero-element; instead, they argue that, when the head noun is omitted, the function of head is taken on by another element in the NP (Halliday & Hasan 1976: 147), for instance a quantifier or determiner.

Finally, as briefly discussed in Chapter 3, the TS provided by the head can be further specified by a CLASSIFIER (Halliday 1994: 184–185). This can be an adjective, e.g. *an electric train*, but also a noun, e.g. *a garden flower*. In both cases, the premodifier subclassifies the type denoted by the head, thereby restricting the head's denotative scope (Adamson 2000: 57). Classifiers are the most direct modifiers of the head (Breban & Davidse 2016: 224). This is shown by the fact that no other elements can be inserted between the classifier and the head (e.g. \**an electric fast train*). Moreover, as Davidse & Breban (2019: 334) argue, classifiers add semantic elements to the TS but do not designate qualities (see also Bolinger 1967: 11–17; Bache 1978, 2000: 235; Quirk et al. 1985: 436–437). This is evidenced by the fact that classifiers are not gradable and, therefore, do not support degree modification (e.g. \**a very electric train*), which quality-denoting modifiers do (e.g. *a very fast train*). Structurally, the classifier-plus-head can therefore be considered as forming a "composite noun" (*ib*: 335), whose semantic function is to give a "composite type description" (Breban & Davidse 2016: 224).

---

**58** Halliday & Hasan (1976) list a number of other uses of *one* in addition to the substitute *one* and the quantifier *one*. They consider, for instance, the use of *one* as a generic pronoun (e.g. *One never knows what might happen*) or as a "pro-noun" with the schematic meaning of 'person' or 'people' (e.g. *Now, my dearest ones; gather round*) (*ib.*: 98–104). In the second case, pro-noun *one* is similar to the substitute in that it functions as the head of an NP; unlike substitute *one*, however, pro-noun *one* does not establish a cohesive link to the preceding text (*ib.*: 102).

## 4.1.2 Premodifiers

The elements in the premodifier zone do not apply to the TS but to the instance designated by the NP. Four functions can be distinguished, viz. epithets, adjective-intensifiers, noun-intensifiers and metadesignatives.

The premodifiers that occur closest to the head, or the composite head, are the 'DESCRIPTIVE MODIFIERS' (Bache 2000: 239) or 'EPITHETS' (Halliday 1994: 184), e.g. *a beautiful pink flower*. The function of epithets is not to subclassify the general type but to ascribe qualities to the entity denoted by the NP. This is demonstrated, Breban & Davidse (2016: 224) argue, by the fact that these premodifiers alternate with descriptive predicative adjectives, e.g. *The flower is beautiful and pink*.[59] The quality expressed by an epithet can be objective, e.g. *pink*, but also subjective, e.g. *beautiful* (Quirk et al. 1972: 924–926; Ghesquière 2014: 30–31). In the first case, the quality is "objectively recognizable, purely descriptive and potentially defining" (Ghesquière 2014: 30). In the second case, the quality is "of an evaluative, often affective, nature, expressing a subjective, personal stance of the speaker [towards the instance being described]" (*ib.*).

Epithets, or descriptive modifiers, may themselves by submodified by ADJECTIVE-INTENSIFIERS, e.g. *a very beautiful flower* or *a rather tall man*. Their function is to modify the degree to which the quality expressed by an epithet obtains. Adjective-intensifiers are structurally integrated with the epithet they submodify (Breban & Davidse 2016: 225), so that the submodifier and modifier can be analysed as together occupying one functional slot in the NP structure.

In addition to adjective-intensifiers, NOUN-INTENSIFIERS can be distinguished as a separate kind of premodifier. Noun-intensifiers are used to "qualitatively change the descriptive meaning of the unit they relate to, more specifically its scalar properties" (Davidse & Breban 2019: 348), e.g. *pure luck*. The unit over which the intensifier

---

[59] The argument that predicative use of an adjective is proof of its qualifying function may not be entirely uncontroversial. It is, for instance, possible to find examples of classifying premodifiers for which predicative alternates are attested, e.g. *an electric car* > *Porsche's first car is electric* (Google), *a legislative procedure* > *the procedure is legislative and not quasi-judicial* (Google), *military men* > *he is military at heart* (Google). This raises the question: does the predicative use of these classifying adjectives make them descriptive, or can predicative adjectives also serve a classifying function? A thorough discussion of the issue is beyond the scope of this book, but I would tentatively argue in favour of the second hypothesis: none of the examples appear to support degree modification (e.g. *\*Porsche's first car is very electric, the procedure is very legislative*, or *he is very military at heart*). What is more, the three examples all seem to concern what 'subtype' the subject can be classified as. I will leave the issue for future research and conclude, for now, that gradability may be a better recognition criterion for the distinction between classifiers and epithets than predicative alternation.

has scope[60] always includes the head and, potentially but not necessarily, classifiers and epithets (*ib.*). The scope of the noun-intensifier is indicated by its position in the NP: all the elements that occur to the right of the intensifier fall within its scope. Hence, according to which elements the noun-intensifier scopes over, it can occur at various positions within the NP structure, e.g. *pure unashamed luxury* or *a large-scale pure computer fraud*.

Davidse & Breban (2019: 360) introduce a fourth type of premodifier, which they refer to as 'METADESIGNATIVE' modifiers. Metadesignatives "[assess] the relationship between (parts of the) designation and referent" (*ib.*). The assessment of this relationship can be in terms of the goodness-of-fit between a referent and the description by which it is referred to, or the appropriateness of using a certain description for a referent, e.g. *a true friend* or *a so-called friend*. But it may also be in terms of temporal, modal or evidential relations, e.g. *the future king of England*, *a likely winner* and *an alleged rapist* respectively. Furthermore, as Davidse & Breban (2019: 363) point out, metadesignatives can apply to three elements in the NP, viz. the head designating the general type and any classifiers and/or epithets that modify it. Unlike noun-intensifiers, metadesignatives can take scope over each of those three elements individually. In *a so-called "good" widow*, for instance, the metadesignative *so-called* comments on the evaluation expressed by *good* rather than the composite *good widow* as a whole (Vandelanotte 2002: 250). Likewise, the metadesignative may apply to the type alone without having scope over other potential premodifiers: since the metadesignative is placed before the element it modifies, it can occur at various positions in the NP, e.g. *the troubled former child star*. Finally, metadesignatives can be realised by adjectives, e.g. *former, likely*, but they can also be adverbs, e.g. *then* in *the then accepted belief*.

### 4.1.3 Post-head dependents

While English premodifiers have been discussed at length in the literature, post-head dependents (i.e. modifiers and complements following the head noun) have received much less attention. One of the few studies that have proposed an analysis of different post-head dependents is Bache (2000: 235). Since Bache's (2000)

---

**60** McGregor (1997: 64–65), whose interpretation of 'scope' is used here, indicates that he uses the term 'scope' differently and more broadly than in the formal semantic tradition, where it pertains, for instance, to interpretations of quantifier scope over propositions. McGregor uses the notion in terms of the relation between a scoping element and the domain it scopes over to characterise syntagmatic relations in which the former "applies over a certain domain" thus shaping it to "indicat[e] how it is intended to be taken or viewed by the addressee" (*ib.*: 210).

discussion of premodifier functions is similar to the one outlined in Section 4.1.2, his model of post-head functions will be used to ensure consistency in the description of modifiers and complements in general.

Bache (2000: 235) distinguishes between four potential functions that post-head elements, *viz.* (i) determination, (ii) qualification (or 'modification'), (iii) categorisation, and (iv) complementation. DETERMINING postmodifiers, firstly, help to identify the instance referred to by the NP, e.g. *the dog of my neighbour*. They typically take the form of a genitive *of*-phrase, which, unlike the prenominal genitive phrase (e.g. *my neighbour's dog*),[61] does not serve as primary determiner but performs a secondary determining function.

QUALIFYING postmodifiers ascribe qualities to the instance designated by the NP (e.g. *the naval officer with the nice smile*). In that sense, they serve a similar function as qualifying epithets (cf. *the smiling naval officer*). Qualifying postmodifiers can be realised by members of various grammatical classes, including PPs (e.g. *with the nice smile*), relative clauses (e.g. *one issue I would like to discuss*), participial clauses (e.g. *a man fighting for his life*), the occasional postmodifying adjective or adjectival phrase (e.g. *the stars visible* or *a masterpiece worth up to $1 million*), and adverbs (e.g. *the man downstairs*).

CATEGORISING postmodifiers are functionally similar to classifiers in premodifier position: they specify a subtype of the type referred to by the head noun. This can be illustrated with examples like *the queen consort*, *the attorney general* or *a professor emerita*, in which the postnominal adjectives give a subclassification of the general type expressed by the noun.

POST-HEAD COMPLEMENTS, finally, are defined by Bache (2000: 33, 161) as "filling out the meaning of the unit complemented" (*ib.*: 33), e.g. *a visit to her parents*. He (*ib.*) points out that the complementation relation often holds between a noun that implies a process, e.g. *visit*, and a complement in which a participant or a circumstance of that process is expressed, e.g. *her parents* (cf. *they visited her parents*). The complementation function can, however, be seen more broadly. Keizer (2007: 241, 257), for instance, observes that 'relational' nouns in general, not just deverbal nouns, often take a complement. Unlike non-relational nouns, relational nouns can only be used meaningfully in relation to another entity (or entities): "they need a complement to complete the denotation of the head noun" (Keizer 2007: 220; see also Löbner 1985: 292). Such non-verbal relational nouns include kinship names

---

[61] Not all prenominal genitive phrases have a determining function, as Willemse (2007) points out. Non-determining prenominal genitives like *a women's magazine*, for instance, serve a classifying function. With non-determining prenominal genitives, therefore, some other element in the NP is responsible for the determiner function, as indicated by the use of *a* in *a women's magazine*.

(e.g. *daughter*), body parts but also abstract nouns like *type*, *sort* and *kind*, which do not imply processes but do take complements, e.g. *a type of plant*. Davidse (2018) makes a similar case specifically for nouns designating emotion, discovery, locutions and ideas, e.g. *the idea that she was guilty*. The complementational function of these post-head dependents is shown by the fact that, when they are not overt, their content is retrieved from the preceding discourse and brought into the interpretation of the head noun (*ib.*). Since the function of these post-head dependents fits in with Bache's (2000: 33) description in terms of "filling out the meaning" of a head noun, I will include the examples described by Keizer (2007) and Davidse (2018) in the category of post-head complements.

I propose to add one more type, namely PARTITIVE constructions (e.g. *one of the pitfalls*). The function of the partitive is to code a set-membership, or subset-set, relation between the head, or NP$_1$, and the set of entities expressed by the plural NP$_2$ in the *of*-phrase (Keizer 2017). Structurally, partitives consist of a quantifier (typically *one*) + elided head noun + post-head *of*-phrase. Since the elided head noun 'inherits' its TS from the NP in the *of*-phrase, the head noun of this second NP has been called the 'secondary head' of the partitive. While partitive constructions could be considered a special case of Bache's (2000) post-head complements, the fact that the semantic specifications of the partitive are given entirely in the *of*-phrase makes the status of the *of*-phrase as a complement controversial (Keizer 2017). However, for the interest of this study, it is useful to set partitives apart from other post-head dependents without taking them out of the equation altogether.

### 4.1.4 Determiners and focus markers

The outermost layer of the English NP is the determiner zone. Determiners are found in the most leftward position in the NP. Their meaning generally involves positioning the instance designated by the NP relative to the speech context and, potentially, to other (implied or given) instances in that context. A distinction can be made between primary determiners, secondary determiners and, finally, focus markers.

PRIMARY DETERMINERS are concerned with the 'identification' of the instance designated by the NP (Langacker 1991: 53). Their function is to signal the epistemic or cognitive status of the designated instance in a given speech context (Langacker 1991: *ib.*; Gundel, Hedberg & Zacharski 1993): that is, they tell the hearer whether and how s/he can retrieve the instance from the discourse. They do this generally by giving an indication of whether the designated instance is uniquely identifiable in the given speech context or not (Langacker 1991: 98, 103). These meanings are coded respectively by definite vs indefinite determiners. Determiners can be articles (*the*, *a*, *some*), demonstratives, possessive pronouns, but also quantifiers like *one*, *many* and *every* (Davidse 2004). Quantifiers, however, only serve as primary determiners when they are not preceded by an article or a demonstrative (*ib.*): for instance, the quantifier *one* is used as a primary determiner in *one problem* but not in *the one problem*. A further difference can be made here between absolute and relative quantifiers (Langacker 1991: 83; Davidse 2004): the first denote the magnitude of an instance along a measuring scale (e.g. *many*, *few*); the second assess the magnitude of a subset relative to a full or finite set (e.g. *most*, *all*). Cardinal numbers like *one* fall under the category of absolute quantifiers (Langacker 1991: 86), since cardinality is not assessed relative to a finite set. Finally, in indefinite plural NPs, the identifying function can also be expressed by a 'zero-determiner', e.g. *cats*. This zero-element can be interpreted in terms of a paradigmatic choice within the system of determiners, in which the choice for 'nothing' has a semantic value in contrast with the other potential options (e.g. the cats, three cats). Davidse (2004: 529) illustrates this, for instance, by comparing the use of plural NPs in existentials like *there are Ø/three/many other problems*, where the zero-option Ø is shown to stand in complementary distribution with other determiners like *three* and *many*.

SECONDARY DETERMINERS assist in the primary determiner's identifying function by adding more specific referential information (Davidse, Breban & Van linden 2008: 476–477; Breban 2011: 59, who further refines Halliday & Hasan's [1976: 80] and Halliday's [1994: 183] definition of 'postdeterminers'). Secondary determiners can express deictic as well as discursive relations, such as *usual* in (3) and *same* in (4).

(3) The plane had deviated from *the usual route*. (WB)

(4) SAGITTARIUS. November 23 December. The spotlight is on partnerships and an on/off relationship can change into a permanent, loving one. But *the same Venus magic* can bring just the kind of love you need into your life. (WB)

The notion of secondary determination is used as a cover term for both predeterminers, e.g. *all the pretty horses*, and postdeterminers, as in (3) and (4). As determiners – primary and secondary – are the last layer to be integrated in the NP structure (Langacker 1991: 432), they occur in the NP's outermost layer. Davidse & Breban (2019: 354–355) argue that primary and secondary determiners form a composite unit, which has scope over the entire NP (see also Davidse 2004: 529): because of their unithood it is not possible, they claim (*ib.*: 353), to insert representational or quality-intensifying modifiers before or between primary and secondary determiners, e.g. *\*the strong usual cup of coffee*, *\*the complete two fools*.

It is possible, however, for multiple secondary determiners to be used in combination, as in *the usual three cups of coffee*.⁶²

The difficulty with many adjectives that can be used as secondary determiner is that they can often also be used to serve a different function. The adjective *former*, for instance, is used as secondary determiner in (5) but as a metadesignative modifier in (6).

(5) DeLancey pointed out that the difference between (66a) and (66b) does not concern the difference in certainty. *The former example* . . . (Davidse & Breban 2019: 353)

(6) He had to watch *his former colleagues* become consultants while he trained for something else. (*ib.*)

More frequently, the kinds of adjectives that can be used as secondary determiner can also be used as an epithet, e.g. *different, identical, usual, regular, certain, odd, famous, well-known, typical, obvious*. Halliday & Hasan (1976: 159–160) argue that the secondary determiner uses can be distinguished from the epithet (i.e. qualifying) uses by the different orders in which they combine with numerals. They provide the following examples (*ib.*: 160):

| Secondary determiners | Epithets |
|---|---|
| the *identical* three questions | the three *identical* questions |
| the *usual* two comments | the two *usual* comments |
| a *different* three people | three *different* people |
| the *odd* few ideas | the few *odd* ideas |
| the *obvious* first place to stop | the first *obvious* place to stop |

---

**62** Authors who have studied the function of secondary determination generally include cardinal and ordinal numeratives in this category (e.g. Quirk et al. 1985: 261; Crain & Hamburger 1992; Matthews 1997: 289; Wardhaugh 1997: 38; Bache 2000: 239; Denison 2006; Davidse, Breban & Van linden 2008: 476). For ordinal numeratives (e.g. *second, fifth*), the inclusion in the class of secondary determiners is straightforward: they indicate the position of the instance denoted by the NP vis-à-vis others and thereby facilitate identification. Cardinal numeratives, on the other hand, quantify an instance by specifying its cardinality, i.e. the number of component entities it comprises (Langacker 1991: 81): in the absence of a primary determiner, however, cardinal numbers (and other absolute quantifiers) are solely responsible for the identifying function (Davidse 2004: 526–531), e.g. *three little bears*. In combination with a primary determiner (which is then necessarily definite), cardinal numeratives serve a secondary determining function, *viz.* to indicate how many individuals are subsumed by the referent of the definite NP (e.g. *the three cups of coffee I drank today*).

Against this, Davidse & Breban (2019: 355) hold that such polysemous adjectives can be either epithets or secondary determiners when they follow a numeral, "with the context often disambiguating the two possible readings" (*ib.*). For instance, *three different people* may mean that the three people that are mentioned are very different from each other, in which case *different* is used as an epithet. The same NP may also contrast the 'three people' that are introduced with 'three other people' that were previously mentioned: in this case, *different* serves as secondary determiner as it facilitates identification of the referent of the NP. For the study in this chapter, I therefore stick to Davidse & Breban's (2019: 353) recognition test to differentiate between two uses of polysemous adjectives, namely the expected impossibility to insert representational modifiers between primary and secondary determiners. I supplement this test with another criterion, namely the fact that epithets are gradable (e.g. *three very different people*), while secondary determiners are not (e.g. *\*very different three people*). This means that, in all potentially ambiguous cases where gradability presented itself as an option, I made the 'conservative' choice to code the adjective as an epithet.

Finally, the last element in the determiner zone is the FOCUS MARKER. Its function is to put special focus on the entity it modifies by "indicating how the [entity] fits into the framework of knowledge and expectations" relevant to what is being said (McGregor 1997: 210). Focus markers often do so by contrasting the 'focus value', i.e. the entity they scope over, with alternative (implied) values relevant to the proposition (Davidse & Breban 2019: 358–359). In (7), for instance, the focus marker *mere* emphasises the 'mention of food' as sufficient to trigger off hunger pangs, implicitly contrasting it with other (stronger) expected triggers.

(7) The mere mention of food had triggered off hunger pangs. (WB)

Structurally, focus markers occur in a more leftward position than noun-intensifiers (Breban & Davidse 2016: 225), e.g. *the mere utter silence*. They can be recognised by the fact that focusing adjectives tend to alternate with focusing adverbials (*ib.*), i.e. Quirk et al.'s (1985: 604–612) "focusing subjuncts", e.g. *merely the mention of food*.

In conclusion, the English noun phrase forms a composite structure of different component structures, which each construe a distinct function with respect to the whole. In the remainder of this chapter I will investigate how the semantic function of the indefinite NP in predicative and specificational clauses, and the pragmatic meanings thereby triggered, influence the lexicogrammatical realisation of the indefinite NP. More specifically, the corpus study will answer the question whether statistically significant differences can be found between indefinite predicate nominatives and indefinite variable NPs in terms of the distribution of structural elements (e.g. the different functional types of modifiers set out in this section) and their lexical realisation. The answers to these questions will be related to the larger process-participant constellations in which the indefinite NPs figure, as set out in Chapter 3.

## 4.2 Method

In this section, I will describe the methodology for the case study of the NP in the three construction types. In Section 4.2.1, I will first recapitulate the research questions raised in the introduction and formulate hypotheses for them. In Section 4.2.2, I will explain how the data were collected, to then give an overview of how they were analysed in Section 4.2.3. The results of the case study will then be presented in Section 4.3, where I will interpret them in answer to the research questions.

### 4.2.1 Questions and hypotheses

This study examines the nominal construal of the indefinite specificational variable and the indefinite predicate nominative. Firstly, I examine if the different semantic functions the NPs serve within their respective clausal structures, predicative complement versus variable, are reflected in their internal functional structure, i.e. in the head nouns, modifiers and determiners they take. Secondly, I investigate whether the grammatical function of the indefinite specificational variable influences its construal: more specifically, are there differences between the indefinite variable subject and the indefinite variable complement, or are the two NPs similarly construed, both contrasting as such with the indefinite predicate nominative. The answers to these questions are expected to offer new insights into the construal of the indefinite specificational variable – as subject or complement. As argued in Chapter 3, I do not view specificational clauses with indefinite variables as marginal phenomena whose felicity depends on factors that bring them as close as possible to specificational clauses with definite variable. Rather, I have argued that they provide the speaker with the positive option of construing specification with a non-exhaustive implicature in contrast with specificational clauses with a definite variable, which carry an implicature of exhaustiveness.

**Research questions**
As outlined in the introduction to this chapter, the corpus study seeks to answer the following research questions:
(i)  Are there statistically significant differences in **distribution** of **structural elements** (e.g. different functional types of modifiers) and their **lexical realisation** (e.g. more abstract or concrete nouns as head) in predicative and specificational clauses?
(ii) Are the same functions (e.g. epithet) associated with **comparable lexical sets** (in terms of lexical types and lexical subclasses), or is for instance the lexical set of the same function more restricted in the one copular type than in the other?
(iii) If there are differences, do they support the posited **semantic contrast** between predicative and specificational clauses? Can these differences plausibly be related to the posited semantics of the two clause types, and do they put more semantic flesh on the semantic account proposed in Chapter 3?
(iv) Finally, does this systematic study lead to greater insight to **interpret contextualised data**? Can we, for instance, elucidate different semantic functions of what at first sight might seem similar elements (e.g. the adjective 'good' in *He's a good man* vs *A good example is* . . ., in which *good* ties in with the 'criterial' component of the variable)?

**Hypotheses**
In answer to the research questions presented above, the following hypotheses can be formulated. First, based on previous observations (e.g. Declerck 1988: 19; Mikkelsen 2005: 154) that indefinite variables often include modifiers that express 'old' information, indefinite variable NPs are expected to frequently use secondary determiners, which signal how a referent can be retrieved. The predicate nominative, by contrast, is said to introduce new information (*ib.*), which makes secondary determiners less likely to be used.

Instead, predicate nominatives may attract classifiers and epithets, which can contribute additional subclassifying and qualifying features to the characterisation that the predicate nominative gives. Moreover, as NP predicates structurally allow the attribution of qualities to the subject, I also expected to find a high incidence of intensifiers.

There is no expectation that the indefinite variable will use classifiers and epithets more or less frequently than the predicate nominative; however, the lexical sets that are associated with these elements may be more restricted for the variable NP than for the predicate nominative. This hypothesis is based on Quirk *et al.*'s (1985: 1388) finding that the variable in specificational pseudoclefts attracts adjectives like *important*, *crucial*, *key*, etc. (e.g. *What is important is this*). Given the similar function of the variable NP, similar lexical sets can be expected.

In addition, a difference may also be found in the distribution of abstract and concrete nouns in predicate nominatives and variable NPs: since the TS of the variable NP are often supplemented with TS retrieved from the preceding context, it can be expected that the head of the variable NP is more likely to be an abstract noun that instructs the hearer to look at the context to 'fill in' the meaning of the head (e.g. 'relational' nouns [Keizer 2017], or nouns designating emotion, discovery, locutions and ideas [Davidse 2018]).

Furthermore, it is probable that variable NPs will more frequently take the form of a partitive construction than predicate nominatives: the set-membership relation expressed by the partitive is expected to accord with the non-exhaustiveness implicature triggered by the indefinite variable NP.

Finally, no major differences are expected to be found between variable subjects and variable complements. In this respect, I hypothesise that the different distributions of structural elements and their lexical realisations provide support for the posited semantic contrast between predicative nominatives and specificational variables.

The hypotheses formulated here will be tested in the corpus study. However, by taking a bottom-up approach in the data analysis, I will allow for other potential patterns that were not predicted prior to the corpus study to also come out.

### 4.2.2 Data collection

In this study, I compared three kinds of copular clause, focusing, on the one hand, on the distinction between indefinite predicative and specificational clauses, and, on the other hand, on the distinction between non-reversed (subject variable) and reversed (complement variable) indefinite specificational clauses. For predicative clauses and non-reversed specificational ones, I examined 500 examples, all taken from the 'Times' (UK Times newspaper) and 'BrSpoken' (British Spoken) subcorpora of Wordbanks*Online* (WB). For reversed specificational clauses, which were less frequent, I looked at 300 examples. The data were collected from an initially large set of concordances for the verb *be* (100,000 examples): after filtering out all specificational and predicative clauses (based on the criteria set out in Chapter 3), I selected the first 500 examples of predicative and non-reversed specificational clauses and the first 300 reversed specificational clauses from the randomised dataset.

The resulting 1,300 examples were analysed in terms of four variables, corresponding to the four zones in the nominal structure (cf. Section 4.1). The specific categories for the data analysis will be outlined in Section 4.2.3.

### 4.2.3 Data analysis

The discussion of English NP structure in Section 4.1 will be operationalised into the categories that will be considered in the case study. In this section, I will first describe the categories of interest for the 'head' of the NP and the different values that were annotated for each category. Then I will discuss the categories and their values for premodifiers and post-head dependents, after which I will give an overview of how the elements in the determiner zone were examined.

Starting at the centre of the NP, I looked at the types of HEAD NOUN that typically occurred in the variable NP and in the predicate nominative, focusing on two subfactors. In the first step, I used Lyons' (1977: 442–447) distinction between 'first-order', 'second-order' and 'third-order' entities to probe for the 'abstractness' of the meaning of a head noun. According to Lyons (1977: 443), first-order entities are "physical objects", which are typically perceivable through the senses and located in "a three-dimensional space". Second-order entities are states-of-affairs, "which are located in time [...] and said to take place" (*ib.*: 443). Third-order entities, finally, are "unobservable" and refer to "such abstract entities as propositions, which are outside space and time" (*ib.*: 443). The three kinds of entities can be placed on a scale from concrete to abstract.

In a second step, I looked at the semantic domain under which the head noun lemmas were classified in *WordNet*, an electronic lexical database for English. *WordNet* identifies twenty-six semantic domains ('lexnames'):

> acts, animals, artifacts (man-made objects), attributes, body parts, cognition, communication, (natural) events, feelings, food, groups, locations, motives, (natural) objects, people, (natural) phenomena, plants, possessions, (natural) processes, quantity, relations, shapes, states, substances and time.

The lemma *pie*, for instance, is categorised in WordNet as having two senses, namely (i) <food> *pie* 'a dish baked in a pastry-lined pan often with a pastry top' and (ii) <communication> *Proto-Indo European, PIE* 'a prehistoric unrecorded language that was the ancestor of all Indo-European languages'. For each example, I determined the relevant sense and, hence, the relevant domain of the head noun.

The last factor of interest for the head of the NP was the frequency of CLASSIFIERS in predicate nominatives, variable subjects and variable complements to see how often a subclassification of the TS was given in each kind of NP.

In the second structural zone (i.e. of PREMODIFICATION), I coded how frequently premodification occurred with each of the three types of NP. First, I probed for the presence or absence of premodifiers in general. If a premodifier was used, the premodifier was then classified according to the four functional types described in Section 4.1.2 (*viz.* epithets, adjective intensifiers, noun intensifiers, metadesignatives). However, because adjective-intensifiers submodify another modifier with which they occupy one slot within the NP structure, I looked at them as SUBMODIFIERS rather than include them as a separate premodifier of the noun.

For the POST-HEAD zone, I likewise examined the general presence or absence of post-head dependents. If present, these elements were then coded for the five functions discussed in Section 4.1.3: qualifying, complementational, categorising, determining, and partitive post-heads.

The last factor I looked at was DETERMINATION. Here, I coded primary determiners and any secondary determiners and/or focus markers that were present. Within the primary determiners, I distinguished between indefinite articles (e.g. *a cat*), absolute quantifiers (e.g. *one cat*, but not substitute nouns, e.g. *a furry one*), negative quantifiers (e.g. *no cat*) and, finally, the 'zero'-determiner, which is found in indefinite NPs with uncount noun (e.g. *cat food*) and in plural count noun (e.g. *cats*).[63]

In addition to primary determiners, the other two elements in the determiner zone were also coded for, namely SECONDARY DETERMINERS – e.g. *another* (where primary and secondary determiner have functionally coalesced), *a different* – and FOCUS MARKERS – e.g. *a mere formality*.

The results of the case study will be discussed in Section 4.3, where I will analyse them in terms of the research questions formulated in Section 4.2.1. The results will be described for each zone of the English NP individually. The discussion will start with the head (Section 4.3.1) and continue with premodifiers and post-head modifiers and complements (Section 4.3.2) to end with the determiner zone (Section 4.3.3). A summarising conclusion will be given in Section 4.4.

## 4.3 Results

### 4.3.1 The head noun and classifiers

Indefinite predicate nominatives and indefinite specificational variables differ considerably as to the types of head noun they take. A first distinction between nouns designating first-, second- and third-order entities shows that indefinite

---

[63] Predicative clauses with a bare noun complement (e.g. *Persephone is queen of the underworld*) were not taken into account for the purpose of this study because it focuses on contrasting full NPs. Note that bare nouns are also found in what appear at first sight to be specificational clauses such as *Point is, it's safe*, cf. (Schmid 2001). As convincingly argued by Keizer (2016), expressions like *thing is* have grammaticalised into discourse markers and the constructions in which they occur are non-specificational.

predicate nominatives typically take head nouns that designate either first-order (44%) or third-order (43%) entities, e.g. (8) and (9) respectively.

(8) Dr Rohan Gunaratna is <u>a terrorism specialist at the Centre for the Study of Terrorism and Political Violence, University of St Andrews</u>. (WB)

(9) If you put a hundred pounds into bonds at the end of the year you get a hundred and four pounds back. Other things being equal, if that's er *if it's <u>a question of holding money for a year or holding bonds for a year,</u>* er the natural er choice is to hold the bonds, okay? (WB)

Indefinite specificational variables, by contrast, strongly preferred more nouns denoting third-order entities, which accounted for 83% of the ones construed as subject and for 81% of those functioning as complements, as illustrated in (10) and (11) respectively.

(10) The ITV partners, squeezed by a fall in advertising revenue, appear to have accepted that the losses incurred by ITV Digital cannot continue. *One option is to close the business altogether*, plugging a hole that has already cost the partners £800 million. (WB)

(11) What can we rely on in these uncertain, straitened times? *The conspicuous consumption of Donatella Versace would be a pretty safe option.* (WB)

The differences between the three kinds of NP are significant ($X^2(4)=220.21$, $p < 0.001$; Cramer's V: 0.291), and are presented in Figure 9.

**Figure 9:** The function of the indefinite NP influences the type of head noun it takes.

The different preferences for different types of noun are linked to the variation in SEMANTIC DOMAINS that the head nouns exhibit. The boxplots in Figure 11 illustrate this variation based on the absolute frequency of examples for each of the twenty-six domains: the frequency for each domain was taken as a data point, so that the boxplot displays the distribution of the data across these data points. The different cut-off points in the boxplots provide a means for interpreting whether the data are distributed symmetrically, how tightly they are grouped, and if the data are skewed. The first (lower) quartile Q1 represents the cut-off point between the 25% least frequent domains and the 75% most frequent ones. Q2 represents the median frequency. The third (upper) quartile Q3 splits off the 75% least frequent from the 25% most frequent domains. The data between Q1 and Q3 – i.e. the interquartile range (IQR)[64] – represents the middle 50% of the data and is taken as a measure of statistical dispersion: the smaller the IQR, the more tightly the middle 50% are grouped together and, hence, the smaller the dispersion, and vice versa. Because the data distribution can be skewed by particularly high or low data points, the boxplot provides a measure of indicating these points as 'outliers' (illustrated as dots in Figure 11). These outliers represent all the datapoints that are located either 1.5 x IQR below Q1 or 1.5 x IQR above Q3: these numbers form the 'inner fences' between which all datapoints that do not diverge extremely from the middle 50% are situated. Figure 10 gives a standard boxplot representation of these statistics, against which the visualisation of the dataset in this study can be interpreted.

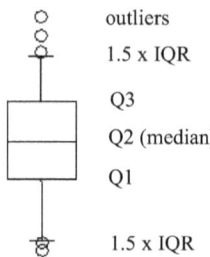

outliers

1.5 x IQR

Q3

Q2 (median)

Q1

1.5 x IQR

**Figure 10:** General display of distribution in a boxplot.

As a measure of variability across the twenty-six possible domains, the interquartile range (IQR) for the data distribution of each NP was higher for predicate

---

**64** The interquartile range (IQR) is visualised, in Figures 10 and 11, by the height of the boxes, i.e. the distance between the bottom of the box (Q1) and the top of the box (Q3).

nominatives (20.5) than for the indefinite specificational variables (*viz.* 13 for indefinite variable subjects and 9 for indefinite variable complements).

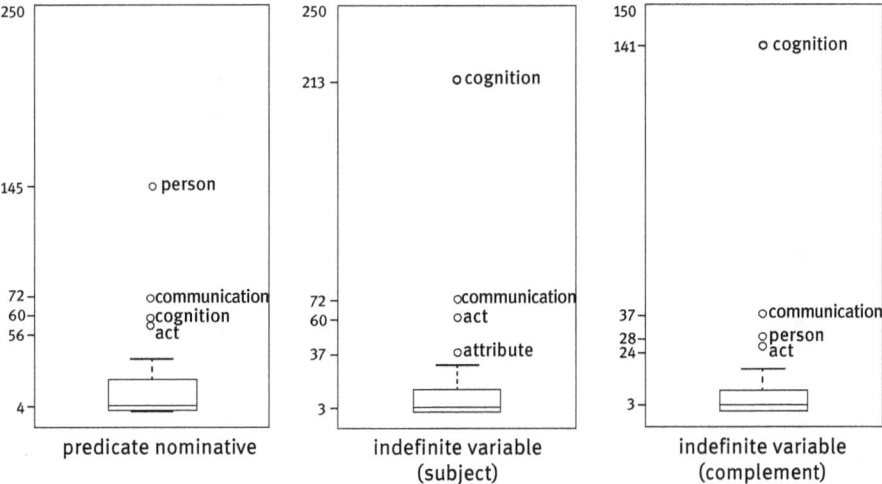

**Figure 11:** Boxplots illustrating the variation of absolute frequencies of the twenty-six domains.

The interquartile ranges indicate that the head nouns of the predicate nominatives, for which the IQR is higher, are distributed more evenly over the different domains. As shown in Figure 11, the higher IQR for the predicate nominatives is mostly due to its Q3 being higher, which suggests that the absolute frequencies for the middle 50% of the datapoints range higher than for the indefinite variables. By contrast, the middle 50% of the datapoints for the specificational variables do not only have a lower median absolute frequency but also a lower Q3. This means that the semantic domains that are included between Q1 and Q3 (i.e. the middle 50% of the data) have an overall lower frequency than the ones for the predicate nominative. In other words, roughly speaking, the noun tokens that are used in the predicate nominative are distributed more evenly across different semantic domains than the tokens for the variable subject and complement. As shown in Figure 11, this is due to the noun tokens used in the variable NP being concentrated in a few domains, notably the domains of 'cognition' and 'communication', as exemplified respectively by *problem* in (12) and by *answer* in (13).

(12) One problem with British wine lists is that they seesaw in quality, from the Petrus to the plonk. (WB)

(13) The patients felt that the hospital-based occupational therapy concentrated on tasks that were too repetitive, unrewarding and failed to give the opportunity for patients to mix with local communities. *Running a bicycle shop seemed to be <u>an answer</u>.* (WB)

The concentration of the specificational data in the domain of 'cognition' is shown in Figure 11 where the domain of 'cognition' is a clear outlier in both specificational variables. This indicates that a very high number of the indefinite variable NPs had 'cognitive' head nouns, *viz.* 213 of the indefinite variable subjects (43%) and 141 of the indefinite variable complements (47%). The data for the predicate nominatives, on the other hand, were not as skewed towards one category, even though a preference for head nouns relating to 'people' can be observed, e.g. *vice-president* in (14): 145 of the predicate nominative's head nouns (29%) were concentrated in the domain 'person' (as illustrated by the outlier in Figure 11).

(14) Mum goes to work at the bank, *where she's <u>a vice-president</u>*. (WB)

The strong attraction of nouns from the abstract domain of 'cognition' to specificational variables accounts, to a large extent, for their higher percentage of nouns denoting third-order entities. The great semantic variability of nouns in the predicate nominative, in combination with its preference for the more concrete domain 'person', is in line with the observation that predicate nominatives frequently take nouns denoting either first- or third-order entities (cf. Figure 9).

Thirdly, considerable differences can be observed between the token-frequencies of head nouns used in the different NPs. Unlike with predicate nominatives, a handful of noun tokens recurred highly frequently in the specificational dataset, with comparable results for variable subjects and variable complements. For indefinite variable subjects, seven tokens occurred at least 10 times (which jointly account for 35% of the dataset):

*thing* (73 times), *problem* (26 times), *way* (25 times), *reason* (20 times), *example* (12 times), *question* (10 times) and *solution* (10 times).

Since in the data sets used there were fewer indefinite variable complements (i.e 300) than variable subjects or predicate nominatives (i.e. 500 each), the threshold for a domain to be considered as frequent was set at 6 occurrences rather than 10 (since 10/500 = 6/300). Only six noun tokens had a frequency of at least 6 occurrences and together make up 32% of the variable complements:

*thing* (30 times), *example* (19 times), *reason* (18 times), *way* (13 times), *option* (10 times) and *problem* (6 times)

By contrast, very few nouns in predicate nominatives stood out as being highly token-frequent: two exceptions were *thing*, which occurred 16 times, and *person/ people*, which occurred 10 times. Together, these token-frequent nouns represent only 5% of the predicative examples.

Finally, significant differences were found in the frequency of use of CLASSIFIERS in the three NP types (Table 6, Figure 12). Predicate nominatives are shown to use these premodifiers significantly more frequently (13%) than variable subjects (3%) or complements (1%) ($\chi^2(2)= 85.348, p < .001$; Cramer's V: 0.256).

**Table 6:** The frequency of classifiers in the three NP types.

|  | presence | | absence | |
|---|---|---|---|---|
| predicate nominative | 64 | 13% | 436 | 87% |
| variable subject | 17 | 3% | 483 | 97% |
| variable complement | 3 | 1% | 297 | 99% |

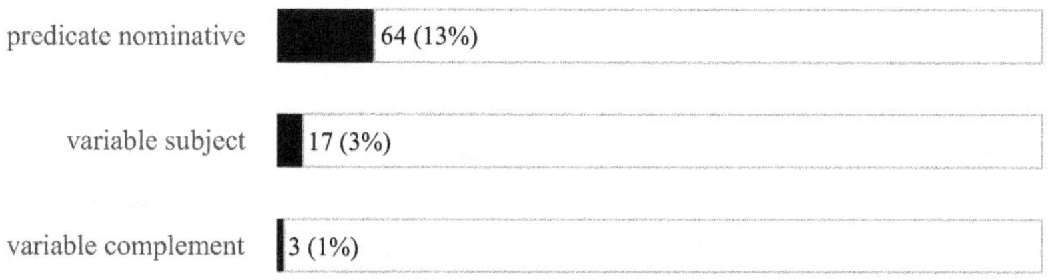

predicate nominative ▮ 64 (13%)

variable subject ▮ 17 (3%)

variable complement ▮ 3 (1%)

**Figure 12:** The frequency (in black) of classifiers, relative to the total number of data per construction type.

While overall classifiers do not occur very frequently in any of the NPs in the three clause types, the higher percentage for predicate nominatives fits in with their descriptive function. Since the predicate nominative is used to attribute TS features (and, potentially, qualities) to the subject referent, it was expected that they would be likely to integrate subclassifying information. In this way, the predicate nominative can describe the subject referent in terms of a more fine-grained TS, e.g. *prose writer* in (15).

(15) Mary Woolstonecraft [sic] is not a particularly good prose writer in my opinion. (WB)

In the following paragraphs, I compare in more detail how specific classes of head nouns are used in the predicate nominative (Section 4.3.1.1) and indefinite variable NP (Section 4.3.1.2).

### 4.3.1.1 Head nouns in the indefinite predicate nominative

Since the predicate nominative is 'non-referential' (i.e. construed as relational), its function is to conjure up a 'mental representation' of an instance, rather than pick out an individual entity from a set (see Chapter 3). Head nouns are selected for the purpose of providing a description. The description can be objective, based on the subject-referent's matter-of-fact membership of a certain class, e.g. (16). The description can be further supplemented with objective or subjective qualities, e.g. *old Jewish* in (17) and *horrible* in (18) respectively. Alternatively, the head noun itself can also provide subjective TS to express the speaker's evaluation of the subject referent, e.g. *weirdo* in (19).

(16)  He's a postgrad. (WB)

(17)  Her mum was an old Jewish lady. (WB)

(18)  Blackmail's a horrible thing. (WB)

(19)  He's a weirdo. (WB)

The semantic variation of the head nouns attested in the corpus suggests that the descriptive function of the predicate nominative imposes no particular bias on the choice of head noun. As I will argue in Section 4.3.1.2, this is not the case for the head nouns in the specificational variable.

Still, the 'direction of fit' of the predicate process (see Chapter 3) can be expected to be reflected in the choice of head nouns. Particularly, the marked type where the describee is fitted to the description, as in (20), seems to favour the class membership type.

(20)  The Mischling Test refers to the legal test under Nazi Germany's Nuremberg Laws to determine *who was a Jew*. (http://www.jewishwikipedia.info/who_is_a_jew.html)

In (20), the class noun *Jew* is selected within the context of an article on Jewish identity and is chosen for the purpose of categorising instances whose identity the interrogative subject probes for. In this type, the noun chosen is typically discourse-given (Kaltenböck 2005), i.e. either evoked in the preceding text or retrievable from it. If entities falling under a categorisation are being looked for, that category can be expected to be discourse-given. In the case study, only four of the predicative examples (i.e. less than 1%) could be interpreted as displaying such a direction of fit, e.g. (21) and (22). (An additional five examples were ambiguous between the two directions of fit.)

(21) The Strategic Rail Authority's role appears to have been marginalised: it will have the power to appoint one just one non-executive director. [. . .] An unspecified number of members would play the role of shareholders in holding the board accountable, "but would have no additional powers." *Construction firms, train operators, passenger groups and employees were all possible members.* (WB)

(22) Coleridge tries to demonstrate that Shakespeare is a subtle-souled psychologist. And there's only way in my opinion in which you can demonstrate that *anybody is a subtle-souled psychologist*, that is, you look in to yourself and see if it touches you. (WB)

On the other hand, if the description is fitted to the describee (as is usually the case), head nouns can be chosen to indicate objective class membership of the describee, e.g. (23), or to give the speaker's own evaluation, expressing a subjective assessment, e.g. *tosser* in (24), both constituting discourse-new categorisations.

(23) My brother in law is a test pilot. (WB)

(24) The public is full of people who think *Henman is a tosser*. (WB)

The head noun can also be discourse-given, e.g. in (25). Here, the fact that the referent of *you* is a member of the class of 'people' is evident from the semantics of *you*, and the referent has already been mentioned in the prior context. The focus of the description is, therefore, on the qualification of *you* as a 'generally nice' and 'hard-working' instance of the class 'people', rather than on the classification itself.

(25) You are a pretty fortunate person erm you are courteous and industrious erm you know... you... *you are a generally nice person who works hard*. (WB)

When the head noun is the substitute noun *one*, the predicate nominative instructs the hearer to retrieve its TS from the prior context. Two examples in the set of predicative examples used substitute *one*. In both cases, the TS of the predicate nominative were the same as the TS of the subject referent, e.g. *a tragic one* in (26) and *a tough one* in (27). The TS of the predicate nominative, therefore, do not add new information about the subject referent, so that the main point of the description is the qualification expressed by the premodifiers.

(26) Her life has been <u>a tragic one</u>. (WB)

(27) The game in Istanbul will be <u>a tough one</u> but we have to go there with the belief that we can score. (WB)

In sum, the predicate nominative allows for a wide variation of head nouns with different meanings. While having a slight preference for nouns expressing 'people', the predicate nominative's descriptive function imposes few conditions on the NP's type specifications, which differ according to the semantic features of the describee, the speaker's evaluation of the describee, and relation to the preceding text. The marked subtype in which the describee is fitted to the description selects mainly nouns that express contextually relevant, and most likely objective, categories.

### 4.3.1.2 Head nouns in the indefinite variable NP

Unlike the predicate nominative, the specificational variable was found to select head nouns from restricted lexicosemantic domains. Most of the head nouns, in both variable subject and complement NPs, were likely to have more abstract semantics, typically denoting third-order entities rather than first- or second-order entities. This was reflected in the predominance of nouns relating mainly to the domain of 'cognition' but also that of 'communication', e.g. *choice* in (28) and *response* in (29).

(28) Eggs baked with cheese and chutney calls for a fully-flavoured wine. *A Provence Rose, which is much more full-bodied and higher in alcohol than most other roses, is <u>a good choice</u>*. (WB)

(29) The abduction of a newly born baby from a maternity ward at Wordsley Hospital in Stourbridge in the West Midlands over the weekend has provoked a predictable chorus of demands for tightening up hospital security. But given that hospitals are already as well-guarded as prisons, surely <u>a more sensible response</u> would be to abandon security measures altogether? (WB)

These preferences were explained, to a large extent, by the high frequency of a small number of nouns, such as *thing, problem, way, reason, example, question, option* and *solution* (which were used in 35% of the variable subjects and 32% of the variable complements). Authors such as Halliday & Hasan (1976: 274–277), Francis (1986), Flowerdew (2003) and Aktas (2005) have drawn attention to the cohesive role that can be played by such 'general' or 'abstract' nouns. Flowerdew

(2003), for instance, argues that the meaning of such nouns "can [in fact] only be made specific with reference to the context" (*ib.*: 2). This they do by setting up phoric links to the preceding and/or following discourse (Francis 1986, 1994: 83). In doing so, they can serve a textual function and promote cohesion in the text (Aktas 2005: 8, with reference to Halliday & Hasan 1976). These nouns are considered what Schmid (2000, 2001) has termed 'shell nouns', which "create conceptual shells for complex pieces of information expressed by clauses or even longer passages somewhere else in a text or discourse" (Schmid 2001: 1531).

The use of such abstract 'phoric' nouns is consistent with the argument that the variable NP expresses a generalised instance. This generalised instance is a virtual entity, or mental representation, that involves making a local generalisation over more concrete instances (Breban 2011: 513). Generalised reference is ad-hoc and text-bound: the semantic specifications that feed into the conception of the generalised instance are interpreted with reference to the local discourse context. In (28), the explicit general type specifications of the variable NP, *(a good) choice*, have to be further filled out from the preceding discourse as *choice of a fully-flavoured wine*. At the same time, *a good choice* pragmatically refers to a new instance in the actual domain of instantiation, which the value NP specifies as *a Provence Rose*. This explains why variable NPs attract such abstract 'shell' nouns: not only do such nouns capture a generalisation at a higher level of abstraction, they also help to realise the textual function of the variable. This is illustrated in (28) and (29), in which the general type expressed by *choice* and *response* has to be further fleshed out with information from the prior discourse, as explained above.

The text-bound nature of the generalised instance thereby enables the variable's 'discourse-connective' function (which Mikkelsen [2005: 157] considers an essential condition for the variable NP). The use of 'shell nouns' in the variable NP ensures a link with the preceding discourse. At the same time, Tadros (1994: 71–73) and Hinkel (2001: 115) point out that shell nouns can also introduce information that is elaborated further in the discourse. This is the case when the variable is subject and precedes the value: in a way, the very function of the value is to 'elaborate' on the information that the variable introduces, since the value specifies what concrete information can be understood by the variable. For instance, in (29), the variable links up with the prior context via its text-bound type 'response to the abduction of a newly born baby, etc.'. This is then elaborated by the value *to abandon security measures altogether*, which is specified in contrast with the earlier mentioned instance *demands for tightening up hospital security*. In this respect, the meaning of these nouns in itself can serve a discourse-organising 'cohesive' function, allowing for a new topic to be introduced in relation to what has already been said, as is particularly the case with *problem, reason, solution*, etc.

Furthermore, some of the most frequently used head nouns in indefinite variable NPs have a meaning that would appear to lend itself particularly well to the 'exemplifying' function that is commonly associated with specificationals with an indefinite variable (e.g. McGregor 2003: 148–149; Halliday & Matthiessen 2004: 235). Particularly nouns such as *example, instance* and *option*, but also ones like *choice, aspect, possibility, problem, reason, way* and *question* are often used to construe an indefinite variable NP triggering the non-exhaustiveness implicature, which indicates that one or a few examples will be specified, rather than the exhaustive set of values, as illustrated in (30).

(30) *One of the many intriguing aspects of new information and telecommunications technologies is their scope for creating entirely new types of work. An example is the growth of telephone counselling:* busy and stressed-out professionals can call a sympathetic listener, who will give them advice about how to get through difficult meeting [sic] or deal with career problems. *Another possibility would be the development of professional takers-in of parcels to serve the growth of online shopping.* (WB)

Finally, the type specifications of the indefinite variable were also found to be commonly coded by substitute noun *one*, e.g. (31), or by quantifier *one* when the head noun is elided, e.g. (32). Variable subjects used substitute *one* in only 1 case but a quantifier (with elision of the head noun) in 206 cases (41%); variable complements had substitute *one* as head in 17 cases (6%) and quantifier *one* (with head noun elision)[65] in 79 cases (26%).

(31) This deep-seated association between direct linearity and the seat of a monarch or leader finds expression, if now subconscious, in even recent landscape schemes. *Examples are legion, but a classic one is the palace of Versailles with its radiating straight lines.* (WB)

---

[65] Following Halliday & Hasan (1976: 147), I take it that, when the head noun is elided, the function of the head (i.e. type-specification) is not realised by some zero-element; instead, the function of the head is realised by another element in the NP (see also Section 4.1.1), for instance quantifier *one*.

(32) There are still a few companies that pay a decent rate of interest without too much risk to your capital – *and one is Cahoot*. (WB)

Halliday & Hasan (1976: 92, 94) point out that the substitute *one* and the antecedent it substitutes for have the same function in structure and the same class, viz. head noun plus any modifiers it may have. Substitute *one* is in this sense a strictly grammatically defined unit, even though the semantic content it carries is primarily lexical. The substitute *one* anaphorically refers to a type specified in the prior context, e.g. 'example of a recent landscape scene that reflects this deep-seated association, etc.' in (31). *One* carries over this lexical meaning and inserts it in a new context, involving additional or contrastive features, e.g. *a classic one*. With quantifier *one* + head noun elision, the type specifications also have to be retrieved from the surrounding (typically preceding) context, e.g. *companies that pay a decent rate of interest*, etc. in (32). In this case, the cohesion relation is not achieved through substitution but elision of the head (Halliday & Hasan 1976: 105). In different ways, therefore, the use of substitute *one* and of 'quantifier *one* + head noun elision' in variable NPs both activate the discursive schema of 'exemplification'. The effect is different than with the uses of substitute *one* in the predicate nominative, where it replays the noun in the subject, as in *Her life has been a tragic one*, where subject and predicative complement are both construed as instances of the same type specifications (see Section 4.3.1). By contrast, the type specifications in the variable, e.g. *a classic one*, 'example of a recent landscape scene that reflects this deep-seated association', in (31), are at a higher level of generality than those of the value, e.g. *the palace of Versailles*.

In sum, the preference of indefinite variable NPs for third-order entities can be explained in terms of the generalising and phoric force of such nouns, which fit perfectly with the generalised reference of variable NPs. These 'shell' nouns bring out the text-bound nature of the variable's abstract generalised entity. A relatively small number of nouns such as *problem*, *reason*, *option* and *example* occur frequently in the indefinite variable. The meaning of these nouns was argued to serve a discourse-organising function, simultaneously linking up with the preceding text and pushing the communication forward by serving as a base for introducing a new entity. The meaning of the noun can evoke exemplification, which is commonly associated with specificationals with indefinite variable (e.g. *example, option, possibility*). Both kinds of noun – i.e. shell nouns and 'exemplifying' nouns – thereby promote cohesion in the text. This cohesive function is found both for variable subjects and for variable complements, between which few and only minor differences appear. Both can be contrasted, therefore, with the predicate nominative, where the choice of head noun was not as constrained by preferences for particular lexical types or tokens.

### 4.3.2 Pre- and postnominal dependents: Modification and complementation

The next two functional NP zones to be considered for the nominal construal of indefinite predicate nominatives and specificational variables are the pre- and postnominal zones. Taken together, premodifiers and postnominal dependents (i.e. modifiers and/or complements) are frequent in all three constructions, mostly so in the indefinite variable subjects: 76% of the indefinite variable subjects contained at least one modifier or complement, compared to 71% of the ones functioning as complement. In indefinite predicate nominatives, a modifier and/or complement was used in 73% of the cases. In other words, as far as the frequency of premodifiers and/or postnominal dependents in general is concerned, the three NPs do not differ significantly ($\chi^2(2) = 3.0615$, $p = 0.2164$) (see Table 7).

**Table 7:** The frequency of pre- and postnominal modifiers/complements and submodifiers.

|  | predicate nominative | | variable subject | | variable complement | |
| --- | --- | --- | --- | --- | --- | --- |
|  | presence | absence | presence | absence | presence | absence |
| **modifier/complement** | 363 (73%) | 137 (27%) | 382 (76%) | 118 (24%) | 214 (71%) | 86 (29%) |
| prenominal | 222 (44%) | 278 (56%) | 87 (17%) | 414 (83%) | 74 (25%) | 226 (75%) |
| postnominal | 212 (42%) | 288 (58%) | 343 (67%) | 157 (33%) | 162 (54%) | 138 (46%) |
| **submodifier** | 40 (8%) | 460 (92%) | 16 (3%) | 484 (97%) | 6 (2%) | 294 (98%) |

When we focus on PREMODIFICATION alone, however, a significant effect of the semantic role of the NP does emerge ($\chi^2(2) = 92.325$, $p < .001$; Cramer's V: 0.266). In indefinite variable subjects, a premodifier was used in 17% of the cases. That number is slightly higher for indefinite variable complements, i.e. 25%. By contrast, for predicate nominatives, premodification was much more frequent and occurred in 44% of the examples.

In the case of POST-HEAD MODIFICATION and/or COMPLEMENTATION as well, a significant difference between the three NPs can be noted ($\chi^2(3) = 69.591$, $p < .001$; Cramer's V: 0.231). Interestingly, while for this factor the predicate nominative has the lowest scores (i.e. 42%), a divergence can be observed here between the indefinite variable construed as subject (67%) and as complement (54%). While the indefinite variable subject shows a clear preference for postnominal modification/complementation, the indefinite variable complement seems to be relatively neutral to presence or absence of post-head dependents.

In addition, as SUBMODIFIERS, adjective-intensifiers were coded as a separate category from premodifiers. Here too, significant differences were found between the three copular clause types ($\chi^2(2) = 19.267$, $p < .001$; Cramer's V: 0.122). While overall not very frequent, adjective-intensifiers were found more in predicate nominatives (8%) than in indefinite variable subjects (3%) or indefinite variable complements (2%).

While the mere absence or presence of pre- and postnominal dependents already shows significant differences between the copular types, the most significant difference pertains to the semantic functions those elements have in the noun phrase, i.e. predicate nominative versus variable. This difference is most notable for the TYPES OF PREMODIFIERS, which are summarised in Table 8.

**Table 8:** The frequency of different premodifier functions in the NPs in the three constructions.

|  | presence | | absence | |
|---|---|---|---|---|
| **epithets** | | | | |
| predicate nominative | 215 | 43% | 285 | 57% |
| variable subject | 88 | 18% | 412 | 82% |
| variable complement | 70 | 23% | 230 | 77% |
| **noun-intensifier** | | | | |
| predicate nominative | 12 | 2% | 488 | 98% |
| variable subject | 0 | 0% | 500 | 100% |
| variable complement | 1 | 0% | 299 | 100% |
| **metadesignative** | | | | |
| predicate nominative | 4 | 1% | 496 | 99% |
| variable subject | 2 | 0% | 498 | 100% |
| variable complement | 5 | 2% | 295 | 98% |

For EPITHETS, a significant difference can be found between the NPs in the three constructions ($\chi^2(2)$=84.307, $p$ <.001; Cramer's V: 0.255). While 18% of the variable subjects and 23% of the variable complements use epithets, the frequency of these premodifiers is roughly twice as high in predicate nominatives (43%). The use of epithets, which were the most frequent type across the three NPs, is illustrated in (33) for the predicate nominative and in (34) and (35) for the variable subject and complement respectively.

(33)  Tamara Rojo, our star on Tuesday night, is <u>a terrific dancer</u>. (WB)

(34)  It's all very well to bemoan children falling victim to advertising, without looking at the problem of parents all-too-easily becoming slaves to their children's desires. It is not particularly original or brave to attack corporations either; *<u>a bolder move</u> would have been to attack feeble-minded adults*. (WB)

(35) Some banks and building societies are, however, taking steps to get better returns. *Lloyds TSB is a good example*. (WB)

The numbers for NOUN-INTENSIFIERS and METADESIGNATIVES were overall too low for reliable statistical analyses. Nonetheless, Table 8 shows that noun-intensifiers were used slightly more frequently in predicate nominatives (2%) than in the two types of variable NP, where only 1 attestation was found for the variable complement.

Finally, significant differences can also be observed in the different POST-HEAD DEPENDENTS that the NPs take, the frequencies of which are summarised in Table 9 and visualised in Figure 13.

**Table 9:** The frequencies of different types of post-head dependents in the three constructions.

|  | predicate nominative | | variable subject | | variable complement | |
| --- | --- | --- | --- | --- | --- | --- |
|  | presence | absence | presence | absence | presence | absence |
| determining | 2 (0.5%) | 498 (99.5%) | 3 (0.5%) | 497 (99.5%) | 1 (0%) | 299 (100%) |
| qualifying | 93 (19%) | 407 (81%) | 39 (8%) | 461 (92%) | 35 (12%) | 265 (88%) |
| categorising | 0 (0%) | 500 (100%) | 1 (0%) | 499 (99%) | 0 (0%) | 300 (100%) |
| complementing | 100 (20%) | 400 (80%) | 132 (26%) | 368 (74%) | 56 (19%) | 244 (81%) |
| partitive | 17 (3%) | 483 (97%) | 168 (34%) | 132 (66%) | 70 (23%) | 230 (77%) |

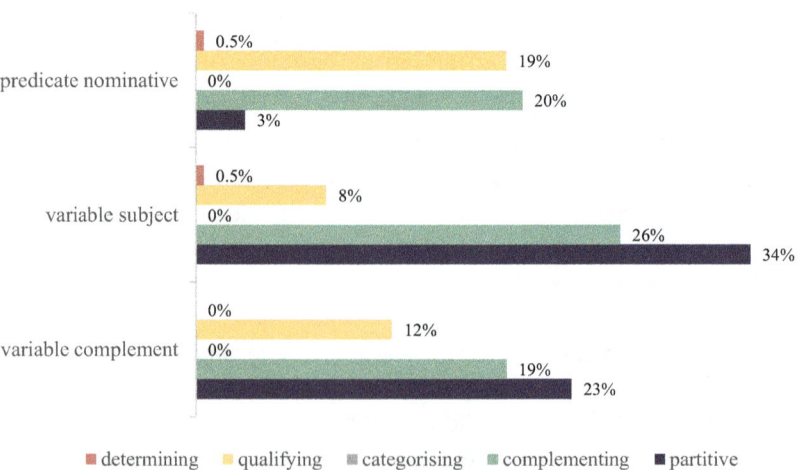

**Figure 13:** The relative frequencies of postnominal functions in the three indefinite NPs.

Firstly, categorising and determining post-heads were rarely used. For categorising post-heads, there was only one attestation, namely for the variable subject. Determining post-heads were only slightly more frequent, with two attestations for predicate nominatives, three for variable subjects and one for variable complements. These numbers are too low to allow for reliable statistical analyses.

Secondly, the use of qualifying postmodifiers was significantly more frequent in predicate nominatives (19%) than in variable subjects (8%) or complements (12%) ($\chi^2(2)$= 26.53, $p$ < .001; Cramer's V: 0.143). This is in line with previous observations from premodifiers that predicate nominatives attract qualifying information, e.g. (36).

(36) You're a generally nice person <u>who works hard</u>. (WB)

Such qualifying information can also be added to variable subjects and complements, even though this is less frequently the case, e.g. (37) and (38). When qualifying postmodifiers are used in the variable NP, they contribute to the 'criteria-stipulating' function of the variable by adding more specific qualities that the value must meet to satisfy the variable.

(37) You don't need a flashy office to sell something. More often what you do need are local partners, and it is just as important to listen to and understand customers as to sell to them. *<u>One small company in the league table that demonstrates this point</u> is Boiler Management Systems (BMS), a power-station software and systems developer.* (WB)

(38) Small companies are also feeling the pinch of rationalisation by service providers such as banks and post offices. They point to poor co-ordination between government departments, rural development agencies and local authorities. *Peter Roberts, a potter from Tywyn in Mid Wales, is <u>one business owner who has felt the full force of rural decline</u>.* (WB)

Thirdly, partitive constructions were, as expected, much more frequent in variable subjects (34%) and complements (23%) than in predicate nominatives (3%) ($\chi^2(2)$ = 291.32, $p$ < 0.001; Cramer's V: 0.515).

(39) <u>One of the strongest reasons for electing Labour</u> was its care and concern for the NHS. (WB)

(40) A lot of clubs in the SPL are now placing emphasis on youth. I know Motherwell is <u>one of those</u>. (WB)

(41) Turner was <u>one of those men who prefer statistical models to real life because they are neater and don't complain</u>. (WB)

The reason partitive constructions are particularly common with indefinite variables is that they structurally code a subset/set relation between the head, typically *one* as in (39)-(40) and the NP in the *of*-phrase. In doing so, these constructions simultaneously assert the existence of one instance and of a set of other instances of the same type, from which the former is selected. As variable NPs, which are referential (see Chapter 3), indefinite partitive NPs as in (39)-(40) have an implicature of non-inclusive reference: there may be more instances besides the one designated with the relevant type specifications. Such an implicature is not carried by the predicate nominative, as its 'non-referential' NP designates an instance got up only for attributing type specifications to the subject. Therefore, partitive constructions are much less frequent with predicate nominative (3%). When they do occur, e.g. (41), the larger set from which a subset, or 'one' instance in (41), is selected is typically not anchored to the prior text. Instead, the partitive construction is used here to describe the subject referent as being a member of a set which the hearer is assumed to have prior knowledge of, e.g. *those men who prefer statistical models to real life*, etc. In (41), the effect of the partitive construction is, in addition, that the use of the distal demonstrative *those* allows the speaker to psychologically distance her- or himself implicitly from this set of 'men'.

Finally, post-head complements were frequently used in all three of the NP types. They did, however, occur significantly more in variable subjects (26%) than in predicate nominatives (20%) or variable complements (19%) ($\chi^2(2) = 8.6876$, $p = 0.013$), although the size of the effect is relatively small (Cramer's V: 0.082). The higher frequency of post-head complements with variable subjects can be understood in terms of the clause-initial position of the variable subject. The initial position is where the clause 'links up' with the preceding discourse and where coherence is typically signalled, e.g. by *this study* in (42).

(42) An important trial published in the New England Journal of Medicine in 1997 called the DASH study [. . .] had impressive results in reducing high blood pressure with diet alone. *<u>One aim of this study</u> was to emulate aspects of the higher-fibre, higher-potassium and magnesium diets of vegetarians, who often have lower blood pressure.* (WB)

The indefinite NP singles out a newly introduced instance, e.g. *one aim*, via its association with a recoverable entity, e.g. *this study*. The post-head complement thereby refines the denotation of the noun and, in doing so, anchors it to the preceding discourse.

In the following paragraphs, I look in more detail at the differences in distribution of modifier types manifested by the predicate nominative and indefinite variable NP.

### 4.3.2.1 Modification and complementation in the indefinite predicate nominative

As discussed in Chapter 3, it is crucial to recognise that its form as a full NP gives the predicate nominative a meaning potential that is different from either adjectival or bare noun predicative complements, e.g. (43) and (44) respectively.

(43)  Tony Blair was jubilant last night after the IRA finally committed to peace. (WB)

(44)  Macmillan rose to be prime minister in 1957. (WB)

Predicative clauses with adjectival complements describe an entity by ascribing qualities to it, e.g. *jubilant*. The ones with a bare noun complement describe an entity by making a type-attribution, e.g. the type *prime minister*, which cannot take further modifiers expressing qualities. When the predicative complement is realised by an indefinite NP, however, it can ascribe both type specifications and qualities to the subject instance, as in (45)-(47). The qualities ascribed to the subject referent can also be graded, as with *very unnatural* in (46).

(45)  Nature is a prestigious British science publication. (WB)

(46)  Bear in mind that *the university is a very unnatural state of existence*, there isn't such a thing in nature. (WB)

(47)  Laurent Robert is a French left winger blessed with gifts that have quickly won him a place in the hearts of the fans who are so desperate to see their club turn years of promise into fulfilment. (WB)

The relation between the type specifications and the subject referent that is described can be commented on by means of a metadesignative modifier (Davidse & Breban 2019: 341). In (48), the metadesignative modifier *true* comments on the appropriateness of the type specifications *British Hero* to describe the subject referent. In (49), the metadesignative *former* expresses that the type *Miss World* applies only in the past to the subject referent.

(48) He just gets on with it. *He's a true British hero*, an old school British gent who is cool and calm in the face of such pressure. (WB)

(49) Wilnelia is a former Miss World. (WB)

As the results from the case study show, this meaning potential is exploited in the vast majority of the predicative examples: this was evidenced by the high frequency of pre- and postnominal modifiers and/or complements (73%) in the attested predicate nominatives, with 44% of them taking a premodifier and 42% a post-head dependent. In addition, the results from the case study showed that, like the variable NP, predicate nominatives were likely to use post-head complements, e.g. (50).

(50) Research is being carried out to find out if *pigs might be carriers of BSE-type diseases*. (WB)

Unlike the variable NPs, however, predicate nominatives also had a preference for qualitative postmodifiers, which were equally frequent as post-head complements (both 19%). In (51), for instance, the postmodifying participial clause *dressed unexpectedly in slacks...* serves to supplement the description, *a middle-aged man*, with further individuating information.

(51) He was a middle-aged man dressed unexpectedly in slacks, a pressed short-sleeved workshirt, and tie. (WB)

We can conclude that, in my data, the predicate nominative goes in a great majority of cases beyond merely describing the subject as an otherwise undefined member of a class.

### 4.3.2.2 Modification and complementation in the indefinite specificational variable

Indefinite variable subjects and complements are roughly equally likely to have a modifier and/or complement – respectively 76% and 71% – as predicate nominatives (73%). However, while the predicate nominative had no distinct preference for premodifiers (44%) or post-head dependents (42%), the variable NPs strongly favoured the use of post-head modifiers or complements over premodifiers: 67% of the variable subjects and 54% of the variable complements took a post-head modifier or complement, while only 17% of the first and 25% of the second took a premodifier. The only frequently used type of premodifier is formed by epithets, which account for practically all of the premodifiers used by the variable subject (17%) and by the variable complement (25%). Moreover, variable NPs used a smaller set of frequently used lexical types (e.g. *good, common, prime, major*). These lexical types illustrate the preference of the variable for subjective epithets, especially the ones making a qualitative comparison between instances. Finally, the variable did not share with the predicate nominative its preference for qualitative postmodifiers but instead strongly favoured post-head complements and partitive constructions.

To describe the specific semantic function of epithets in indefinite variable NPs, I first briefly reproduce the account given in Chapter 3 of the semantic-pragmatic contribution of the latter to the specification relation. I proposed that the variable NP designates an abstract criterial entity and implies reference to a concrete instance of it. It conveys these CRITERIAL semantic specifications, explicitly in the head and potential classifiers, while often also giving instructions to retrieve more type specifications from the preceding text. It is from these criterial semantic specifications that the notion of A SET OF QUALIFYING ENTITIES, i.e. values, is INFERRED. This inferred set is in principle delimited and finite: it contains ALL the entities that correspond to the criterial specifications, one or a larger number. Specificational copulars with indefinite variable NP carry a non-exhaustiveness implicature, i.e. there is no implicature that they specify all the values in the inferred set. Discursively, indefinite specificationals are used in contexts where the speaker is not willing or able to identify all the qualifying entities, or to distinguish qualifying from non-qualifying entities. This is where the function of epithets in indefinite variable NP comes in. In examples like *common*[66] in (52) and

---

[66] Premodifiers like *common* in *a common example of a rock formed in this way* in (52) have sometimes also been considered secondary determiners: Halliday (1985: 162), for instance, comments that secondary determiners can facilitate identification of an instance "by referring to its fame or familiarity", not just by indicating "its status in the text, or its similarity/dissimilarity to some other designated [instance]". However, if we consider predicative alternation (e.g. *one example is common, namely sandstone*) and gradability (e.g. *a very common example*) as grammatical recognition criteria to distinguish between secondary determiners and epithets (Breban & Davidse 2003: 272), *common* is best interpreted here as providing qualitative rather than referential information. The same is true for other polysemous adjectives like *prime* and *major*, which can also be used as epithets (e.g. *the Mexican Museum is a very prime example of what I'm talking about* (Google); *A very major concern is that double vaccinated people. . . are still getting the virus* (Google)). Moreover, they also support predicative alternation, e.g. *The worldwide possibility from the brand-new variant is very prime* (Google); *This is major* (Google). (For comparison, a secondary determiner like *further* behaves differently: e.g. *\*a very further difficulty*, *\*a difficulty is further*; see Section 4.1 on the structures and functions in the English NP.)

*good* in (53) the epithets delineate within the set of entities that qualify as values in terms of mere representational specifications, a SUBSET of qualifying entities satisfying EXTRA QUALITATIVE criteria. It is then from this restricted subset that the entity designated by the value NP is selected.

(52) A rock which has been formed by the consolidation of sediment derived from pre-existing rocks. *Sandstone is <u>a common example of a rock formed in this way</u>; mudstone and shale are <u>other examples</u>.* (WB)

(53) Styles shift so quickly and what was cutting edge three months ago has already been overtaken. *<u>A good example</u> is last season's gypsy look.* (WB)

The meanings which these epithets acquire in the context of specificational constructions hinge on notions such as 'criteria-meeting' (coming up very clearly to the criteria specified by the variable), e.g. *good* in (53) or (54), 'typicality' (being a frequently attested value of the variable), e.g. *common* in (52), and 'prominence' (standing out from less obviously qualifying values), e.g. *notable* and *very important* in (55) and (56).

(54) Hatred eats you up and takes you over, whilst being tolerant and understanding will make your heart swell with pride. *<u>A good way to deal with racism</u> is to ask yourself, 'If we were all blind what would we hate each other for?'* (WB)

(55) Today's search for Martian life brings to mind the false claims of the past. *<u>A notable one</u> was the "discovery" by amateur astronomer Percival Lowell that the "canals" on Mars were part of an irrigation system.* (WB)

(56) What are the four components that taken together define an emotional experience? Although cognitions, physiology, and overt behavior are involved in an emotional reaction, there seems to be little doubt that *<u>a very important aspect</u> is the subjective-feeling component.* (WB)

The stricter criteria expressed by epithets such as 'good', 'notable', etc. form the basis for implicitly *comparing* the entities that qualify 'well' or 'notably' for the criteria of the variable with those entities that do not. In other words, the qualities expressed by adjectives like *notable, good, common*, etc. provide a stricter basis for selecting qualifying entities from the set of potential ones. These epithets comment on the speaker's motivation for singling out one value from among other potentially qualifying instances. They imply comparison between one or more prototypical values focused on by the speaker and a fuzzy set of entities of which it is less clear that they qualify for the variable. In this way, the opposites of the epithets, 'not notable', 'not or less good', 'uncommon', characterise the implied set of other potential values, from which the speaker does not choose the values. This is, of course, the set which, by the non-exhaustiveness implicature of specificational clauses with indefinite variable, is implied to exist.

The use of the comparative form of epithets, e.g. *bolder* in (57) and *better* in (58), has the same semantic-pragmatic effect of comparing a subset of values that in some sense stand out with an implied set of potential values that do not. For instance, *bolder* in (57) locates the newly introduced instance in a more restricted subset of 'bolder move' in contrast with other instances given elsewhere in the context, e.g. *bemoan children* and *attack corporations*. In (58), *better* adds an explicitly comparative qualification to indicate the well-suitedness of the subject referent as a value for the variable vis-à-vis a previously mentioned instance, e.g. *Germany* in (58). In addition, if other qualifying entities are specified in the local discourse context, as is the case in (58), this also gives salience to the interpretation of the indefinite NP as a variable rather than a description.

(57)  It's all very well to bemoan children falling victim to advertising, without looking at the problem of parents all-too-easily becoming slaves to their children's desires. It is not particularly original or brave to attack corporations either; *a bolder move would have been to attack feeble-minded adults*. (WB)

(58)  Only yesterday police in Stourbridge stormed a mosque to detain and expel two Afghans to Germany, where their original claim was being processed before they decided *Britain was a better option*. (WB)

Finally, the case study showed that, more so than predicate nominatives (42%), indefinite variables were likely to incorporate post-head dependents in their nominal structure, both as subject (67%) and as complement (54%). Partitive constructions were particularly frequent, used in 34% of the variable subjects and in 23% of the variable complements, e.g. (59) and (60).

(59)  The Tories are unlikely to lose their status as Her Majesty's Loyal Opposition, but *one of Iain Duncan Smith's first acts as leader was to set up a unit to deal with the Lib Dem threat*. (WB)

(60)  Er happiest child memories. . . Can't think of any. No erm. . . *Playing apple fights I think is probably one of them*. (WB)

As noted in the discussion of predicate nominatives, partitive constructions grammatically code a subset-set relation between the head of the construction and the set of referents expressed by the plural NP in the *of*-phrase. As part of the variable NP, the effect of the partitive is to define a subset within the set of qualifying entities, though in a different way than we saw for the epithets. The subset introduced by the partitive is not specified by qualities imposing stricter selection criteria but by quantifying instances, typically only *one*, within the explicitly coded set of qualifying entities.

Apart from partitive constructions, post-head dependents of the complementing type in Bache's typology (see Section 4.1.3) are also common in variable NPs, used in 26% of the variable subjects and in 19% of the variable complements. Post-head complements have to be considered in the light of Patten's (2012) claims that lexical modifiers and/or complements as a rule "lexically imply uniqueness" (Patten 2012: 55) and that such implied uniqueness is necessary to make indefinite variable NPs acceptable. Specifically about relative clauses, Patten (2012: 53–54) claims that they make the indefinite variable "noncommittal with respect to inclusiveness and exclusiveness" (*ib.*: 54). In Chapter 3, I argued contra Patten (2012) that variables construed by indefinite NPs generally do trigger the implicature of 'non-inclusive' reference that there may be other instances corresponding to the relevant type specifications. In the following paragraphs, I argue for this position by considering the semantics coded by restrictive relative clauses and complement clauses and the contextual effects observed in examples of specificationals whose variables contain postmodifiers of this kind.

As argued by Langacker (1991: 432), a restrictive relative clause "restricts the head noun's type specification" (Langacker 1991: 432), that is, it further narrows down the general type designated by the head noun, i.e. *reason that's given for disliking Shelley* in (61). This narrowed down subtype is then structurally integrated with the determiner, which happens to be *another* in (61). The complex determiner *another* in fact explicitly codes the non-uniqueness of this instance of *reason that's given for disliking Shelley*.

(61)  There's also. . . aspects of Shelley that perhaps put people off reading him. One is the thought of the martyred image of himself the man with the persecution complex that he presents . . . <u>Another reason that's given for disliking Shelley</u> is often the lack of substance in his writing. (WB)

Post-head PPs and complement clauses serve a similar type-restrictive function as restrictive relative clauses, as shown in (62) and (63) respectively. Moreover, the postmodifiers in (62) and (63) do not just narrow down the general type into a more elaborate subtype, but they also set up cohesive links to the prior discourse, e.g. *the [abortion] pill* in (62) and *the EU* and *this stance* in (63). In neither case, however, does the postmodifier "lexically imply uniqueness" (contra Patten 2012: 55).

(62) Abortion is never a happy matter. It is a horrible, it is horrible for a woman to have to wait when she has made this decision. *An overriding reason for developing and using the [abortion] pill is*, she pointed out, *that women have always wanted a method like this*, but it is not a miracle she emphasized and must never be sold at the chemist. (WB)

(63) The single factor most likely to stop the talks dead is the European Union's stance that the "environment" must be on the table, too. This is code for wanting the right to ban imports, in advance of scientific evidence of any harm to people or the environment, a policy many countries think is no more than protectionism. *French farmers are one main reason why the EU has taken this stance*. (WB)

A final observation is that indefinite variable subjects take post-head dependents (67%) more frequently than variable complements (54%). In terms of the specific functions of both premodifiers and post-head dependents, the variable subjects and complements nevertheless show few differences. This suggests that the premodifiers and post-head dependents are generally used with the same semantic functions in the two grammatical positions and that other factors must be considered to account for the different frequencies of post-head dependents between the two. In Chapter 7, I will propose that the discourse-embedding of the indefinite variable in the two different grammatical positions can provide insights into the higher frequency of post-heads with variable subjects.

In conclusion to the discussion of modification and complementation, significant differences were found between predicate nominatives and variable subjects and complements as to the frequency and function of the modifiers and/or complements they used. Predicate nominatives used modifiers generally more than the two variable NPs and had a specific preference for qualitative modifiers ascribing qualities to the designated instance (e.g. epithets and qualitative postmodifiers). Variable subjects and variable complements, on the other hand, used premodification less frequently and resorted to a more restricted lexical set of premodifiers (e.g. *good, notable, common*). Post-head modifiers and complements were found to be used more frequently by the two variable NPs. This was mainly due to the high frequency of partitives, which code a subset-set relation, and of post-head complements, which restrict the type-specifications of the head and often link them to the preceding text.

### 4.3.3 Determination

The final functional zone to be considered for the contrast between the indefinite predicate nominative and variable is the determiner zone. Determiners provide information about how the instance denoted by an NP relates to the speech context and its participants, or the 'ground' (Langacker 1991, 2004; Davidse 2004).

Turning first to primary determiners, the different referential statuses of the indefinite predicative and variable NPs (see Chapter 3) was found to correlate with significant differences in the choice of specific determiners for the two NP types ($\chi^2(4) = 412.71, p < .001$; Cramer's V: 0.399)[67] (see Table 10, which is visualised in Figure 14).

**Table 10:** The frequency of different determiners in the NPs in the three construction types.

|  | predicate nominative | | variable subject | | variable complement | |
| --- | --- | --- | --- | --- | --- | --- |
|  | abs. freq. | % | abs. freq. | % | abs. freq. | % |
| indefinite article | 416 | 83% | 172 | 34% | 166 | 55% |
| zero | 59 | 12% | 8 | 2% | 10 | 3% |
| no | 7 | 1% | 0 | 0% | 0 | 0% |
| quantifier | 18 | 4% | 320 | 64% | 124 | 42% |

By default, indefinite identification is realised by an indefinite article in the singular or by the zero-article in the plural.[68] Predicate nominatives conform to this: 83% of the examples included an indefinite article in singular NPs, e.g. *a failure* in (64), and 12% were plural NPs with the zero-article, e.g. *glamorous figures* and *rejects [. . .]* in (65). Together, these forms of indefinite grounding represent 95% of the predicative data.

(64)   If we think we are going to be <u>a failure</u>, we shall be <u>a failure</u>. (WB)

---

[67] The data for the negative quantifier *no* were not included in the chi-square test, since there were not enough attestations to ensure statistical reliability.

[68] As argued by Davidse (2004: 527), the zero-article occupies a specific value in the paradigm of indefinite plural articles: it can systematically be replaced by unstressed *some*. By contrast, bare generic plurals are truly 'determinerless' as shown by the impossibility of systematically replacing them by any determiners, including *all* (Carlson 1978: 33, 196): *Koalas/\*all koalas are on the verge of extinction*. Bare generics give direct mental access to the class with the type specifications named by the bare common noun as such (see also McGregor 2003; Davidse 2004: 527; Langacker 2017a: 236–237).

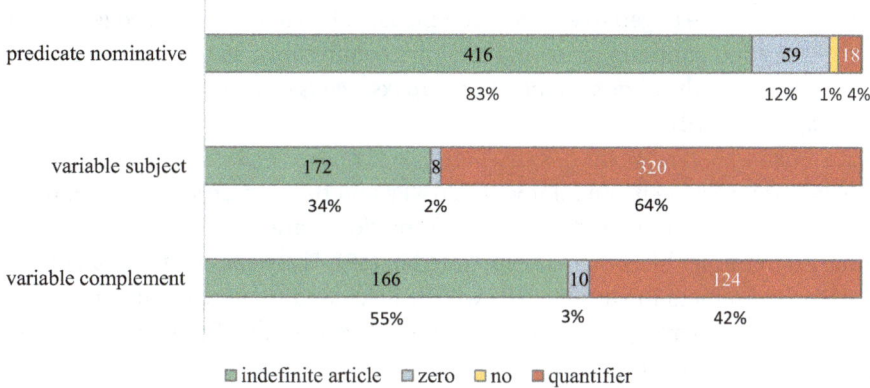

**Figure 14:** The frequencies of different indefinite determiners in the indefinite NPs.

(65) Most of France's wartime heroes were not <u>glamorous figures</u> but <u>rejects who, by reason of age or infirmity, were unfit even for forced labour</u>. (WB)

Indefinite variables, by contrast, depart from this default. The indefinite article is used in only 34% of indefinite variable subjects and in 55% of the complements, e.g. (66) and (67).

(66) Fellowes wrote a draft of the [Queen's] speech [following Princess Diana's death], Crawford adding to it. *<u>A key question</u> was the phrasing of the Queen's admission that the royal family could benefit from the princess's example.* (WB)

(67) Wistful reveries and meandering monologues constituted the bulk of the hour-long set [by Jarvis Cocker]. *The opening number, Weeds, was <u>a case in point</u>.* (WB)

Plural NPs occurred in only 2% and 3% of the indefinite variable subjects and complements respectively, e.g. (68) and (69).

(68) By 2003 it is predicted a third of us will be living on our own, and so trend-spotter Marks & Spencer has brought out a range of single-portion comfort food. *<u>Winners in our household</u> were the Lamb Shank with White Wine Garlic and Rosemary Glaze, £3.99, the Chicken Confit with Cannellini Beans, Bacon and Thyme and the Ham Hock with Spicy Lentils, both £2.99.* (WB)

(69) Beds can be edged in any way you please. I like to use a solid edge of brick that soon supports moss and mellows comfortably, as terracotta will, too. *Treated timber, bricks, hooped wire, rocks, shells or woven saplings are <u>other options</u>.* (WB)

The indefinite article in singular variable NPs and the zero-article in the plural – which both offer minimal identifying information – are often followed by a secondary determiner like *other*, as illustrated in (69). The semantic function of secondary determiners in variable NPs will be discussed in more detail below. Yet, as the NPs in (67) and (68) illustrate, variable NPs with indefinite primary determiner only are also found.

Besides by indefinite articles, the grounding function of the indefinite variable is commonly fulfilled by a cardinal number. 64% of variable subjects and 42% of variable complements are grounded by cardinal numbers, e.g. (70) and (71) respectively.

(70) <u>One dimension of organizational fairness</u> is pay level. (WB)

(71) The word 'Wende', meaning a turning point or time of seismic change, is not used lightly in the German language. *The nation's reunification in 1989 was <u>one occasion</u>,* but rarely before has it been used in a sporting context. (WB)

Of the cardinal numbers, *one* is the most frequent choice for grounding the generalised instance in both variable subjects and variable complements in terms of a quantifier; the only uses of another cardinal number were all with *two*, which occurred in 3 of the variable subjects and only 1 of the variable complements. This contrasts with the use of *one* in predicate nominatives, where they were attested in 4% of the data.

Finally, the predicate nominative can also be grounded by a negative quantifier, which was the case in 7 examples (1%), e.g. *no artiste* in (72). In the specificational variable, by contrast, no such NP-internal negation was attested. This is readily explained by the presupposition of existence that attaches to the specificational variable (Chapter 3).

(72) When it comes to putting on make-up, I am <u>no artiste</u>. (WB)

When we now turn to the secondary elements in the determiner zone – i.e. secondary determiners and focus markers – the contrast between predicate nominative and variable appears under a different light than when the primary determiners only are considered. The quantified results are summarised in Table 11.

**Table 11:** The frequency of secondary determiners and focus markers.

|  | predicate nominative | | variable subject | | variable complement | |
| --- | --- | --- | --- | --- | --- | --- |
|  | presence | absence | presence | absence | presence | absence |
| 2nd determiner | 25 (5%) | 475 (95%) | 412 (82%) | 88 (18%) | 200 (67%) | 100 (33%) |
| focus marker | 11 (2%) | 489 (98%) | 0 (0%) | 500 (100%) | 6 (2%) | 294 (98%) |

As Table 11 shows, SECONDARY DETERMINERS were found significantly more frequently in variable subjects (82%) and complements (67%) than in predicate nominatives (5%) ($\chi^2(2)$ = 668.13, $p$ < .001; Cramer's V: 0.717). For FOCUS MARKERS, the absolute frequencies were too small to carry out a reliable statistical test. The data do show, however, that, while they are not attested at all for the variable subject, focus markers can be found in some of the predicate nominatives (2%) and equally frequently in the variable complements (2%), as illustrated in (73) and (74) respectively.

(73) Human life is just a blink in the cosmos. (WB)

(74) There's no hiding the fact that the 2004/05 season has probably been South Africa's worst since the end of isolation and in that regard Smith must bear at least some responsibility. He hasn't been helped by administrative inefficiency that has seen him play his trade as skipper under two different coaches, two different selection conveners, and the various changes to playing personnel (*Gary Kirsten's retirement being just one example*, the doling out of five new caps in the last three months being another). (WB)

The complex determiner *another* is used more frequently in variable subjects (15%) and variable complements (21%) than in predicate nominatives, where it is hardly used at all (i.e. in 3 cases, or less than 1%). The complex determiner *another* signals that new instances of a phorically given type are introduced (Breban et al. 2011: 2689). However, in the context of the predicate nominative, *another* gives different instructions for retrieval of the type than in the specificational examples. In the predicate nominative in (75), *just another drama* describes the instance as one of countless other examples of its type. The secondary determiner *other* in this case refers to implied instances that are part of culturally shared knowledge (homophoric retrieval in Martin's [1992] terms).

(75) [Review of *Acorn Antiques*] But *generally it is just another drama about friendship, ambition, adultery and betrayal*, and I find it very hard to care less about any of them. (WB)

In the variables in (76) and (77), by contrast, *another* expresses comparative reference to an instance in relation to instances of the same type evoked in the preceding discourse. The retrieval of this type is anaphoric.

(76) Can't borrow at home because the banks won't lend. They've said we're not allowed to lend er when we've reached our credit ceiling. *Well then <u>another way of getting money</u> is to go abroad, okay?* (WB)

(77) We have five life career roles. Home and family is one of them. *Employment is <u>another</u>. Study is <u>another</u>.* Voluntary work and leisure. And I'm sure there are others. (WB)

Besides *other*, secondary determiners used in variable NPs include *further*, *next*, *final*, and ordinal numbers like *first*, etc., e.g. (78).

(78) Graeme Garden's translation of Georges Feydeau's "Le Mariage de Barillon" sees Griff Rhys Jones... as the eager bridegroom Barillon. It is his wedding day, but unfortunately his bride Virginie (Diana Morrison) is in love with Patrice (Eliot Giuralarocca), who threatens to kill himself if the wedding goes ahead. *<u>A further difficulty</u> is his mother-in-law-to-be (Alison Steadman), who fancies him,* and he also needs to avoid the mayor, whom he has challenged to a duel. (WB)

All these secondary determiners set up 'COMPARATIVE REFERENCE' with previously evoked instances of the same type (McGregor 1997: 322; Breban & Davidse 2003). This comparison is a textual one: these secondary determiners specify the designated instance's position in the discourse with respect to another instance or a sequence of instances in the context. In doing so, secondary determiners like *further*, *final*, etc. set up phoric links: the new instance introduced by the indefinite variable NP is integrated in the discourse by positioning it with respect to prior information. Moreover, Breban & Davidse (2003: 281) and Breban (2011: 513) argue that secondary determiners, like *another*, *further* but also *different* and *similar* can function as markers of generalised reference. In (79), for instance, *similar* in *a similar such word* indicates "comparative reference" based on the "likeness" between the earlier instance *"no can do"* and a new non-recoverable instance (Halliday & Hasan 1976: 77). *A similar such word* instructs readers to abstract away from the individual entities and create a more abstract entity that generalises over them based on their commonalities. In this way, the variable NP introduces a generalised entity that captures the commonalities of more concrete instances. The very high frequency of secondary determiners in variable NPs can be explained by their construing the generalised reference, which, as argued in Chapter 3, is the referential status of indefinite variable NPs.

(79) "No can do" originally emerged in the 19th century to mock Chinese immigrants because of what is called the "pidgin English," which are forms of English that immigrants have used to make it easier for them to communicate in America. *A similar such word is* "Long Time No See", which was used to mock the English of Native Americans. (https://medium.com/lessons-from-history/common-words-you-never-knew-had-such-an-offensive-history-b630b187340)

While indefinite variable subjects and complements were found to mostly align in terms of their preferences for different types of premodifiers, a small but interesting difference between them was the absence of focus markers in variable subjects, while they did occur in a small number of variable complements. In fact, all 11 cases of focus marking in the variable complement involved *only* or *just*, e.g. (80).

(80) *The corpus is only one area that we look at* and the real world is another. (WB)

As Davidse & Breban (2019: 329–330) point out, focus markers like *only* position a focus value against alternative values, which in example (80) is mentioned explicitly. This corresponds, at the clause-level, to the implicature that other values than *the corpus* can also qualify for the variable, not that 'only one' variable determines *the corpus* as a fitting value.

In the following paragraphs, I look in more detail at the differences in distribution of determiner types manifested by the predicate nominative (Section 4.3.3.1) and indefinite variable NP (Section 4.3.3.2).

### 4.3.3.1 Determiners in the indefinite predicate nominative

The strong preference for an indefinite article (83%) or the plural zero-article (12%) in predicate nominatives can be explained by the fact that both have "minimal semantic content" (Lyons 1999: 36) compared to *one* and the complex determiner *another*. This preference fits in with the 'non-referential' status of the indefinite predicate nominative as discussed in Chapter 3. The instance designated by a predicative indefinite NP carries no presupposition of existence and has no individuality: it is a purely 'virtual' instance got up to carry the type specifications and often also the qualities which are attributed to the subject referent.

Other ways of grounding the predicate nominative are very infrequent. The absolute quantifier *one* is used in 4%. In an example like (81), *one* stresses the unity of the *state*. In (82), the subject referent is described not simply as 'a' way of earning money, but as 'one' way in addition to implied others. If *one* is part of a partitive construction as with *one of the fastest-growing businesses in luxury goods* in (83), the subset-set relation is explicitly coded: the type specifications and qualities attributed to the subject referent also apply to other businesses.[69]

(81) Karinov justified remaining in the CIS and the rouble zone. "*Until recently CIS members were <u>one state geopolitically and administratively</u>,*" he observed. "If all connections are broken, it would damage and destabilize the region and the international arena." (WB)

(82) The marriage lasted 15 months and, when it ended, Gulzar lost no time in selling intimate stories about their relationship. ("*I suppose it's <u>one way of earning money</u>,*" she says grimly.) (WB)

(83) Bulgari is <u>one of the fastest-growing businesses in luxury goods</u>. (WB)

### 4.3.3.2 Determiners in the indefinite variable NPs

As shown in Tables 10 and 11 above, the most common way of grounding the indefinite variable NP is by indefinite determiner + secondary determiner, e.g. *another*, and the second most common by cardinal numbers, e.g. *one*. It is not uncommon for the two to co-occur in the same context, as in (84).

(84) If most of your stress derives from your boss's way of working you have several options. <u>One is to say there is nothing you can do and suffer</u>; <u>another is to change bosses</u>; or, more constructively, you may try to confront him or her with the problem. (WB)

Much less commonly, the indefinite variable is grounded by an indefinite article only, i.e. in 15% of the variable subjects, e.g. (85), and in 30% of the variable complements, e.g. (86). As (85) and (86) illustrate, in most of these cases, the variable NP uses a modifier. Only exceptionally does the indefinite variable NP use an indefinite article without then also using a modifier, i.e. in 2% of the variable subjects and in 7% of the variable complements.

---

[69] In the context of a specificational variable – as I will discuss below – the subset-set relation has the purpose of singling out one value from the larger set of values (see Section 4.3.3.2).

(85) **A.** Is there anything you recommend for colds?
**B.** For colds yeah erm <u>a very good remedy</u> is fruit mixed with er like I used to put almond oil and you rub it into the chest and into the back in a kind of circular up motion which helps to release the fluids in the bronchials. (WB)

(86) But another point I'd like to make is that erm <pause> proportion of the prisons in this country were built in the nineteenth century er a period of time when prisoners weren't exactly spoilt. Erm *Birmingham Winson Green is <u>a good example</u>.* (WB)

As in the section on modifiers in variable NPs above, I will consider these three types of grounding in the light of Patten's (2012) claims that implied uniqueness is necessary to make indefinite variable NPs acceptable. According to Patten (2012: 49), "the kinds of indefinite NP predicate to occur in the specificational inversion construction would be those that share most in common with definite NPs". On this account, variable NPs with an indefinite article do *not* carry the exclusiveness implicature that typically attaches to indefinite NPs (Hawkins 1978: 186, 1992). Rather, they are "noncommittal with respect to inclusiveness and exclusiveness" (Patten 2012: 54). In Chapter 3, I argued against Patten (2012) that indefinite variable NPs do trigger the implicature of 'non-inclusive' reference, i.e. there may be other instances corresponding to the relevant type specifications in the context. This implicature of 'non-inclusiveness' is demonstrated clearly by the use of a focus marker in the indefinite variable complement, as in (87). Here, *just* focuses on 'one' example and contrasts it with implied alternatives, one of which is specified in the next (specificational) clause.

(87) There's no hiding the fact that the 2004/05 season has probably been South Africa's worst since the end of isolation and in that regard Smith must bear at least some responsibility. He hasn't been helped by administrative inefficiency that has seen him play his trade as skipper under two different coaches, two different selection conveners, and the various changes to playing personnel (*Gary Kirsten's retirement being <u>just</u> one example*, the doling out of five new caps in the last three months being another. (WB)

In what follows, I will discuss how the three types of grounding attested in the indefinite variable NPs work with regard to the exclusiveness implicature. I will also touch on the discursive schema of (non-exhaustive) *enumeration* of values that is often associated with these grounding types.

The most common type of grounding is the indefinite article (*a* or the zero article) plus a secondary determiner, e.g. *further* in (88) and *similar* in (89).

(88) Graeme Garden's translation of Georges Feydeau's "Le Mariage de Barillon" sees Griff Rhys Jones. . . as the eager bridegroom Barillon. It is his wedding day, but unfortunately his bride Virginie (Diana Morrison) is in love with Patrice (Eliot Giuralarocca), who threatens to kill himself if the wedding goes ahead. *A further difficulty is his mother-in-law-to-be (Alison Steadman), who fancies him*, and he also needs to avoid the mayor, whom he has challenged to a duel. (WB)

(89) Similar in function to the *boulē* was the Spartan council of elders (selected men over age 60) known as the *genousia*, which had certain legal powers as well as the two Spartan kings as members. Similar bodies of elders existed in Corinth and Stymphalos. *In Athens, the Areopagus was a similar such council*, where elders were made members for life. (https://www.commonlit.org/texts/greek-government)

In such examples, the secondary determiner helps construe the generalised reference which I argued in Chapter 3 is the referential status of the variable NP. I further argued that the variable NP involves the pragmatic phenomenon of "dual reference" (Ward & Birner 1995), i.e. reference to a general concept and implied reference to concrete instances of it. According to Breban (2011: 530), indefinite primary determiners + secondary determiner apply 'distributively' to the implied concrete instances. The lexical type specifications – present in the variable NP and/or to be retrieved from the discourse – construe the generalisation, e.g. 'difficulties associated with Barillon's wedding' in (88). This general description generalises over the earlier instances in the context (his bride is in love with another man; this man wants to kill him) as well as over the new concrete instance it implies, which is specified by the value NP as being 'his mother-in-law fancies him'. Hence, the NP's lexical meaning refers to a notion not associated with one spatiotemporal occurrence but abstracting over many different occurrences. Reference to the instances is conveyed by the indefinite determiner and the secondary determiner, which apply distributively to these concrete instances.

Adjectives used as secondary determiners in my data include *other, further, additional, added* as well as ordinal secondary determiners like *first*. All these secondary determiners invoke *comparison* and features shared between the concrete instances. This is because the abstraction process from specific antecedent to generalised concept and back to a new specific instance, as with *a further difficulty* in (88), is based on *shared* general type specifications. Secondary determiners like *other, further*, etc. focus on the new instance being introduced, but their meaning implies comparison. Comparative adjectives like *similar*,[70] which can be used either as secondary determiner or as epithet, explicitly index the similarity between the antecedents and the new instance (Breban & Davidse 2003). All of them involve type-phoricity: the indefinite variable NP introduces a new instance of a generalisation that has at least one other instantiation in the discourse, which creates a phoric link between the features generalising over the two instances. The distributive effect conveyed by indefinite determiner + secondary determiner makes the exclusive, non-unique implicature of the indefinite variable NP explicit. The very use of *another, a further* signals explicitly that the concrete instance implied by the variable NP is *not* the only one in the context.

The high frequency of this grounding type thus supports the claim made in Chapter 3 that specificational clauses with indefinite variable are not something semi-aberrant for which conditions making them acceptable have to be specified, as Patten (2012) claims. Rather, they offer the speaker a contrastive option to specificational clauses with definite variable and exhaustiveness implicature. Specificational clauses with indefinite variable allow the speaker to express a specificational relation with a non-exhaustiveness implicature, based precisely on the exclusive (non-unique) of the indefinite variable NP, which is made explicit by the secondary determiner.

Secondly, indefinite variable NPs that are grounded by *one* always convey a subset-set relation. As was explained in Section 4.3.2.2, this subset-set relation is coded explicitly when *one* is used as the head of a partitive construction. The value is then situated in a more restrictive subset of the set of qualifying entities coded by the plural NP in the *of*-phrase, e.g. (90). This mechanism is similar to the delineation of a subset by means of modifiers (Section 4.3.2.2). With the partitive, however, the more restrictive subset is not delineated in terms of extra qualitative criteria but by means of quantification.

(90) More than half the population of America is overweight. *One of the really worrying aspects* is how much younger the patients are now. (WB)

When *one* stands on its own, as in (91), the subset-set relation is not explicitly coded but still implied by the use of *one*. The larger set from which *one* delineates a subset that needs to be inferred from the preceding text (Brems & Davidse 2003). The argument that *one* here is similar in meaning to the partitive construction is supported

---

[70] Cases of *similar* used as a secondary determiner did not occur in the dataset, although the examples in (79) and (89) indicate that *similar* can appear unambiguously as secondary determiner in indefinite variable NPs.

by the fact that it can alternate with a partitive construction (e.g. *one of the explanations for the apparent ease*, etc.). (The difference in meaning between the two is in terms of the explicit- or implicitness of the subset-set relation.) In addition, *one* also has phonetic prominence, which is in line with Milsark's (1977) criteria for a 'strong' (i.e. partitive) reading of cardinal numbers and absolute quantifiers.

(91)   Various explanations have been advanced for the apparent ease of heterosexual transmission in Africa, although none has been proved conclusively. *One is that the prevalence of untreated sexually transmitted diseases, especially genital ulcer disease, may augment the transmission of HIV*. (WB)

Finally, when the indefinite variable NP is not grounded by 'indefinite article + secondary determiner' or by *one*, the NP typically includes a modifier to delineate a subset in terms of extra qualitative criteria (Section 4.3.2.2). As mentioned earlier in this section, indefinite variables are only rarely grounded by an indefinite article without a further indication of a more restrictive qualitative subset (i.e. in only 2% of the variable subjects and 7% of the variable complements). But even in such rare cases, the interpretation of a subset-set relation can be implied by the semantics of head nouns like *example, option, alternative,* etc., e.g. (92) and (93).

(92)   One of the many intriguing aspects of new information and telecommunications technologies is their scope for creating entirely new types of work. *An example is the growth of telephone counselling*: busy and stressed-out professionals can call a sympathetic listener, who will give them advice about how to get through difficult meeting or deal with career problems. (WB)

(93)   Small squares of glass mosaic arc as popular as they are expensive, but their colour is usually ugly and their tiny scale is out of place in the open air. All these tile or marble finishes are expensive, but once installed need no replacement. *Paint is an alternative*, but a pool may need repainting every second or third year. (WB)

To sum up this section, I supported the position that the predicate nominative and the indefinite variable NP have different referential statuses as a result of their different functions in the clause and that this is reflected in the types of indefinite determiners they typically take. The predicate nominative is non-referential. This is reflected in a preference for an indefinite article or the 'zero-article', which have minimal semantic content (Lyons 1999: 36). The variable NP, by contrast, is referential and denotes a generalised instance. It is often grounded in such a way to either code or imply a subset-set relation. This is in line with the argument made in Chapter 3 that the variable's generalised instance triggers the inference of a set of qualifying entities, from which one (or more) is/are selected. This goes against Patten's (2012: 54) claim that indefinite variable NPs are "non-committal with respect to inclusiveness and exclusiveness." Instead, indefinite variable NPs form a positive choice motivated by the implicature of non-exhaustiveness, which is brought out by primary and secondary determiners that signal that no inclusive reference is made to all the instances within the set of entities qualifying for the variable.

## 4.4 Conclusion

In this chapter I presented an in-depth quantitative and qualitative study of the lexicogrammatical realisation of the indefinite NP in predicative and specificational clauses. The study focused specifically on how the functions of the NPs in the whole clause impact on the various internal functions of the NPs, coded by the head, modifiers and complements, and determiners.

The case study demonstrated that there are statistically significant differences between the predicate nominative and the variable NP in the distribution of different structural elements and their lexical realisation. For instance, unlike the predicate nominative, the specificational variable selects head nouns from restricted lexicosemantic domains, which are typically more 'conceptual', often with a 'verb-like' quality to them (e.g. *solution*, *response*, *reason*). The type-specifications expressed by these head nouns are further restricted by content retrieved from the prior discourse or, more often, explicitly expressed in the form of post-head complements.

Support for the argument that the predicate nominative is not a 'property' NP (see Chapter 3) was found in the frequent use of epithets. This is evidence that the predicate nominative typically exploits the meaning potential of the NP structure to go beyond the function of mere type-attribution and also ascribe qualities to the designated instance. Variable NPs use epithets less frequently and are more restrictive in their choice of specific adjectives. This smaller lexical set typically included adjectives that imply a qualitative comparison between instances (e.g. *notable*, *important*). I argued that these adjectives were used to stipulate extra qualitative criteria that the value that satisfies the variable has to meet.

A similar delineation of a more restrictive subset within the set of entities that qualify for the variable can also be observed for the indefinite determiners that the variable NPs typically use. While the predicate nominative almost exclusively takes the indefinite article or the 'zero-article', the indefinite variable NP has a strong preference for 'indefinite article + secondary determiner' and for the quantifier *one*. Both grounding types are often used to comment on the non-inclusiveness, or non-uniqueness, that is implied by the indefinite NP. This was raised as evidence for the claim made in Chapter 3 that the indefinite variable NP is not something semi-aberrant (contra, for instance, Patten 2012); instead, it offers a contrastive option to the definite variable NP that is motivated by the implicature of non-exhaustiveness that the indefinite variable triggers.

In conclusion, the case study in this chapter supports the posited semantic contrast between predicative and specificational clauses described in Chapter 3. The difference in the NP construal of the predicate nominative and the indefinite variable NP were shown to be related to the functions of these NPs in their respective clause types and to the referential status they thereby acquire.

# Chapter 5
# Aspect and modality in the copular clause

In Chapter 3, I presented a functional-structural analysis of predicative clauses with indefinite predicative NP and specificational clauses with indefinite variable NP in terms of their different process-participant configurations, their different mood structures and textual structures. In presenting my analyses of these three structural layers in predicative and specificational clauses, I argued against the claim that "specificational meaning is quite literally the *inverse* of specification" (Patten 2012: 243). The claim that the difference between predication and specification involves 'inverse' focus-assignment was countered by prosodic evidence (Van Praet & O'Grady 2018): specificational clauses typically assign information focus to both the variable and the value, so that a binary clause-level background-focus contrast is not tenable. In other words, the two semantic relations of predication and specification are coded lexicogrammatically, but not prosodically. Within specific contexts of use, these semantic relations can give rise to a wide range of (prosodically coded) information structures, as I will argue in Chapter 6. Chapter 4 offered a qualitative-quantitative corpus study of how the different process-participant relations manifest themselves in the lexical realisation of the indefinite predicate nominative and indefinite variable. The statistically significant different selection patterns of head nouns, modifiers/complements and determiners further supported the view that predication and specification constructions are categorically different.[71]

This chapter[72] will examine if and how the different semantics-pragmatics of predicative and specificational clauses influence choices made in the meaning potential of the VP: it considers, more specifically, which kinds of aspect and modality are attracted to, or repelled by, predicative versus specificational copulars. To study this, I will carry out collostructional analyses (e.g. Stefanowitsch & Gries 2003) which measure the degree of attraction of specific aspectual and modal meanings to predicative and both reversed and non-reversed specifica-

---

[71] When I state that predication and specification are categorically different, I mean that they are different categories of copular clause with different semantics (contra the 'inverse' approach, see Chapter 3). I do not mean that they are different in all respects – they are, after all, *sub*-types of the same basic clause type – i.e. copular clauses – or that there can be no examples that are ambiguous between the two types. This is consonant with the idea in cognitive-functional approaches that categories need not be discrete and allow for both typical and peripheral instances.
[72] Substantial parts of this chapter are an elaborated version of sections in Van Praet (2019b).

tional clauses with definite and indefinite variable. These attractions are interpreted with respect to (i) the different process-participant configurations of the copular clauses and (ii) the pragmatic mechanisms that they trigger (e.g. (non-)exhaustiveness implicature), and (iii) the discursive functions they serve in specific contexts of use.

By focusing on the realisation of VP structures, the study in this chapter fills a gap in the literature, which has focused mostly on the function and status of the pre- and post-copular NPs of predicative and specificational clauses. This is mainly due to the common assumption that the 'copula' *be* provides a mere structural 'link' or 'supportive device' between the subject and the complement (e.g. Dik 1983: 142; Williams 1983; Huddleston 1984: 183; Partee 1986a) or is a "meaningless lexeme whose syntactic function is to convert whatever it combines with into a verbal (i.e. predicative) expression" (Lyons 1977: 471). The advantage of this position is that it provides a uniform account of *be*, contra positions that treat *be* as a 'multiply ambiguous' or 'polysemous' verb that has different meanings in different constructions (e.g. of class-membership, identification). However, on a cognitive-functional account, the treatment of a linguistic expression as 'meaningless' is theoretically suspect since all expressions are necessarily meaningful. Instead, as discussed in Chapter 3, Langacker (1991: 65) ascribes to *be* a highly schematic meaning, which is elaborated by the integration of *be* with other elements. *Be* expresses "the continuation through time of a stable situation characterized only as a stative relation" (Langacker 1991: 65). This stative relation is rendered specific by the elements it takes as subject and complement. This implies that "*be* is a meaningful element" and that, as head of the clause, the composite expression – i.e. the whole copular clause – "inherits its processual character" (Langacker 1991: 65). This position, therefore, develops the idea that *be* is, in some way, a 'supportive' element (e.g. Dik 1983: 142), without postulating, as Lyons (1977: 471) does, that it is therefore meaningless.

In Chapter 3, I defended the view that predicative clauses are intransitive: only the subject is a participant, the describee, while the non-referential complement specifies the content of the descriptive predicate (Langacker 1991, 2015). Specificational clauses are transitive configurations whose participants stand in a relationship of variable, i.e. an abstract entity carrying criteria to be met, and value, the more concrete entities meeting these criteria. The different nature of these two copular relations explains, I will argue, why predicative clauses allow, under special circumstances, for certain aspectual and modal meanings that specificational clauses do not allow for. The different discursive functions that the two copular types can serve will also be shown to affect the attraction of different kinds of modality. In addition, more specific constructional differences, such as the (in)definiteness of the variable and the construal of the variable vs the value as subject, also set different preferences for modal meanings. These differences will be analysed with regard to the pragmatic implicatures of (non-)exhaustiveness and (non-)contrastiveness respectively.

The structure of this chapter is as follows. In Section 5.1, I provide a general outline of aspect and modality. In Section 5.2, I present a quantitative and qualitative case study of aspect and modality in predicative and specificational clauses: at the centre of the study will be the analysis of specificational clauses with an indefinite variable NP, which I compare with predicative clauses with an indefinite NP complement but also with specificational clauses with definite variable NPs. These two types of specificational clauses will be examined in their non-reversed construal (with variable/subject) and their reversed construal (with value/subject). In Section 5.3, finally, I will sum up the findings of this corpus study with respect to my general account of predicative and specificational clauses.

## 5.1 Background

### 5.1.1 Aspect

As a grammatical category, the system of aspect is concerned with the representation of the internal temporal structure of a situation or event (Declerck 2006: 28). Aspect expresses how the process – i.e. an event or state – denoted by a verb extends over time and, thus, provides a means for adjusting how the process is perceived (Langacker 2015), e.g. as stable, habitual, ongoing. In English, grammatical aspect is coded by "markers on the verb (i.e. suffixes, auxiliaries or a combination of the two)" or the absence of such markers (Declerck 2006: 28). Three basic aspectual meanings are distinguished: simple, progressive and perfect aspect.[73]

The baseline for grammatical aspect is a 'simple' verb form (Langacker 2015: 7): it is characterised by the absence of special aspectual markers. The 'simple' form

---

[73] As Declerck (1991: 57) points out, grammatical aspect should be distinguished from lexical aspect or 'Aktionsart'. Grammatical aspect concerns the representation of a situation's internal temporal constitution and is coded by particular grammatical VP forms, e.g. auxiliary *be* + present participle. Aktionsart, on the other hand, has to do with the meaning potential of the verb as a lexical item, that is "how the lexical material inherently represents the situation", for instance as static or dynamic, punctual or durative, etc. (Declerck 1991: 57). Declerck (1991: 57) concludes that the aspectual interpretation of a sentence depends on the interaction between grammatical aspect and Aktionsart, i.e. between the meaning coded by the grammatical 'aspect' construction (e.g. *be* V-*ing*) and the lexically coded meaning of the particular verb V that is used with it. In this section, I take 'aspect' to refer to 'grammatical aspect'.

merely expresses that a situation, state, or action occurs – or does not occur – at the 'vantage time' (i.e. the time at which a State-of-Affairs, henceforth SoA, holds). As Declerck (2006: 33) explains, this vantage time may be expressed explicitly by a temporal adjunct, as with *now* in (1), or it may be implied by the kind of tense that is used. The location in time of the vantage point therefore may vary according to the tense of the VP, as illustrated in (1)-(3).

(1) Mr Milosevic's agreement to open Kosovo to the Organisation for Security and Co-operation in Europe mission now effectively passes the financial burden of dealing with the refugees to others, including international aid organisations. (WB)

(2) The Queen ate her breakfast in curlers and Prince Charles chatted to his plants. (WB)

(3) My vibes say he'll move south, will study in a huge university (Birmingham perhaps) and will take his artistic talents to huge heights. (WB)

Huddleston (1984: 154) adds that such simple, non-progressive forms present a situation as obtaining rather than taking place: the situation may be either static or dynamic, and in the latter case, the situation is presented in its temporal totality, hence as an event (*ib.*). In the present, such simple forms are used when there are no limitations on the extension of the situation through the present into the past and future time (Quirk *et al.* 1972: 85), e.g. (4).

(4) Her hair smells of roses. (WB)

The progressive – formed by a form of *be* and the present participle, e.g. (5) – represents a situation as 'ongoing' (Declerck 2006: 29). It is conceived of as being more or less dynamic, as opposed to wholly static, and implies the potential for continuation (Huddleston 1984: 153). The situation is therefore not viewed in its "temporal totality" but at some 'subinterval' of time (*ib.*). Langacker (1991: 207–211) explains this as taking an 'internal perspective' on the process expressed by the verb: the immediate 'scope' of the designated relation is restricted to a series of component states from which the initial and final states are excluded. The process is thus represented "from the midst, as it were, as on ongoing activity" (McGregor 1997: 124).

(5) The idea of living in a small and picturesque rural community is becoming increasingly popular among Britain's city-dwellers. (WB)

The progressive correlates with the distinction between perfectivity and imperfectivity (e.g. Comrie 1976: 32f; Declerck 1979; Langacker 1987a,b, 1991: 207–211; Huddleston & Pullum 2002: 163), illustrated respectively in (6) and (7).

(6) a. Sam is building a house.
    b. *Sam builds a house.

(7) a. Sam knows French.
    b. *Sam is knowing French.

Perfective verbs like *build* express a situation that can be viewed as a single whole (Comrie 1976: 21) and thus can be conceived of as a bounded process with a beginning and ending (Langacker 1991: 551). Imperfective verbs like *know*, by contrast, lexically code situations that are viewed from within (Comrie 1976: 24): the VPs in which these verbs are used designate unbounded processes (Langacker 1991: 208). Imperfectives, in other words, refer "to part of the internal temporal structure of the situation" by "not refer[ring] to the complete situation, but only to its beginning, middle or end" (Declerck 2006: 32). In general, verbs that express inherently perfective processes, like *build*, are used with progressive present-tense forms (6a) but not with the simple present tense (6b), except on a special interpretation (e.g. to refer to a habit, as in *Sam builds a house once every ten years*, or a job, as in *Sam builds houses*), but never to indicate one instance of the designated process situated at the time of speaking (Langacker 1987b: 79). By contrast, inherently imperfective processes, like *know*, occur, by default, in the simple present tense (7a), but typically not in the progressive (7b), even if the latter is marginally possible (e.g. *I feel I'm knowing the city for the first time*, Halliday 1994: 116). This can be explained by the fact that the progressive *be* V-*ing* construction is 'imperfectivising' (Langacker 1991: 207–209): it takes a perfective process and construes it as imperfective. Its effect is one of 'zooming in' on a bounded activity by excluding its initial and final states from the conception of the designated process, which is thereby presented as unbounded (Langacker 1991: *ib.*). It is because a bounded relation is reconstrued as unbounded that the progressive represents a situation or process as 'ongoing' (Declerck 2006: 29). In Section 5.2.3.1, I will return to some subtle issues with the interaction between (im)perfectivity and progressive meaning, focusing specifically on the use of the progressive in predicative and specificational clauses.

In addition to the non-progressive vs progressive contrast, Quirk et al. (1972: 90–92) and Huddleston (1984: 158–164) also include the perfect as an aspectual category in English. If used with a present tense, the perfect "indicates a period of time stretching backwards into some earlier time" (Quirk *et al.* 1972: 91), e.g. (8).

A past perfect, by contrast, has the meaning of "past-in-the-past" (*ib.*: 92), that is, of the situation occurring or obtaining prior to a past vantage point, e.g. (9).

(8)  The Dalai Lama has lived in exile in Dharamsala, India since 1959. (WB)

(9)  Deborah had lived with Jim for six years before they married. (WB)

According to Declerck (1991), there are two kinds of aspectual interpretation that the perfect allows for. The CONTINUATIVE perfect (Declerck 1991: 100) describes a situation that started in the past and continues into the present (and possibly beyond), e.g. (10). Since the continuative perfect expresses that a situation (still) obtains at the time of utterance and implies that it may extend into the future, the situation is represented as unbounded, and hence as imperfective.

(10) Jay and Heidi have known each other for more than ten years. (WB)

The other aspectual reading is referred to as the INDEFINITE perfect (or existential perfect). It indicates that a situation has occurred at least once (or has not occurred) within a period between a past point and the present (Declerck 1991: 100), e.g. (11).

(11) HSBC, Britain's biggest bank, has blasted doom-mongers for talking the world into a recession. (WB)

The indefinite perfect is normally used to refer to bounded situations: as such, the situation occurring in the pre-present is strictly speaking past, but the use of a present perfect tense implies some 'current relevance' to the time of utterance. If no indication is given about the time lapse between the occurrence of the situation and the present, the span is interpreted as relatively short (Declerck 2006: 305), as in (11). This 'current relevance' implicates that the situation, while finished, still has some result in the present (Quirk et al. 1972: 91; Declerck 2006: 38). Declerck (1991: 102) points out that this conversational implicature is cancellable, when the lapse of time between the past situation and the present is relatively long, as illustrated in (12).

(12) This gate *has been locked* in the past, but now nobody bothers to do so any more. (Declerck 2006: 304)

The quantitative study in Section 5.2 will focus on the distinction between simple, progressive and perfect aspect, the distinction between which is structurally apparent and hence objectifiable. In the qualitative analysis I will, however, take into account the semantic distinction between indefinite and continuative perfect too.

### 5.1.2 Modality

While aspect is concerned solely with the representation of a situation, 'modal' expressions can be either content-related or speaker-hearer-related (Verstraete 2001: 1506). For Halliday (1970b: 349), the two options, in fact, represent two different systems, one being the system of modality, while the other, though sharing some similarities with modality, is better explained as a form of 'modulation' (or modification) of the designated process. On Halliday's account, modality is, by definition, interpersonal: it "is external to the content, being a part of the attitude taken up by the speaker" (Halliday 1970b: 349). Modulation, on the other hand, pertains to what Halliday calls the 'ideational' (i.e. representational) function of the clause: it is related "to transitivity and the grammar of processes and participants" (Halliday 1970b: 350). Narrog (2005a: 184) proposes an alternative interpretation of modality in terms of 'factuality': "a state of affairs is modalized if it is marked for being undetermined with respect to its factual status, i.e. is neither positively nor negatively factual" (*ib.*). Narrog's (2005a,b) definition of modality therefore allows for both "event-orientation" and "speaker-orientation" (Narrog 2005a: 685) and, hence, differs from Halliday's definition in viewing content-related 'modulation' as part of the modal system. In this chapter, I will refer to both content- and speaker-hearer-related expressions as 'modals', while taking into account the important distinctions Halliday (1970b) proposes.

Interpersonal (i.e. speaker-hearer-oriented) modality includes both epistemic modality and some forms of deontic modality. Epistemic modals, as in (13), offer an assessment of the likelihood of a SoA or, in other words, the probability or possibility of a proposition being the case (McGregor 1997: 228; Nuyts 2001: 21–22; Verstraete 2001: 1506; Van linden 2012: 20–21). Hence, as the term suggests, epistemic evaluations are concerned with the speaker's knowledge of the validity of the proposition in declarative clauses or with the hearer's knowledge in interrogative clauses. This is a matter of degree, going from high certainty, e.g. *must* in (13), via intermediate stages of probability, possibility and improbability, to impossibility, e.g. *can't* in (14) (e.g. Nuyts 2005: 10; 2006: 6).

(13) The doctor must not have been too busy because a few minutes later he showed up at the front desk. (WB)

(14) It <u>can't</u> have been easy for her, living here. (WB)

Deontic modals, on the other hand, are concerned with the actualisation of a SoA, which has traditionally been defined in terms of 'obligation' or 'permission' (Kratzer 1978: 111; Palmer 1986: 96–97). As argued by Nuyts (2005: 9), Verstraete (2005: 1405) and Van linden (2012: 17), however, the notion of deontic modality is explained more accurately in terms of the desirability that a SoA is realised. In (15), for instance, the speaker evaluates the SoA in which 'all Iraqis are equal in their rights' and 'no Iraqi is prohibited from casting his vote' as desirable. The example does not, however, involve an illocutionary act of issuing obligation or permission.

(15) All Iraqis <u>should</u> be equal in their rights, no Iraqi <u>should</u> be prohibited from casting his vote. (WB)

Deontic modals have been argued to allow for both subjective and objective assessments (e.g. Lyons 1977; Coates 1983; Palmer 1986). For Lyons (1977: 797–801), the distinction hinges on whether the deontic assessment stems from the speaker or hearer (in declarative or interrogative clauses respectively) or from an external source (such as a moral or legal rule): in the former case, the speaker creates an obligation; in the latter case, the speaker makes a statement about the existence of such an obligation (Lyons 1977: 828–833), as is the case in (16).

(16) The opening ceremony [of the Olympic games in Barcelona in 1992] contained different displays to represent Catalonia and Spain. Each announcement <u>had to</u> be made in four languages – not just French, Spanish and English, but Catalan as well. (WB)

Verstraete (2001: 1517) notes that in declaratives with subjective modal auxiliaries, the speaker assumes a modal position here and now, 'performatively' (Nuyts 2001: 39–40), to the propositional content, e.g. (15). In interrogatives, the speaker shifts the responsibility for the modal position to the hearer, as in (15'), where the hearer is construed as the modal source of *should*. By contrast, objective modals do not shift the commitment from the speaker in declarative clauses to the hearer in interrogative ones, e.g. (16').

(15') <u>Should</u> all Iraqis be equal in their rights? [subjective]

(16') Did each announcement <u>have to</u> be made in four languages? [objective]

As shown by the past tense form *had to* in (16), objective modals are also subject to tense, while subjective modals are not (Verstraete 2001: 1518). Because objective deontic 'modals' lack performativity, they are content- rather than speaker-hearer-related: they are part of the propositional content (Verstraete 2001: 1525; Nuyts 2006: 15). Therefore, in Halliday's (1970a) approach, such expressions are not actually part of the modal system, but involve modulation of the ideational, or representational, meaning of the clause.

A third type of modal meaning is dynamic modality. Dynamic modality is concerned with modal notions that can be thought of as 'forces' related to a participant or situation, viz. ability/possibility, need/necessity, volition/power. The term "dynamic modality" derives from Greek δυναμις 'power', 'strength'. Dynamic modality describes the existence of such forces and is always content-related. Traditionally, participant- internal, participant-imposed and situation-oriented dynamic modals are distinguished (Palmer 1986; Van linden 2012: 13). Participant-internal modals subsume ability, as in (17), in which 'Barbie' is ascribed the remarkable ability to speak 'American', and need, as in (18), in which the need to pee is ascribed to the subject referent.

(17)  Well, Barbie can speak American! (WB)

(18)  I had to pee so bad I was ready to pop. (WB)

Participant-imposed dynamic modality includes necessity (19), imposed for instance by local circumstances partly beyond the control of the participant (19), and 'situational possibility' (20) (Nuyts 2006: 3; Van linden 2012: 14). In (19), the need to 'pull out of previous England games' is imposed on the subject referent by the external circumstances of 'family bereavement and a car accident'. In (20), for instance, no ability is ascribed to the subject referent (which, as an inanimate entity, lacks controllability): instead, the meaning of (20) is that the conditions of most 'waters in England and Wales' make it impossible for big fish to grow naturally under such circumstances.

(19)  I feel particularly sorry for Chris. He has had to pull out of previous England games because of a family bereavement and a car accident. (WB)

(20)  Few waters in England and Wales can grow big fish naturally. (WB)

I follow authors such as Hengeveld (1988: 234) and Palmer (2001: 76–79) in considering volition as part of dynamic modality, on the basis that the will, desire or intention (not) to carry out some action or bring about some situation is ascribed to the subject entity, e.g. (21). The corresponding situational notion is the description of a natural law or habit, e.g. *Oil will float on water.*

(21)  Police <u>will not</u> say how or when Quinney died. (WB)

Finally, there is the category of evidentiality, which has been discussed in close relation to the modal system, though its inclusion in it is a topic of ongoing debate (Cornillie 2009). Evidentiality is defined as marking the basis for the information in a proposition (Bybee 1985: 184; Aikhenvald 2004: 3), as illustrated by *is alleged to* in (22). As pointed out by McGregor (1997: 232–233), it is a form of authorisational modification, by which the speaker specifies the authority on which a proposition is based: the speaker indicates the source of their knowledge or belief (e.g. personal experience, inference or presumption, hearsay or quotative, etc.).

(22)  He <u>is alleged to</u> have stolen a jewelled daffodil motif brooch valued at £5,000. (WB)

Aikhenvald (2004) distinguishes roughly between two types of evidential modification: either the basis for the information in the clause is made explicit (e.g. hearsay) (i.e. direct evidentiality) or it is implied (i.e. indirect evidentiality). While Aikhenvald (2004) considers evidentiality a category in its own right that is distinct from modality, she does acknowledge that evidentiality may interact with epistemic modality, in that an indication of evidence may correlate with the negotiation of reliability and certainty of the proposition. In this sense, while direct evidentiality, as in (22), indicates evidence that is external to the speaker (and, hence, is objective), indirect evidence like in (23) may suggest a subjective epistemic implication of tentativity, with the speaker not fully committing to the proposition.

(23)  At the moment, Tony Blair <u>seems to</u> be evading the issue. (WB)

For the purpose of this study, evidential marking will be discussed together with the expression of epistemic, deontic and dynamic modality.

## 5.2 Case study

The research in this chapter compares random samples of predicative clauses with an indefinite NP complement and specificational clauses with an indefinite or definite variable NP, to examine the use of aspect and modality in each clause type. The aim is to find out if the semantics of the clausal relations, the pragmatic meanings these trigger, and the discursive functions of the clauses interact differently with these two forms of 'modification'. To this end, I carried out collostructional analyses (Stefanowitsch & Gries 2003), which measure the strength of attraction or repulsion of a linguistic expression to a slot in a given construction. This implies comparing the use of aspect and modality in the three copular clause types to their use in non-copular clauses, which served as a control group against which meaningful interpretations of VP behaviour in the copular clauses could be made.

In Section 5.2.1, I will formulate hypotheses about the expected patterns in the different constructions, based on the background information detailed in Section 5.1. In Section 5.2.2, I will explain the research design, including the data collection and adopted methodology. In Section 5.2.3, I will report on and interpret the results.

### 5.2.1 Hypotheses

For aspect, the typically stative character of the copular relation led me to assume that both clause types would favour a 'simple' non-progressive form. For modality, I expected diverging preferences between predicative and specificational clauses. More specifically, specificational clauses were predicted to attract epistemic and evidential modals. As we saw in Chapter 3, specificational constructions are always used in contexts where entities that qualify as value of the variable have to be distinguished from ones that are potential candidates but ultimately do not qualify as values. In such contexts, one expects that the speaker will sometimes modify the proposed specificational relation as not certain (epistemic modality) or as based on inference or hearsay (evidentiality). In particular, it was noted in Chapter 3, specificational clauses with an indefinite variable, which are associated with a non-exhaustiveness implicature, may be used when the speaker is unable or unwilling to identify all the qualifying entities, or to distinguish qualifying from non-qualifying entities. Hence, they were expected to be more likely than specificational clauses with definite variable to occur with epistemic modals, e.g. *An example would be this sentence*. The implicature of non-exhaustiveness can be captured in a paraphrase of the form *There's this sentence that would be an example (but there are others too)*, as compared to paraphrases of the form *It's Darryl Wakelin (and only Darryl Wakelin) that is the winner*, which capture the meaning of specificational clauses with definite variables. For deontic modality, no particular attractions were expected. Expressions of participant-inherent dynamic modality notions such as ability, need or volition were expected to be slightly more frequent in predicative than specificational clauses because some descriptions can be related to the describee in terms of ability, need or volition.

## 5.2.2 Data collection and coding

For the purpose of this study, I examined datasets of predicative clauses with an indefinite NP complement and specificational clauses with an (in)definite variable NP, in their non-reversed and reversed construal (i.e. with the variable as subject or complement respectively). The data that I used are the data taken from the *Times* subcorpus of Wordbanks*Online*, which I reported on in Chapter 2. These data were collected by taking an initial large randomised extraction of 100,000 hits for the verb *be* in the *Times* subcorpus. As described in Chapter 2, this yielded a total of 7,504 predicative clauses with indefinite predicate nominative, 650 specificational clauses with indefinite variable (of which 438 non-reversed and 182 reversed), and 3,161 specificational clauses with definite variable (of which 2,494 non-reversed and 667 reversed).

These data included some examples that were not relevant for the study in this chapter, namely copular construction realised as gerunds (e.g. *I love being a superstar; most of the important decisions . . . had been taken by a group of us, myself being a dominant factor*). Since gerunds are nominalisations (i.e. verbal forms reclassified as nominal), I excluded them from the discussion of the VP. This resulted in the dataset summarised in Table 12.

**Table 12:** Summary of the dataset for the study of VP construal.

| predicative | | | 7,375 |
|---|---|---|---|
| specificational | indefinite variable | total | 617 |
| | | non-reversed | 437 |
| | | reversed | 180 |
| | definite variable | total | 3,143 |
| | | non-reversed | 2,478 |
| | | reversed | 665 |

The data in Table 12 were used in the collostructional analyses for modality, aspect and polarity. Collostructional analyses (Stefanowitsch & Gries 2003) examine the attraction or repulsion of an expression *e* to a specific construction *X* by comparing the frequency of expression *e* in *X* to the frequency of *e* in all other constructions in a dataset that are not *X*. Therefore, it was necessary to know the frequency of specific patterns of aspect and modality in a random sample of non-copular examples, which was collected by extracting 100,000 examples containing a random verb in any form (also from the *Times* subcorpus of WB). From the non-copular dataset, I excluded all false hits (i.e. where a form was not actually used as a verb, e.g. *according to*; *the sitting room*; etc.) as well as all copular uses of *be* – but I kept the auxiliary uses. The resulting dataset totalled 67,840 relevant examples.

For the collostructional analyses, the copular clauses were systematically compared to all and only non-copular clauses: for the behaviour of one copular type, e.g. predicative clauses, the other copular types were therefore not included in the comparison set. This was important because of the choice to distinguish between non-reversed and reversed specificational clauses as well as between specificational clauses with indefinite and definite variable NP: if, for instance, reversed specificationals with an indefinite variable were compared to a set including all other specificational clauses, this could obscure notable observations due to the similarities between the other specificational clauses. The choice to keep the comparison set constant thus allowed for a more consistent tracking of the similarities/differences in the attraction/repulsion of aspect and modality to the individual copular types.

To prevent potential skews in the collostructional analyses (which rely on relative frequencies within a dataset), attraction and repulsion were measured by means of Odds Ratios (OR), i.e. the odds that an outcome (e.g. a specific form of aspect/modality) will occur in a given clause type, compared to the odds that the outcome occurs in all other cases. Unlike the more commonly used Fisher's exact test (see, for instance, Stefanowitsch & Gries 2003, 2005), the OR measure is not affected by sample sizes (Schmid & Küchenhoff 2013), making it a more reliable statistic for the purpose of this study. The results can be interpreted as follows: an OR of 1 means that the odds of a specific pattern occurring are the same in the target construction as they are in all other constructions (i.e. there is no attraction/repulsion of an outcome by the target construction). If OR > 1, the odds of an outcome occurring are higher in the target construction, compared to other constructions: in such cases, the *higher* the OR is, the more strongly the construction *attracts* the outcome. If OR < 1, the odds of the outcome occurring are lower in the target construction: in this case, the *lower* the OR is, the more strongly the construction *repels* the outcome.

For the coding of aspect, I distinguished first between simple, perfect and progressive aspect, in each of the copular and non-copular examples.[74] For the coding of modality, I looked at the presence of modal auxiliaries in copular and non-copular clauses. For each modal verb, I subsequently determined its modal meaning, for which I distinguished between epistemic, deontic and dynamic modality and, in addition, coded for evidential marking as well. For matters of time and space, modal adverbs were not taken into account.

---

**74** Gerunds – e.g. *the fridge stopped working* – were distinguished from actual progressive *be* V-*ing* constructions, since they do not have the same meaning of representing a situation as 'ongoing'. Rather, gerunds are nominalisations expressing reified situations.

## 5.2.3 Quantitative and qualitative case study

In this section I will argue that divergent frequencies of aspect and modality in predicative and specificational clauses can be explained by their different semantics-pragmatics. The different degrees of attraction of polarity and modality can be explained partly by the discursive functions that the predicative and specificational clauses can serve in specific contexts of use and partly by the pragmatic inferences triggered by the lexicogrammatically coded meaning of the clauses (e.g. (non-)exhaustiveness, (non-)contrastiveness).

### 5.2.3.1 Aspect

The absolute and relative frequencies of simple, progressive and perfect aspect in each of the clause types are listed in Table 13 and visualised in Figure 15. At first glance, few differences appear between the different copular types, which all strongly prefer a simple aspectual construal. The most notable observation is that the progressive is very rare in all copular clauses, occurring in only one predicative example while not attested at all in any of the specificational clauses. The perfect form does occur in all clause types, except in reversed specificational clauses with a definite variable. It is, however, not used frequently in any of the copular clauses.

**Table 13:** Absolute and relative frequencies of aspectual construals across copular clause types.

|  | *simple* |  | *progressive* |  | *perfect* |  |
|---|---|---|---|---|---|---|
| predication | 7,000 | (95%) | 1 | (0%) | 374 | (5%) |
| specification: indef. variable |  |  |  |  |  |  |
| non-reversed | 420 | (96%) | 0 |  | 18 | (4%) |
| reversed | 176 | (98%) | 0 |  | 4 | (2%) |
| specification: def. variable |  |  |  |  |  |  |
| non-reversed | 2,419 | (98%) | 0 |  | 59 | (2%) |
| reversed | 651 | (98%) | 0 |  | 15 | (2%) |
| **non-copular** | 55,144 | (81%) | 2,532 | (4%) | 10,164 | (15%) |

The collostructional analyses, summarised in Table 14, confirmed that all copular clause types attract simple aspect.[75] The strength of attraction differs across the

---

[75] A threshold of OR > 1.5 was taken as an index of attraction and a threshold of OR < 0.5 for repulsion. While attraction and repulsion are matters of degree, represented by the OR as deviation from the standard 1, such thresholds ensure meaningful interpretation of the results. Any numbers surpassing these thresholds were marked in bold and include an indication of attraction (A) or repulsion (R).

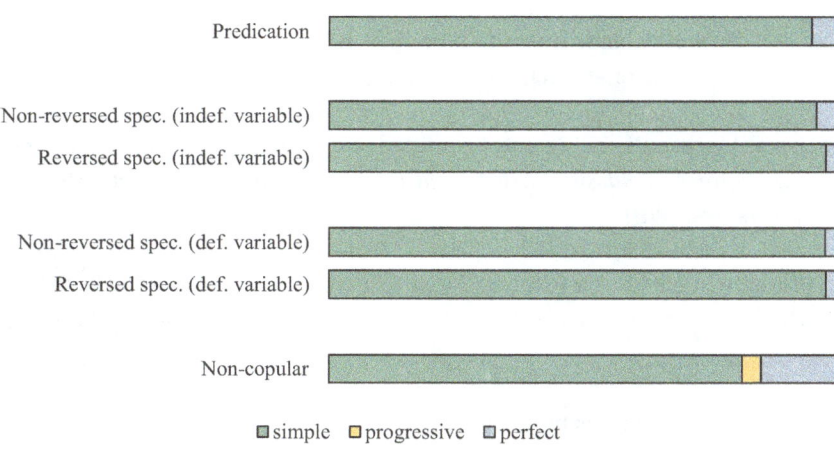

**Figure 15:** The relative frequencies of simple, progressive and perfect aspect in copular and non-copular clauses.

copular clause types on two counts: (i) it is generally higher for specificational clauses than for predicative ones; (ii) it is slightly less high for non-reversed specificationals with indefinite variable/subject, which had a slightly higher proportion of perfect forms. Furthermore, all copular clause types repel both the perfect and the progressive. The ORs are particularly low for the progressive in all clause types, suggesting strong repulsion. For the perfect, however, the relatively high OR for the predicative construction suggests that the repulsion is relatively weak; whereas in specificational clauses, the repulsion of the perfect is much stronger.

**Table 14:** Odds ratios for different attractions (A) to and repulsions (R) of aspectual construals.

|  | *simple* | *progressive* | *perfect* |
|---|---|---|---|
| **predication** | 4.2924 (A) | 0.0052 (R) | 0.3035 (R) |
| **specification: indef. variable** | | | |
| non-reversed | 5.2333 (A) | 0.0294 (R) | 0.2496 (R) |
| reversed | 9.0007 (A) | 0.0717 (R) | 0.1451 (R) |
| **specification: def. variable** | | | |
| non-reversed | 9.3625 (A) | 0.0052 (R) | 0.1395 (R) |
| reversed | 9.6775 (A) | 0.0193 (R) | 0.1350 (R) |

It is not surprising that the most common realisation of both predicative and specificational copular constructions is by means of a simple verb form. 'Simple' aspect merely expresses that the clausal relation holds at the time of orientation (i.e. past, present, future, as encoded by tense marking). It gives no indication of how the relation extends over time, neither in terms of its progression nor in terms of its beginning or ending, e.g. (24) and (25).

(24) [Isaiah] Jackson's skills are not confined to music. *He is a brilliant academic with degrees in Russian history and literature from Harvard and Stanford universities.* (WB)

(25) Property in the 'wrong location' – *one example is London Town's The Bridge*, which sits next to a gasworks, railway line and very busy road in Battersea. (WB)

Since copular constructions typically express temporalised stative relations, they are, by default, imperfective. That is, the situation they express is unbounded, in the sense that the designated process does not make reference to its initial and final states. Moreover, both predicative and specificational clauses imply that the processes they designate are 'homogeneous' (Declerck 1991: 59): no change is implied from one component state to the other (Langacker 1987a: 256). The question of how the copular relation evolves over time is, therefore, typically not an issue, in a way similar to other imperfectives like *know* in *Sam knows French*. This explains why all copular clause types attract simple aspect, while repelling the progressive as well as the perfect forms.

One aspectual difference between predicative and specificational clauses is the – admittedly rare – occurrence of the progressive in predicative clauses. In the case study, no progressive aspect was attested in specificational clauses, while one occurrence was found for the predicative ones. This suggests that predicative clauses allow, under special circumstances, for a progressive construal, e.g. (26).

(26) I shut her out of my life. *I was being a selfish bastard really.* (WB)

The use of the progressive with predicative clauses, like (26), coerces them into a reading where the subject is temporarily exhibiting behaviour that warrants the description given in the predicate: in (26), the quality of 'being a selfish bastard' is not presented as intrinsic to the subject 'I' (and thus unchanging); rather, the subject referent is described as carrying out a controlled action (Davidse 1999: 185–87) in accordance with the description given by the predicate nominative, i.e. '*acting like* a selfish bastard'. The progressive construal of the predicative relation thus imposes boundaries on the described process. If the relation expressed by the composite predicate cannot be conceived of as a bounded episode of controlled behaviour, then the progressive is not possible, e.g. (27) and (28).

(27) ?Martin is being a Belgian.

(28) *Martin is being tall.

In specificational clauses, the use of the progressive appears to be extremely marginal if not impossible. This is due to the specificational relation being inherently imperfective and stative: unlike in the predicative construction, *be* does not integrate with the specificational complement to form a composite predicate which can be conceived of as a bounded episode of controlled behaviour, e.g. (29a,b).

(29) a. *The favourite for the post [of Defence Secretary] <u>was being</u> John Reid, then Secretary of State for Scotland.
b. *John Reid <u>was being</u> the favourite for the post...

Specificational clauses also appear to oppose, or at least disfavour, the use of an indefinite present perfect, as illustrated in (30).

(30) *One by-product of fame <u>has just been</u> that you get to meet your heroes relatively easily.

I propose that this is due to the incongruence between the 'boundedness' meaning of the indefinite perfect and the semantics of the specificational clause. The use of an indefinite perfect would imply a (recent) past endpoint to the specificational relation, thus inappropriately imposing a boundary on the imperfective specificational relation. Still, rare examples of specificational clauses with an indefinite can be found, as suggested by the use of *recently* in (31) and (32).

(31) Fast forward 40 years and American foreign policy hawks are again calling for wars of "regime change" or "surgical de-nuclearization", this time on Iran on the pretext of the latter's alleged (but as yet unconsummated) nuclear weapons aspirations. *One such strident voice <u>has recently been</u> that of Mitt Romney, the Republican presidential nominee, who has surrounded himself with neoconservative advisers.* As for the Obama Administration, like its GW Bush predecessor, it continually claims that it will "use all elements of American power to prevent Iran from developing a nuclear weapon". (https://theconversation. com/stabilising-the-middle-east-lessons-from-the-us-rapprochement-with-china-8547)

(32) E-money provides faster and more comfortable transactions compared to the cash money, especially for the small-amount transactions. With e-money, every transaction is simpler, cheaper, and easier both for the buyers and sellers. *One of the government interventions* <u>has recently been</u> *that every highway transaction can only be paid using e-money*. This policy has resulted in a various response from the consumers or society at large. (https://e-journal.unair.ac.id/JMTT/article/view/10024/0)

What is interesting about the examples in (31) and (32) is that they locate the specificational relation in the recent past, but they do not imply that the relation itself no longer holds at the temporal zero-point (i.e. the moment of encoding and/or decoding), which we would expect with an indefinite perfect. In (31), for instance, there is no implication that the value *Mitt Romney* currently no longer exemplifies the variable *one such strident voice*, nor does the value in (32) no longer qualify as *one of the government interventions*. Instead, the temporal adjunct *recently* implicitly locates what is described in the variable in the recent past, e.g. 'some people have recently voiced their opinion pro war, and one such voice is Mitt Romney' in (31) or 'there have recently been government interventions, and one of them is that . . .' in (32). The use of the indefinite perfect in (31) and (32) appear to involve what Declerck (2006: 572) calls a 'shift of temporal focus'. Such a shift happens when "the discourse switches from focus on one time-zone to focus on another" (*ib.*), for instance from the present to the recent past in (31) and (32). One reason for shifting the temporal focus may be that the speaker wishes to represent a situation which encompasses both past (or pre-present) and present from a past point of view (*ib.*: 582). For instance, when a speaker, recounting a hike, says: "we had difficulty climbing, because the hill was very steep", s/he does not mean to say that the hill is no longer steep, but s/he simply shifts the temporal focus to the past situation when s/he experienced the hill as being steep. I would argue that such a shift of temporal focus is what accounts for the rare and marked examples of specificational clauses with an indefinite perfect.

In contrast with the indefinite perfect, a continuative perfect is more compatible with the specificational semantics. A continuative perfect construal merely states that a relation originates in the past and continues up till the temporal zero-point and potentially beyond. It does not require the designated relation to be bounded and is thus compatible with the semantics of the specificational clause, e.g. (33).

(33) Our main target since day one <u>has always been</u> to win the championship. (WB)

Finally, as with the progressive, predicative clauses can be coerced into an indefinite perfect construal, even if such a use is not attested in the corpus and would appear more marginal than progressive predicative clauses. It is nonetheless possible to imagine a predicative sentence like (34), in which the described event is bounded. Note that, here too, the use of the indefinite perfect appears to involve a shift of temporal focus: the speaker is not stating that s/he is no longer a victim of robbery but rather shifts the focus to the moment in the recent past when the robbery happened.

(34)  I've just been a victim of robbery.

In sum, the possibility of progressive and indefinite perfect aspect in predicative clauses is motivated by special bounded senses of controllable behaviour and bounded events which can be construed for *be* + predicate nominative. The specificational process, by contrast, cannot be represented as bounded, nor can the variable or the value be presented as temporarily exhibiting controllable behaviour their warrant their relation to the other participant. This makes the meaning of the specificational clauses incompatible with the progressive and at least awkward with the indefinite perfect.

### 5.2.3.2 Modality

Table 15 and Figure 16 give the distribution of modal meanings across predicative clauses with indefinite predicative nominative, the different specificational clause types and non-copular clauses. Clearly, the use of modal auxiliaries is overall not common in copular or in non-copular clauses.

**Table 15:** The absolute and relative frequencies of modal meanings in copular clause types.

|  | *non-modal* | *deontic* | *dynamic* | *epistemic* | *evidential* |
|---|---|---|---|---|---|
| **predication** | 6,696 (91%) | 57 (1%) | 95 (1%) | 387 (5%) | 140 (2%) |
| **specification: indef. variable** | | | | | |
| non-reversed | 411 (94%) | 1 (0%) | 0 | 25 (6%) | 0 |
| reversed | 165 (92%) | 0 | 1 (0%) | 14 (8%) | 0 |
| **specification: def. variable** | | | | | |
| non-reversed | 2,367 (96%) | 18 (0%) | 6 (0%) | 64 (3%) | 23 (1%) |
| reversed | 618 (93%) | 5 (1%) | 2 (0%) | 38 (6%) | 2 (0%) |
| **non-copular** | 61,621 (91%) | 1,668 (2%) | 2,027 (3%) | 1,961 (3%) | 563 (1%) |

While predicative clauses appear to be similar to non-copular clauses in the frequency of non-modal uses, specificational clauses are generally less likely to

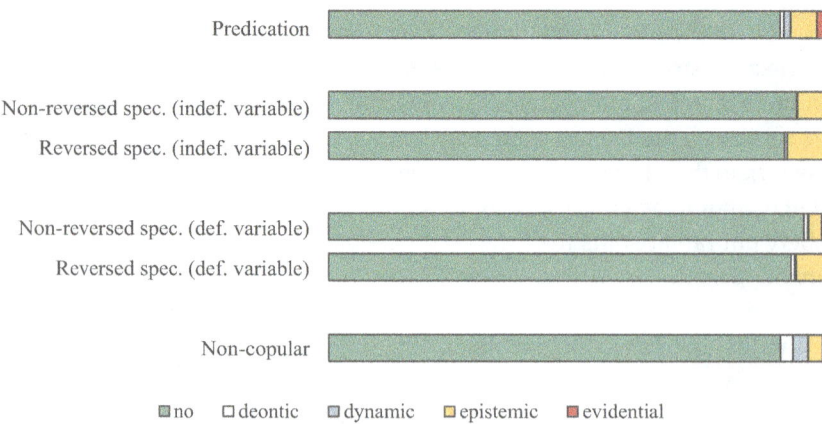

**Figure 16:** The relative frequencies of modal meanings in copular vs non-copular clauses.

take a modal, except in reversed ones with indefinite variable. Of the latter, 8% occurred with a modal verb; compared to 7% with reversed clauses with definite variable, 6% with non-reversed clauses with indefinite variable and 4% in the non-reversed ones with definite variable. In general, epistemic modality was the most frequently used modal meaning in all clause types (e.g. [35]-[38]), but it was – relatively – most frequent in reversed specificational clauses with an indefinite variable (8%), e.g. (35).

(35) **reversed specificational clause with indefinite variable**
King has been hyped as a potential late World Cup entrant, but in Holland his customary assurance deserted him. He let himself down with several poor passes, suggesting that *Dean Richards, his Spurs defensive partner, might be a better outside international bet*. (WB)

(36) **non-reversed specificational clause with indefinite variable**
The problem with the wife as biographer is one of wilful ellipsis: she's got the dope and she's not telling. I wanted more on the drunken first marriage to Iris, and what happened to her; more – forgive me, father – on Billy's coyly mentioned sexual "experiments with other men" [. . .] *A clue might be the reuse of the phrase "holding court" to describe his demeanour at social gatherings in Los Angeles with his chums Erics Idle and Clapton, Steve Martin, Dustin Hoffman, etc.* (WB)

(37) **reversed specificational clause with definite variable**
On hearing that neither of the "heavyweight theories" may explain the mammoth's disappearance 11,000 years ago, many of us feel guilty that so

much passion has been spent in vain; and in secret. It seems that *disease may have been the true culprit.* (WB)

(38) **predicative clause**
A little rainfall *might* not be a bad thing before tonight's Champions League match away to Boavista, the Portuguese champions, since the home team believe they can expose a "sluggish" Liverpool defence if the weather stays dry. (WB)

Furthermore, deontic and dynamic modality are overall not frequent at all, especially in specificational clauses with an indefinite variable, where they are virtually absent, except for the odd example of each of the modal meanings. Evidentiality, finally, was also rare in all clause types, with only predicative clauses having a slightly higher percentage (2%), e.g. (39), than non-copular clauses.

(39) It would be politically difficult to continue relations with a country *proven to* be a sponsor of terrorism. (WB)

The varying distributions of modal meanings in the different clause types are reflected in the different degrees of to which they are attracted to the copular constructions.[76] These attractions/repulsions of different modals to the copular clause types are summarised in Table 16.

**Table 16:** The attraction and repulsion of modals to specificational and predicative clauses.

|  | no | deontic | dynamic | epistemic | evidential |
|---|---|---|---|---|---|
| predication | 0.9947 | **0.3116 (R)** | **0.4258 (R)** | **1.8623 (A)** | **2.3184 (A)** |
| specification: indef. variable |  |  |  |  |  |
| non-reversed | **1.5673 (A)** | **0.1363 (R)** | **0.0371 (R)** | **2.0762 (A)** | **0.1364 (R)** |
| reversed | 1.0777 | **0.1099 (R)** | **0.2713 (R)** | **2.9249 (A)** | **0.3307 (R)** |
| specification: def. variable |  |  |  |  |  |
| non-reversed | **2.1431 (A)** | **0.2982 (R)** | **0.0853 (R)** | 0.8972 | 1.1427 |
| reversed | 1.3142 | **0.3302 (R)** | **0.1223 (R)** | **2.0607 (A)** | **0.4499 (R)** |

---

[76] A threshold of OR > 1.5 was taken as an index of attraction and a threshold of OR < 0.5 for repulsion. While attraction and repulsion are matters of degree, represented by the OR as deviation from the standard 1, such thresholds ensure meaningful interpretation of the results. Any numbers surpassing these thresholds were marked in bold and include an indication of attraction (A) or repulsion (R). (The same measure was also taken for Table 14 above, where all the values surpass their respective thresholds.)

As shown in Table 16, non-reversed specificational clauses, i.e. with variable/subject, generally prefer non-modalised VPs (i.e. OR = 1.5673 for the ones with indefinite variable and OR = 2.1431 for the ones with definite variable). Nevertheless, one type of modal meaning, namely epistemicity, is attracted to specificational clauses: this is shown by the high OR > 2 with generally all specificational clauses. Only non-reversed specificationals with definite variable did not attract epistemic modals (OR = 0.8972). In fact, no modal meanings at all were attracted to non-reversed specificationals with definite variable. Furthermore, evidential marking is repelled from all specificational clauses, except the non-reversed ones with definite variable, e.g. (40).

(40) Take yesterday's news about the Government's reorganisation of Railtrack. The original privatisation was flawed since Railtrack is a monopoly dependent on huge government subsidies, but with weak links to rail customers and with a poor top management concerned with maintaining shareholder dividends. [. . .] The Tories lack credibility on the issue. They were responsible for the botched structure now being ended. *Their answer to every question has appeared to be: bring in the private sector, even when big state subsidies are needed.* (WB)

Finally, deontic and dynamic modals are also repelled from all specificational clauses. In fact, the only kind of dynamic meaning that was attested at all in specificational clauses was situational possibility, e.g. (41). Deontic and dynamic modality were also repelled from predicative clauses. Here, however, the occurrences of dynamic modality were not just of situational possibility, e.g. (42); predicative clauses with participant-internal and -imposed dynamic modality were also attested (in small numbers, *viz.* 8 attestations), e.g. (43).

(41) Arrange at least two specific times in the day for sitting on the potty or toilet. It's best to do this at the time that he is most likely to go. Every child is different; for your son it might be after breakfast, lunch, or exercise. *Sometimes the problem can be that a child does not like sitting on the or potty or lavatory, so make the experience enjoyable.* Put up posters in the bathroom, let him have a toy to play with, read his favourite book

(42) Many people don't realise that *garlic can be an irritant, even in minuscule doses*, which makes it a fairly common cause of contact allergies. (WB)

(43) Jane is distraught at having her past revealed and concludes that *she will never be a witness again.* (WB)

In the following paragraphs, I will interpret these interactions of modal meanings with the functions of specification and predication. I will focus on three points. First, I will discuss why all copular clauses repel dynamic and deontic modality. Secondly, I examine the attraction of epistemic modality to (i) both kinds of specificational clauses with an indefinite variable, in (ii) both kinds of reversed specificationals, and (iii) predicative clauses. I will propose that those three environments present different conditions for attracting epistemic modals. Finally, I discuss why evidentiality is repelled from all specificational clauses but the non-reversed ones with definite variable, and why it is attracted to the predicative construction.

In general, we have to bear in mind the distinction between content-related modals that bear on the representation of the copular relation (e.g. objective deontic and dynamic modality) and speaker-related modals that construe a position with regard to the status of the proposition or the authority on which it is based (epistemic and subjective deontic modality, evidentiality). I will argue that, in the former case, the felicity of the modal expression depends, like with aspect, on its compatibility with the semantics of the copular clause. In the latter case, the modal or evidential markers have scope over the entire proposition: their attraction/repulsion is not a question of (in)compatibility with the representational meaning but is instead motivated by the particular discursive functions that the predicative or specificational clauses can serve and with pragmatically implied meanings (e.g. non-exhaustiveness, contrastiveness).

A first observation from the case study was that all copular clauses repel both dynamic and deontic modality, with very few examples being actually attested for specificational clauses in particular. Especially for dynamic modality, however, there seems to be a difference in the specific kinds of dynamic modal meanings that are compatible with predicative and specificational clauses. The use of situational possibility is acceptable in both predicative (44) and specificational clauses (45). The speaker can commit to the theoretical possibility of the description (44) or the value-variable assignment (45).

(44) *Wearing a hat can be a joy* if you find a shape and style that suits your face. (WB)

(45) In China, *the Taklamakan desert temperature in summer can be 90 degrees Fahrenheit (32 degrees Celsius)*, but in winter it falls to 25F (-4C). (https://sciencing.com/cold-desert-plants-animals-5263593.html)

By contrast, participant-oriented dynamic modality occurs with some frequency in predicative clauses, as shown by the attested examples of ability (46), need (47) and volition (48). Volition and ability are possible but highly infrequent and marked in specificational clauses with subject/value, as in (49)[77] and (50b), and seem to be excluded altogether in specificational clauses with subject/variable, as illustrated by (50c), (51), (52) and (53).

(46) *I can't be a shining example to you*, but at least let me be an awful warning. (WB)

(47) You just had to be a hero, didn't you? (Google)

(48) If I'm a social pariah I shall be a social pariah. (WB)

(49) I think of all the contemporary American poets and artists who represent their outlook on this strange country and I find myself beginning to realize that *I shall be one of them*. (Google)

(50) a. Jim Prentice [. . .] is first out of the blocks in the race to lead the new Conservative Party of Canada, [w]hile Canadian Alliance Leader Stephen Harper and Tory Leader Peter MacKay are widely expected to mount campaigns in coming weeks [. . .]. I think the critical issue here is winnability – *who can be the leader of this new party* and inspire Canadians with hope and with an agenda? (WB)
b. **Jim Prentice** can [= has the ability to] be the leader.
c. *The leader can [= has the ability to] be **Jim Prentice**.

(51) *Property in the 'wrong location' – one example can [= is able to] be London Town's The Bridge.

(52) *One of them shall [= is willing to be] be me.

(53) *Property in the 'wrong location' – one example needs to [= has the need to] be London Town's The Bridge.

The point made in Chapter 3 should be recalled here that the subject is not a purely formal category but functions semantically as "the entity in respect of which the assertion is claimed to have validity" and "in whom is vested the

---

[77] The example in (49) is an attested example, and while the clause is ambiguous between a predicative and a specificational reading, it is meaningful that the specificational reading is not excluded, even when *shall* is indeed taken to be an expression of volition.

success or failure of the proposition" (Halliday 1985: 76). Therefore, the construal of the variable or value as subject of the specificational clause is a meaningful choice, coding different matching relations between the two entities they denote. When the variable is subject, the validity of the proposition is asserted based on the criteria that the variable sets up; we can call this the 'criterial' perspective on specification. But when the value is subject, the perspective construed is that of the value 'qualifying as' the variable.

What seems to be involved in the selection restrictions on dynamic modality in copular clauses, then, is the possibility of relating the complement to the subject in terms of an internal dynamic 'force'. Participant-internal and participant-imposed dynamic modals both involve attributing a dynamic force – i.e. ability, need or volition – to the subject referent (which need not be an agent, e.g. *I will not be overawed*) (Nuyts 2006: 3). With participant-internal modality, this implies that the subject referent has control over the process designated by the VP (Palmer 2003: 7; Gisborne 2007: 51); with participant-imposed modality, the control over the process is conditioned by external circumstances, so the subject referent only has partial power over the property s/he is ascribed (Nuyts 2006: 3).

The infelicity of (50c) shows that, regardless of whether the variable/subject denotes an animate entity (e.g. *the leader*) or not, it cannot be a controlling participant in a specificational clause. To the abstract entity that the speaker sets up with the variable NP cannot be ascribed any participant-inherent force like ability, volition or need. The felicity of (50b), on the other hand, suggests that to the concrete value/subject participant-inherent forces like ability, volition or need can be ascribed, though only under special circumstances. These circumstances are, firstly, that the value/subject must be an animate entity (which is required for the attribution of an ability, need or volition to it, see Verplaetse [2003: 159– 160]); and, secondly, that this entity has control over the qualities that sanction its qualifying as a value for the variable. Such special circumstances, however, appear to be rare, as dynamic modality is not attested in the examples of either non-reversed or reversed specificational clauses in my sample. This suggests that the use of dynamic modality to attribute some disposition to the value is only very marginally compatible with the meaning of reversed specificational clauses but not compatible at all with that of non-reversed ones.

The repulsion of deontic modality by all copular clause types can arguably be related to the discursive functions for which they are employed rather than to their representational meaning. In predicative clauses, it is highly infrequent but possible for the speaker to express the opinion that the subject entity should exhibit certain qualities or representational features. In (54), for instance, the subjective belief that the quality of being 'a solemn occasion' is presented as desirable or even required for 'the swearing in of a government'; in (55), the obligation for 'every Labour MP' to be 'a member of a trade union' is presented as an objective social rule in the Labour party.

(54) The swearing in of a government <u>should</u> be a solemn occasion. (WB)

(55) For all its Red Rose rebranding, New Labour is still Old Labour when it comes to strikes. *Every Labour MP <u>has to</u> be a member of a trade union*. (WB)

Specificational clauses are less likely to involve desirability judgements. In the rare cases that they do, the deontic evaluation was always found to be subjective in my sample, e.g. (56). We find the 'criterial' perspective on specification. The speaker vests his or her subjective stance of desirability to the specificational relation in the criteria stipulated by the variable/subject.

(56) A first step towards combating the threat of biological weapons <u>must</u> be to strengthen the norms against their use and make doubly clear that that form of terrorism, like all others, is unacceptable. (WB)

In contrast with deontic and dynamic modality, all copular types – except non-reversed specificationals with a definite variable – attract epistemic modality. In predicative clauses, epistemic modals would appear to occur mostly in two contexts. First, in cases like (57), the modalised proposition does not so much imply speaker uncertainty about the predicative relation as reticence to take personal responsibility for the assertion.

(57) John Boyle <u>might</u> be a brilliant businessman, a philanthropist, an enthusiast – but he can also be a right numpty as his bonkers plan to merge Airdrie to death proves. (WB)

In such contexts, the epistemic modal has the effect of echoing an opinion expressed or implied elsewhere in the discourse context. When subjective modals are used congruently (non-echoically), the speaker hic et nunc assumes a position of commitment with respect to the propositional content of the utterance (Verstraete 2001: 1517–1518). When the speaker does not take responsibility for a subjectively modalised proposition, the implication is that someone else is responsible for it and that the speaker merely echoes the proposition, which s/he neither denies nor confirms, as in (57).

Second, epistemic modal auxiliaries are also commonly used in predicative clauses to make a hypothetical statement, as in (58) below. Palmer (1990: 172) points out that the apodosis (i.e. main clause) of an unreal conditional sentence, future or past, "must contain a modal verb", typically *would* (see also Declerck 2006: 166), as is the case in (58). But in non-conditional predicative sentences, like (59), the epistemic modal also most commonly expresses a hypothetical and even counterfactual SoA: in such cases, the speaker does not waive responsibility for the proposition but presents the description in the predicative clause as obtaining only under the unreal circumstances specified in the context (e.g. the protasis of the conditional sentence in [58] or the hypothetical event described by the subject in [59]).

(58) I would be a charlatan if I pretended I knew how the political and military situation would evolve. (WB)

(59) "For me to leave now while the club is in this state would be a big shame," Roberts said. "I'm a local boy and I've got a love for the club." (WB)

In specificational clauses, two generalisations can be made about the use of epistemic modals: they are attracted, firstly, to specificationals with indefinite variable and, secondly, to reversed specificationals, i.e. with value/subject. In reversed specificationals with indefinite variable, to which both conditions apply, the attraction of epistemicity is the strongest (OR = 2.9249, compared to OR = 2.0762 for non-reversed specificationals with indefinite variable and OR = 2.0607 for reversed specificationals with definite variable). Let us look at these two constructional environments in order.

Specificationals with indefinite variable, with their implicate of non-exhaustiveness (Declerck 1988: 31; Lambrecht 2001: 508), are used when the speaker does not specify the values exhaustively. This may be because the speaker lacks the information to distinguish all qualifying values from potential, but non-qualifying, values, or the 'best' values from 'less good' ones. This may cause the speaker to convey reticence about the specification by modifying it in terms of epistemic modality. Thus, in (60), the use of the epistemic modal does not question the validity of the value, e.g. *Dean Richards*, as a specification of the variable; rather, the tentativity expressed by the modal has to do with comparing different values as good or 'better' examples of the variable. Similarly, in (61), the speaker does not so much doubt that the value counts as "one of the reasons for this" but rather weighs the importance of the specified value as one of the contributing factors to the fact that poorer dioceses rely more on donations from parishioners.

(60) King has been hyped as a potential late World Cup entrant, but in Holland his customary assurance deserted him. He let himself down with several poor passes, suggesting that *Dean Richards, his Spurs defensive partner, might be a better outside international bet.* (WB)

(61) Robin Stevens, national stewardship officer, said it was clear that people in poorer inner-city dioceses were giving more of their income than parishioners in richer areas. He said: "One of the reasons for this <u>may</u> be that, in the past, richer dioceses have had their own independent income and so the need to give has not been so great as in poorer areas." (WB)

In other words, the modalised expressions in (60) and (61) do not so much question *that* the value is a possible specification of the variable, but rather give an evaluation of *how appropriate or relevant* it is as a value for the variable in comparison to other (explicit or implicit) potential values.

In reversed specificational clauses with value/subject, the comparison of the value to other implied, or explicitly mentioned, potential values is given added prominence. Not only is the success of the proposition vested in the value/subject qualifying for the criteria expressed by the variable, but the informational-structurally marked clause-initial position also gives it a 'contrastive' reading (Halliday 1967b: 228–229). The implied comparison of the value to others invites epistemic evaluations both when the variable NP is indefinite, e.g. (60), and when it is definite, e.g. (62).

(62) During the 1950s, with a junior officer called Peter Wright, Martin had become convinced that there were still Soviet moles at large in all areas of British life, that MI5 was being infiltrated at the highest levels, and that a serious investigation was needed. [...] To make matters more complicated, Martin and Wright were beginning to think that *Roger Hollis, now MI5's director*, <u>might</u> *be their prime suspect*. (WB)

To the definite variable attaches an inclusiveness (i.e. uniqueness) implicature (Hawkins 1978: 161), which triggers the implicature at clause-level that the specified value is the only one qualifying as the variable. However, while the use of an epistemic modal *emphasises* the non-exhaustiveness implicature of specificationals with indefinite variable, it *weakens* the exhaustiveness of specificationals with definite variable. By not committing to one value as the appropriate specification, the speaker leaves open the option that other potential values qualify better than the definite variable, e.g. *Roger Hollis* vs other potential 'Soviet moles' in (62).

Finally, it is interesting that, despite the commonly observed interaction between evidentiality and epistemicity, expressions of evidentiality were not attested and, hence, repelled from specificational clauses with indefinite variable – both non-reversed and reversed ones – and from reversed specificationals with definite variable. In non-reversed specificationals with definite variable, by contrast, evidential markers occurred 23 times: evidentiality was not repelled from these clauses, although the OR comes to close to 1 (i.e. OR = 1.1427) to really talk about an attraction. Of the 23 occurrences, only six were examples of hearsay, e.g. (63); all the others were inferential examples with either *seem* or *appear*, e.g. (64).

(63)     The JCR's [i.e. 'Junta Coordinadora Revolucionaria', an alliance of leftist South American guerrilla organisations] chief commanding officer in Europe is reported to be Fernando Luis Alvarez, who is married to Ana Maria Guevara, sister of the Latin Revolutionary, Che Guevara.

(64)     It seems online recruitment needs to reconsider its remit. *The way forward seems to be the growth of specialisation across sectors and functions.* (WB)

In this respect, specificational clauses contrast with predicative clauses, which strongly attract expressions of evidentiality. Unlike with non-reversed specificationals with definite variable, the evidential markers used in predicative clauses typically invoke hearsay, e.g. (65). Expressions of inferential evidentiality, such as *seem* and *appear*, only make up 18% of the evidential examples with predication, e.g. (66).

(65)     The married Old Etonian [i.e. Brian Robin Wyldebore-Smith] was said to have been a heavy drinker with severe liver disease. (WB)

(66)     Much of what has been said by Conservative Members today seems to be a rearguard attempt to protect the Home Secretary and his sinking reputation. (WB)

In the majority of cases, the speaker does not take a position with regard to the validity of the proposition in the predicative clauses – i.e. s/he neither questions nor commits to it – but merely indicates that the evidence for the proposition comes from an external source, e.g. hearsay in (65). While the high frequency of such evidential markers can be explained by the 'newspaper' genre of the examples (taken from *The Times*), it is worth noting that predicative clauses, in particular, invite such authorisational modification. In cases like (65), the motivation for avoiding responsibility for the proposition seems to be the controversial nature of the defamatory claim. In other cases, the speaker may indicate a lack of conclusive evidence for a temporary conclusion, as in (67). Or s/he backs up a somewhat subjective evaluation by presenting it as based on external evidence, as in (68).

(67) Mr Ashcroft said three men living in Detroit, whose detention was already known, were "suspected of having knowledge of the September 11 attacks". [. . .] The three Arab immigrants, *believed to be members of Osama bin Laden's al Qaeda network*, were living, or had previously lived, at an apartment in Detroit. (WB)

(68) The war on terror has proved to be a bonanza for America's inventors, entrepreneurs and old-fashioned snake-oil salesmen. (WB)

In specificational clauses, such authorisational modification is rare and even not attested in those with an indefinite variable. This may be because the latter, in view of their implicature of non-exhaustiveness, intrinsically require less commitment on the part of the speaker. In other words, specifying *a* value for a variable is a more tentative assertion than specifying *the* (sole) value for a variable, and hence is not likely to be further attenuated by evidential markers.

Summing up, I have argued in this section that the use of modal verbs in predicative and specificational clauses differs on two counts. First, when the modal expression is content-related and ascribes a property to the subject referent (i.e. participant-internal or -imposed dynamic modality), it can only occur in predicative clauses or, very marginally, in reversed specificational ones. This I explained in terms of the controllability of the coded relation. Secondly, modal expressions that have scope over the entire proposition were found to be compatible with the meaning of all copular clause types. The attraction of epistemic modals to the predicative clause type was often motivated not so much by speaker uncertainty as by the speaker's reluctance to assume responsibility for a (subjective) description. In specificational clauses, epistemic evaluations are invited by (i) the non-exhaustiveness implicature triggered by the indefinite variable NP and (ii) the emphasis on comparing the value subject to other potential values in reversed specificationals.

## 5.3 Conclusion

In this chapter, predicative and specificational clauses were shown to differ in their use of aspect and modality. These differences, I proposed, could be correlated with the different semantics-pragmatics of predication and specification, and their different discursive functions in specific contexts. Different degrees of attraction for aspect and modality, as identified in collostructional analyses, were also found between non-reversed and reversed specificational clauses and between specificational clauses with definite and indefinite variable. I analysed these results in terms of (i) the different perspectives on the specificational relation that are coded by non-reversed vs reversed clauses and (ii) the different implicatures of (non-)exhaustiveness triggered by the definite vs indefinite variable NP.

For aspect, I argued that the progressive is possible with predicative clauses but not with specificational ones. I suggested that, in predicative clauses, the composite predicate formed by *be* + NP can, under special circumstances, be construed as respectively bounded episodes of behaviour or perfective events, thereby allowing for a progressive construal. By contrast, in specificational clauses, the inherently imperfective stative relation cannot be presented as a bounded episode of controllable behaviour of neither variable nor value. The indefinite perfect, it was argued, can be found in both clause types, even if it is very rare and always appears to involve what Declerck (2006: 572) calls a 'shift of temporal focus': both in predicative clauses and in specificational ones, the use of the indefinite perfect, therefore, did not appear to imply that the copular relation no longer holds at the temporal zero-point, but rather the speaker shifts the focus to a moment in the recent past when the specificational relation was particularly pertinent.

The attraction of other modals to the copular clause types was motivated by multiple factors. First, certain forms of dynamic modality – i.e. participant-internal and -imposed – are not possible with non-reversed specificational clauses, though marginally acceptable with reversed ones. The construal of the variable vs the value as subject was shown to be a meaningful choice, prompting different felicity judgements for dynamic modals. With the variable as subject, the 'success' of the proposition is vested in the *criteria* the speaker sets up with the variable NP. No participant-inherent force like ability, volition or need can be ascribed to the abstract criterial entity designated by the variable NP. With the value as subject, on the other hand, the perspective is one of the value *qualifying as* the variable: if the value is an animate entity and has control over the qualities that make it a fitting specification, it is possible for the value to be ascribed ability, need or volition. Since the use of dynamic modals remains nevertheless only marginally acceptable, the fact that predicative clauses more readily accommodate such modals is further proof of the point that predicative and specificational clauses are different categories with different semantics.

Secondly, predicative clauses attract epistemic modals and evidential markers. The discursive function of description was argued to invite a subjective evaluation on the part of the speaker. (See also the frequent use of epithets in predicate nominatives, which are often subjective, e.g. *he's a <u>terrific</u> dancer*, see Chapter 4.) This, I argued, is in line with the subjectivity of epistemic modality, which implies different degrees of speaker commitment to the validity of a proposition. The use of evidential markers was found to typically have the opposite effect: the speaker often refrains from taking responsibility for the subjective evaluation by citing an external source as evidence for the proposition.

In specificational clauses, such evidential markers were rare and not attested at all when the variable NP was indefinite. The 'weaker' commitment (Lyons 1999: 261) associated with the non-exhaustiveness implicature triggered by the indefinite variable was put forward as a potential explanation for the repulsion of evidentiality: the speaker would appear less likely, in such cases, to 'hedge' the assertion by citing 'external' evidence. The very implicature of non-exhaustiveness tallies with contexts in which the speaker is not able or willing to specify all the values exhaustively or distinguish qualifying entities (real values) from potential, but failed candidates. This was also raised as a factor in the attraction of epistemic modals to 'indefinite' specificational clauses, where they convey epistemic tentativity.

In sum, the findings from the collostructional analyses of VP-related resources in this chapter adduce further evidence for the semantics-pragmatics of predication and specification proposed in Chapter 3 and for the different discursive meanings they can express.

# Chapter 6
# The prosodically coded information structure of specificational and predicative copular clauses

In this chapter[78] I examine the prosodically coded information structure of specificational and predicative clauses. In previous studies, information structure has been interpreted in terms of a semantic-pragmatic relation between a 'presupposition' and a 'focus' (e.g. Chomsky 1969: 26; Akmajian 1970, 1973: 218; Lambrecht 1994: 213). This interpretation, which I have argued against in Chapter 3, has led to the erroneous belief that specificational clauses are syntactic structures that grammatically code a 'presupposition-focus' relation (e.g. Heycock & Kroch 2002: 147; den Dikken 2006: 83; Heycock 2012: 217–218). Specificational clauses have, therefore, been argued to have a 'fixed' information structure (e.g. Higgins 1976; Partee 2000; Mikkelsen 2005; Patten 2012, 2016), in the sense that the variable is claimed to be always 'presupposed' and the value necessarily 'focal'. The information structure of predicative clauses, by contrast, has been characterised as 'free', so that either the describee or the description can be 'presupposed' or 'focal' (e.g. Patten 2016: 81).

As argued in Chapter 3, the semantic-pragmatic interpretation of 'presupposition' and 'focus' that has led to the idea of a 'fixed' specificational information structure is problematic, because it conflates different layers of coded and pragmatic meaning. Firstly, the information structural notion of 'focus' has been collapsed with the role of the value in the specificational relation. This goes back to the idea that the 'presupposition' is the part of the sentence that expresses an open proposition with a semantic 'gap', or variable, that is filled, or specified, by the so-called 'focus' (e.g. Chomsky 1969: 26; Akmajian 1979: 195, 221; Prince 1986: 207). The 'focus' is then claimed to be the constituent "which contains the intonation center, i.e. the position of highest pitch and stress" (Akmajian 1979: 190; see also Chomsky 1969: 26; Patten 2016: 80): this sets the focus apart from the non-focal presupposed remainder of the sentence "as being semantically special and important" (Akmajian 1979: 191).

Secondly, the notion of the pragmatic presupposition often seems to get amalgamated with the information structurally presupposed material. According to Akmajian (1979: 192), "the use of the term 'presupposition' reflects the intuitive feeling that [prosodically] non-focal material is generally indeed presupposed by

---

[78] Parts of this chapter are an elaborated version of sections in Van Praet & O'Grady (2018) and Van Praet (2019a).

the speaker to be known to the hearer, and thus is material which is non-informative." Lambrecht (1994, 2001: 474) develops this idea further. He defines 'pragmatic presupposition' as what "the speaker assumes the hearer already knows or believes or is ready to take for granted at the time the sentence is uttered (the 'old' information)" (Lambrecht 2001: 474). Contrasting it with 'presupposition', he interprets 'focus' as the "semantic component of a pragmatically structured proposition whereby the assertion differs from the presupposition" (Lambrecht 1994: 213): the focus, in other words, is the "unpredictable part" that makes a proposition into an assertion (2001: 474). Furthermore, Lambrecht (1994) "insist[s] on the fundamental importance of prosody in the marking of focus structure" (*ib.*: 225): prosodic prominence correlates with "the relative communicative importance of the prosodically highlighted element", so that "the prosodic peak" points to the "communicatively most important element in the utterance" (Lambrecht 1994: 242). At the same time, Lambrecht (1994: 213) sharply distinguishes his notion of focus – as a 'semantic-pragmatic' function – from how it is formally expressed. Rather than viewing prosodic prominence, specifically 'pitch accentuation', as coding focus itself, he claims that the assignment of pitch accents marks the 'activation state', or retrievability, of a piece of information: an expression is unaccented, if "the speaker assumes that [its] referent can be construed as ratified in the discourse", i.e. that it is "taken to be predictable to the addressee at the time of the utterance" (*ib.*: 479). By contrast, accentuation, or pitch prominence, implies the opposite, *viz.* that the accented expression presents unpredictable 'new' information. In sum, for Lambrecht (1994), the correlation between prosodic prominence and information focus involves, on the one hand, pitch accentuation marking new information as communicatively important and, on the other hand, the interpretation of focus as the part of a proposition that is presented as 'new' in relation to the presupposed remainder of the clause.

Finally, presupposition and focus have often been interpreted in terms of 'given' and 'new' information (Akmajian 1979: 196). The term 'new', or non-recoverable, information is used not necessarily "in the sense that [the information] cannot have been previously mentioned, although it is often case that it has not been, but in the sense that the speaker *presents* it *as* not being recoverable from the preceding discourse" (Halliday 1967b: 204, italics mine). For Akmajian (1973: 218, 1979) and Lambrecht (1994: 211–213), this means that it is not necessarily the 'focus constituent' itself but the relation between the focus and the presupposition that is new. Halliday (1967b: 207) himself proposes a more nuanced analysis: he distinguishes between two different relations that the focus can have to the other material in the information unit. In the first, unmarked type of information structure, the information focus simply marks the 'point of culmination' in the information unit: while the focus is presented as new, the remainder of the information unit can be either given or new (Halliday 1967b: 208). For instance, the information unit in (1) has unmarked focus on *the shed*, which is presented as new but gives no indication of whether the remainder of the unit is (partly) given or new. Examples with unmarked information structure are probed by general verbs like *do* or *happen*. For (1) the interrogative probe can either be 'What did John do?' – so that only *paint the shed* is new information – or 'What happened?' – so that the entire proposition is new.

(1)    // John painted **the shed** // (Halliday 1967b: 208)

In the second, marked type, the focus relates to PRESUPPOSED INFORMATION and is contrastive in a general sense – either with lexical items or with grammatical options (Halliday 1967b: 207–208). The focus is probed by a WH-interrogative inquiring about one specific element, e.g. (2).

(2)    a.    (Who painted the shed yesterday?) // **John** painted the shed yesterday // (Halliday 1967b: 208)
       b.    (What did John do to the shed yesterday?) // John **painted** the shed yesterday // (*ib.*)
       c.    (When did John paint the shed?) // John painted the shed **yesterday** // (*ib.*)

Only in cases like in (2a,b,c) does the focus explicitly relate to an information-structural 'presupposition' (Halliday 1967b: 208).

In this chapter, I will critically and empirically examine the correlation of the focus with the value and of the variable with the pragmatic presupposition, which has been posited in so much of the literature on specificational copular clauses (e.g. Higgins 1979: 234–236; Declerck 1988: 12; Heycock & Kroch 1999: 394; Partee 2000: 199; Mikkelsen 2005: 133). To come to a better understanding of the actual information structure of both specificational and predicative clauses, it is crucial, I argue, to disentangle the different layers of lexicogrammatically coded and pragmatic meaning that have been collapsed in previous studies. To this end, I propose to distinguish: (i) the semantics of the constituents and structural relations coded at lexicogrammatical level; (ii) pragmatic presuppositions and implicatures triggered by linguistic signals at level (i); (iii) the information structural meanings, both relational (i.e. focal vs non-focal material) and referential (*viz.* identifiability, discourse-givenness).

The semantics of predicative and specificational clauses at level (i) were analysed, in Chapters 3 to 5, as respectively involving an intransitive process in which only the subject referent participates, while the predicate nominative serves a relational (non-participant) function and a transitive process between a variable and a value. It was further argued that the predicate nominative is non-referential, while the variable has generalised reference, which, via the mechanism of dual reference, implies reference to more concrete entities, to which a presupposition of existence applies (e.g. Delahunty 1984; Declerck 1988: 14). This existential presupposition cannot be conflated with information-structurally 'presupposed' material (in the sense of Halliday [1967b: 208] described above).

Information structure, at level (iii), has, since Gundel (1988), been analysed as involving two dimensions: the referential and the relational. The referential dimension concerns the marking of the activation state of referents in the discourse, which includes (i) the identifiability of referents (e.g. Halliday & Hasan 1976; Langacker 1991; Martin 1992; Gundel, Hedberg & Zacharski 1993) and (ii) their discourse-givenness (e.g. Prince 1981b; Kaltenböck 2005). This dimension will be discussed in detail in Chapter 7. The relational dimension, on the other hand, is concerned with the relation between focal and non-focal information in the information unit. Following Halliday (1967b: 204–207) (but also, for instance, Tench [1996], Verstraete [2007], O'Grady [2017]), I assume the information unit to be demarcated by the tone unit (TU). Within each TU, the placement of the tonic marks the focal information. To avoid confusion with the actual discourse-givenness of information, I will refer to the meaning of the focus as the 'point' or 'points' in the TU that are presented as most informative or noteworthy, rather than in terms of 'newness' or 'unpredictability'. Moreover, the meaning of focus as signalling NOTEWORTHINESS more accurately captures its interpersonal function (McGregor 1997: 274–275; Verstraete 2007: 81–88), i.e. to direct the hearer's attention to information that the speaker presents as important in light of the message s/he wants to convey.

Therefore, to analyse the information structure of specificational and predicative clauses – and specifically the marking of focus (or foci) – one needs to pay close attention to the prosodic patterns with which specificational and predicative clauses are uttered in spoken discourse. This chapter will be devoted to the study of attested spoken data, the analysis of which will allow for a detailed inspection of what exactly the information structure of specificational and predicative clauses is and whether it serves as a recognition criterion to distinguish one clause type from the other.

## 6.1 Background

A pervasive assumption in studies of information structure is that the focus in a declarative clause can be probed by a WH-interrogative, in which the WH-pronoun inquires into the focal constituent in the corresponding declarative clause (e.g.

Mikkelsen 2005: 33; den Dikken 2006: 294). Usually, predicative clauses are not probed at all (Declerck 1988: 55), but when they are, it is typically by means of a question that asks for a description of the describee, e.g. (3a). As I pointed out in Chapter 3, they can also be probed by a question that inquires into entities that can be characterised in terms of the type-specifications given by the description, as in (3b).[79]

(3)  a.  What's he like? – *He's **a big fella, a bit of a Fancy Dan**, he has silver armbands.* (WB)
     b.  As Bush passed by, the protesters chanted, "Who is a terrorist, ***Bush** is a terrorist*." (WB)

Specificational clauses, by contrast, are probed only by WH-interrogatives that seek (a) fitting value(s) for the variable, e.g. (4).

(4)  What is your favourite part of the house? My favourite part of the house is **the big deck out the back.** (WB)

However, against the assumption that WH-interrogatives reveal the focus of information, I argued in Chapter 3 that interrogatives like the ones in (3a,b) and (4) do not probe for information structure but for the 'direction of fit' of predicative and specificational relations. This direction of fit concerns the logical order in which the two entities in the copular clause are related, or associated, with each other (Austin 1970; Davidse & Van Praet 2019). It is intrinsic to the meaning of the specificational process that the variable logically precedes the value: the direction of fit always goes from variable to value. Hence, as the interrogative probe for the specificational clause indicates, it is always the value that accords with the variable, not the other way round. The meaning of predicative clauses, by contrast, imposes no logical order, or direction, onto the designated process: their corresponding interrogative probe can either ask for a description that captures the characteristics of the describee, e.g. (3a), or it can inquire into entities that can be characterised in terms of the type-specifications given by the description, e.g. (3b). In the first case, the description is fitted to the describee; in the second case, the describee is fitted to the description. The direction of fit does not necessarily correlate with the information structure of the two clause types.

---

**79** The interrogative probes for the predicative clauses in (3a,b) and for the specificational clause in (4) figured as such in the original attested examples and, hence, were not simply added later for illustrative purposes.

To understand how the semantics and the information structure of specificational and predicative clauses interact as distinct levels of meaning in their own right, we have to take seriously the notion of focus as an information structural 'attention-directing' mechanism. Halliday (1985: 277) views the meaning of the focus as signalling to the hearer 'attend to this, this is news'. He interprets focus as operating at the textual level: for him, primary importance goes to the 'newness' of the focal information and, hence, to its status in the text or context. Against this, McGregor (1997: 274–275) and Verstraete (2007: 81–88) argue that focus marking and information organisation are genuine speaker-hearer phenomena: the speaker assesses "newness" or "newsworthiness" by evaluating the hearer's (assumed) state of knowledge within a given discourse context and, on that basis, marks information as important to be attended to. Moreover, because the speaker can assess information as attention-worthy regardless of whether it is actually new to the discourse or not, I will refer to the function of the focus as signalling NOTEWORTHINESS, rather than newness, predictability or newsworthiness.[80]

Noteworthiness is signalled, in spoken discourse, by the utterance's intonation structure (e.g. Bolinger 1954, 1989; Halliday 1967b,c, 1970c; Crystal 1969, 1975; Tench 1988, 1996). Halliday (1967c: 18), and others with him (e.g. Crystal 1969, 1975; Tench 1988, 1996; Cruttenden 1997), interpret intonation in terms of three systems, or distinct meaningful (sets of) choices: (i) tonality, (ii) tonicity, and (iii) tone. TONALITY concerns the segmentation of an utterance into prosodic units, called tone units (TUs) (or, alternatively, tone groups, intonation units, etc.) (Halliday 1967c: 20–24; 1967b: 199–211). Each TU marks a pitch contour, i.e. a single pitch movement (Halliday 1970c: 6), which presents the information thereby expressed as one unit of information (Halliday 1967b: 203). Each TU consists minimally of one obligatory part, namely the 'tonic'. The assignment of the tonic accent to a syllable in the TU is referred to as TONICITY. The system of tonicity marks the focus in each information unit: each pitch contour has one (major) point of culmination that "carries the main burden of the pitch movement" in the TU (Halliday 1970c: 4), e.g. *worry* in (5). This special prominence signals where the noteworthy information lies. The tonic may, furthermore, correlate with increased loudness and reduced speed (Halliday 1970c: 4; Halliday & Greaves 2008), which add to the phonological prominence signalled by pitch movement.

---

**80** As argued in Chapter 3, in opting for the term 'noteworthiness', I am not stating that newness plays no role at all in the noteworthiness of information. I merely wish to avoid the confusion that the function of the focus would be to code actual discourse-newness, which is not the case.

(5)  ^I'm getting too old to !w\orry a_bout it# (LLC)[81]

As pointed out in the introduction, Halliday (1967b,c) distinguishes two types of information structure.[82] In the first, UNMARKED type of information structure, tonic prominence marks the focus "without an associated presupposition" (Verstraete 2007: 82): the focus is, therefore, NON-CONTRASTIVE. Such information structures allow "only . . . generalized interrogatives like what happened?" (*ib.*). In this type of information structure, the tonic prominence is "on the last element of grammatical structure that contains a lexical item" (Halliday 1967c: 22), e.g. on *worry* in (5). In this unmarked information structure, Halliday (1967c: *ib.*) notes, the tonic will typically not fall on e.g. personal pronouns like *it*, *some* or *one*: these are not considered 'lexical items', or content words, since they form options in a closed system. In the second, MARKED type of information structure, the focus does relate to presupposed information and is contrastive in a general sense – either with lexical items or with grammatical options (Halliday 1967b: 207). Such a marked CONTRASTIVE information focus may be placed on any lexical element in the tone group as well as on grammatical items, e.g. on *I* and *they* in (6), or twice on *that* in (7). In both examples, the marked foci signal contrastiveness (Halliday 1967b: 208), i.e. between *I* and *they* in (6) and between *that* and implied alternatives in (7).

---

**81** The more precise prosodic marking in LLC includes the following symbols: ^ silent onset; . brief pause; - unit pause of one stress unit; ' normal stress; " heavy stress; : higher pitch level than preceding syllable; ! booster higher than preceding pitch prominent syllable; [] partial words or phonetic symbols; {} subordinate tone unit; * simultaneous talk; (()) incomprehensible words; VAR various speakers.

**82** These two types of information structure, i.e. unmarked with non-contrastive focus and marked with contrastive focus, have inspired similar classifications of information structure in later studies. Citing Halliday (1967b,c), Kiss (1998) distinguishes, for instance, between 'information focus' (unmarked) vs 'identificational focus' (marked). Lambrecht's (1994: 221–223) account too is heavily influenced by Halliday (1967): his 'argument focus' corresponds to Halliday's marked (contrastive) focus, while 'sentence focus' and 'predicate focus' are similar to Halliday's unmarked (non-contrastive) focus with broad vs narrow domain respectively. Finally, Dik's (1997: 331–335) classification of focus types also takes over the general distinction between non-contrastive and contrastive focus, reminiscent of Halliday's original account. Dik (1997: *ib.*), however, further elaborates the contrastive focus type into further subtypes (e.g. parallel focus, counter-presuppositional focus, which he subdivides into rejecting, replacing, expanding, restricting, and selecting focus). These different subtypes of contrastive focus may be useful to describe, in specific contexts of use, what a speaker tries to achieve when s/he expresses a contrast. But these subtypes merely present different strategies inferrable from a context; they are not coded prosodically. For that reason, they will not be included as a further subclassification of the prosodically coded information structure described and used in this study.

(6) ^but !\/I'm pre_pared to# and as ^long as *!th\/ey're pre_pared to# (LLC)

(7) ^never !thought of th\/at# - ^never !thought of th/at# (LLC)

The information focus can but need not be limited to the one syllable that carries the tonic accent. Rather, the focus has scope over a certain 'domain', which normally extends over the "highest rank constituent" of which the last accented syllable is assigned the tonic accent (Halliday 1967b: 207). In the unmarked option, there may be indeterminacy to the focus domain, as in *I'm getting too old to worry about it* in (5), where the boundary of the focus domain may be interpreted in terms of what "was mentioned in the preceding clause" (Halliday 1994: 297). This means that unmarked information structure can have either 'broad focus', taking the entire information unit in its scope, or it can have 'narrow' but non-contrastive focus on part of the information unit (Wells 2006: 116). In the marked option, by contrast, the domain is restricted to the specific constituent of the information unit corresponding to the implied WH-interrogative, and involves contrast with "some predicted or stated alternative" (Halliday 1967b: 208), e.g. *I* and *they* in (6) and twice *that* in (7). Marked focus is, therefore, always 'narrow' and contrastive.

Both an utterance's tonality (i.e. the segmentation into TUs) and its tonicity (i.e. the placement of the tonic within a TU) are interlinked in a speaker's strategy to present different pieces of information as noteworthy or not. For instance, the more information an utterance adds to the discourse, the more TUs the utterance will likely be segmented into and, hence, the more tonic accents the clause will have. This is illustrated in (8) where one sentence is split up into three TUs, whereby tonic prominence is given to *s\eeing*, *v/\iva* and *W/\ednesday*.

(8) ^you'll be s\eeing him# at ^[dhi] at ^[dhi] . v/\iva# . ^on W/\ednesday# (LLC)

Finally, the choice of TONE – that is, the direction of the major pitch movement within the TU – also plays a role in the presentation of information. Tone typically serves an illocutionary function and/or an attitudinal one (e.g. Halliday 1967c: 40–47; Tench 1996: 16–20). For instance, while declaratives typically end in a fall, polar interrogatives are more likely to be uttered with a final rising tone (Halliday 1967c: 26). This illocutionary function of tone is related to its attitudinal function: falls can also be used, for instance, to convey speaker certainty, while rises express speaker uncertainty or deference to the hearer (Tench 1996: 98). Thus, the choice of tone can have different 'values' (Halliday 1967c: 41), or signal different 'information statuses' (Tench 1996: 80), in interaction with different speech functions (e.g. statements, questions, commands). The English tone system distinguishes between three 'simple' tones, *viz.* falls '\', rises '/' and level

'-' tones. Two additional 'complex' tones can be derived from the former two, namely fall-rise '\/' and rise-fall '/\'.

(i)  fall: \, e.g. *the only shift of contact is th\ere#*
(ii) rise: /, e.g. *is this a spare p/aper#*
(iii) level or low rise: - or = , e.g. *oh to hell with th=is#*
(iv) fall-rise: \/, e.g. *I think he's a s\/erious candidate#*
(v)  rise-fall: /\, e.g. *well he's such a d/\ynamo#*

The first two tones – namely falls and rises, illustrated in (9) and (10) respectively – have often been characterised as having contrasting values, e.g. the expression of certainty vs uncertainty (Halliday 1970c: 23), but also completeness vs incompleteness (or continuation) (Tench 1988: 80); definiteness or dominance vs non-commitment or deference (Tench 1996; Cruttenden 1997: 177); telling vs not telling (Brazil 1997; Gussenhoven 2004; O'Grady 2010), etc.

(9)  well I'm quite ^c\ertain that they _do# (LLC)

(10) it`s ^for five p/ounds# . ^r/ight# (LLC)

Furthermore, rise-falls can express finality, definiteness, etc., but also convey additional 'impressed' or 'challenging' meanings (Cruttenden 1997: 92–93), as in (11).

(11) ^that's for the :b/\ank# ^not the tr/\ain# (LLC)

Fall-rises are considered by some as variants of rising tones (e.g. Brazil 1997; Cruttenden 1997), but by others as independent tones which signal a variety of meanings. Fall-rises have been said (i) to give 'major prominence' to a piece of information (Sharp 1953), (ii) to connect a discourse entity to others (Hirschberg & Ward 1985: 449), which Ladd (1980: 153) describes as 'focus within a set', (iii) to signal a reservation (Halliday 1967c; Halliday & Greaves 2008) or (iv) to present information as "the speaker's personal opinion offered for consideration" (Tench 1988: 172), as illustrated in the sequence of fall-rises in (12).

(12) ^one of the :things that oc:curs to :m\/e# ^is _[dhi:] [@:m] !student :n\/urses# at"^tending ":family "!s\/essions# ^in [dhi] - !hospital that they're _actually !tr\/aining 'in# (LLC)

The level tone, finally, can present a particular piece of information as "being dependent on something else – provisional, tentative, afterthought and so on"

(Halliday 1994: 303), or obvious or to indicate that the speaker is not engaging communicatively (e.g. Brazil 1997; Tench 2003), e.g. (13).

(13)   ^y=es# of ^c=ourse# (LLC)

Despite the importance that many studies of copular clauses attribute to information structure and specifically to focus marking (e.g. Akmajian 1970; Declerck 1988; Lambrecht 1994, 2001; Mikkelsen 2005; Patten 2012, 2016), there has been little study of the actually coded information structure in spoken data. The idea – put forward by Chomsky (1969: 26) and Akmajian (1979: 190) – that what they call the 'semantically focal' constituent is also intonationally the focus is picked up in Declerck's (1988: 12–13) analysis of specificational clauses. He claims that, in a sentence like *the bank robber is John Thomas*, "*John Thomas* is the focus and *the bank robber* is the presupposition", from which "it follows that the tonic accent of the sentence falls on *John Thomas*" (Declerck 1988: 12). In contrast with specificational clauses, Declerck (1988) does not discuss information structure as an essential characteristic of predicative clauses. He merely mentions that, in predicative clauses, the subject tends to express old information and the predicative complement new information (*ib.*: 61), but he does not link this to a distinction between presupposition and focus, as he does for specificational clauses. Declerck (1988: 69) further theorises that predicative clauses are expected to normally have a 'neutral' intonation pattern (i.e. with the nuclear accent falling on the last lexical item). They can thus be distinguished from specificational clauses, which Declerck (1988: *ib.*) assumes to have contrastive accent on the value constituent.

Similarly, Patten (2012: 35, 2016: 81) argues that the function of specification is signalled by marking the value as focus. On her 'inverse' account, however, focus marking can be achieved in two ways, depending on the syntactic structure of the clause. When the value is complement (yielding what Patten [2012, 2016] calls an 'inversion construction'), the "focus is consistently placed on the post-copular element [*viz.* the value]" (Patten 2016: 81). In other words, the construal of the value as complement, e.g. *Diane and Carla* in (14) (cited also in Chapters 1 and 3), results in a syntactic structure with a "fixed information structure" (*ib.*).[83]

---

[83] Mikkelsen (2005: 134) makes a similar argument for a 'fixed' specificational information structure. On her account, however, 'focus' is contrasted with 'topic', which Mikkelsen (2005) links to discourse-familiarity of information (following Vallduví [1992: 21]). In addition, since Mikkelsen (2005) associates the topic with the grammatical subject of the clause, the assumption of a 'fixed' information structure of specificational clauses means that they are also fixed syntactically. Therefore, unlike Patten (2012, 2016), Mikkelsen (2005) does not acknowledge the possibility that specificational clauses allow for the variable to be the complement. Therefore, ultimately, Mikkelsen's (2005) only diagnostic for focus marking is syntactic structure, not intonation.

(14) The waitresses were Diane and Carla. (Patten 2016: 81)

When the value is subject, however, the syntactic structure of the clause is ambiguous between a predicative and a specificational interpretation. This ambiguity can be resolved, Patten (2016: 81) claims, via intonation: the specificational reading is brought about by placing the tonic accent on the subject, as illustrated by the small caps in (15). Hence, in such cases, it is not the syntactic function of the value but its prosodic realisation that is deemed responsible for marking the value as focal.

(15) DIANE and CARLA were the waitresses. (Patten 2016: 80, original caps)

Halliday (1967b: 226), by contrast, does not interpret information structure as a defining criterion of the specificational clause type. Halliday (1967b: 226) does expect the value to normally be the focus, marked in bold, in such cases, as in (16). In examples with an intonation as in (16), we find what Halliday views as the marked information structure, in which a contrastive narrow focus, corresponding to the implied WH-interrogative, relates to presupposed information. However, he explicitly points out that specificational clauses may be structured into two or more information units (Halliday 1967b: 226). Both the variable and the value are then marked as focus in (17a,b) – so that there is no one-to-one correspondence between the semantic roles of variable and value and the information-structural distinction between non-focal and focal information.

(16) 'which is the leader?', // the leader is **John** //, // **John** is the leader // (Halliday 1967b: 226)

(17) a. // the one who painted the **shed** last week // was **John** // (Halliday 1967b: 226)
b. // **John** // was the one who painted the **shed** last week // (*ib.*)

Moreover, even when the variable and value are uttered within one and the same TU, it is not necessarily the value that is assigned the tonic accent. Halliday (1967b: 226) notes one common exception to this tendency. When the value is realised as a non-contrastive anaphoric demonstrative, the focus is not expected to fall on the value but, instead, on the last lexical item in the TU, e.g. *meant* in (18).

(18) [what you've just said] // that's what I **meant** // (*ib.*)

In Halliday's (1967b) analysis, therefore, focus placement is not a recognition criterion of specificational clauses. Not only is the value not necessarily the focus of the clause, e.g. (18), in such examples the variable is also not coded as presupposed. Halliday (1967b, 1985, 1994) has always stressed that the participant roles in the specificational process and the information structural functions of presupposition and focus are "independently variable" (Halliday 1967b: 226).

In this chapter, I follow Halliday (1967b) in distinguishing between the participant roles in the specificational process – as coded by the lexicogrammar – and the information structural marking of focus – as coded by the intonation pattern of the clause. I adhere, in other words, to the view that information structure is coded prosodically and that two kinds of information structure can be distinguished, i.e. unmarked information structure with non-contrastive focus and marked information structure with focus contrasting with the presupposed remainder of the information unit. The distinction between specification as a lexicogrammatically coded relation and information structure as prosodically coded challenges the oft-made assumption that the variable and the value contrast, by definition, as being respectively presupposed and focal. The challenge to this assumption raises the question how the two distinctions do relate to each other. To answer this question, I examined attested spoken data from the London-Lund Corpus of Spoken English (LLC). The design and results of this study will be set out in Section 6.2. These results will be analysed in more detail in Section 6.3, which homes in on the question whether focus marking forms a useful empirical basis for distinguishing between predicative and specificational clauses and, if so, in what way. The chapter will end with a conclusion in Section 6.4.

## 6.2 A usage-based study of focus marking

### 6.2.1 Data collection and data analysis

This study aims to provide a descriptive qualitative analysis of the prosodically coded information structure of predicative and specificational clauses, in which the latter are looked at both in their non-reversed and reversed order. The data were collected from the London-Lund Corpus of Spoken English (henceforth, LLC), the prosodic annotation of which was based on Crystal (1969) (see Chapter 2). The transcriptions in LLC are divided into TUs, i.e. the domain of the pitch movement, the boundaries of which are indicated by the symbol #, as in (19).

(19)  well my !v\ague am'bition# is to ^get ^y\es# is to ^get an ad:ministrative 'post h\ere# (LLC)

In addition, the LLC also marks the location of the tonic accent by placing the symbol for tone on the tonic syllable, e.g. *v\ague* in (19). The symbol for tone indicates the direction of the pitch movement (*viz*. fall \, rise /, level or low rise – or =, fall-rise \/, and rise-fall /\). Other symbols include the onset (^) of the TU (i.e. the first prominent syllable of the TU), short and long pauses (symbolised respectively as . and -), two types of stress (*viz*. normal stress ' and heavy stress "), and, finally, boosters ! (i.e. syllables pronounced with a higher pitch than the preceding pitch prominent syllable).

In addition to the three simple and the two complex tones, the LLC also recognises 'compound' tones, which are essentially "simple tones and complex tones in various combinations (e.g. fall+rise, rise-fall+rise)" (Halliday & Greaves 2008). Contrary to complex tones, compound tones are considered binuclear, having a sequence of two accents – a primary accent followed by a secondary one – within one TU.

(vi)   fall+rise, e.g. *that's a good p\oint of yours R/eith#*

The theoretical grounds for acknowledging compound tones are, however, shaky. Halliday's (1970c: 12) initial argument was based on the notion of 'fusion', or the idea that the two tones have become fused in a single tone group, with no possibility of introducing additional pre-tonic prominence before the second tonic in the compound. The compound tone, therefore, has two tonic accents, marking "two places where the speaker has decided to focus the information in the information unit, instead of one" (Halliday 1970c: 43). The two tonic accents are not equal in value: the first, e.g. on *p\oint*, signals 'major' information; the second, e.g. on *R/eith*, expresses 'minor' information that is "subsidiary" to the "principal new information" of the first tonic (*ib*.). However, Watt (1992: 153) – whose study supplements auditory, impressionistic analyses of tonicity with an instrumental analysis of acoustic factors like fundamental frequency (F0) – found little evidence for the existence of compound tones. In addition, TU boundaries are sometimes difficult to identify (Barth-Weingarten 2016), particularly when one has to decide whether a sequence of two tonic elements forms one compound tone – with no boundary between them – or a sequence of two separate TUs. In addition, Tench (1990: 168–170) argues that the compound tones 'fall + rise' or 'rise-fall + rise' do, in fact, allow, in certain cases, for a pre-tonic segment to be inserted between the first and the second tonic. He illustrates this by citing examples from Halliday (1970c) in which a sequence of two tones was interpreted as forming a compound despite the presence of pre-tonic prominence between the two tonics. Tench (1990: *ib*.), therefore, rejects the necessity of interpreting 'fall + rise' and 'rise-fall + rise' as compound tones. Furthermore, Tench (1990: *ib*., 1996: 81) and O'Grady (2017: 151–152) also object to the idea that one TU can be interpreted as having one 'primary' (or major) and one 'secondary' (or minor) point of information. The analysis of one TU having two foci, albeit of different status, compromises the very idea that a TU marks one unit of information (O'Grady 2017: 152). A similar argument is made by Cruttenden (1986: 29–30, 94; 1997: 37), who notes that the meaning of the so-called compound tone, *viz.* that the second tonic signals information that is dependent on the first tonic, can also be expressed as a sequence of two TUs, in which the second tone (i.e. the rise) signals 'additional' information that modifies what comes before. Hence, he considers it more sensible to regard so-called compound tones as sequences of two independent TUs. For the reasons presented here, I follow Tench (1990), Cruttenden (1997) and O'Grady (2017) in analysing compound tones as a sequence of two separate TUs, in which each TU is interpreted as a single unit of information, rather than a compound representing "one and a half information units" (Halliday 1967c: 37). Hence, the compound tones annotated in the LLC, e.g. (vi), were adapted into sequences of two separate TUs, as in (vi').

(vi')   that's a good p\oint of yours# R/eith#

The dataset I focus on for this study comprises 545 predicative and 455 specificational examples (cf. Table 17), manually collected from the LLC according to the recognition criteria set out in Chapter 2. Of the specificational examples, 393 have the variable as subject (of which 81 were indefinite NPs and 312 definite NPs); 62 specificational examples have variable complements (of which 20 are an indefinite NP and 42 a definite one). The initial data collection searched for the examples in the prosodically annotated transcriptions, for which I subsequently extracted the sound files from the original recordings in Praat.

**Table 17:** The distribution of copular clause types in the dataset.

| | PREDICATIVE CLAUSES 545 | | |
|---|---|---|---|
| | SPECIFICATIONAL CLAUSES 455 | | |
| non-reversed 393 | | reversed 62 | |
| *indefinite variable* 81 | *definite variable* 312 | *indefinite variable* 20 | *definite variable* 42 |

To examine the prosodic realisation of information focus, a number of factors were taken into consideration. First, I determined the clauses' tonality, that is, the number of TUs each clause was segmented in. If the clause was packed into one TU, I examined whether the tonic accent fell on (part of) the semantically more specific NP (*viz.* the specificational value or the describee), on the semantically more general NP (*viz.* the variable or the description), or, marginally, on (part of) the VP (*viz.* copula *be* or, possibly, an auxiliary verb).

For clauses spoken on more than one TU, I counted the number of TUs the clause, and its two nominal elements, were segmented into, and I registered on which tone(s) (e.g. falls, rises) each nominal element was uttered. With respect to the marking of focus in clauses of multiple TUs, I considered two options. First, it often occurred that the two NPs – variable and value or describee and describee – were each segmented in their own separate (sequences of) TUs, e.g. (20). If that was the case, the two NPs did not contrast by one being focal and the other non-focal.

(20)  'one of the !best ways of :d\/oing 'that# will ^be to have a !strong 'Scottish de'velopment :\/agency# . ^which would be !\/answerable# to the ^Scottish As!!s\embly# (LLC)

The second option was that only one of the two NPs spread over multiple TUs while the other NP was packed together with part of the other NP. This is illustrated in (21), in which the describee *she* is non-focal, while the description carries two foci, as marked by the placement of the tonic accents on \*oldest* and *l*\*ist*.

(21)  ^she's . 'one of the :\oldest 'persons# ^on the !l\ist# (LLC)

In cases like (21), the copular clause was analysed as exhibiting a clause-level background-focus contrast between its two NPs, even though – technically – the NP 'in focus' actually carried multiple foci, e.g. *one of the* \*oldest persons# on the l*\*ist#*.

In addition to the segmentation in TUs and the placement of the tonic accent (marked by the main pitch change), two additional factors of prosodic prominence – *viz.* relative pitch height and intensity – were considered, following, for instance, Ladd (2008). The rationale for including relative pitch height and relative intensity is as follows. First, if one part of an utterance is uttered with a considerably higher pitch than the other parts in the surrounding context, then that part has prosodic prominence and, hence, attracts special attention. The difference between the pitch height with which two elements are uttered is technically referred to as "pitch excursion". How great a pitch excursion should be to count as significant is a complex question. Grabe, Kochanski & Coleman (2007: 295) point out that a difference of 0.2 normalised F0 units – i.e. 0.2 times a speaker's mean fundamental frequency (F0) – is substantially larger than the psychophysical just-noticeable-difference (i.e. the amount that the pitch should be changed for a difference to be noticeable). This measure was, therefore, taken as the threshold for prosodically prominent pitch excursions. Mean F0 was computed automatically with Praat. The differences in pitch between the two NPs were then calculated by measuring – with Praat – the highest pitch value for each NP. If the difference between the two values was larger than 0.2 times the mean F0, the NP with the highest pitch value was coded as having prosodic prominence over the other. To illustrate, in Figure 17, the highest pitch value on the variable 'one of the 'troubles you 'run up ag\/ainst is on ag\/ainst (200 Hz), while the highest point for the value is on !t\ell (237 Hz): since the speaker's mean F0 was 166 Hz, the threshold for a prominent pitch excursion was 33 Hz. Therefore, the difference between the highest pitch values for the two NPs in the specificational clauses (viz. 237 Hz − 200 Hz = 37 Hz) was assessed as substantial enough (because 37 Hz > 33 Hz). Hence, for the example in Figure 17, the value was coded as having prosodic prominence over the variable for the factor 'pitch height'.

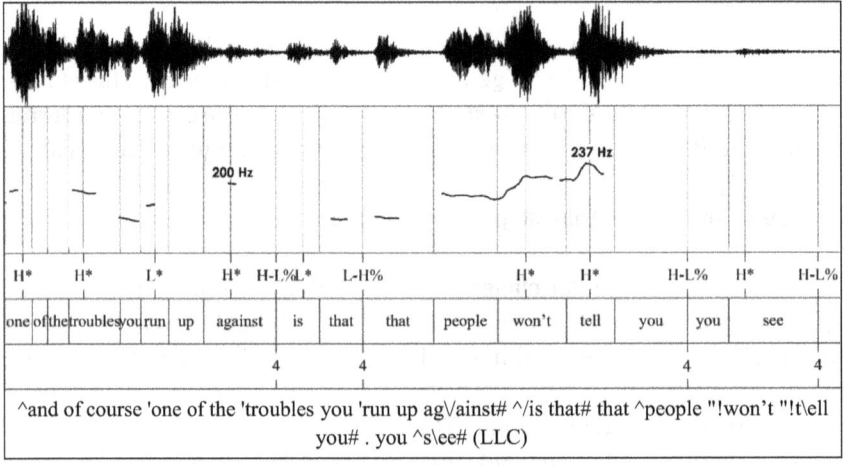

**Figure 17:** Praat picture indicating the highest pitch values for the variable and the value in the given specificational clause.

Secondly, for the factor 'intensity' (measured in decibel dB), I followed a similar procedure. Here too, I measured, for each NP in the copular clause, the highest intensity level in Praat. Since differences in intensity of 3 dB are only just perceptible and differences of 5 dB are generally clearly noticeable (Hansen 2001: 41), the threshold for a substantial difference in intensity between the NPs was taken at 5 dB. The Praat picture in Figure 18 visualises the intensity curve for the specificational example ^one of th/ese# . is a ^w\/eight# . ^bouncing 'up and 'down

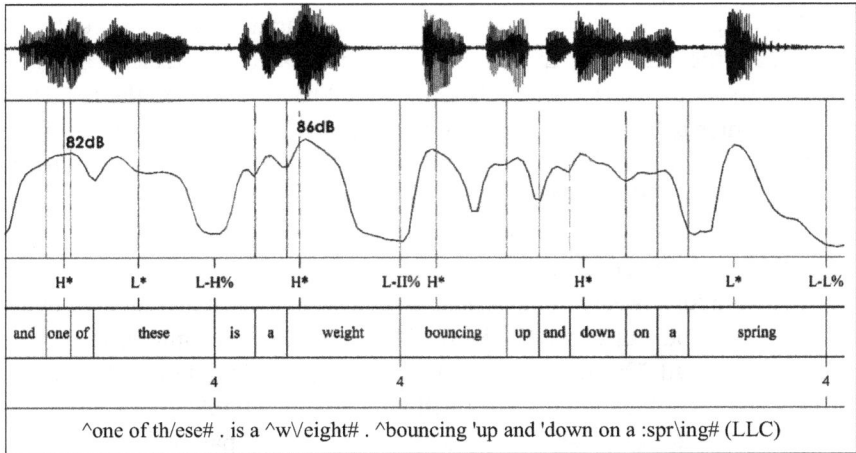

**Figure 18:** Praat picture indicating the values for the highest intensity peaks for both NPs in the given specificational clause.

*on a :spr\ing#*. The highest intensity levels for the variable (82 dB) and the value (86 dB) do not, however, differ substantially to result in a clearly noticeable difference in intensity (since 86 dB – 82 dB = 4 dB < 5 dB). Hence, for the example in Figure 18, the difference in intensity was coded as insignificant and as not lending prominence to one NP over the other.

As shown in Figures 17 and 18, the Praat pictures for pitch and intensity include – below the pitch and/or intensity curves – an annotation of so-called 'tonal events' in the ToBI transcription system (i.e. Tones and Breaks Indicates) (Pierrehumbert & Hirschberg 1990; Silverman et al. 1992; Beckman & Ayers Elam 1993). I provided these annotations based on the acoustic evidence from Praat. In the ToBI model, prosodic transcriptions include – below the pitch and intensity curves – (i) a tones tier (with the indication of H(igh) and L(ow) tonal events), (ii) a words tier, in which the speech chain is cut up into different words, (iii) a break-index tier, which shows the strength of the juncture (from 0 to 4), and (iv) a 'miscellaneous' tier, which I used to provide the prosodic annotation from LLC. The tones tier presents an analysis of the utterance in terms of PITCH ACCENTS (i.e. highs H* and lows L*, regardless of whether they are tonic in the British tradition or not), BOUNDARY TONES H% and L%, and PHRASE ACCENTS H- and L-, which are between pitch and boundary accents. The latter two roughly indicate the direction of pitch in a tone group, the boundary of which is indicated by a 'break'. The strength of the break is indicated by a number from 0 (i.e. the absence of a break, e.g. between *I* and *'m* in *I'm*), 1 (i.e. a word break), 2 (i.e. perceived juncture without pause), 3 (i.e. intermediate break, possibly with pause), to 4 (full intonation phrase, roughly corresponding to the boundary of a TU in the British tradition). For the analysis in this chapter, I only indicated the breaks of strength 4, marking the boundaries of the TUs as indicated in the LLC, and the breaks of strength 3, which are associated with a phrasal accent H- or L- and, hence, correlate with changes in the pitch contour. Since breaks of 0, 1 and 2 are not directly relevant to the analysis of information structure, I did not include them in the transcription to reduce the amount of information in the Praat pictures.

Finally, non-reversed specificational clauses in which both NPs in the copular clause carried a tonic accent and, hence, were segmented in separate TUs. I analysed on which tone – or which final tone, in case of multiple tonic accents – the variable was uttered. The aim was to examine the inter-TU relations signalled by tone, focussing specifically on the transition from the variable to the value. For the analysis, I looked at indefinite and definite variables separately.

## 6.2.2 Results

The prosody of copular clauses exhibits important cross-constructional differences, not just between predicative and specificational clauses, but among different specificational subtypes as well. In this section, I will first examine the tonality, or segmentation into TUs, that is typical of each copular type (Section 6.2.2.1), to which I will then relate the question of tonicity, i.e. the placement of the tonic accent in a TU (Section 6.2.2.2). The likelihood that the copular clause is segmented into multiple TUs will be shown to differ between predicative and specificational clauses. The consequent possibility of one clause having multiple foci challenges the assumption that the information structure of copular clauses neatly distinguishes specificational clauses – with a 'fixed' focus on the value – from predicative ones – with a 'free' focus on either NP (e.g. Declerck 1988; Valldují 1990; Mikkelsen 2005; Patten 2012, 2016). If such a hypothesis proves untenable in the light of the evidence from focus marking (by the tonic), can we observe other ways in which the specificational value is informationally foregrounded vis-à-vis the backgrounded variable? This will be investigated, in Section 6.2.2.3, by examining differences in pitch height and intensity levels as other (potential) factors of prosodic prominence (e.g. Ladd 1978: 213; Gussenhoven 2004; Kochanski et al. 2005). Finally, in Section 6.2.2.4, I will consider the use of different tones, such as falls and rises, by which the speaker assesses the textual relations between successive information units (e.g. (in)completeness) as well as different speaker attitudes towards the information expressed within each unit (e.g. (un)certainty).

### 6.2.2.1 Tonality, or the segmentation in TUs

Firstly, if we consider only predicative clauses – in which the more specific NP, *viz.* the describee, is subject – and non-reversed specificational clauses – in which the subject is the more general variable – the two clause types are found to differ significantly in their segmentation into TUs ($\chi^2(1)$ = 317.69, $p$ < 0.001) (cf. Table 18).

**Table 18:** The segmentation in TUs of predicative and (non)reversed specificational clauses.

|  | one TU or less |  | more than one TU |  |
|---|---|---|---|---|
| **predicative clauses** | 403 | (74%) | 142 | (26%) |
| **specificational clauses** |  |  |  |  |
| *non-reversed (total)* | 58 | (15%) | 335 | (85%) |
| indefinite variable | 10 | (12%) | 71 | (88%) |
| definite variable | 47 | (15%) | 265 | (85%) |
| *reversed (total)* | 43 | (69%) | 19 | (31%) |
| indefinite variable | 13 | (65%) | 7 | (34%) |
| definite variable | 31 | (71%) | 11 | (29%) |

As shown in Table 18, predicative clauses are typically packed into one TU (i.e. in 74% of the examples), while only 15% of the non-reversed specificational ones are not segmented into multiple TUs. The two clause types are illustrated respectively in (22) and (23), each of which consists of one TU.

(22)  ^PMLA's a :l\ousy _maga_zine# (LLC)

(23)  the ^only 'subject I 'wanted to 'do was :Fr\ench# (LLC)

In addition, the preference to be segmented in multiple TUs is found in clauses with a definite variable as well as in the ones with an indefinite variable. No significant differences in tonality are observed between these two clause types ($\chi^2(1)$ = 0.19535, $p$ = 0. 6585).

Between non-reversed and reversed specificational clauses, on the other hand, tonality is a significant distinguishing factor ($\chi^2(1)$ = 89.293, $p$ < 0.001; Cramer's V: 0.451): in contrast with non-reversed clauses, reversed ones are generally much more likely to be uttered on one TU or less (i.e. in 69% of the cases), e.g. (24).

(24)  **A.**  ^had she 'any [@:m] ((oh)) ^what \is the _word# for [@:m . @] ^personal :\impact#
  **B.**  cha^r\/isma#
  **A.**  ^y\eah# - ^y\eah# . cha^risma is the :word I was l\ooking for# (LLC)

In this respect, reversed specificational clauses are more similar to predicative clauses, with which they share the fact that the more specific term (i.e. the value and describee respectively) is construed as subject. It is therefore meaningful that no significant difference in tonality is observed between predicative and reversed specificational clauses ($\chi^2(1) = 0.38933$, $p = 0.5327$). (The difference between indefinite and definite variables does not affect the tonality of reversed specificational clauses in any significant way ($\chi^2(1) = 0.17232$, $p = 0.6781$).) In sum, the segmentation into TUs shows that predicative and reversed specificational clauses have more in common than reversed and non-reversed specificationals. While the former two are typically no longer than one TU (thus having only one tonic accent), the latter typically spread over multiple TUs. Since each TU has its own focus, the possibility of one clause spreading over multiple TUs problematises the notion that each clause has one information focus and that the assignment of this focus serves as a recognition criterion of specificational clauses.

The next question to consider is which part of the sentence (i.e. describee or description, variable or value) tends to be segmented into multiple TUs in each clause type. Table 19 represents the tonality of the describee/description or variable/value in each construction, by comparing how often each NP is segmented in one TU or less and how often it is spread over more than one TU. Given that predicative and reversed specificational clauses are most likely to be uttered on one TU, it is not surprising that their two NPs tend to be shorter than one TU. More noteworthy are the findings for non-reversed specificational clauses. Firstly, the value complement is more likely than not to be segmented into multiple TUs: this is the case both when the value is specified for an indefinite variable (65% of the cases) and when it is specified for a definite variable (54%). (While the value is slightly more likely to be longer than one TU in the first case than in the second case, the difference is not significant ($\chi^2(1) = 3.232$, $p = 0.07$).) The segmentation of the variable itself, however, differs significantly depending on its (in)definiteness ($\chi^2(1) = 42.01$, $p < 0.001$; Cramer's V: 0.335). As shown in Table 19, the indefinite variable is more likely than the definite one to spread over more than one TU (namely in 46% and 13% of the cases respectively), as illustrated in (25) and (26) respectively.

(25) ^one of the pr\/oblems# ^in your m\/arriage# ^is that the 'things !y\ou have f/aith in# ^she !!d\oesn't have f/aith in# - and the ^things that !sh\e has 'faith in# ^y\ou don't have *'faith in# (LLC)

(26) ^the \only# gl\immer# of - of ^hope on the ho:r\izon# - was the ^invitation to !Y\ork# for ^which I did not ap!pl\y# . I was ^just in!v\ited# (LLC)

The significant differences in segmentation between the two variables can be interpreted against the observations of the discourse-embedding of the variable in Chapter 7: indefinite variables are typically less recoverable than definite ones (in terms of actual discourse-familiarity as defined by Kaltenböck [2005]). Their typical discourse-familiarity, I will argue in Section 6.3, influences the segmentation of the two variables: the typically less familiar indefinite variable, in that sense, is marked as consisting of multiple units of information (each with its own focus) and, hence, of multiple units that the speaker wants the hearer to attend to in 'setting up' the variable. The definite variable being typically more familiar to the discourse is segmented in fewer information units, which suggests that it adds less newsworthy information to the discourse. This suggests that the indefinite variable is presented as requiring more processing effort than the definite variable.

**Table 19:** The tonality of the individual elements in predicative and specificational clauses.

| | described subject | | predicate nominative | |
|---|---|---|---|---|
| **predication** | | | | |
| | 537 (99%) | 8 (1%) | 442 (81%) | 103 (19%) |
| **non-reversed specification** | variable subject | | value complement | |
| indefinite variable | | | | |
| | 44 (54%) | 37 (46%) | 28 (36%) | 53 (64%) |
| definite variable | | | | |
| | 272 (87%) | 40 (13%) | 145 (46%) | 167 (54%) |
| **reversed specification** | variable complement | | value subject | |
| indefinite variable | | | | |
| | 19 (95%) | 1 (5%) | 13 (65%) | 7 (35%) |
| definite variable | | | | |
| | 31 (74%) | 11 (26%) | 34 (81%) | 8 (19%) |

*legend:* ■ one TU or less    more than 1 TU

### 6.2.2.2 Tonicity, or the placement of the tonic

The tendency of non-reversed specificational clauses to be segmented into multiple TUs means that it is often impossible to identify only one information focus in the clause. Still, the question remains whether copular clauses of one TU or less exhibit the hypothesised focus marking, which is believed to distinguish between specificational clauses, with focus on the semantically more specific value, and predicative ones, with focus on the more general description. This question will be addressed in this section.

The answer to the question is nuanced, as can be seen on Table 20. In Table 20, each row gives, per clause type, the absolute and relative frequencies of the placement of the tonic – i.e. on the semantically more specific NP (viz. describee, value), the more general NP (viz. description, variable), or another clause component (e.g. copula, adverb) – in clauses of one TU (or less). In predicative clauses, firstly, the tonic accent is most likely to fall on the description (95%) – as illustrated in (27) and in (22) above – while the describee is rarely focal (1%), e.g. ^whore its\elf in (28).

(27) my pro^fessor is an :in!compre'hensible n/itwit# (LLC)

(28) A. I was ^on a 'bus 'just 'going 'down to the _British Mu!s\eum 'not so 'long a'go# - and ^there - were !two 'girls just :g\/etting 'on the 'bus# and ^flirting with the . con:d\/uctor# - and ^one of them 'said to the :\/ other# . ^you're a 'dirty !wh\/ore# and ^she said !no I /ain't# I'm a "^cl\ ean 'whore#
B. ^whore it!s\elf is a 'euphemism# (LLC)

Table 20: Tonic placement in predicative and (non-)reversed specificational clauses of 1 TU.

| predicative clauses | describee | | description | | other | |
|---|---|---|---|---|---|---|
| | 5 | (1%) | 384 | (95%) | 14 | (4%) |
| **specificational clauses** | | | | | | |
| | variable subject | | value complement | | other | |
| non-reversed (total) | 1 | (2%) | 56 | (98%) | 0 | (0%) |
| indefinite variable | 0 | (0%) | 10 | (100%) | 0 | (0%) |
| definite variable | 1 | (4%) | 46 | (96%) | 0 | (0%) |
| | value subject | | variable complement | | other | |
| reversed (total) | 2 | (5%) | 42 | (95%) | 0 | (0%) |
| indefinite variable | 0 | (0%) | 13 | (100%) | 0 | (0%) |
| definite variable | 2 | (6%) | 29 | (94%) | 0 | (0%) |

Secondly, non-reversed specificational clauses are shown to have a similarly strong preference for a specific focus assignment, viz. on the value in 98%, e.g. (29). (No significant differences[84] hold between indefinite and definite variable subjects, both of which are illustrated in [29].)

---

[84] The fact that all but one example focus on the value means that a chi-square test is not possible, since the numbers of 'focus on the variable' and 'focus on some other clause component' are too low for statistical reliability.

(29) ^we have at the :m\/oment# ^and !have 'had 'for . for m\onths# !p\/ast# [@_m] a ^serious - cl\ash# be^tween !two points of 'view in 'in the :m\anagement# ^one . is – we'll !t\ell them what to d/o# and the ^other is – we'll !let them !d\o it# (LLC)

The caveat, of course, is that the data in Table 20 are only representative of the 15% of non-reversed specificational clauses that are not longer than one TU, whereas they account for 74% of the predicative clauses. The results, therefore, present a good overview of the typical information structure of predicative clauses, but it presents only a small piece of the puzzle for non-reversed specificational clauses.

Moreover, in reversed specificational clauses of one TU or less, 95% of the cases have non-focal values and focal variables, e.g. \one of them in (30).

(30) there are ^certain+ 'areas of the s/yllabus# where the ^students [@:m] ^which the 'students queue !\up for# - it's ^very !p\opular# [@:m] . the Ro^mantics is 'obviously \one of them# (LLC)

This finding invalidates the hypothesis that specificational clauses consistently have focal values. This has two important consequences. First, it marks a contrast between non-reversed and reversed specificational clauses ($\chi^2(1)$ = 85.382, $p$ < 0.001), with an almost absolute separation between them, as shown by the extremely high effect size of the correlation (Cramer's V: 0.94). Second, the regular placement of the tonic in reversed specificationals on the variable complement raises the question if focus marking can even be considered a tendency that can help distinguish specificational clauses from predicative clauses.

The typical focus marking on the variable complement, such as on \one of them in (30), also discredits the assumption that the variable is, by definition, informationally presupposed. On Halliday's (1967b) account, information is only presented as presupposed within one TU vis-à-vis a 'marked' focus, which relates to an implied WH-interrogative. In reversed clauses, however, the variable follows the value: on the hypothesis that the clause-initial value is focal and the clause-final variable non-focal (see, for instance, Patten 2016: 80), the reversed construal would be the only context in which we would expect the variable to be prosodically coded as presupposed information (in the sense of Halliday [1967b: 207]).[85]

---

**85** On Halliday's (1967: 207) account (but see also e.g. Verstraete 2007: Chapter 3), Speakers present information as 'presupposed' through prosodic means: the 'presupposition' is the part of the marked information structure that falls outside the scope of the narrow contrastive focus. What is directly relevant, therefore, is not whether information can be 'pragmatically presupposed', in the sense of e.g. Stalnaker (1974), but that the speaker explicitly codes it as such (see also Section 6.1).

Only two examples in the entire set of specificational clauses (0.4%) actually exhibit a focus-presupposition pattern in which the variable is both non-focal and presupposed,[86] *viz.* (31) and (32).

(31) I ^don't 'think :G\illian# ^or \/Ingeborg# . ^are !\on the 'board this y/ear# - ^so - well "^G\illian# - could [k] could ^carry /on you 'see# . ^giving those !l\ectures# <u>^th\/at's the i'dea#</u> (LLC)

(32) I sup^pose it's :reasonable to ex:p\ect# ^y\/ou 'know# ^every ^every . :person :reading :\English# to have "^b\ought 'or# ^somehow to have been :given their :own 'copies of :Sh\akespeare# . ^but [@:] <u>"!th\/at isn't the 'point#</u> the ^point 'is that you've got "!m\asses# of cr\iticism# to ^r\ead# (LLC)

Both examples have demonstrative pronouns (*that*) as value. The marked tonic placement on the demonstrative makes the value contrastive (Halliday 1967b: 231–32) and presents it vis-à-vis alternative values. These alternative values can be implied (31) but also explicitly given (32). Most of the other reversed clauses are examples of Halliday's (1967b: *ib.*) prediction that anaphoric demonstrative values will not be focal when used non-contrastively, e.g. (33). Here, the non-tonic demonstrative is presented as not requiring special attention, since it is discourse-familiar and is not contrasted with implied alternatives. As such, it falls outside the domain of the focus.

(33) A. I ^wondered if the !pl=ugs# ^need 'cleaning \up# and ^new 'ones 'putting \in# per^haps you'd ch\eck those#
B. oh ^that was an!\other  thing I was  going to  do# I was ^going to !take them all \out# (LLC)

In all other cases – where the value subject was not a demonstrative pronoun, e.g. *the Romantics* in (30) above or *charisma* in (24), restated here as (34) – no focus-presupposition relations of the type predicted by Patten (2016: 80) were observed in the dataset.

(34) A. ^had she 'any [@:m] ((oh)) ^what \is the _word# for [@:m . @] ^personal :\impact#
B. cha^r\/isma#
A. ^y\eah# - ^y\eah# . <u>cha^risma is the :word I was l\ooking for#</u> (LLC)

---

[86] Patten (2016: 80) claims that this information pattern is criterial for reversed specificational clauses.

If the value was explicitly recoverable from the prior context, as is the case for *charisma* in (34), its discourse-familiarity motivates why the value is not given focus. In the case of *the Romantics* in (30), however, the value has not been explicitly mentioned in the prior context but is presented *as if* it is familiar, either because it fits in, or coheres, with the information in the prior context or because it introduces information that can be readily accepted as familiar to both speaker and hearer upon first mention. (That this is the case for *the Romantics* is illustrated, for instance, by the use of the stance marker *obviously*.) Here, the scope of the focus domain is ambiguous. Does the focus extend over the entire specificational clause to present the value as part of the non-recoverable, noteworthy information? Or does the value fall outside the focal domain and is it presented as recoverable? I will come back to this question in Section 6.3.3 and argue that the ambiguity of the value being presented as familiar or unfamiliar information may be part of the function of the reversed specificational construction.

### 6.2.2.3 Relative pitch and intensity as potential factors of prosodic prominence

In the previous section, I have shown that the assumption that the prosody of specificational clauses codes a clear binary distinction between 'presupposed' variables and 'focal' values is problematic when faced with the evidence of foci marked by tonic accents (main pitch change) in both non-reversed and reversed specificational clauses. As we saw, the default is for both value and variable to be segmented into separate tone units and, hence, for both to carry information focus. In this section, I will consider the question if there is any evidence that the focus on the value is prosodically more prominent than that on the variable. The markers of prosodic prominence that will be examined are relative, *viz.* difference in pitch height and intensity. The question I will investigate is if these factors show that specificational values are relatively more prominent than the variable and if they can thus be discerned from predicative clauses.

To ensure the feasibility of the work-intensive study for each of these two factors, I worked with a random subset of 300 examples of the large set of predicative data. The specificational data being less frequent, all the specificational examples were included in the analysis. For the two kinds of non-reversed specificational clauses, 6 examples of the ones with definite variable and 19 of the ones with definite variable were not analysable in Praat (due to simultaneous talk which makes the values for pitch and intensity unreliable, problems with the recording, etc.).

Firstly, the findings for the pitch excursion with which different elements in the clause are uttered, as determined by fundamental frequency (F0), are presented in Table 21. Here, each row presents, per clause type, the absolute and relative frequencies of three possible outcomes: (i) the first NP is uttered with a significantly higher intensity (with a difference of more than 5 dB) than the second one, (ii) the second NP is uttered with a significantly higher intensity, or (iii) no significant differences in intensity are attested between the two NPs.

**Table 21:** Pitch excursion on one of the NPs in the copular clause types.

| predicative clauses | describee | | description | | insignificant | |
|---|---|---|---|---|---|---|
| | 49 | (17%) | 100 | (33%) | 151 | (50%) |
| **specificational clauses** | | | | | | |
| | *variable subject* | | *value complement* | | *insignificant* | |
| non-reversed (total) | 190 | (52%) | 63 | (17%) | 115 | (31%) |
| indefinite variable | 43 | (57%) | 8 | (11%) | 24 | (32%) |
| definite variable | 147 | (50%) | 55 | (19%) | 91 | (31%) |
| | *value subject* | | *variable complement* | | *insignificant* | |
| reversed (total) | 19 | (31%) | 11 | (18%) | 32 | (52%) |
| indefinite variable | 7 | (35%) | 2 | (10%) | 11 | (55%) |
| definite variable | 12 | (29%) | 9 | (21%) | 21 | (50%) |

In both predicative and reversed specificational clauses, pitch height differences appear to have only minor importance for marking prominence: in roughly 50% of the cases, no significant pitch differences are attested between the two NPs in either clause type. This lack of significant pitch excursion in the two clause types is illustrated in Figure 19 – which presents the Praat picture, with pitch curve, for the predicative clause in (35) – and in Figure 20 –for the reversed specificational clause in (36).

(35) [di] he was ^only a '[ka] a :f\orest worker# (LLC)

(36) ^sort of a . a !fl\eet# I supp/ose# . would ^be a b/etter de'scription# (LLC)

In cases where significant differences are attested between predicative and reversed specificational clauses, the first were more likely to have a pitch peak on the description (33%), while the second were more likely to lend prominence to the value

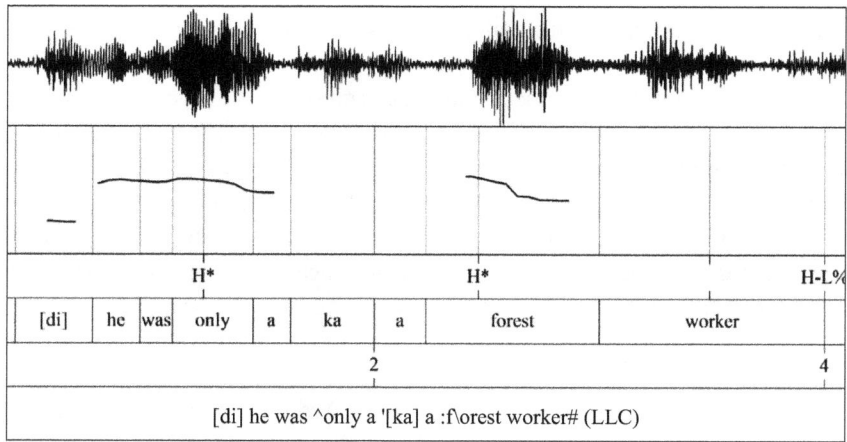

**Figure 19:** Praat picture, including the pitch curve, for the predicative clause in (35).

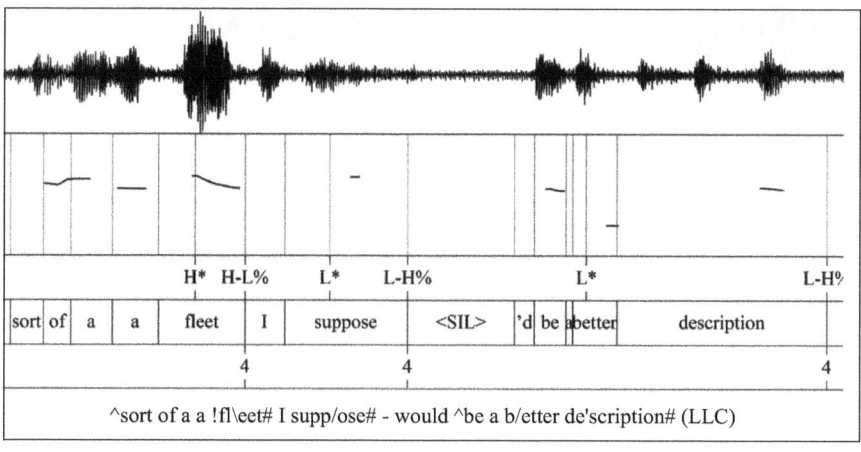

**Figure 20:** Praat picture, including pitch curve, for the reversed specificational clause in (36).

subject (31%). This makes the contrast between the two clause types significant ($\chi^2(2) = 9.6927$, $p = 0.007857$),[87] even if the effect size of the correlation is small (Cramer's V: 0.164). Therefore, pitch differences could be a minor cue for contrasting predicative and reversed specificational clauses based on which NP – the semantically more specific or general one – is most likely to be prosodically prominent.

---

[87] The chi-square test takes into account the absolute data for the predicative clauses and for the total of reversed specificational clauses (i.e. taking together the ones with indefinite and definite variable).

Furthermore, in non-reversed specificational clauses, the percentage of non-significant pitch differences between variable and value is much smaller (31%). Instead, the non-reversed specificationals are more likely to have a significantly higher pitch peak on the variable (52%) but much less so on the value (17%). The variable's prominence is illustrated by the Praat picture in Figure 21, which presents the pitch curve for the specificational clause in (37). While the tendency to give pitch prominence to the variable is slightly stronger when the variable NP is indefinite (57%) than when it is definite (50%), no significant differences are observed between the two kinds of non-reversed specificational clause ($\chi^2(2) = 2.9015$, $p = 0.2344$).[88]

(37)　^one of [dhi:] :main [@] \arguments# that ^you put f\/orward# . ^is that !\/other methods# ^are in 'fact 'less 'cruel than !h\unting# (LLC)

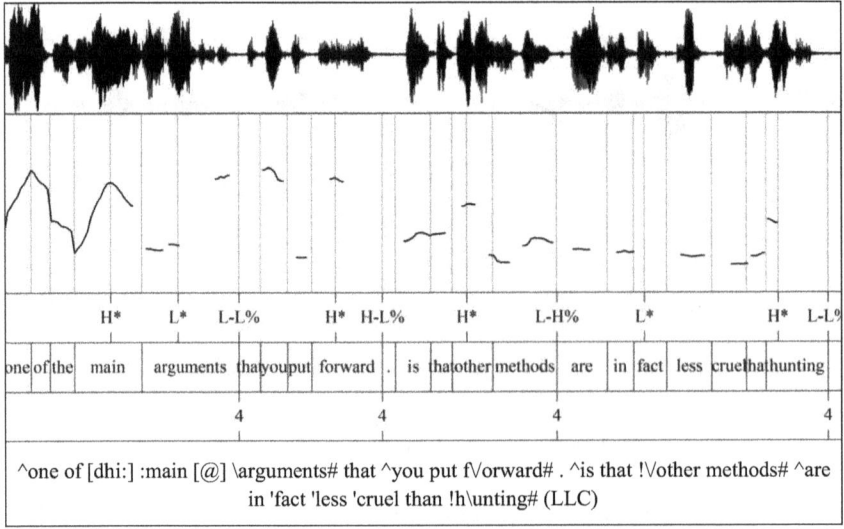

Figure 21: Praat picture, with pitch curve, for the specificational clause in (37).

Taken together, the results for pitch reveal two points. Firstly, from the pitch differences in predicative and specificational clauses, the hypothesised prominence pattern – with prominence on the description and the value respectively – cannot be confirmed. Predicative and reversed specificational clauses do have a ten-

---

[88] The chi-square test compares the absolute frequencies for non-reversed specificational clauses with indefinite vs definite variable.

dency to display such a pattern when significant pitch differences are found; in only half the data, however, the pitch differences between the two NPs are substantial enough to be noticeable. This suggests that the importance of such pitch differences is only minor in those two clause types. Secondly, in non-reversed specificational clauses, substantial differences in pitch are (more) common. Here, however, it is actually the variable, not the value, that is marked as prosodically prominent by pitch. The fact that 52% of the non-reversed clauses have 'pitch-prominent' variables suggests that pitch height is likely to have a significant communicative function, even if it is not to signal the importance of the value over the variable. I will return to this observation in Section 6.3, where I will explain that these pitch differences signal prominence relations at the discourse level rather than at the clause level.

The second potential marker of prosodic prominence that is advanced in the literature is intensity, perceived as loudness (e.g. Gussenhoven 2004; Kochanski et al. 2005). Here, however, the results are more diffuse, as can be seen in Table 22. Each row presents, per clause type, the absolute and relative frequencies of three scenarios (similar to the scenarios found for pitch differences): (i) a significantly higher intensity peak on the first NP (compared to the second NP), (ii) a significantly higher intensity peak on the second NP, and (iii) the absence of significant differences in intensity between the two NPs.

**Table 22:** Intensity as a potential cue to mark the more specific vs general 'copular' NP as prominent.

| predicative clauses | *describee* | | *description* | | *insignificant* | |
|---|---|---|---|---|---|---|
| | 71 | (24%) | 172 | (57%) | 57 | (19%) |
| **specificational clauses** | | | | | | |
| | *variable subject* | | *value complement* | | *insignificant* | |
| non-reversed (total) | 138 | (34%) | 83 | (21%) | 182 | (45%) |
| indefinite variable | 18 | (24%) | 1 | (11%) | 55 | (75%) |
| definite variable | 120 | (36%) | 82 | (25%) | 127 | (39%) |
| | *value subject* | | *variable complement* | | *insignificant* | |
| reversed (total) | 21 | (33%) | 13 | (21%) | 29 | (46%) |
| indefinite variable | 8 | (38%) | 5 | (24%) | 8 | (38%) |
| definite variable | 13 | (31%) | 8 | (19%) | 21 | (50%) |

First, a distinction can be observed between predicative clauses, on the one hand, and both types of specificational clause, on the other. In the first case, most examples were uttered with a significant difference in intensity between the two NPs. Here, the description was most likely to have a higher intensity than the describee (57%). In predicative clauses, intensity therefore aligns with the typical pattern of focus marking, i.e. main pitch change (and, to a lesser extent, pitch height) to present the description as having prominence over the describee. This is illustrated in the Praat picture for the predicative clause in (38), with an intensity peak on (part of) the description (i.e. on *:d/\ynamo*) in Figure 22.

(38)    ^well he's 'such a :d/\ynamo# (LLC)

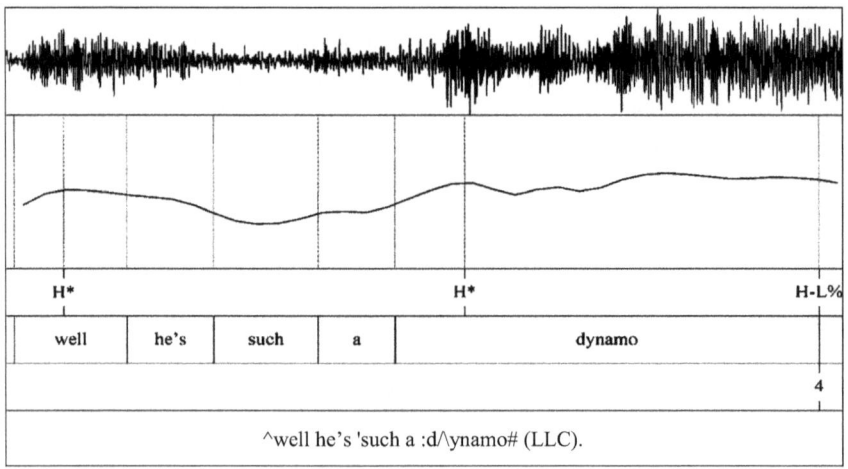

**Figure 22:** Praat picture, with intensity curve, for the predicative clause in (38).

In specificational clauses, however, intensity is far less likely to signal a substantial difference in prominence between variable and value: in 45% of the non-reversed clauses and in 46% of the reversed ones, no significant intensity differences were attested between the two NPs. In cases where a significant difference can be found, non-reversed specificationals are slightly more likely to lend prominence to the variable subject (34%) than to the value complement (21%). In reversed specificational clauses, however, it is the value subject that is more likely to be uttered with more intensity (33%), while the variable complement only has a significant pitch peak in 21% of the cases. The meaningful generalisation seems to be that specificational clauses – whether they are non-reversed or reversed – are more likely to have increased intensity on the subject rather than on the complement. This is illustrated in Figure 23, which presents the Praat picture for the non-reversed specificational clause in (39), and in Figure 24, for the reversed specificational clause in (30).

(39)    and ^one of the con:ditions of my :taking the :j\/ob with 'Frank 'Morgan# ^was that I . re:m\ained# a ^Ph'D 'student 'under 'Peter !K\ennedy# (LLC)

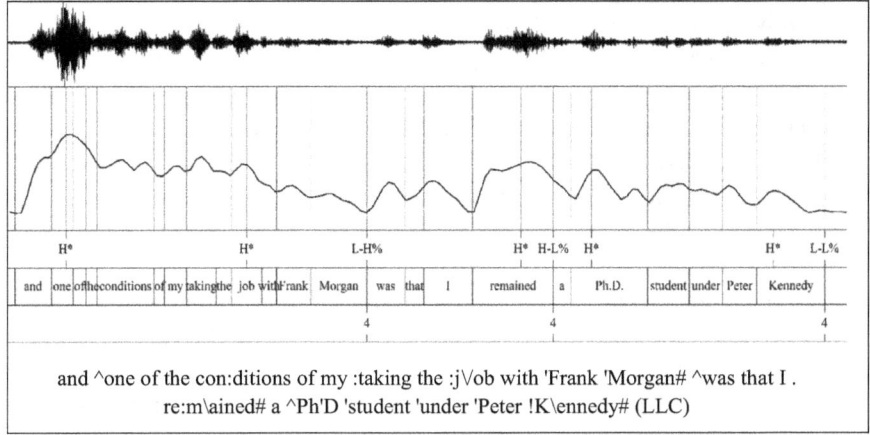

**Figure 23:** Praat picture, with intensity curve, for the specificational clause in (39).

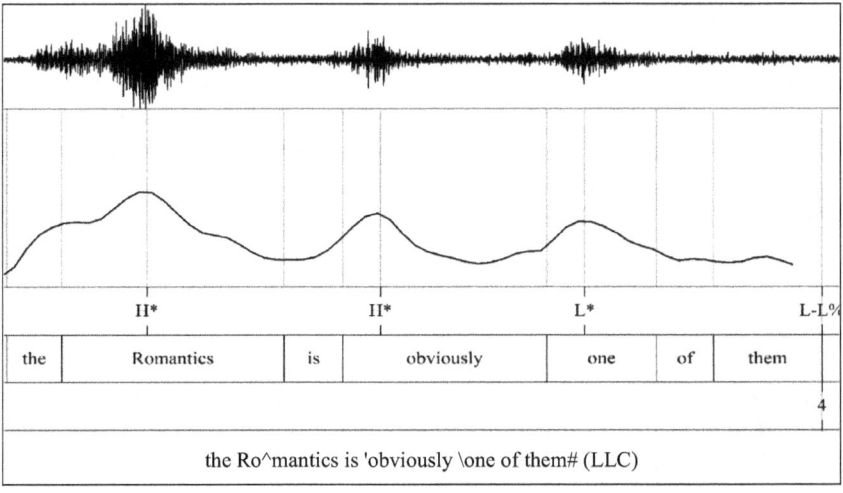

**Figure 24:** Praat picture, with intensity curve, for the reversed specificational clause in (30).

The visualisations in Figures 23 and 24 illustrate that the more important contrast is between specificational clauses, on the one hand, and predicative clauses (e.g. Figure 22), on the other hand. In non-reversed and reversed specificational clauses alike, the variable and the value typically each have their own peaks in intensity. Both the variable and the value are, hence, given prominence by means of intensity. This is the case even when there are no substantial differences in the level of intensity between these two peaks. In predicative clauses, by contrast, the describee, or subject referent, typically had no peak in intensity. Therefore, if predicative clauses are highly likely to have a substantial difference in intensity between describee and description, it is because the describee is typically not marked as prominent by intensity at all. Furthermore, both types of specificational clause were likely to have an intensity peak on the subject, regardless of whether the subject was the variable or the value. This suggests that the factor 'intensity' is not so much used to mark a difference in prominence between the participant roles (i.e. between variable and value). Rather, I propose that the typical clause-initial intensity peak in specificational examples marks the clause as standing out vis-à-vis the prior context. It appears that it is in this respect that specificational clauses can be contrasted with predicative clauses: the clause-initial intensity (and pitch) peak in specificational clauses presents the entire clause as attention-worthy in the unfolding discourse. By contrast, the absence of such clause-initial peaks in predicative clauses presents the clause – or, at least, the first part of it (*viz.* the describee) – as fitting in, or cohering, with the prior context.

Taken together, the results for pitch and intensity suggest that these factors only play a minor role in marking prominence differences between the NPs in predicative and specificational clauses. In predicative clauses, the hypothesised alignment between the semantic roles of describee and describee and the respective background-foreground contrast was borne out by all factors of prosodic prominence. For specificational clauses, however, neither the tonic accent nor relative pitch and intensity differences unambiguously confirmed the hypothesis that the value is necessarily more prominent than the variable. This led to the conclusion that the potential function of pitch and intensity is not so much to mark prominence contrasts between the variable and the value; instead, the two factors appear to be used to signal the prominence of the specificational clause as a whole in relation to the prior discourse context. Moreover, contrary to the assumption that specificational variables are informationally presupposed, they were found to be explicitly presented as prominent in most cases: the evidence from tonality (i.e. segmentation into TUs), tonic placement, pitch excursion and relative intensity, therefore, seems to converge in marking the variable as particularly noteworthy. In Section 6.3, I will elaborate on this observation, arguing that the variable typically cannot be considered presupposed but that it is set up as information that requires special attention within the unfolding discourse.

### 6.2.2.4 Tone as a factor in signalling inter-TU relations

The results so far exposed serious issues with the assumption that specificational clauses can readily be contrasted with predicative clauses in terms of a fixed background-foreground pattern in which the value consistently has more prosodic prominence than the variable. Especially for copular clauses consisting of multiple TUs, the hypothesised patterns of information structure have proven untenable. In such cases, the question remains how the separate TUs relate to each other and if an intersegmental prosody can be found that ties together the sequence of TUs as one composite specificational intonation structure. The choice of tone has been advanced – in non-copular clauses – as one potential factor in tying consecutive TUs together (e.g. Tench 1996): for instance, while falling tones are often interpreted as signalling completeness, rising tones can be used to indicate that the information in a TU will be elaborated on in the following units (i.e. a so-called 'continuation rise'). The function of tone is, in that case, interpreted as not purely attitudinal (i.e. as marking the speaker's attitude towards the information being conveyed), but it includes signalling inter-TU relations: Tench (1996: 80), for instance, describes this particular function of tone in terms of their potential to 'manage' the discourse by organising consecutive TUs into a coherent stretch of discourse. In this section, I will home in specifically on non-reversed specificational clauses, which were most likely to divide into more than one TU. In non-reversed clauses, the variable precedes the value, both logically and linearly: in other words, the variable is not only logically prior to the act of specification (see Chapter 3), but, when functioning as subject, it also precedes the value temporally in spoken language production (or spatially in written text). Hence, the interest of this study is to examine the tone(s) with which the variable is uttered and to investigate how the information thereby conveyed is to be interpreted vis-à-vis the prior and the following discourse context, particularly in relation to the value.

The results for the variable's choice of tone are summarised in Table 23. The numbers presented here only take into account the data in which the variable takes up one TU or more. In other words, all the data presented in Table 23 come from specificational clauses that were segmented into more than one TU (see Table 18 above). However, not all specificational clauses of more than one TU necessarily realise the variable and the value in their own separate TUs: in 22 of the 'longer' non-reversed specificational clauses (i.e. > 1 TU), the variable was packed together with part of the value as forming one TU, while the value itself was segmented into more than one TU. This is illustrated in (40), in which the value is shown to split into two parts, one of which (i.e. *that hunting is unneces!s\/arily*) is grouped together in one TU with the variable *the first . suggestion* and the second part (i.e. *cr\uel*) is uttered on its own separate TU.

(40)  the ^first . sug'gestion 'is that 'hunting is 'unneces"!s\/arily# ^cr\uel# (LLC)

In the 22 cases that were segmented in this way, the variable did not carry a tonic accent. These cases were, therefore, not included in the data in Table 23.

**Table 23:** The (final) tone of the variable in non-reversed specificationals of more than 1 TU.

|  | falling tone | | rising tone | | |
| --- | --- | --- | --- | --- | --- |
|  | fall | rise-fall | rise | fall-rise | level(-rise) |
| indefinite variables | 18 (26%) | 0 | 21 (30%) | 27 (39%) | 4 (5%) |
| definite variables | 102 (42%) | 3 (1%) | 69 (28%) | 67 (28%) | 3 (1%) |

For the clauses in which the variable and the value were divided into separate TUs, Table 23 shows that definite and indefinite variables differ considerably in terms of the choice of tone on which they are uttered. While definite variables showed no strong preference for either falling (43%) or rising tones (57%), indefinite variables strongly favoured rising tones (74%): the two variables, hence, differ significantly when it comes to a broad distinction between falling and rising tones ($\chi^2(1) = 6.1395$, $p = 0.01$). If we make a more fine-grained distinction between the different tones, definite variables were most likely to end in a fall (42%) as on j\ob in (41); whereas indefinite variables favoured fall-rises (39%), as on j\/ob in (42), or rises (30%), e.g. on c/ountry in (43). In Section 6.3, I will interpret these different preferences for specific tones as motivated by the different epistemic speaker assessments of the variable-value relation in specificational clauses with definite and indefinite variable.

(41) their ^j\ob 'is# to . [@:] ^think the :ways of :doing the b\/est# for [e] +^each+ 'child as an :indiv\idual# (LLC)

(42) ^one of the con:ditions of my :taking the :j\/ob with 'Frank 'Morgan# ^was that I . re:m\ained# a ^Ph'D 'student 'under 'Peter !K\ennedy# (LLC)

(43) ^one of [dhi:] !major 'difficulties of this c/ountry# is the ^growing 'im!b\ alance# ^[?]of the bu!r\/eaucracy# [?] and ^st\ate interf/erence# ^whether [w] it 'be with :{\industry or with} !\anything /else# - [@] ^which we s/ee# as an acc\/eler'ating# - [@] :pr\/o'gramme# ^under !this !g\overnment# (LLC)

To sum up Section 6.2, the quantitative-qualitative analysis outlined here highlighted significant differences in the information structure of predicative, non-reversed specificational and reversed specificational clauses. The results warrant a nuanced interpretation of focal and non-focal information in predicative and specificational clauses. While predicative clauses confirm the expected information structure, specificational clauses conform much less to the hypothesised marking of information focus and other prominence relations proposed in much of the literature.

In non-reversed specificational clauses, the examples of one TU or less did in fact largely confirm the hypothesised information structure in which the value has tonic prominence and the variable does not. Those 'short' clauses (i.e. ≤ 1 TU), however, made up only 15% of the dataset of non-reversed specificational examples. In the other 85%, the segmentation in multiple TU made the focus pattern more complex: one clause contains multiple foci, so that the variable and the value cannot be contrasted based on which NP is focal and which one is not. Moreover, my data analysis showed that the value cannot be argued either to be more prosodically prominent than the value in terms of greater pitch differences or intensity. Against the expectation, it was the variable subject rather than the value complement that was more likely to be given greater relative prominence.

Reversed specificational clauses did not conform to the patterns generally predicted in the literature either. With this type, the clauses tended to be shorter – and, hence, realised in one TU – so that a background-focus contrast was, in principle, possible. However, against the claim that the specificational value is consistently focal (e.g. Declerck 1988; Heycock & Kroch 2002; Mikkelsen 2005; Patten 2012, 2016), it was predominantly the variable, not the value, that was marked as focus in reversed clauses. Not only does this raise questions about the characterisation of specificational clauses as having a 'fixed' information structure (e.g. Mikkelsen 2005), but it also problematises those accounts in which the distinction between reversed specificational clauses and predicative ones hinges on the assignment of focus (e.g. Patten 2012, 2016).

In all, the findings of the corpus studies demonstrate that there are serious issues with the existing assumptions about the information structure of copular clauses. These assumptions are, therefore, in need of revision based on an empirically founded characterisation of the information structure of specificational and predicative clauses. In Section 6.3, I will explain that the prosodic realisations of the two clause types are motivated by discursive factors rather than purely by the lexicogrammatically coded semantics of specification and predication (as was implied by the analyses in Chomsky [1969: 26] and Akmajian [1970, 1979]). While these levels interact, the semantics of the two clause types merely set preferences for typical intonation patterns. These preferences are implemented, in specific contexts of use, into more complex information structures marking not only the speaker's choices of the most noteworthy information but also discursive relations external to the information units.

## 6.3 The prosodic marking of information focus

In this section, I will argue that the results of the corpus research challenge two preconceptions commonly found in the literature. First, I will raise issues with the oversimplification of interpreting focus marking as determined by the semantic relations in the clause (contra, for instance, Chomsky 1969; Akmajian 1979) or by the pragmatic inferences thereby triggered (contra, for instance, Lambrecht 1994). Secondly, I propose that the disentangling of information structure and semantics, on the one hand, and pragmatic inferences, on the other, allows for a more accurate description of the function of focus in copular clauses. Finally, I home in on the choice of tone on which the variable is uttered in non-reversed specificational clauses. The significant differences between indefinite and definite variables, I put forward, are motivated by different epistemic assessments of the variable-value relation in the two constructions. More specifically, the non-exhaustiveness implicature triggered by the indefinite variable often correlates with a reticence, on the part of the speaker, to fully commit to the variable-value relation. This is reflected in a preference for rising tones, which bring out this tentativity.

The structure of this section is as follows. In Section 6.3.1, I home in on short clauses of one TU or less, in which we find a simple distribution of non-focal versus focal constituents. In Section 6.3.2, I turn to the more complicated longer sentences, in which one clause is not restricted to one information unit. Here, I will examine the evidence from pitch, intensity and choice of tone as potential markers of suprasegmental textual relations (i.e. relations that go beyond the TU-internal distinction between focal and non-focal information). Finally, in Section 6.3.3, I concentrate on reversed specificational clauses, where the assumption that the value is focal in clauses of one TU or less requires modification.

### 6.3.1 Focus marking in predicative and non-reversed specificational clauses of one TU or less

The information structure of copular clauses uttered on one TU is straightforward to interpret. The TU represents a single information unit (Halliday 1970c: 3). Therefore, the packing together of the describee and the description, or the variable and the value, presents the entire copular clause as one manageable piece of information (Tench 1988: 21–22). The information that the clause adds to the unfolding discourse can be processed as having one point of interest in which the message culminates: this is signalled by the placement of the tonic accent (Bolinger 1954: 152; Halliday 1967c: 13; Crystal 1969: 263). Within one TU, multiple syllables may be accented by means of (smaller) peaks in pitch or intensity reflecting the relative importance of information (marked in Pierrehumbert & Hirschberg's [1990: 286] ToBI system by highs H* and lows L*). It is, however, the tonic accent that indicates the "point" of the message, "where there is the greatest concentration of information" (Bolinger 1954: 152). In this section, I will describe, for copular clauses that are uttered on one TU or less, what part of the clause they mark as the focus or noteworthy 'point' of the message.

In predicative clauses, the focus is typically the description (i.e. in 95% of the predicative clauses of one TU or less), e.g. *such a pain in the neck* in (44) and *a tenth rate nation* in (45). The describee, by contrast, does not have tonic prominence and is presented as background information.

(44)   she ^must have been !such a 'pain in the n\eck# (LLC)

(45)   in ^ten !years' t\ime# ^England 'will be a "!t\enth 'rate 'nation# (LLC)

In (44), the describee *she* refers anaphorically to a previously mentioned instance. In (45), the describee *England* was not mentioned in the preceding text,[89] nor was it inferable from previously evoked information. It does, however, introduce an entity that can be assumed to be familiar to the hearer. Prince (1981b: 235) considers such information to be 'unused', i.e. known to the hearer but new to the discourse. She argues that 'unused' information is less recoverable than explicitly evoked information but more recoverable than information that needs to be inferred from other pieces of information. The prosodic pattern in (45) seems to support this claim: the 'unused' information *England* has secondary accentuation (since it is the onset ^ of the TU), which the previously evoked describee *she* in (44) does not have; neither of the describees, however, has tonic, or primary, accentuation so that both are presented as not particularly noteworthy.

In short non-reversed specificationals, it is almost exclusively the value on which the tonic accent falls (98%), e.g. *H\ocking* in the specificational clause with indefinite variable in (46) and *H\erman* in the one with definite variable.

(46)   ^so 'far we've :only got "!two other n/ames# ^and [@:] !one is H/ocking#
       and the ^other's !H\erman# (LLC)

---

[89] The recordings from the LLC took place in England, so in a sense the describee *England* could be taken as situationally evoked. Without prior mention of 'England' or matters of national interest, the immediate speech context of a conversation does not generally make salient the entire country where the conversation takes place. Therefore, I assume that *England* in (45) does not present evoked information, but information that needs to be explicitly introduced in order to be activated.

In (46), the variables in the two consecutive specificational clauses, viz. *one* and *the other*, are both evoked in the prior context via the mention of *two other names*. Their relative discourse-familiarity prompts the speaker to mark them as not requiring special attention. This is coded prosodically by the absence of tonic accentuation. Instead, the tonic falls on the corresponding values, which are marked as the most noteworthy point in the two clauses. Note, in addition, that the first indefinite variable *one* is realised with a pre-tonic accent (H*), which gives it pre-tonic prominence (see Figure 25): the indefinite variable in (46) is given partial prominence by a step up in pitch on *!one* (symbolised by "!"). By contrast, since the first specificational clause has revealed one of the 'two other names', the second variable *the other* is (more) predictable. The definite variable *the other* is prosodically backgrounded (e.g. by the absence of (pre-)tonic accenting and the low pitch with which it is uttered). The information expressed by *the other* is thereby presented as not noteworthy in relation to the immediately relevant context.

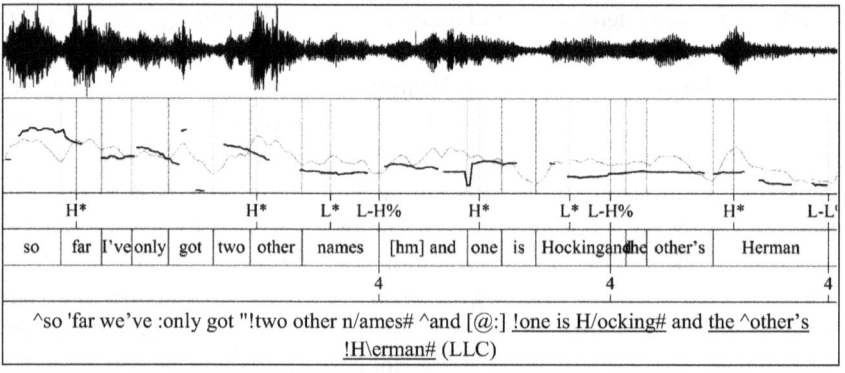

**Figure 25:** Praat picture, with pitch (bold) and intensity (light grey) curve, for the specificational clauses in (46).

Even though tonality is partially determined by physiological constraints (e.g. taking pauses to breathe), it is possible to compress relatively long strings of words into one TU. In such cases, the presentation of the sentence as one bigger unit of information becomes all the more remarkable, since the tonic accent then marks the focus vis-à-vis a larger chunk of information. For instance, while the two clauses in (46) each present relatively little information, the specificational sentence in (47) packs together the relatively long variable and the value into one TU, presenting it as one big information unit in which the variable is intonationally backgrounded in contrast with the focal value. Particular emphasis is on *aw\/ay* as marking the concentration of information in the message (as marked by the step-up in pitch "!", see also Figure 26): the choice of a fall-rise tone brings out a contrastive relation between the wish to get away and the inability to do so – as expressed in the following TU (Ladd 2008).

(47)   in the !\/end# the ^only thing you !want to do is to get a"!w\/ay from the 'people# and you +"^c\an`t# (LLC)

To compress both variable and value in one TU, the marking of the variable as non-prominent requires the former being produced with increased speed.[90] This is illustrated in Figure 26, in which the length of the waveform presents extension in time: the increased speed with which the variable is produced is evidenced by the fact that it comprises a bit more than a third of the total length of the sentence (i.e. 0.71 seconds of the total of 1.81 seconds), despite the fact that it counts more words than the value. The lack of tonic prominence on the variable is all the more remarkable because the information it expresses is not recoverable from the prior discourse context: it has neither been explicitly mentioned in the prior context, nor is it inferable from previously evoked information. Hence, the fact that the variable is discourse-new and yet not given tonic prominence is evidence that both the segmentation into TUs and focus marking in each TU reflect a genuine choice on the part of the speaker. While the (actual) discourse-familiarity of the information may, to a large extent, influence the segmentation into TUs, the correlation between the two is ultimately mediated by the speaker's deliberate choice whether or not to present information as one individual piece of information. By packing together the variable and the value in one TU, the speaker can then mark the value as focal, while presenting the variable as backgrounded (less noteworthy) information.

As Halliday (1967b: 209) points out, focus-marking in a TU can be unmarked or marked (see Section 6.1). Marked (i.e. narrow and contrastive) information focus is characterised by its relation to presupposed information. The tonic accent may be on any lexical grammatical item in the TU: in such cases, the information that follows the focus is presented as informationally presupposed and contrasted as such with the focal information. By contrast, with an unmarked (i.e. broad or narrow non-contrastive) focus the rest of the information unit in the TU is not presented as presupposed. The domain of the focus is, in this case, ambiguous, since it can take the whole information unit in its scope ('broad focus') or only a part of it ('narrow focus') (Halliday 1967b: 208). If the entire information unit

---

**90** See Crystal (1969: 152–156) for a more elaborate discussion of speed, or what he calls 'tempo'.

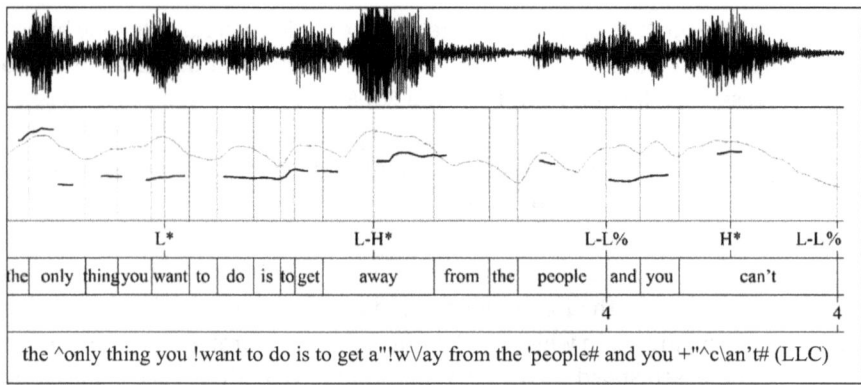

**Figure 26:** Praat picture, with pitch (bold) and intensity (grey) curves, for the non-reversed specificational clause in (47).

is presented as noteworthy information, then the whole information unit falls within the scope of the information focus (Halliday 1967b: 208).

In fact, if we look at the pitch and intensity curves for predicative and specificational clauses of one TU or less, differences do appear in the prosodic prominence of the non-tonic material in the two clause types. In predicative clauses, the describee was often a pronoun (92%), typically a personal pronoun (70%): as illustrated in the Praat picture in Figure 27 (which visualises the predicative clause in [48]), the pitch and intensity with which the describee *he* is uttered do not make it stand out from its immediately surrounding context. The absence of prosodic prominence – for tonicity, pitch and intensity combined – suggests that *he* falls outside the domain of the focus, which is, instead, restricted to the description (or, in this case, to the noun phrase *absolutely "gr\and chap*).

(48)   I'm ^told he's an absolutely "gr\and chap# (LLC)

If we compare this to the pitch and intensity curves in non-reversed specificational clauses of one TU or less, the non-tonic variable is typically still given prominence in the form of pitch and intensity peaks. This may be largely due to the fact that the variable is, by default, a full noun phrase, e.g. *the last enemy* in (49): unlike a proform such as *he*, full noun phrases are more likely to introduce new information (see Figure 28). But the Praat picture for the specificational clause with indefinite variable in (50) also shows (see Figure 29) that even when the variable consists of only one word, such as quantifier *one*, it is still likely to be given prosodic prominence by the pitch and intensity with which it is uttered.

## 6.3 The prosodic marking of information focus — 245

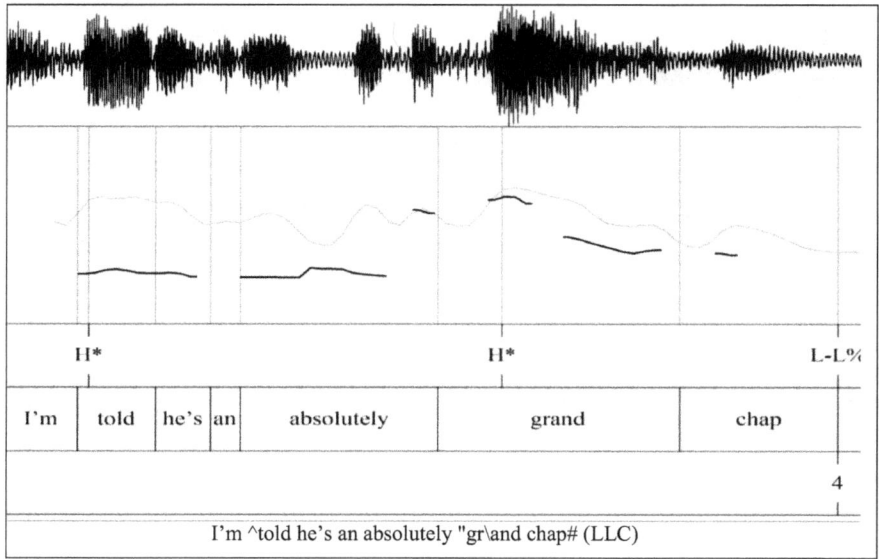

**Figure 27:** Praat picture, with pitch (in bold) and intensity (in light grey) curve, for the predicative clause in (48).

(49)  ^they say <u>the :last enemy that shall be conquered is :d\eath</u># (LLC)

(50)  ^I mean ^we [hae?] ^we have at the :m\/oment# ^and !have 'had 'for . for :m\onths# !p\/ast# [@_m] a ^serious - cl\ash# be^tween !two points of 'view in 'in ((the)) :m\anagement# <u>^one . is - we'll !t\ell them#</u> <u>what to d/o#</u> and the ^other _is - we'll !let them !d\o it# (LLC)

To sum up this section, in predicative and non-reversed specificational clauses uttered on one TU or less, the focus pattern as hypothesised in the literature can be found. Predicative clauses typically place the tonic accent on the description, while the describee is non-prominent; non-reversed specificational clauses assign the tonic to the value, while the variable is not tonically prominent. In predicative clauses, the describee often takes the form of a personal pronoun and does not stand out from its immediate context in terms of pitch or intensity: this suggests that predicative clauses often take narrow (but non-contrastive) focus having scope only over the description. In specificational clauses, by contrast, the variable NP is more likely to be given (non-tonic) prominence by pitch and intensity: this implies that specificational clauses uttered on one TU are, therefore, likely to have broad focus, with the entire clause falling within the scope of the focus.

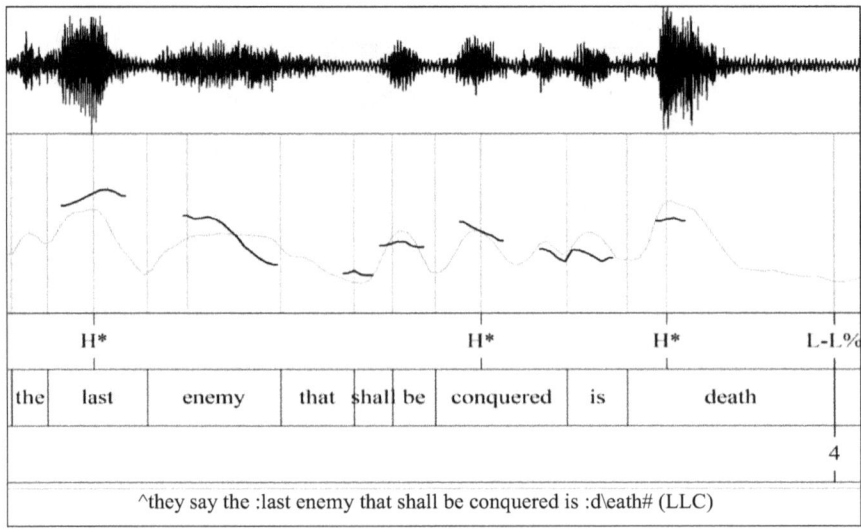

**Figure 28:** Praat picture, with pitch (bold) and intensity (grey) curves, for the specificational clause in (49).

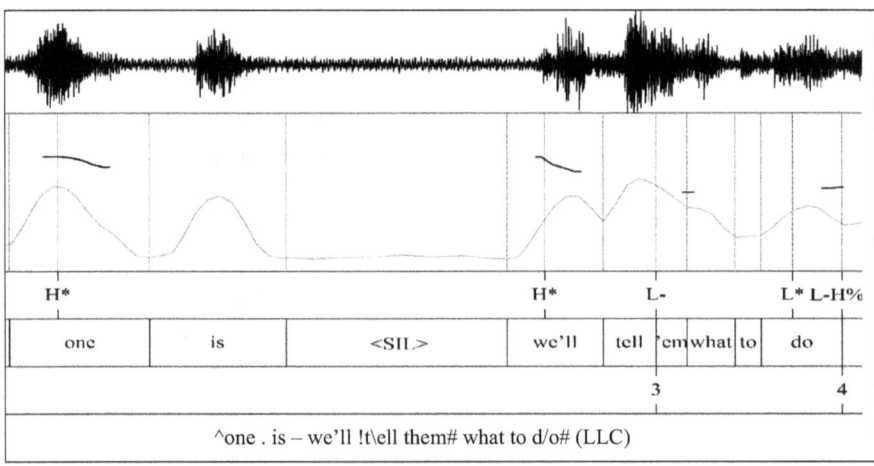

**Figure 29:** Praat picture, with pitch (bold) and intensity (grey) curves, for the specificational clause with indefinite variable in (50).

## 6.3.2 Beyond focus marking: prosodic prominence and discursive organisation

In this section, I turn to the discussion of copular clauses longer than one TU, which mostly include non-reversed specificational clauses: 85% of the non-reversed specificational clauses were longer than one TU, compared to 31% of the reversed ones and 26% of the predicative clauses. In clauses of more than one TU, both NPs in the copular clause are normally assigned focus within their own separate information units. This challenges the assumption that the value is always presented as communicatively more important than the variable. The evidence from relative pitch and intensity further contradicts this assumption: both factors typically lend prominence to the variable rather than to the value. The more intricate patterns of prominence marking in copular clauses of more than one TU will be discussed in Section 6.3.2.1. Here, I will describe, firstly, what can motivate the assignment of multiple foci in the copular clause and, secondly, what factors like pitch height and intensity contribute to the presentation of information as communicatively important. In Section 6.3.2.2, I will then consider the function of different tonal choices and how these choices interact with the different pragmatic meaning associated with the indefinite and definite variable NPs.

### 6.3.2.1 Prominence marking in copular clauses of more than one TU

The finding that (non-reversed) specificational clauses very often segment the variable and value into separate TUs challenges the idea that one is presupposed and the other 'the' focus of information (contra Chomsky 1969; Akmajian 1970; Declerck 1988). Converging evidence from tonality, tonicity, and relative pitch excursion and intensity demonstrates that, in most non-reversed specificational clauses, the variable is not informationally backgrounded but, instead, explicitly brought to the hearer's attention. This requires us to rethink the way in which the semantics of predicative and specificational clauses, their discourse-embedding and, ultimately, their intonation patterns interact. I will take the view that the intonation of copular clauses is essentially motivated by the speaker's evaluation of the communicative importance of information to the development of the discourse. The findings for pitch excursion and intensity will be advanced as evidence that specificational clauses often steer the discourse in a new direction, which is reflected by the prominence of the clause-initial variable subject. Finally, I will show that indefinite variables often contribute more to the development of the discourse than definite variables, which is reflected in their intonation pattern.

In predicative clauses, firstly, the typical distribution of prosodic prominence is for the describee to have little, or no, prosodic prominence, while the description stands out as prominent (95%), not only because of its tonicity, but also by its higher pitch and intensity. This typical pattern, however, is not fixed. It is possible, for instance, to find predicative clauses in which both the describee and the description introduce new unfamiliar information. This is the case, for instance, in (51), so that the describee and the description are, accordingly, both marked as noteworthy.

(51) ^this chap !\opposite# ^y\/ou know# that ^lives . in !D\/anny's 'old 'house# is an ^expert on :th\/ese 'things# (LLC)

Moreover, other factors than discourse-embedding may also influence the choice to mark information as prominent or not. In (52), for instance, the three predicative clauses uttered by Speaker B all have focus on both the describee and the description. Only the last describee (*Andrew Layman*), however, is new to the discourse (though possibly familiar to the hearer). Hence, the choice to mark the describees as focal cannot be motivated by discourse-newness. Instead, all three of the predicative clauses have a direction of fit in which fitting describees are sought (and given) for the previously evoked description. In answer to Speaker A's question about the English professor's membership of the board of studies of the 'other' (i.e. archaeology) department, Speaker B asserts that both the English and archaeology professors are members of the board of studies of each other's departments. Subsequently, speaker B continues to list the membership of both boards of studies, in which he includes himself (i.e. \*I*) and *Andrew L\ayman*. Since the predicative processes here imply fitting a describee to a description, the describee can be expected to have relatively high communicative importance.[91] This is reflected in the speaker's decision to give prosodic prominence to *both the prof/essors*, \*I* and *Andrew L\ayman*. Therefore, not only discourse-embedding but also the pragmatically inferred direction of fit can influence the speaker's choice to present information as noteworthy.

---

[91] Despite the consecutive predicative clauses in (52) listing membership of the 'boards of studies' with the members carrying information focus, they are not specificational clauses (contra, for instance, Patten 2012: 35, 2016). This is evidenced by the fact that the same descriptive listing pattern can be glossed alternatively as: "the professors are members of both (boards), and so am I, and so is Andrew Layman". The use of the relational anaphoric proform *so* is a diagnostic that the NP *a member of both* is not an indefinite variable for which the subject NPs provide specification: as discussed in Chapter 3, the specificational variable is a referring expression and, unlike the non-referential predicate nominative, is not referred back to by means of a proform with relational semantics like *so*.

(52) A. Is the professor of English language not a member of the board of studies of the other department
B. ^y\/es# ^both the prof/essors# ^are !members of +b\oth you see# - . and ^\I'm# a 'member of b/oth# . and [@] ^almost 'over 'Riven's 'dead :b\ody# but ^st\ill# ^and Andrew !L\ayman# is a ^member of !b\oth# because ^he 'did some 'medieval :t\/eaching you 'see# (LLC)

Unlike in predicative clauses, both NPs in non-reversed specificational clauses are, by default, marked as focus within their own information units (*viz*. in 85% of the cases, compared to 16% of the predicative clauses). Despite the variable being logically prior to the specificational process (Davidse & Kimps 2016: 135), the variable is typically not explicitly given in the prior discourse context; instead, it often presents new information that is in some way 'anchored' to the context (in the sense of Prince [1981b]) or needs to be inferred from it. (Taken together, indefinite and definite variables express 'new-anchored' information in 58% of the cases and 'inferrable' information in 35%, as will be shown in the corpus research in Chapter 7.) The typical discourse-newness of the variable is illustrated in (53), where the speaker is lecturing students on the use of perfused tissues in biochemical experiments: the indefinite variable *^one of the !s\/implest# and ^least de-!m\/anding prepa'rations* shifts the discussion from the abstract theoretical discussion of 'this type of perfusion experiment' to a particular subtype. This new-anchored variable needs to be 'set up': the speaker presents it as a separate chunk of information, requiring the hearer's attention before the value's new, further specifying information, e.g. *the intact profused rat heart*, can be introduced. More specifically, in setting up the variable, the speaker shifts from the general type of 'perfusion experiments' to a particular instance of that type that stands out as by its 'simplicity' and its 'least demanding' character. These two selection criteria are drawn attention to as being important, before the speaker specifies which more concrete instance meets those criteria, *viz. the :in'tact pro'fused :r\at 'heart*.

(53) it is ^possible for a :sh\ort 'time at l/east# ^after the re!m\oval of the _organ from the /animal# - ^to be'lieve that it be'haves in 'very much the !s\ame w/ay# . ^as it :would d/o in !v\ivo# - ^and ind/eed# ^much _useful inform/ation# . ^has been der/ived# ^fr/om# ^this 'type of per'fusion ex-!p\eriment# - ^one of the !s\/implest# and ^least de!m\/anding prepa'rations#. ^is the :in'tact pro'fused :r\at 'heart# (LLC)

In addition, the variable's typically high communicative importance is not only signalled by tonic prominence, but it is also reflected in the pitch – and, to a lesser extent, the intensity – with which the variable is often uttered: the variable subject was produced with a substantial peak in pitch in 52% of the cases, and with a peak in intensity in 34%. (Only in 17% and 21% of the cases was there a substantial peak in respectively pitch and intensity on the value.) The Praat picture in Figure 30 illustrates the substantial peak in pitch – and, to a lesser extent, in intensity – on the variable in example (53).

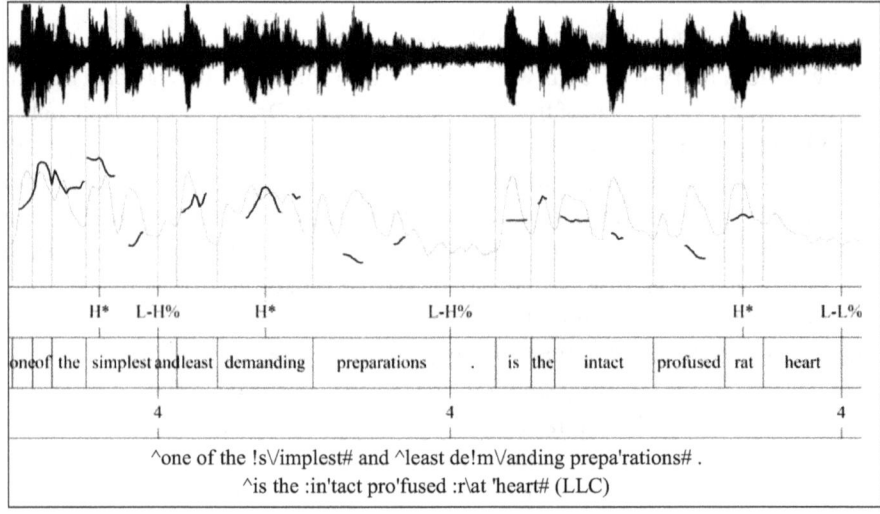

**Figure 30:** Praat picture, with pitch (bold) and intensity (grey) curve, for the specificational clause in (53).

The fact that the variable is given prosodic prominence by pitch and intensity does not accord with the prominence pattern that we would expect from the semantics of specification: given that the variable is logically prior in the specificational process, the process of specification implies a direction of fit by which the value is expected to contribute most to the development of the discourse. The fact that prosodic factors like pitch and intensity do not reflect this expected pattern suggests that these factors do not signal communicative importance at the clause-level but at a higher level of discursive organisation.[92]

I propose that the prosodic prominence of the variable can be accounted for by what Wichmann (2000: 5, 24, 102–122) calls 'paragraph intonation', which con-

---

[92] To compare, in predicative clauses, pitch and intensity were more likely to peak on the description (resp. 33% and 57%) than on the describee (resp. 17% and 24%): the prosodic prominence of the description, hence, aligns with the expect pattern in which the description is marked as communicatively more important than the describee.

cerns the role of pitch (and, to a lesser extent, intensity) in signalling relations between larger stretches of discourse. In non-reversed specificational clauses, for instance, the frequent and typically high step-up in pitch on the variable can be seen as marking a shift in discourse-topic. This is also emphasised by the increased intensity on the variable. As Wichmann (2000: 24) observes, "the most common prosodic correlate of a new topic or 'conceptual paragraph' is an extra high pitch reset", with "the speaker speaking high in his pitch range and speaking loudly" (Brown, Currie & Kenworthy 1980: 26). In specificational clauses, the shift in topic usually concerns a new subtopic within an already ongoing discussion, so that the variable typically introduces a new entity in relation to the prior discourse. In example (54), for instance, the speaker shifts the conversation from travel writing as a record of subjective impressions to a problem s/he identifies with that: by introducing the variable, the speaker first establishes the existence of a problem with what has just been said, to then specify what the problem is, with the specificational value thus elaborating on, or refining, the newly raised subtopic.

(54) **A.** ^everything that 'James t\ells me# about :Fl\orence# ^or a_bout . Mil/an# or ^V/enice# . or a^bout the Fr/ench 'towns he 'visited# - [i?i?] ^is a a subj/ective# acc/ount# . [p?] of the "^\/impact# . ^of this exp\/erience# and ^his re!c\ording# of 'this exp/erience# ^just as one 'has of :W\/ordsworth# . ^s=o# I'm ^not s\ure# r/eally# ^what ^whether you're _not _setting 'up an Aunt "!S\ally h/ere *and that# ((that)) we ^never !!d\o# ex'pect f\acts# - - ^as I !s\ay# a^part from [@] /altitude# and ^popul/ation# - . ^number of b/uses there *'are# and ^s/o on#
**B.** *(laughs - )* - I ^think <u>my :problem :th\/ere# in ^answer to :th\at# ^w/as that [@:m]# - I'd ^like to dis:cuss - with'in the 'confines of the :same b\ook# . [@:m] . bi^ographies and . !\/autobi'ographies# ^which . [@:] . to :some ext\ent# . "^do purport to re'cord :f\act#</u> (LLC)

Finally, as shown in the case studies in Section 6.2.2.1, a significant difference in tonality can be observed between indefinite variables, like (53), and definite ones, like (55).

(55) **A.** a ^lot of the ex'ams are 'multiple :ch\oice ((1 to 2 sylls))#
**B.** well a ^lot of the ex'ams are 'multiple :ch\oice ((1 to 2 sylls))# not logical th\inking# - - in ^medicine the :two go very 'much :hand in !h\and# . because ^if there's !so much !st\uff# . that <u>the ^only 'way you can !l\earn it# . is to ^think !l\ogically# . and ((syll)) and ^y\ou know# to ^systematize [dh@] . infor:m\ation#</u> (LLC)

Indefinite variables are much more likely to be themselves segmented into multiple TUs (46%) than the definite variables (13%). Unlike definite variables, indefinite variables are therefore presented as consisting of multiple units of information, each with its own focus marking. In this respect, the segmentation of the indefinite variable into a larger sequence of TUs suggests that it contributes more noteworthy information to the discourse than the definite variable. This can be attributed to the typically higher 'informativity' of the indefinite variable (Ariel 1990: 34, 80), i.e. the amount of lexical material that an NP includes to direct the hearer's attention to the intended referent of the NP (see also Chapter 7). Since the indefinite variable NP does not imply contextually unique identifiability and tends to be less familiar to the discourse than the definite variable NP, it typically incorporates more lexical material. As we saw in Chapter 3, from the type specifications of the indefinite variable the addressee often infers not just the delimitation of all qualifying entities, but also the delimitation of a subset delimited by extra criteria, e.g. *one of the simplest and least demanding preparations* in (53). The indefinite variable is, therefore, typically presented as contributing more to the development of the discourse than its definite counterpart.

In conclusion to this section, the disentangling of the different layers of coded and inferred meaning that have been conflated in various ways in the literature raises questions about how information structure actually relates to the semantics and the discourse-embedding of copular clauses. The evidence from the corpus study suggests that there is interaction between the different layers of meaning, as was demonstrated by the fact that typical intonation patterns emerge for each of the different copular clause types. The lexicogrammatically coded meanings of the different clauses set preferences for different typical discourse-embeddings (see Chapter 7). In predicative clauses, the describee is likely to be discourse-familiar and the description discourse-new. In non-reversed specificational clauses, the variable subject and value complement are both likely to be discourse-new. (As will be argued in Section 6.3.3, in reversed specificational clauses, on the other hand, the value subject is often discourse-familiar, as it is frequently realised by a demonstrative.) These different typical patterns of discourse-embedding consequently set different preferences for prosodic prominence marking, by which the speaker indicates the communicative importance of information for the development of the discourse. However, while the semantic and the contextual factors may influence the choice to mark information as communicatively important or not, it is ultimately the speaker who decides which information, and how much information, s/he presents as noteworthy.

## 6.3.2.2 Choice of tone and the information status of indefinite and definite variables

In the discussion so far, I advanced that rather than being informationally backgrounded, the specificational variable is – more often than not – given prosodic prominence by (i) its segmentation into a separate (sequence of) TU(s), (ii) focus marking, and by (iii) relative pitch and intensity peaks. By presenting variable and value as separate pieces of information uttered in their own (sequences of) TUs, the information structure of specificational clauses gives no direct indication of how the pieces of information expressed by variable and value interact with one another. (This distinguishes them from predicative clauses, whose tonicity, or focus marking, typically does allow for describee and description to be contrasted on those grounds.) However, as described in Section 6.2.2.4, tone can serve as a means for signalling relations between successive TUs (Tench 1988, 1996). The choice of tone can indicate, for instance, that the information presented in one TU does not complete the speaker's message and that the communication will be continued in the subsequent TU(s). Hence, while tone is typically interpreted as conveying the speaker's attitudinal position towards the information, it can also express the speaker's assessment of the status of the information in a TU as part of the larger discourse (Tench 1996: 80–81). Tone can thus serve a subjective function (e.g. expressing (un)certainty, annoyance), but also a discursive one (which involves the speaker assessing how the information in a TU relates to its immediate context). In this section, I examine the relations that are signalled by the use of tone in non-reversed specificational clauses of more than one TU. The focus will be specifically on the (final) tone with which the variable is uttered, since it is this tone that marks the transition from variable to value and, hence, signals how the two are linked together. Finally, by comparing the use of tone in indefinite and definite variables, I will advance that the choice of tone also interacts with the different pragmatic implicatures that the two variables trigger (*viz.* of (non-)exhaustiveness): I will argue that the different strengths of speaker commitment that the implicatures of (non-)exhaustiveness invite are reflected in the different subjective meanings that are signalled by the tone with which the variable is uttered.

**Variables ending in rising tones**

In the corpus study, a broad distinction between falling and rising tones showed that longer non-reversed specificational clauses are typically uttered with a rising tone on both the indefinite and definite variable (i.e. in 74% and 57% of the respective variables). The preference for rising tones (i.e. rises, fall-rises, or level-rises) can be explained by one function associated with them: rising tones, especially rises, are often used to indicate non-finality, also described as incompleteness or a 'look forward' (e.g. Bolinger 1989; Pierrehumbert & Hirschberg 1990; Cruttenden 1997). This meaning accounts for the high frequency of rising tones in both definite and indefinite variables, which, in non-reversed specificationals, occur in non-sentence-final position. The rising tones are therefore commonly used as 'textual glue' indicating that the speaker will elaborate on the TU's point in the next TU. In (56), the context leading up to the specificational clauses discusses Croydon Council's plan to evict tenants with joint incomes amounting to over twenty pounds a week, which, the speaker argues, will lead to segregation. Against this 'modern conception' of public housing, the speaker introduces *the old idea* as new-anchored information, presented as an individual unit of information. The rise on *idea*, however, signals the incompleteness of the communication, for which the value's TU provides completion. As Fox (1986) notes, two consecutive TUs in which the first has a continuation rise and the second a fall often realise such a completion pattern, in which the two TUs stand in a 'complementary' relation to each other. In (57), the indefinite variable likewise introduces new-anchored information. Here, the variable spreads over two TUs, each having a rising tone: these rising tones signal incompletion, which is eventually resolved in the final TU of the specificational clauses by the fall on *sh\ip*.

(56)  ^housing est/ates# . ^should be :l\/imited# . to ^people of a :certain \income# - it's an ^argument for . :segreg\ation# - ^segregating the p/oor# from [dhi:] . ^reasonably well-to-d/o# . from the ^r\ich# . it's a ^modern con:c\eption# - the ^old id/ea# was to ^build a v\illage# - a ^v/illage# where ^/everybody# whether they were ^rich or p/oor# . ^lived as :n\eighbours# (LLC)

(57)  ^as you s/ee# we're ^l\ooking# at a ^model sh/ip# - ^out on the :l\ake# - - ^and you can s/ee# that it's ^more or less !st\ationary# at the m/oment# . it ^hasn't 'got any :\energy# - - ^one w/ay# . in ^which we could :give it some /energy# - ^would b/e# to ^set up a p/ump# - and ^actually di'rect a :stream of w\/ater# - to^wards the !sh\ip# (LLC)

Interestingly, however, the preference for rising tones, especially fall-rises, was much greater with indefinite variables (74%) than with definite ones (57%). This suggests that the meaning of rising tones in the latter is not restricted to signalling continuation, but that the indefiniteness of the variable is conducive to some other meaning(s) expressed by rising tones.

One such meaning is the expression of the speaker's reservation or uncertainty towards the claim s/he is making. In (58), for instance, the speaker is advising the hearer on the latter's marital problems and on the option of marriage counselling.

(58) ^w/ell# I ^think it 'may 'well b\e# that - ^one of the pr\/oblems# ^in your m\/arriage# ^is that the 'things !y\ou have f/aith in# ^she !!d\oesn't have f/aith in# - and the ^things that !sh\e has 'faith in# ^y\ou don't have *'faith in# (LLC)

The speaker hedges the sensitive topic by presenting it as her own belief (via the modalised use of *I think*) which she downplays by means of the modal expression *it may well be that*, etc. The specificational clause, which falls within the scope of the modal expression, is thereby presented as a possible State-of-Affairs rather than an actual one. The non-uniqueness implicature of the indefinite variable *^one of the pr\/oblems# ^in your m\/arriage#* further foregrounds the epistemic uncertainty associated with the specification. This is reflected in the use of the fall-rises on the variable (i.e. 39% of the indefinite variables and 28% of the definite ones), which, as Tench (1988: 20) points out, can be used to signal that the proposition represents the speaker's personal opinion. The use of the rising tone, therefore, invites the hearer to confirm or reject the suggestion being made, by emphasising the subjectivity and tentativity of the statement. In this respect, the non-exhaustiveness implicature of the indefinite variable and the use of rising tone can both be used as distinct but interacting strategies for the speaker to waive responsibility for the proposition. The non-exhaustiveness implicature presents the specified value as (only) one of multiple possible instances qualifying for the variable: the speaker can thereby leave open the option that other possibly more fitting instances qualify for the variable. The rising tone can serve a similar function, with the additional implied meaning that the speaker hesitates to take full responsibility for the value as a valid specification of the variable.

Note that the argument being made here is different from Patten's (2012: 57–58) claim that the felicity of indefinite variable NPs depends on their being "non-committal or evasive with respect to inclusiveness". As argued in Chapter 3 and 4, the non-exhaustiveness implicature is one of the main reasons for realising the variable by means of an indefinite NP. The kind of speaker-reticence that I am talking about has to do with the speaker acknowledging that the variable can be exemplified in multiple ways yet having to choose 'one' fitting example from amongst others. In (58), for instance, the speaker actually codes that there is a set containing multiple 'problems in your marriage'; the reticence comes in when s/he selects a specific value: the fact that the speaker chooses one value over other potential ones could be interpreted as meaning that this value (e.g. *that the things you have faith in, she doesn't have faith in*, etc.) is somehow more important or more fitting than the others. The speaker may choose to hedge this by presenting the choice for the specified value as subjective.

Another related meaning of the fall-rise is that it connects a discourse entity with other entities in the discourse (Hirschberg & Ward 1985: 449). Ladd (1980: 159) describes this as 'focus within a set', as expressed in (59).

(59) ^\/one of the 'things that # ^one of the :m\/any 'things the 'books brings _out# very ^cl\/early 'is that# they ^w\ere de'cisively de'feated# ^in the "!f\ield# - ^b\/y the _Allied _armies# (LLC)

Example (59) starts off with a falling-rising tone on the indefinite pronoun *one*, thus emphasising its exclusiveness whereby the speaker shifts the focus towards a single instance of a set, the size of which is left unspecified. The restart – i.e. *^one of the :m\/any 'things...* – deaccents the indefinite pronoun to give prominence to *many*, thus explicating and underscoring the possibility of multiple instantiations by giving a description of the magnitude of the reference set from which the instance under discussion is drawn. The focus on the relation between *one* instance and the set of *many things the book brings out* is reinforced by the use of the fall-rise: in the case of the indefinite variable, this emphasises the non-contrastiveness of the specificational relation.

Finally, though relatively rarely, the variable may also be realised with (a series of) level-rises, as in (60) and (61).

(60) ^one of [dhi:] . :matters we'll "!turn to !l=ater# is the ^question of :trade 'union m\embership# (LLC)

(61) the ^basic :tr=uth# a^bout !m=en# . is that ^men . 'like to 'be with 'other :m\en# (LLC)

Halliday (1970c) points out that the sequence of level tones followed by a falling TU does not merely link two or more pieces of information but signals that the relation between them is almost self-evident and, hence, expected to be obvious to the hearer. In (60), the indefinite variable *one of the matters we'll turn to later* thus marks the specificational relation as obvious: the speaker takes the hearers to know the agenda of the meeting and merely reaffirms it as common ground in relation to which he subsequently develops the point he wants to make. In (61), the speaker, a woman, presents her belief as an objective 'basic truth' to be taken for granted. This serves as a solid argument against mixed colleges (i.e. the topic of discussion). The speaker does not invite her hearer, also a woman, to agree or disagree. But neither does she underscore her own (lack of) authority on the matter. Interestingly, later on in the discourse, when the speaker is not present, the hearer comments on the statement, explicitly saying she did not agree with it herself but felt "it wouldn't have been very tactful to argue" with "this sort of rationalisation".

**Variables ending in falling tones**
In contrast with rising tones, falling tones typically signal finality or completion. Despite the fact that the variable does not complete the non-reversed specificational clause, falling tones were used relatively commonly: especially when the variable was definite, falling tones were almost as frequent as rising tones (respectively 43% and 57%), e.g. (62).

(62)  I said if ^you make a statistical an:alysis of the "!overs/\eas# ^c\andidates# - the ^candidates who !p\ass# . are ^those candidates who are :getting :thirteen :fourteen !fifteen m\arks# . on ^those . !two qu=estions# and ((that's)) ^usually the clause an:\alysis _question# (LLC)

In (62), the speaker and hearer are discussing which essay questions count most in deciding whether university applicants pass an entrance examination. The clause preceding the specificational clause narrows down the discussion from candidates in general to the overseas ones in particular. The rise-fall on *"!overs/\eas* indicates that the new content moves beyond the existing content: that is, the new information expands the shared knowledge from the previous context (Knowles 1984: 235). In relation to *the "!overs/\eas# ^c\andidates#*, the specificational variable subsequently demarcates *the ^candidates who !p\ass* as a subset of the former. The tonic accent and, hence, the informational focus is on *!p\ass*, which as part of the restrictive relative clause functions not only to identify the relevant subset but also to contrast it with the set of failed candidates. This contrast is conveyed by the extra emphasis that the raised pitch on *!p\ass* adds. The value, spread over two TUs, adds two main pieces of information, namely (i) the 'marks' candidates get and (ii) the questions that weigh most in the grand total. Finally, the falling tone on the variable is used to signal an interpersonal meaning rather than a textual one: the falling tone does not express completion of the message, but the speaker's certainty and authority in asserting that the specified value is the one corresponding to the variable.

The expression of certainty and assertiveness is particularly clear in (63), where the variable is realised as a series of three (relatively short) TUs, each produced with a fall.

(63) the ^tr\ouble# with ^these p\eople# - ^who !advocate :mixed c\olleges# . ^is that they have !absol\utely# ^n/\o# - - ^underst/anding# of the ^n\eeds# of :m\en#

The choice to set apart *the ^tr\ouble* as a single TU and, hence, a separate information unit reflects the speaker's insistence that there is in fact a problem both with mixed colleges and with their advocates. The pauses after the second and third TU add a sense of resoluteness to the utterance, leaving time to let the information sink in. Likewise, in the value, the compartmentalisation of the information into many small TUs gives prominence to the individual pieces of information, as if to hammer each of them in (i.e. *absol\utely – n/\o – ^underst/anding – n\eeds – m\en*). The use of a rise-fall on *no* further adds to its prominence by signalling not only a sense of definiteness or firmness but also increased emotional involvement, for instance challenging some (implied) assumption (Bolinger 1947: 136; Cruttenden 1986: 101, 1997). This implicitly signals the speaker's view of the opinions of those advocating mixed colleges.

Much less frequent is the use of a rising-falling tone on the variable itself, which only occurred in three cases of all non-reversed specificationals, all of which were examples of definite specificationals, e.g. (64).

(64) *but ^Mr Nab/\arro#* we "^know that you be:l/\ieve _this# . the ^str/\ange fact is# that you ^still haven't given us a !r\eason for it# (LLC)

In (64), the speaker presents Mr Nabarro's previously mentioned argument as a mere 'belief', the content of which is challenged, as expressed by the rising-falling tone. The variable *the ^str/\ange _fact* consequently marks a contrast with this belief, both prosodically by means of the rise-fall on *str/\ange* and lexically by means of the opposition between 'fact' and 'belief'. While not explicitly contradicting Mr Nabarro, the speaker in (64) points out the incongruity of Mr Nabarro presenting an apparently logical argument in the absence of any overt evidence. In that sense, the rise-fall on *strange* adds a touch of sarcasm (Cruttenden 1986: 102, 1997): the contextually relevant interpretation of the specificational clause is not that the speaker actually finds Mr Nabarro's failure to produce evidence strange, but rather that he believes the latter's argument to be false.

In conclusion to this section, falling tones, unlike rising tones, express certainty or 'definiteness' on the part of the speaker. This is particularly so in the case of the rather infrequent rise-falls. Their meaning potential includes the speaker challenging previous statements or implied assumptions made by other interlocutors. As such, falling tones are typically used to assert the speaker's authority. The exhaustiveness implicature triggered by the definite variable would appear to be more compatible with the expression of speaker certainty and assertiveness than the indefinite variable's exclusiveness. This is why falling tones were relatively uncommon with the indefinite variable (26%), while the definite ones has a relatively similar chance of being uttered with a falling (43%) or a rising tone (57%). Therefore, the meaning that the different tones express allows the speaker to not only assess textual relations between the variable and the value (e.g. incompleteness), but also to convey interpersonal meanings, such as (un)certainty, focus within a set, challenges, etc. The segmentation of the variable and value in separate TUs is, therefore, not necessarily always motivated by the discourse-familiarity of the information they convey, but can be a deliberate choice to bring out such interpersonal meanings.

### 6.3.3 The intonation of reversed specification

The discussion so far has focused mainly on predicative clauses and non-reversed specificational clauses. Since reversed specificational clauses differ considerably from these two clause types, their information structure deserves to be explored in more detail. Unlike non-reversed specificational clauses, reversed specificationals tend be uttered on one TU or less (i.e. in 69% of all the reversed clauses, cf. Table 18 in Section 6.2.2.1). The corpus studies of focus marking indicated that, when uttered on one TU, non-reversed specificational clauses marked the value as the focus. Reversed specificational clauses, by contrast, typically do the exact opposite: in 95% of the clauses of one TU or less, the tonic accent was on the variable rather than on the value. In this section, I will examine what motivates the specific patterns of information structure of reversed specificational clauses.

The main reason for the predominance of non-focal values in subject position is that many of the reversed clauses have an anaphoric non-contrastive demonstrative pronoun as value (*viz.* 34 examples or 55%), e.g. (65). This supports Halliday's (1967b: 231) point that "probably the items which occur with greatest frequency" as the value in specifying clauses "are the demonstratives, particularly *this* and *that*."

(65)　there was an ^aristo!cr\atic e'lite in the /army# - but ^surely !n\ot# ^not an** intel:l\ectual e'lite# [. . .] to ^be an ar:\/istocrat was [@:]# . ^not e:nough to :get you :\/on# . <u>^that was the whole 'purpose of the !st\aff 'system#</u> you s/ee# . and the dis^tinction between :staff and !l\ine# . you could ^be a you could ^get to be a "!g\eneral# to ^be an ar\/istocrat# ^by 'being an ar/istocrat# (LLC)

As Halliday (1967b) observes, such demonstratives tend to not carry a tonic accent, since they are anaphoric and, hence, not new: they therefore tend to not be presented as noteworthy, unless they are used contrastively. Contrastive demonstratives, with tonic prominence, were found in only 4 cases (6%), e.g. (66). While the value *!th\/at* picks up evoked information from the context leading up to (66), it explicitly contrasts that information, by means of a marked focus emphasised by a fall-rise, with the actual 'point' specified in the following TUs. The expression of contrastiveness is more typical of specificational clauses with definite variable NP, which imply exhaustiveness. When the variable NP is indefinite, the NP's exclusiveness typically results in the value being specified non-contrastively, as in (67).

(66) ^but [@:] "!th\/at isn't the 'point# the ^point 'is that you've got "!m\asses# of cr\iticism# to ^r\ead# (LLC)

(67) it ^may have been :one of these :students . "!dr\unk# - . [@:m] . ^either !possibly with a :g=irl# ^coming down_stairs to . !have a !k\iss off her# . ^something of th\at kind# - and ^dr\unkenly# . de^ciding :this might 'be a . 'possible !pl\ace# . ^th\at# might be !\one expla'nation# - but ^I mean :I don't "kn/\ow what the 'explanation 'is# (LLC)

The marking of the demonstrative value as focal in both (66) and (67) therefore realises a subtly different, more general meaning, namely of comparing the focal value vis-à-vis other competitor values. While often contrastive (as in [66]), the comparative relation can be non-contrastive as well, notably when a value is specified for an indefinite variable. The focus on the value, in such cases, then draws attention to the non-exhaustiveness implicature associated with the specification of the indefinite variable. In (67), the failure to commit to one item as being 'the' value for the variable is indicated in the following TU, where the speaker expresses a lack of knowledge of the real value for the variable *the explanation*.

In contexts where no values are compared, Halliday (1967b: 231) argues that the information focus of demonstrative values is determined by their "reference function". Demonstratives can have situational or textual reference, with the latter being backward (anaphoric) or forward (cataphoric). Halliday (1967b: 231) views situational and cataphoric textual reference as expressing 'new' information, while anaphoric demonstratives point to 'given' information. He therefore concludes that the former two will carry focus, while the latter is normally non-focal. This would appear to be true for the majority of the cases, though exceptions do occur. In the context leading up to (68), speakers A and B are talking about fortified wines, which naturally brings them to port and its place in Portuguese culture.

(68)  A.  when did you go to Portugal
      B.  -^sixty- - -:s\even# -
      A.  per^haps th\at's the 'place to 'go to  this  summer# . d'you ^reckon we
          could 'drive to P\/ortugal# (LLC)

Speaker A's conclusion that *th\at's the place to go to this summer* coheres with the prior context only in that the demonstrative value has anaphoric reference to *Portugal*. Yet, even though the value is discourse-given and its variable brand-new to the discourse, it is nevertheless the former that is focal, while the latter is presented as informationally presupposed. The tonicity of the reversed specificational clause, therefore, is not motivated by the discourse-familiarity of the information but, instead, reflects a genuine choice on the part of speaker. The speaker presents the idea of 'going somewhere this summer' as evident and hence presupposed. Against this background information s/he foregrounds the value *th\at* ('Portugal') as (*perhaps*) this year's holiday destination. The focus on the anaphoric demonstrative results in marked focus assignment. This creates an effect of contrastiveness (Halliday 1967b: 206–207), even if no actual contrast is made with other holiday destinations. This contrastiveness is further brought out by the use of a fall-rise on *P\/ortugal* in the following TU, which is used to mark focus within a set. This example thus demonstrates the flexibility that speakers have in presenting information as noteworthy or not. While this choice may be motivated by factors such as discourse-givenness and retrievability, the choices for tonality and tonicity are not a direct effect of those properties. Instead, prominence-marking is a system in its own right, with its own intrinsic meaning – i.e. noteworthiness – which may interact with the actual discourse-familiarity of information in different ways. Halliday (1967b: 211), indeed, explicitly states that "what is new is in the last resort what the speaker chooses to present as new, and predictions from the discourse have only a high probability of being fulfilled." However, with the formulation 'presenting information as new' Halliday ties up the notion of focus to discourse-newness, which may "in the last resort" be cut (*ib.*). A better alternative, in my view, would be to define the meaning of focus as lending prominence to information and thus marking noteworthiness.

A further nuance to the idea that focal demonstrative value subjects express 'new' (or contrastive) information and non-focal ones 'given' information is found in cases that are ambiguous between anaphoric and cataphoric reference. The demonstrative value – and by extension the reversed specificational clause as a whole – is introduced quite frequently as a phoric bridge between the preceding and the immediately following context. The value, in such cases, is not straightforwardly anaphoric, but is instead presented as picking up on prior information which is elaborated on in the immediately following context. The value, then, establishes both anaphoric and cataphoric reference, whereby information from the prior context is further specified by the information that follows the specificational clause. This is illustrated in (69), where the demonstrative value *that* refers anaphorically to hitting upon *lots of people going round Hyde Park Corner* and cataphorically to *those big roundabouts*. The demonstrative's bidirectional phoricity is paired with a 'double specification' in (69), as evidenced by the repetition of the 'being' relation. The anaphoric antecedent of *that* is not sufficiently informative to provide the resolution to the variable *the thing which :fr\ightens me*, so that further specifying information is provided by ^*those big r\oundabouts*, which summarises the situation described in the anaphoric antecedent.

(69) I go ^down Park L/ane# and I ^go 'round 'Hyde 'Park C\orner# and I ^hit _l\ots of people 'going round [@] 'Hyde Park C/orner# . <u>^that's the thing which :fr\ightens me#</u> . is ^those big r\oundabouts# (LLC)

Such cases, though seemingly atypical, were quite common in the dataset of reversed specificational clauses: of the total of 62 reversed specificationals, 25 examples, or 40%, set up a phoric bridge between the prior and the following context. In 5 cases, this led to reiteration of the copula *be* (8%), as illustrated in (69) but also (70). Most cases of such phoric bridging, however, do so in another way, as illustrated by ^*namely* in (71) or the mere use of a specifying *that*-clause in (72).

(70) ^what is . im":p\ortant# and ^\/interesting# is the po^litical . "m\ovement# . of our ^t\imes# - and there's ^absolutely :no question at !\all# that ^socialism "in the !w\orld# ^as a m\ethod# of ^economic :pl\anning# - is "^overtaking c/apitalism# - ^h/and over !f\ist# *- <u>and this is the ^point \ is#</u> the ^eco"!nomic "!pl\anning# which has ^nothing whatso:ever to "d\o# with [dhi] po^litical ":t\yranny# (LLC)

(71) **A.** a^bolish the death sentence alto:g\ether# -
**B.** ^y\es#
**A.** ^or - hang !all murderers who are proved to 'be *((s\ane))#*
**B.** -*I ^think* <u>this is !one point we a:gr\ee /on#</u> ^namely that the !Homicide Act as it stands is extremely a:n\omalous# (LLC)

(72) **A.** I re^gard my_self as _very much _in the col_labor_ation re!s\earch centre# - and I should "^hate "!n\ot to be# . *. ((I mean)) I would ^just . I should ^dry !\up if I w/eren't#*

B. *^y\eah# I ^m=ean# . ^this is . ((the 'best 'part)) of my 'job in !\/Umist#* that I can +^go and 'talk to !P\eter# (LLC)

In reversed specificational clauses where the value is not a demonstrative pronoun, the value tends to express information that is brand-new to the discourse, as in (73). In such cases, the construal of the value as subject serves a rhetorical purpose. The subject being the modally responsible element of the proposition, the entity functioning as subject expresses the information in terms of which the assertion is made. Assigning such responsibility to an entity that is brand-new to the discourse imposes information structure on the clause that overturns the default information flow (i.e. from 'given' to 'new', cf. Birner 1994). Its rhetorical function has an effect similar to the expression of mirativity: the specification of the new value is presented as a 'sudden realisation' (which Aikhenvald [2012: 432], like Adelaar [2013], subsumes under a more broadly defined category of mirativity). The value is, however, specifically not presented as surprising, but instead as readily acceptable: in (73), for instance, despite being brand-new to the discourse, the value *^Brian !St/\atham* introduces information that is 'unused' in Prince's [1981b] terms: though discourse-new, the information is assumed to be familiar to the hearer.

(73) ^he's probably one of these :Lords perf/\ormers# **((1 syll))** ^Brian !St/\atham# was ^\one# ^w\asn't he# (LLC)

Example (73) is taken from a spontaneous commentary on a cricket match, at a point when the commentators are discussing the Australian cricketer Graham McKenzie, lauded here as *one of these :Lords perf/\ormers* (Lord's being a well-known London cricket venue and considered the home of cricket). The implication is that anyone who performs exceptionally well at Lord's is considered among the best in the game. In that context, Brian Statham, one of the leading English fast bowlers in 20th century cricket, is newly introduced into the discourse, but presented as needing no introduction (i.e. as hearer-familiar). The high rise-fall on *Statham* can be glossed here as signalling enthusiasm (Gimson 1980), awe (O'Connor & Arnold 1968; Crystal 1975), special emphasis (Kingdon 1958), or the speaker's admiration for Brian Statham. Hence, the construal of such focal 'unused' information in subject position is exploited here to signal Brian Statham's acclaim: though a sudden realisation, the rhetorical purpose is to mark the assumed obviousness of mentioning *Brian Statham* as *one of these Lords performers*.

To sum up, the intonation structure of reversed specificational clauses provides a challenge, on various counts, to the idea that specificational clauses can be distinguished from predicative ones by the assignment of the tonic accent. Though typically uttered on one TU, reversed specificational clauses often do not mark the value as prominent. This is due to the high incidence of non-contrastive anaphoric demonstratives in these constructions.

## 6.4 Conclusion

This chapter revisited the analysis of the form and function of information structure in specificational and predicative clauses. It centred specifically on the assumption that specificational clauses can be recognised by the fixed assignment of focus to the value, which is contrasted with a presupposed variable. I argued that such an interpretation of information focus hinges on a conflation of different layers of linguistic meaning, viz. (i) the lexicogrammatically coded specificational relation between a variable and a value, (ii) the pragmatic inferences triggered by the meanings at level (i) (notably the pragmatic presupposition of existence, as well as the logical direction of correspondence), and, finally, (iii) the information structure, including focus (and presupposition) marking and discourse-familiarity. I explained that information focus, at level (iii), should be analysed independently of the other layers of meaning, even if interactions with the other layers can occur.

Information focus was then interpreted in terms of McGregor's (1997: 274–275) and Verstraete's (2007: 81–88) reanalysis of Halliday's (1967b, 1985) definition of focus. Halliday defined focus as 'the most important point of the message, presented by the speaker as new information': in foregrounding 'newness' as the function of focus, Halliday interprets information focus as a textual function. McGregor (1997: 274–275) and Verstraete (2007: 81–88), however, correctly point out that the focus function is an essentially speaker-related phenomenon, since it is determined by the speaker's choice of what is to be presented as 'note-' or 'newsworthy' (rather than 'new' per se). In this respect, focus should be regarded as an interpersonal function, namely of the speaker steering the hearer's attention to what is judged to be important information. This is signalled prosodically by the assignment of the tonic accent.

In the case studies, I found that, on this analysis of information focus, only predicative clauses exhibited the hypothesised information structure: the describee was typically non-prominent, while the description was. This suggest that predicative clauses typically have unmarked narrow focus on the description. In non-reversed specificational clauses, the semantic relation between the variable and the value does not reduce to an information structure that can be captured in terms of a binary background-focus pattern. Instead, the variable and the value are typically each presented as individual (sequences of) information units: both elements, therefore, are signalled as sufficiently informative for the hearer to attend to them individually. In cases where the variable and the value do form one information unit, the tonic accent is typically on the value; however, the fact that the variable, in such cases, often has pre-tonic prominence suggests that the domain of the focus covers the entire information unit and not just the value.

What is more, when the variable is segmented into a separate tone unit, its prosodic prominence was often further increased by substantial peaks in pitch and – to a lesser extent – intensity. This indicates, I argued, that the variable is not only presented as communicatively important but often marks a shift in discursive (sub)topic. The variable was, hence, analysed as having high communicative dynamism, making a substantial contribution to pushing the communication forward.

Finally, the observation that reversed specificational clauses are more likely than not to have non-focal values warrants caution in analysing focus assignment to the value as a recognition criterion of specificational clauses. The value's typical lack of tonic prominence can mostly but not solely be attributed to the high frequency of non-contrastive demonstrative pronouns, which are expected not to be focal (Halliday 1967b: 226). But also when the variable was realised by a full NP expressing discourse-new information, the value was not necessarily focal: in such cases, I argued that, despite the value's discourse-newness, its lack of tonic prominence presents the information *as if* obvious or self-explanatory.

In conclusion, the findings in this chapter urge us to reconsider the analysis of specificational clauses as rooted in the assignment of information focus or other factors of prosodic prominence: specificational clauses are distinguished from predicative ones by their distinct semantic relations, which may set default preferences for a certain information structure, but by no means determine it. Hence, the information structure of specificational and predicative clauses is a distinct layer of linguistic organisation and needs to be examined as such.

# Chapter 7
# The discourse embedding of predicative and specificational clauses

In Chapter 6, I showed that the information structure of predicative and specificational clauses is more intricate than commonly assumed in the literature. Empirical data of the prosodic coding of information focus indicated that predicative clauses typically background the describee, or subject referent, while marking the description as focal. Non-reversed specificational clauses, by contrast, rarely display such a background-focus contrast: the variable, as well as the value, is typically uttered as a (sequence of) TU(s), so that both NPs in the copular clause carry information focus. In reversed specificational clauses, the information is typically contained in one TU: contrary to popular belief, however, it is not the value but the variable that is typically marked as the focus of the reversed specificational clause.

This chapter examines how these divergent patterns relate the different copular clause types to specific contexts of use. The main concern is to study how the NPs realising the variable and value, on the one hand, and the describee and description, on the other, are embedded in the discourse. In the literature, the variable has often been described as expressing 'old' or 'given' information for which the value introduces 'new' information (e.g. Kempson 1975; Karttunen 1976; Gazdar 1979a,b; Wilson & Sperber 1979; Declerck 1988: 14). This assumed correspondence of the roles of variable and value with a given-new contrast is based on the belief that the variable is a semantic or pragmatic 'presupposition', to which the value relates as 'new focal' material (e.g. Lambrecht 1994, 2001). This information pattern has been taken as an essential condition for the felicity of specificational clauses and as a point of contrast with predicative clauses, on which no such discourse conditions are imposed (e.g. Mikkelsen 2005; Patten 2012, 2016).

In previous chapters, however, I argued that the traditional 'presupposition-focus' analysis conflates different layers of coded, inferred and information structural meaning. First, the functional-structural analysis in Chapter 3 clarified that the variable does not code a 'semantic' presupposition: instead, the actually coded semantics of the specificational clause trigger the *pragmatic* inference that the role of the variable is logically prior to the value's specifying role. Secondly, the findings for intonation structure in Chapter 6 falsified the assumption that the variable is necessarily *informationally* presupposed or that the value is necessarily focal. Finally, these challenges to the traditional pre-empirical analyses of specificational clauses now raise a final question: to what extent do the existing assumptions about the discourse status of the variable as given and the value as new information hold up, and is discourse status an essential recognition criterion to distinguish specificational from predicative clauses?

This general concern subdivides into the following more specific research questions. First, do specificational clauses always have 'given' variables and 'new' values', or can more variation in discourse status be found for both semantic roles? Can predicative clauses, for which no specific discourse conditions have been posited, be found to display more variation in the discourse status of the describee and the description? In addition, are there differences between the discourse statuses of definite variable NPs and indefinite variable NPs, whose analysis has posed difficulties in past research (e.g. Mikkelsen 2005; Heycock 2012; Patten 2012, 2016). Finally, how do non-reversed and reversed specificational clauses compare to each other in terms of discourse-embedding, and can a motivation for choosing one variant over the other be found in the discourse status of the variable and the value?

To answer these questions, this chapter will provide an empirical analysis of how the predicative and specificational semantics are embedded in the discourse. In Section 7.1, I will provide an overview of how discourse-familiarity has been analysed in past research. The literature study presented there will feed into the categories that will be used in the corpus study in this chapter. The methodology of the corpus studies will be set out in Section 7.3. The findings will be discussed in depth in Section 7.3. A conclusion will be given in Section 7.4, which will wrap up the discussion of the role of information and discourse structure for the description of predicative and specificational clauses.

## 7.1 Background

### 7.1.1 The discourse status of NPs in specificational and predicative clauses

In studies of copular clauses, the widespread idea of a presupposition-focus distinction has not only led to the assumption that the two semantic roles in both specificational and predicative relations are contrasted by their non-focal vs focal status, but it has also been claimed that these roles have different discourse statuses.

Declerck (1988: 14), for instance, argues, for specificational clauses, that "the relation between the notion of old information and that of logical or pragmatic presupposition [of the variable] has been recognized for some time." This means, more specifically, that "in any specificational sentence the value part represents 'new' information while the variable part expresses 'old' information" (Declerck

1988: 14). Declerck (1988: 19) even takes this a step further, arguing that "the variable should not only be known information but should actually be in the hearer's consciousness at the time of utterance." He denies, however, that this suggests that the presupposed variable "must occur verbatim in the preceding context": the variable is "old information only in the sense that it links up with what has already been said" and can thus also be built via "one or more inferential 'bridges'" (*ib.*). Hence, for Declerck (1988), it follows naturally from the variable's presupposition that the information it expresses is discourse-given. While discourse-givenness figures prominently in his discussion of specificational clauses, it is barely mentioned at all in the analysis of predicative clauses. Here, Declerck (1988: 61) restricts his comments to the observation that a "speaker normally introduces [an] entity linguistically before ascribing a property to it": therefore, the subject NP is taken to "represent old information (as is usually the case in a predicational sentence, since it is usually the property that is the new information)" (*ib.*). The very succinct discussion of discourse-familiarity in predicative clauses suggests that Declerck (1988) considers it either as more straightforward or as less important.

Mikkelsen (2005: 135) gives a similar analysis but adds the somewhat bolder claim that "being discourse-old is a precondition for being topic, and hence specificational [variable] subjects must be discourse-old, at least relative to the predicate complement [value]." On her 'inverse' account of specification (see Chapter 3), the assumed relative discourse-familiarity of the variable, in contrast with the value's relative discourse-newness, is key to understanding "why specificational clauses exist at all" (*ib.*). For Mikkelsen (2005), specificational clauses are derived by inversion from predicative clauses. Inversion serves a discourse-connective function, allowing the clause to "present information that is relatively familiar in the discourse before information that is relatively unfamiliar in the discourse" (Birner 1996: 60).[93] Like Declerck (1988), however, Mikkelsen (2005: 143) notes that "what counts in the end is not actual discourse-familiarity, but being treated as discourse-old or discourse-new." The acceptability of an indefinite NP as a specificational variable, therefore, "depends on whether the hearer is willing to accommodate his or her discourse model (in roughly the sense of Lewis 1979), to process this information [i.e. of the variable] as discourse-old."

In both Declerck's (1988) and Mikkelsen's (2005) accounts, the discourse status of the indefinite variable sits awkwardly with their general analysis of specificational clauses. Declerck (1988: 19) notes that, first of all, the variable NP is usually definite

---

**93** Birner's (1996) analysis of inversion does not focus only on specificational clauses, but also includes inversion structures with adjectival and prepositional clauses, e.g. *Particularly important is the promotion of cultural interchange* or *In the distance was the two-tone warble of a police siren.*

(as also argued by Clark & Haviland [1977: 13]): he takes this to follow from "the fact that the presupposition represents old (even given) information" and it is "well-known that indefinite NPs are used to introduce new information" (Declerck 1988: 19). For Mikkelsen (2005: 154), therefore, indefinite specificational variables have to reconcile two conflicting discourse conditions, namely the variable's discourse-connective function and the indefinite NP's discourse-newness (according to Heim's [1982] 'Novelty Condition'). The solution that both Declerck (1988: 19) and Mikkelsen (2005: 157) propose is that indefinite specificational variable NPs introduce overall new information but include modifiers that express old information or information that is somehow linked up with the preceding context. This, Mikkelsen (2005) contends, explains why some indefinite NPs are infelicitous as specificational variable: "these particular indefinites fail to contain any discourse-old material" (*ib.*: 154), for which she cites as evidence example (1).

(1)   #A doctor is John. (Mikkelsen 2005: 159)

However, as pointed out to her by Donka Farkas, "there are still other factors that seem to play a role in determining the felicity of indefinite specificational subjects" (Mikkelsen 2005: 159). This is illustrated by (2), in which the second occurrence of the NP *a doctor* expresses discourse-old information, but despite its indefinite NP form, it apparently fails to introduce a discourse-new referent in a felicitous way. While Mikkelsen (2005: 159) observes that the addition of pre-modifiers such as *another* or *different* makes the indefinite variable NP felicitous, she regrets "to leave these very interesting observations as questions for further research" (*ib.*).

(2)   Bill is a doctor. #A doctor is John (too). (Mikkelsen 2005: 159)

Patten (2012: 50–51) picks up on this question, arguing that Mikkelsen's (2005) discursive motivation of indefinite specificational variables is quite accurate but only "follows from their peculiar function in specificational sentences" (*ib.*: 51). This function is to "assert the existence of [a] set [of entities] and to position this information in relation to the discourse context" in such a way that "it does not rule out a uniqueness (or inclusiveness) interpretation" (Patten 2012: 55). She argues that the condition for indefinite NPs to function as specificational variable is that, like definite NPs, they must "assert the existence of a non-exclusive, restricted set of entities as relevant to the shared discourse environment" (Patten 2012: 51). Unlike definite NPs, however, indefinite variables do not indicate "that the existence of a set of entities that satisfy the description is already known or knowable from the discourse context" but, instead, "*establish* the existence of this set and [. . .] position this information *in relation to* the discourse context" (*ib.*: 53). For the specificational reading to be salient, the number of members of the set denoted by the indefinite NP must be "small enough to be usefully listed" by the value (*ib.*: 48). Hence, while Patten (2012) agrees with Declerck (1988) and Mikkelsen (2005) that the use of modifiers can facilitate the interpretation of an indefinite NP as a specificational variable, she claims that the function of these modifiers is to "provid[e] a more restricted type specification" and to "lexically imply uniqueness" (Patten 2012: 55). The possibility that these modifiers contain discourse-familiar information is, therefore, a by-effect of their function to restrict the contextually relevant reference set established by the indefinite variable.

This chapter examines whether the characterisation of the describee and the variable as discourse-given and of the description and the value as discourse-new is supported by empirical evidence. The analysis of the discourse status of the NPs in the two clause types will focus on a more fine-grained model of discourse-familiarity (Kaltenböck 2005). The point of this study is not to determine the degree of acceptability of indefinite NPs functioning as specificational variable or predicate nominative. Rather, the aim is to describe how the semantic roles in predicative and specificational clauses are 'embedded' in the larger co- and context, i.e. what (typical) patterns of discourse-familiarity of the two NPs are found predicative and specificational clauses.

### 7.1.2 A multifactorial investigation of discourse status: Identifiability and discourse-familiarity

In this section, I discuss two factors by which the relation of linguistic elements to the context can be characterised. The first is the IDENTIFIABILITY status of referents, which is primarily coded by the (in)definiteness of nominal expressions. The meaning of definite and indefinite identification has been discussed at length in Chapter 3: here, I will focus on the different phoricity relations that can be coded by (in)definite NPs (e.g. Halliday & Hasan 1976: 31; Martin 1992: 98). The second is the central factor in this study: the DISCOURSE-FAMILIARITY of nominal referents: this dimension has to do with whether the referents of NPs are related to the situational context or to the preceding discourse. For the analysis of discourse-given-/newness, I will start from Prince's (1981b) influential 'hierarchy of assumed familiarity'. Because of the corpus-based approach of this study, however, Prince's (1981b) hearer-oriented model will be reconceptualised in terms of a model of discourse-givenness (Kaltenböck 2005; Gentens 2016). The text-based approach of this second model has the methodological advantage of providing a more objective basis for interpreting corpus data without having to speculate about the psychological implications of discourse-familiarity.

### 7.1.2.1 The identifiability of discourse referents
The identifiability of discourse referents has to do with the speaker's assessment of whether a nominal description is sufficient to enable the hearer to establish mental contact with a uniquely determined instance corresponding to that description in the current discourse context (Chafe 1976: 37; Langacker 1991: 98). The assumption in question, Chafe (1976: 37) argues, is "not just 'I assume you already know this referent' but also 'I assume you can pick out, from all the referents that might be categorized in this way, the one I have in mind'." This implies that two factors are taken into consideration: the contextual uniqueness of a designated instance (Hawkins 1978: 161, 1991) and the phoric relation(s) of the instance, or its type, to the context (Martin 1992: 98–99). In this section, I will first discuss how identifiability is expressed by NPs (including NPs, proper names, pronouns), after which I will focus on the identifiability of nominalisations, such as gerunds, *that*-clauses and ad-hoc nominal uses of infinitives.

### The identifiability status of noun phrases, pronouns and names
In English, identifiability is expressed by the definiteness or indefiniteness of the NP. The role of both contextual uniqueness and retrievability in the function of identification is summarised nicely by the criteria that Langacker (1991: 98) describes for definite identification:

> (1) the designated instance $t_i$ of [type] T is unique and maximal in relation to the current discourse space; (2) [the speaker] S has mental contact with $t_i$; and (3) either [the hearer] H has mental contact with $t_i$ or the nominal alone is sufficient to establish it (Langacker 1991: 98)

Indefinite identification is traditionally characterised as the opposite of definite identification, not because it involves a negation of *both* contextual uniqueness and retrievability, but because it involves inability to commit to the joint validity of these two factors. Thus, in (3), the indefinite NP *an apple* (in bold) introduces an instance that is, in principle, retrievable from the prior discourse as a member of the set of *red, red apples*. However, because the instance is not contextually unique, it is not assumed to be identifiable to the hearer and, hence, is introduced by means of an indefinite NP. In (4), on the other hand, the referent of *an apple pie* is likely to be the only instance of an 'apple pie' that was thrown at 'me', even if the exclusiveness implicature leaves it open whether there are other such instances (Hawkins 1978: 187, 1991). Still, because the referent is not retrievable from the prior discourse, the NP by which the 'apple pie' is introduced is indefinite.

(3) And then, curious, she moved the cloth to see what else was in the basket, and she saw the red, red apples. They smelled like fresh apples, of course; and they also smelled of blood. And she was hungry. I imagine her picking up an apple, pressing it against her cheek, feeling the cold smoothness of it against her skin. And she opened her mouth and bit deep into it . . . (WB)

(4) This guy rushed down the aisle and threw an apple pie at me. (WB)

The absence of identifiability is straightforward for indefinite NPs with specific reference (e.g. *an apple* in [3] and *an apple pie* in [4]) as well as for the ones with non-specific reference (e.g. *a man* in [5]) (see Chapter 3): both types of expression establish INDIVIDUALISED reference.

(5) If I had children with me at Ascot I would be horrified that they saw a semi-nude woman. If a man had turned up with see-through trousers he would have been arrested. (WB)

With indefinite NPs with generic reference, e.g. *a platypus* in (6), the designated instance is interpreted as a representative instance of its type.

(6) A platypus shuts its eyes and ears underwater but can hunt its prey using its highly sensitive bill.

The instance serves as a proxy for making general statements about the class. For this reason, the generic indefinite NP *a platypus* in (6) differs from indefinite NPs with specific and non-specific reference, in that it has INFERRED IDENTIFI-ABILITY: while the actually designated instance of the indefinite NP is strictly speaking neither unique nor retrievable, its implied referent – i.e. the *kind* of instance it represents – is unique and retrievable based on prior knowledge of the type. Generic contexts, therefore, trigger the inference that the speaker is not talking about any random instance of a certain class but about the class itself, which is identifiable. Hence, in many cases, it is acceptable to substitute a definite NP for the indefinite NP with a similar generic meaning, as illustrated in (6').[94]

---

[94] The fact that definite NPs, indefinite NPs and bare plurals can establish generic reference does not mean, of course, that they code the exact same meaning. Davidse (2004: 519), with reference to Langacker (1991: 70–71), states, for instance, that only definite generic NPs like *the platypus* in (6') refer to the type as such, or rather to the 'type-conceived-of-as-instance'. Indefinite generic NPs like *a platypus* in (6) do not, strictly speaking, refer to a type but to a rep-

(6') The platypus shuts its eyes and ears underwater, etc.

As Halliday & Hasan (1976: 31–34) and Martin (1992: 98–103, 121–127) point out, the RETRIEVABILITY of discourse referents – which is a prerequisite for identifiability – can rely on different kinds of phoricity relation. First, a distinction can be made between referents that can be recovered from the situational context (i.e. the 'speech event' with the speaker and hearer as its participants) and the ones that are recovered from the 'co-text' (i.e. the linguistic context of an expression as part of a stretch of discourse, spoken or written) (Halliday & Hasan 1976: 32). Referents recovered from the situational contexts are characterised as having EXOPHORIC reference (e.g. *I, you*); whereas the ones recovered from the co-text have ENDOPHORIC reference (*ib.*: 33). The instruction given by endophoric reference to recover information from the co-text to interpret an expression can point 'backwards' to previously mentioned information (ANAPHORIC reference) or 'forward' to information following the expression (CATAPHORIC reference) (*ib.*). The difference is illustrated respectively by the backward-pointing *that* in (7) and the forward-pointing *this* in (8).

(7) Who should choose the president, the people or Congress? That was the question facing the framers of the U.S. Constitution more than two centuries ago. (WB)

(8) But the more interesting question is this: Is anti-Semitism on a roll in Germany, 60 years after Auschwitz? (WB)

Moreover, expressions may also have HOMOPHORIC reference, which Halliday & Hasan (1976: 71) describe as a particular type of exophoric reference. Here, the phoric relation is to the cultural knowledge that is assumed to be shared by interlocutors of the same community (Martin 1992: 121). With proper names such as

---

resentative instance of the type; its representativeness allows for the inference that what is said about the representative instance also applies to the type, or rather to other instances of the type (Langacker 1991: 106). Bare plural generics (e.g. *platypuses are widespread in Australia*), finally, "do not simply refer to the kind as such, but can also be used in generic statements focusing specifically on the individuals of the class" (Davidse 2004: 519). Davidse (2004: 520) adds that the notion that bare plural generics point to individual 'members' or instances of a type is bound by a pragmatic implicature of type deixis (this type of. . .), not by one of implied universal quantification (all. . .), e.g. *\*all platypuses are widespread in Australia*. For an indepth discussion of the different ways in which generic reference can be established, I refer the reader to Davidse (2004).

*Mount Everest* or *Elizabeth II*, for instance, speakers rely upon the cultural context to retrieve the discourse referent in question.

Finally, Martin (1992: 123ff) mentions two more types of retrieval: BRIDGING and ESPHORA. Bridging, which is also called indirect or associative anaphora, involves a relation between the phoric NP and its antecedent, which is based on an *associational* relation such as whole-part or contiguity, as in (9), where the event of a murder is associated with *the killer*, which can hence be represented in the discourse as retrievable. Esphora involves 'forward' reference within the same NP (see also Du Bois 1980; Willemse 2005). This is illustrated in (9b), where the referent *the people we met there* is established by a complex NP with a postmodifier which makes the referent uniquely recoverable. Both (9a) and (9b) involve a form of 'bridging reference', whereby a referent is identified through an inference from another referent in the prior context (Willemse 2005: 7). In (9a), the direction of the bridging is 'backwards': *the killer* can be retrieved by linking it to the event of the murder. The bridging in (9b), by contrast, is 'forward': the subject referent of the main clause is endophorically retrievable from the information expressed in the post-modifier.

(9) a. It was dark and stormy the night the millionaire was murdered. <u>The killer</u> left no clues for the police to trace. (Brown & Yule 1983: 258)
 b. <u>The people we met there</u> wanted to get something to eat. (Martin 1992: 123)

Martin (1992: 98–99), who interprets the question of (in)definiteness purely as a matter of recoverability, argues that the 'non-recoverability' coded by indefinite NPs makes them "non-phoric": they "are associated with first mention" (*ib.*: 99). Gundel et al. (1993: 276) observe, however, that successful interpretation of an indefinite NP requires them to be at least "type-identifiable": the hearer is, in that case, "able to access a representation of the *type of object* described by the expression" (*ib.*, italics mine). The indefinite NP, in such cases, relies on linguistic (and cultural) knowledge shared by a speech community: while most speakers of English can easily interpret what *an apple* refers to, it may prove harder to accommodate the discourse referent of an NP like *a Jabberwock* into the discourse model.

Moreover, as Halliday & Hasan (1976: 76–84) point out, indefinite NPs can set up other phoric relations than just type-identifiability. The possibility of indefinite NPs being anaphorically related to the prior context was discussed at length in Chapter 4 and is illustrated here by *another* in (10), which points to a previously mentioned instance of the same type. Example (11) illustrates how a new instance of 'cat', *a similar cat*, can be compared via esphoric reference to *the one we saw yesterday*.

(10) One of the first Vedic Sanskrit aphorisms says Tamasi ma jyotir gama – 'Leave the darkness and come into the light' – while <u>another</u> is Atato brahma jijnasa – 'I am conscious spirit' – the idea being that the better we know ourselves, the happier, more self-fulfilled and powerful we become. (WB)

(11) It's <u>a similar cat to the one we saw yesterday</u>. (Halliday & Hasan 1976: 78)

In addition, an indefinite NP can, in principle, also be used to refer to an entity in the situational context. If a child, for instance, sees a batch of biscuits, she could ask her mother out of the blue: *Can I have <u>one</u>*. In that case, *one* refers exophorically to a non-unique instance singled out from a set of instances available in the situational context.

Finally, indefinite NPs in English can have a zero-article, used with uncount nouns or plural count nouns, as in (12). The zero-article is a positive option with a specific contrastive value in the paradigm of indefinite articles, which also contains unstressed *some*. Hence, the presence of the zero-article can be revealed by its systematic alternation with *some*, as in (12). The zero-article has to be distinguished from the 'bare' generic (Carlson 1978; Davidse 2004), which has no determiner at all, as shown by the impossibility to replace it by *some/all*, as in (13).

(12) Alice drank (some) milk. (Langacker 1991: 103)

(13) The formula for (*some/all) water is $H_2O$. (Langacker 1991: 103)

As bare generic NPs enable mental contact with the class as such they can be considered as designating an identifiable entity: as Davidse (2004: 519) points out, their "'identifying' force stems directly from the criterial qualitative features denoted by the mass [. . .] nouns used in them." Therefore, while NPs with the zero-article introduce a non-retrievable mass, bare generic NPs have inferred identifiability.

In sum, the identifiability status of NPs is determined by two questions: is the instance designated by the NP contextually unique, and is the instance retrievable from the co- or context? Definite NPs, which code identifiable referents, imply a positive answer to both question; indefinite NPs, which code non-identifiable referents, imply that at least one of the two questions cannot be answered affirmatively. An exception to the non-identifiability status of indefinite NPs is the indefinite 'generic' NP: it designates a representative instance that brings about mental contact with the (identifiable) class. Finally, NPs with zero-article do not designate retrievable entities. Bare generic NPs, by contrast, have inferred identifiability.

### The identifiability status of nominalisations

While the discussion so far has focused on the identifiability status of NPs, it is not uncommon for copular clauses to have a nominalised expression as their subject or complement, e.g. *the lighting of a candle* or *lighting a candle* and even *that a candle was lit*. Nominalisations are conceptual reifications of processes (i.e. events or states): they are derived from processes but are reclassified as 'things'.

For nominalisations, a distinction can be made between nominalised finite clauses and nominalised non-finite verb forms. The first express FACTS or REPORTS about states-of-affairs (i.e. PROCESS-INSTANCES located in time). Halliday (1967b, 1968, 1985) describes this distinction in terms of a difference in abstraction: while things and processes are "phenomen[a] of experience" (Halliday 1968: 194), facts and reports are linguistically processed metaphenomena, "with language itself here operating as a participant in the transitivity structure" (*ib.*: 195). Metaphenomena are not 'material' phenomena (like things and processes) but semiotic ones (Halliday & Matthiessen 2014: 205): they are propositions "construed as existing in their own right in the semiotic realm" (*ib.*)

(14)   Girls raised with stepfathers engage in sexual activity even earlier. *One possibility is <u>that the girls learn 'dating' behaviour earlier by mimicking their mothers</u>.* (WB)

(15)   Christine Lo of the Hong Kong Observers questioned, 'How can we expect the Chinese Communists to provide stability and prosperity, when they have never had either?' *A short answer is <u>that China does not have to provide stability or prosperity</u>*: that can be produced only by the Hongkongers themselves. (WB)

Langacker (1991: 149) argues that nominalised clauses like the ones in (14) and (15) take a proposition as their type-specification. Because the clause that forms the basis for the nominalisation is finite and, hence, uniquely related to the time and the participants of the speech events, the derived nominalisation is functionally definite (Heyvaert 2003: 69–70): the referent of the nominalisation is, therefore, taken to be uniquely identifiable to speaker and hearer, not necessarily because the hearer is assumed to be already familiar with the designated process-instance, but because the information in the nominalised clause is sufficient to enable unique identification.

Secondly, nominalisations of non-finite verb forms can be further divided into infinitives, on the one hand, and gerunds, on the other. Since both derive from non-finite verb forms, they are conceptual reifications of PROCESS-TYPES, rather than process-instances that are located in time. The difference between infinitives and gerunds is primarily aspectual: while infinitives imply boundedness, gerunds imply non-boundedness (Kirsner & Thompson 1976; Halliday & Matthiessen 2014: 204). In (16), for instance, the infinitive *to take an aromatic bath each day* undergoes ad-hoc nominalisation, whereby it comes to present the perfective (i.e. bounded) process-type as a concept, *viz.* the 'action, or habit, of taking an aromatic bath every day'. In (17), the gerund *alternating one with the other* likewise expresses an abstract concept of a process-type, which the *ing*-form presents as imperfective (i.e. as unbounded).

(16) Cigarettes and alcohol and tranquillizers have become the methods of relaxation employed by people in the Western world. *A healthy and safe alternative to these measures is <u>to take an aromatic bath each day</u>.* Even if you prefer showering for its speed and economy, think of bathing as a therapy and try to take one or two aromatic baths every week. (WB)

(17) There is what you might call hard interrogation and soft interrogation. Soft interrogation is the person who is nice and friendly to you er says it's gonna be all right. Hard interpretation [sic] is the person who comes and hits you over the head and it has been found that *a very effective technique is <u>alternating one with the other</u>*. (WB)

Not all gerunds, however, express process-types. A further distinction needs to be made between gerunds with and without a determiner. The first are illustrated by *the jailing of a feared gangleader...* in (18) and by *singing and laughing* in (19). The latter has a zero-article, as shown by the possibility to use the non-salient article *some*, e.g. *there was some singing and laughing*. The referent of *singing and laughing* can hence be analysed as non-identifiable.

(18) Liverpool police were today celebrating <u>the jailing of a feared gangland leader at the centre of a bitter underworld gun battle</u>. (WB)

(19) Everybody was happy, there was <u>singing and laughing</u>. (WB)

The second type of gerund – i.e. without a determiner – are so-called 'bare' gerunds, e.g. *dieting* in (20). The fact that they do not have a determiner slot is evidenced by the impossibility to insert the indefinite article *some* (e.g. *\*I'm not obsessed about some dieting*).

(20) I'm not obsessed about <u>dieting</u> because I think you should allow yourself to enjoy your food. (WB)

Only bare gerunds can refer to process-types. They function much like bare uncount nouns (Fonteyn 2016), in that they have generic reference, with inferred identifiability of a class or type as such, e.g. *dieting* in (20).

In gerunds with a determiner, the *ing*-form that denotes the process-type functions as the head of an NP and, hence, serves only to give a type specification, not to designate an instance. As expressed by the full NP structure, this type is then instantiated so that the resulting instance can be further quantified and identified. In other words, gerunds with a determiner are like 'ordinary' NPs, the only difference being that the type is not specified by a noun but by an *ing*-form. Like other NPs, gerunds with a determiner can take a definite or an indefinite identifier, e.g. *the jailing of a feared gangland leader*, etc. in (18) or *a tingling of the spine* in (21): the first express identifiable instances; the second do not.

(21) He switched off the lights, got out of the car, and at the same moment realized, with a tingling of the spine, that the cantilevered door was closing, was already half-closed. (WB)

Hence, since gerunds with a determiner have the same NP structure as other NPs, they can be interpreted as realising the same functions as other NPs and allowing for the same forms of identifiability.

To sum up Section 7.1.2.1, the identifiability status of definite and indefinite NPs, as well as nominalisations, depends on whether the NP introduces a uniquely retrievable instance, or a unique class or kind, in a given discourse context.

### 7.1.2.2 Taxonomy of discourse-familiarity

A seminal study of how discourse referents relate to the co- and context is Prince's (1981b) taxonomy of 'given' vs 'new' information. The study starts from the observation that discourse is characterised by an "informational asymmetry", in that some units convey 'older' information than others (*ib.*: 224). This asymmetry, Prince (1981b) suggests, is not restricted to the boundaries of the individual sentence but can be found on different discourse levels, ranging from the sentence to larger stretches of discourse. For Prince, the linguistically relevant factor is not so much the objective criterion of whether a referent is actually given or new to the discourse; what matters instead is "the tailoring of an utterance by a sender to meet the particular assumed needs of the intended receiver" (1981b: 224). She consequently proposes to interpret the notion of givenness in terms of 'assumed familiarity': what counts as 'given' is therefore what the speaker "assumes the hearer assumes" (*ib.*: 232). Prince's concern is thus essentially with hearer-oriented givenness, i.e. whether a referent is accessible to the hearer; it is, however, the speaker's judgment of this hearer-familiarity that is deemed to be reflected linguistically. In this section, I will first discuss Prince's 'cognitivist' perspective on discourse-familiarity. In the second part, I will consider Kaltenböck's (2005) more 'empiricist' approach, which looks at similar categories of discourse-familiarity but interprets them with a primary focus on the text as a finished product of communication (Gentens 2016: 145).

The model Prince (1981b) proposes distinguishes, in a first instance, between NEW, INFERRABLE and EVOKED discourse referents. When a speaker first introduces an entity in the discourse, it counts as NEW information, which can be either BRAND-NEW or UNUSED. In the first case, the hearer is instructed to create a new entity and add it to the discourse-model (*ib.*: 235), e.g. *a bus* in (22).

(22)   I got on a bus yesterday and the driver was drunk. (Prince 1981b: 233)

(23)   Noam Chomsky went to Penn. (*ib.*)

In the latter case, the hearer is "assumed to have a corresponding entity in his/her model and has to place it (or copy it) in the discourse-model" (*ib.*: 235–236), e.g. *Noam Chomsky* in (23). Prince's (1981b) distinction between brand-new and unused discourse entities thus pertains to whether a discourse-new entity is assumed to be hearer-new or hearer-familiar. It hinges, in other words, on whether the entity can be retrieved via homophoric reference, in which case it is unused, or not, making it brand-new.

Among brand-new entities a further distinction can be made as to whether or not the description by which the entity is introduced contains an 'anchor' that links the entity to another discourse entity. Prince (1981b: 236) reserves the category of BRAND-NEW ANCHORED entities to such cases in which the anchor is explicitly specified – and not merely implied – in the NP, typically as part of a postmodifier. For instance, in (24) the brand-new entity introduced by *a painting I made* is anchored to the discourse by virtue of the evoked entity *I* being included in the indefinite NP; in (25), however, the referent of *a painting made by some French artist* is BRAND-NEW UNANCHORED (or just 'brand-new') as it does not include information linking the referent to the context.

(24)   She wanted to buy a painting I made.

(25)   She wanted to buy a painting made by some French artist.

For this study, I will not interpret brand-new anchored entities as rigidly as Prince (1981b) does: the indefinite NPs *one reason* in (26) illustrates that a brand-new entity can be linked to the prior context by means of an implied anchor, which can be paraphrased here as 'for this' or 'for the fact that Catholic but not Mormon pro-lifers picket SLC's two aborturies'.

(26) Catholic pro-lifers picket Salt Lake City's two aborturies; the Mormons don't. Someone said <u>one reason</u> is that Mormons don't like to be linked to anything the Catholics do. (WB)

At the other end of the taxonomy, the class of evoked entities – i.e. entities that are "already in the discourse-model" (Prince 1981b: 236) – is further differentiated. Prior evocation of a discourse entity can be of two kinds, depending on whether the entity has been explicitly mentioned in the preceding discourse, though perhaps by means of a different description. In (27), for instance, both the second mention of *Charles* and the pronoun *her* (referring back to *Camilla*) can be interpreted as expressing TEXTUALLY EVOKED entities.

(27) Charles and Camilla are a perfect match. So why doesn't <u>Charles</u> marry <u>her</u>? (WB)

Alternatively, SITUATIONALLY EVOKED entities are likewise considered as familiar by virtue of "represent[ing] discourse participants or salient features of the extra-textual context, which includes the text itself" (Prince 1981b: 236). The pronouns *I* and *you* to refer to speaker and hearer are prototypical examples referring to the participants in the speech contexts; other examples would include objects that are physically present in the communicative setting or comments referring to the speech exchange itself (e.g. *what you just said*; *the question you asked earlier*). In other words, as with textually evoked entities, situationally evoked entities need to be explicitly present in the speech context. Information that is shared by both speaker and hearer but that is not part of the preceding context (e.g. entities retrievable via homophoric reference) is not considered as situationally evoked by Prince.

Prince's (1981b) most complex type of discourse-givenness is formed by the INFERRABLES. A discourse entity counts as inferrable "if the speaker assumes the hearer can infer it, via logical – or, more commonly, plausible – reasoning" (*ib.*: 236) from another entity (or entities) in the discourse, a so-called 'trigger entity'. For instance, in (28), the discourse entity introduced by *the driver* is inferrable from the prior mention of *a bus*.

(28) I got on a bus yesterday and <u>the driver</u> was drunk. (Prince 1981b: 233)

As a specific subclass, Prince (1981b) further introduces the CONTAINING INFERRABLES. The difference with Inferrables is that "the entity which triggers the inference is not, as in the case of Inferrables, necessarily in the prior discourse, but is rather *within the NP itself*" (Prince 1992: 307, italics hers). Prince (1981b) illustrates her point with the example reproduced here as (29), arguing that the discourse entity expressed by *one of these eggs* is inferrable from the NP *these eggs*, which can be understood as Situationally Evoked if the eggs are physically present in the communicative setting where (29) is uttered.

(29) Hey, <u>one of these eggs</u> is broken. (Prince 1981b: 233)

In the final analysis, Prince (1981b) ranks the different types of discourse-givenness in her taxonomy on a scale of assumed familiarity, illustrated in (i) from most to least familiar (i.e. Hearer-old).

(i) Evoked (Textual | Situational) > Unused > Inferrable > Containing Inferrable > Brand-New Anchored > Brand-New (Unanchored)

When applied to naturally-occurring text (as illustrated in Prince [1981b, 1992]), however, Prince's model faces a couple of issues. One particular issue concerns the category of 'unused' entities. While the category may be theoretically valid (as being the only one that combines hearer-familiarity with discourse-newness), it poses the empirical challenge that what is discourse-new but shared between speaker and hearer may not be evident to the researcher. For this reason, Kaltenböck (2005: 127) proposes to reconceptualise Prince's (1981b) model and interpret information-status not in terms of assumed familiarity to the hearer, but in terms of 'retrievability' or 'recoverability' from the discourse context (both textual and situational). His 'taxonomy of discourse-familiarity' is summarised in Figure 31.

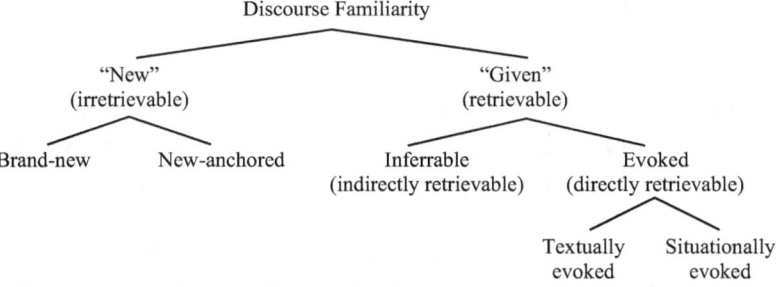

**Figure 31:** A taxonomy of discourse-familiarity (Kaltenböck 2005: 127).

Kaltenböck's (2005) approach "looks at the finished product of the verbal interaction, i.e. the corpus text, and examines the relationship between individual elements" (*ib.*: 126). His model not only leaves out Prince's (1981b) 'unused' category, but also omits the category of 'containing inferrables' (in which the information triggering the inference is contained in the inferrable expression itself). While Kaltenböck (2005) does not comment on the reason for leaving out the latter, Birner (1994: 252) – from whom Kaltenböck (2005) draws inspiration – proposes to interpret the status of the containing inferrable from its trigger entity. If the latter is previously evoked or inferrable, then the former would likewise be treated as "discourse-old" (Birner 1994: 252). If, however, the trigger entity is "discourse-new, the entire NP would be treated as discourse-new" (*ib.*). For instance, in (30), the NP *one of the problems we did not forsee* is a containing inferrable for which the trigger entity *the problems we did not foresee (when we volunteered as leaders for a Jewish youth movement last year)* expresses new-anchored information: the whole NP, therefore, can be characterised as discursively non-recoverable following from the trigger entity's low familiarity. In (31), by contrast, the containing inferrable *one of them* has a textually evoked trigger entity, so that the indefinite NP as a whole can be treated as discursively recoverable.

(30) Three friends and I, all university students in our early twenties, realised we were taking on a challenge when we volunteered as leaders for a Jewish youth movement last year. *One of the problems that we did not foresee was the co-ordination of bladders*. We had to make sure that everyone was drinking enough water to cope with the heat in the Middle East. Impromptu toilet stops soon became an all-too regular necessity. (WB)

(31) So I filled in some job application forms and one of the jobs that I've applied for have taken up you know these references that I've given and *one of them had to be my last employer which was Nat West Bank*. (WB)

An important question for both Prince (1981b) and Kaltenböck (2005) is the information status of indefinite NPs (including NPs, partitives and pronouns). Kaltenböck's (2005) interpretation of 'discourse-familiarity' in terms of retrievability implies a close connection between information status and (in)definiteness. Since definite NPs imply retrievability of a contextually unique instance (see Section 7.1.2.1), we would expect that definite NPs always introduce retrievable referents (either directly or indirectly retrievable). Indefinite NPs, by contrast, normally introduce irretrievable entities, but they can, in principle, also denote entities that are retrievable but not contextually unique. This is illustrated by the containing inferrable *one of them* in (31) above and by the non-containing inferrable *one* (with a similar set-membership meaning) in (32).

(32) Various reasons are given for Egypt's continued religious tensions, which, in recent history, date back to the early 1970s. <u>One is the poor state of the economy</u>. (WB)

While Kaltenböck (2005) does not comment explicitly on the relation between (in)definiteness and information status, Prince (1992: 302–303) points out that the two parameters may be correlated but that this correlation is by no means perfect.[95] She adduces the following three observations. First, Prince (1992) found that, while inferrable entities are normally coded by definite NPs, indefinite NPs can code inferrables as well: this is possible not only when the indefinite NP introduces a member of a previously evoked set (as in [31] and [32]), but also when the set itself needs to be inferred from the prior context. She illustrates this by contrasting the indefinite NP *a cockroach* in (33a) with *a page* in (33b).

(33) a. I picked up that book I bought and <u>a cockroach</u> fell out. (Prince 1992: 306)
 b. I picked up that book I bought and <u>a page</u> fell out. (*ib.*)

In (33a), the existence of *a cockroach* is not inferrable from the prior context and, hence, is assumed to be new information. In (33b), on the other hand, the assumption is that the page in question is not just any page but a page from the book just mentioned (Prince 1992: 307): the existence of 'a page' is thus inferrable from the prior mention of 'that book', since the speaker expects the hearer to believe that 'that book' consists of a set of pages and that s/he will infer that the 'page that fell out' is one of them. The difference between inferrable entities coded by definite vs indefinite NPs can then be formulated as follows: with definite NPs, an entity E is inferrable from a trigger entity T based on the belief that "T typically has an E associated with it", while, for indefinite NPs, "T typically has Es associated with it" and the inferrable entity is a member or a subset of the set of Es (Prince 1992: 318–319).

Secondly, Prince (1992: 302) also notes that definite NPs do not necessarily introduce discourse-old (or retrievable) information (contra what Kaltenböck's

---

[95] Unlike Kaltenböck (2005), Prince (1981b, 1992) does not group inferrables together with evoked entities as forming one general class of given or retrievable information. Instead, she interprets them as a separate intermediate category that is neither retrievable nor irretrievable. Therefore, the possibility of inferrables being coded by either definite or indefinite NPs is not in contradiction with her interpretation of the information status of inferrable entities.

[2005] model appears to imply). Some definite NPs, Prince (1992) argues, can introduce new information (i.e. both discourse-new and hearer-new), for which she cites as evidence the use of *the same people* in (34a,b). Both examples are existential constructions equating the participants at two conferences as being the same set of individuals.

(34) a. The same people were at both conferences. (Prince 1992: 302)
b. There were the same people at both conferences. (*ib.*)

But also in non-existential constructions, it is possible to find definite NPs referring to new entities, as illustrated by the new-anchored NP *the first thing Mr Blair saw as he was whisked over the border from Brazil* in (35). The entity denoted by the definite NP in (35) cannot reasonably be inferred from the prior context, but the information by which it is introduced is presented as sufficient to enable contextually unique identification.

(35) 2 AUGUST 2001 – Argentina's President last night officially ruled out another Falklands invasion after a historic meeting with Tony Blair. President Fernando de la Rua declared he would NEVER send troops into the islands – called the Malvinas by Argentinians – despite his country's claim to own them. He said: "We have made it clear that our claims on the Malvinas are absolutely by peaceful paths." The diplomatic breakthrough came as Mr Blair paid an official visit to Argentina – the first British PM to do so. The first thing Mr Blair saw as he was whisked over the border from Brazil was a roadside sign declaring 'The Malvinas belong to Argentina'. (WB)

Thirdly, indefinite NPs can also introduce 'given' information. Prince (1992: 303) mentions generic indefinite NPs as an example of hearer-old but not discourse-old information (i.e. her 'unused' category), which she illustrates with *bagels* in (36).

(36) I love bagels. (Prince 1992: 300).

But what is more, there is one use of indefinite NPs where it is possible to find both hearer-old and discourse-old entities, namely when the NP is non-referential. As illustrated by the second mention of *a subtle-souled psychologist* in (37), non-referential indefinite NPs can use an already evoked description to reintroduce a virtual instance: because the description is non-referential (i.e. it does not pick out an individualised instance), there is no co-reference between the virtual instances denoted by the first and second mention of *a subtle-souled psychologist* so that both are designated felicitously by an indefinite NP.

(37) Coleridge tries to demonstrate that Shakespeare is a subtle-souled psychologist. And there's only way in my opinion in which you can demonstrate that anybody is <u>a subtle-souled psychologist</u>, that is you look in to yourself and see if it touches you. (WB)

Of course, both generic and non-referential NPs are 'exceptional' cases in that the question of retrievability works differently for them than for 'ordinary' NPs that designate individualised instances. Generic NPs designate representative instances which can be retrieved via homophoric reference. Non-referential NPs instruct the addressee to 'conjure' up a virtual instance so that the questions of referent-tracking and retrievability are not relevant. This has important implications for the discourse-embedding of predicative clauses, in which the information expressed by the predicate nominative can be familiar or new regardless of the non-identifiability of the designated virtual instance.

Taken together, these three observations warrant caution against the idea that (in)definiteness and discourse-familiarity are necessarily interdependent: not only can indefinite NPs, under special circumstances, express familiar information, but it is also possible for definite NPs to introduce new information if the information is sufficient to enable contextually unique identification. Therefore, both indefinite and definite NPs can, in principle, have all the different levels of discourse-familiarity listed by Prince (1992) and Kaltenböck (2005). With these provisions in mind, the research in this study will be based on Kaltenböck's (2005) taxonomy of discourse-familiarity, because it provides a more objective way of analysing the data.

Finally, the discussion so far has focused implicitly on the discourse-familiarity associated with the referents of NPs and pronouns, while the status of nominalisations has not yet been mentioned. Unlike the referents of NPs, the referents of nominalisations are often not objects but facts or reports about process-instances and process-types. As clausal constituents, nominalisations function as 'distributional subfields' with a dual status (Kaltenböck 2005: 128; Firbas 1992): on the one hand, they typically consist of multiple individual 'communicative units'; while, on the other hand, they serve as a single communicative unit at the level of the clause of which the nominalisation realises an argument. As Kaltenböck (2005: 128) points out, when it comes to assessing the information status of such 'subfields', it is not the individual component parts that are evaluated but the status of the composite whole, i.e. of the reification in which the individual components take part. It can be expected, due to subfields typically combining 'given' and 'new' elements, that nominalisations will most frequently introduce new-anchored information (Kaltenböck 2004: 164; Gentens 2016: 149), as with the second *that*-clause in (38).

(38) What's the difference between a woman lawyer and a pit bull? Lipstick. (...) Despite the punch lines, Judy couldn't laugh. She hated that the public made jokes about lawyers, hated <u>that they didn't understand the nobility of the profession, or of the law itself</u>. (WB, as cited in Gentens 2016: 148)

However, as pointed out by both Kaltenböck's (2005) study of extraposed subjects and by Gentens' (2016: 149) analysis of factive complements, nominalisations can be used to convey the whole range from brand-new to explicitly evoked information. This is illustrated by the examples, taken from Gentens (2016: 146–149), in (39)–(42).

(39) TEXTUALLY EVOKED
Even though *giving birth scares me to death*, I like it <u>that it's frightening</u>. (WB)

(40) SITUATIONALLY GIVEN
You have no idea how much it means to me <u>that you're here</u>. (WB)

(41) INFERRABLE
Dejected fans orderly shuffled out of bars and homes in the Charlotte area *after the Super Bowl*, with most saying they were proud of *the Carolina Panthers' performance in a 32-29 loss to the New England Patriots*. [. . .] "I hate <u>that it ended this way</u>. But it was a great season." (WB)

(42) BRAND-NEW
De Pouzilhac [. . .] was born in Sete in the south of France. [. . .]. One of five siblings, he hated school. But his father, a director of a wine company, held lunches with interesting businessman [sic] and felt his children learnt more there. "I love it <u>that in life if you choose the wrong way you pay a penalty</u>," he says. "But in school all you did was learn and repeat – that's French education. (WB)

In sum, the study in this chapter will apply Kaltenböck's (2005) text-based model of discourse-familiarity to analyse the discourse-embedding of the NPs (including nominalisations) in specificational and predicative clauses. In the next section, I will describe how Kaltenböck's (2005) model fed into the methodology for the corpus study. For the discussion in Section 7.3, however, I will not disregard Prince's (1981b) cognitivist model entirely, which, I will argue, raises important questions about what could motivate the choice of one grammatical structure over another.

## 7.2 Methodology of the corpus studies

The research in this study focuses on a comparison of the discourse-embedding of non-reversed specificational clauses with an indefinite variable, which I compare and contrast with (i) predicative clauses with an indefinite complement, (ii) non-reversed specificationals with a definite variable, and (iii) reversed specificational clauses with an indefinite variable as complement. For each construction type 250 examples were analysed. The examples were taken from randomised datasets extracted from the 'Times' and 'British Spoken' subcorpora from Word-banks*Online* (see Chapter 2): both corpora are represented in equal proportions for each clause type.

All examples were analysed in terms of the discourse-familiarity of the information expressed by the two nominal, or nominalised, descriptions (i.e. variable/value, or describee/description). For the reasons outlined in Section 7.1.2, I followed Birner's (1994) and Kaltenböck's (2005) reconceptualisation of Prince's (1981b) account of familiarity in terms of discourse-givenness. In addition, since the category of 'containing inferrables' is taken to be of the same status as its trigger entity (cf. Section 7.1.2), I include the results for containing inferrables in the category of the trigger.

## 7.3 A corpus-based investigation of the discourse-embedding of predicative and specificational clauses

The study of how the elements in the different copular constructions are typically embedded in the ongoing discourse yielded a number of striking observations. Focusing on specificational clauses with indefinite variable, the analysis will centre on three dimensions of contrast: (i) predicative vs specificational clauses with indefinite NP (Section 7.3.1), (ii) specificational clauses with indefinite vs definite variable NP (Section 7.3.2), and (iii) non-reversed vs reversed specificational clauses with indefinite NP (Section 7.3.3). All three distinctions yielded significant differences with respect to discourse-embedding, of which a general overview is given in Table 24.

### 7.3.1 The embedding of predicative vs non-reversed specificational clauses

A first comparison between non-reversed specificational clauses with an indefinite variable and predicative clauses presents a clear difference in the discourse

**Table 24:** Discourse-embedding of the NPs in the four copular clause types.

**a. predicative clauses**

|  | describee |  | description |  |
|---|---|---|---|---|
| brand-new | 10 | (4%) | 118 | (47%) |
| new-anchored | 25 | (10%) | 85 | (34%) |
| inferrable | 17 | (7%) | 26 | (10%) |
| textually given | 180 | (72%) | 21 | (9%) |
| situationally given | 18 | (7%) | 0 | (0%) |

**b. non-reversed specificational clauses with indefinite variable**

|  | indefinite variable |  | value |  |
|---|---|---|---|---|
| brand-new | 6 | (2%) | 92 | (37%) |
| new-anchored | 174 | (70%) | 140 | (56%) |
| inferrable | 70 | (28%) | 8 | (3%) |
| textually given | 0 | (0%) | 9 | (4%) |
| situationally given | 0 | (0%) | 1 | (0%) |

**c. non-reversed specificational clauses with definite variable**

|  | definite variable |  | value |  |
|---|---|---|---|---|
| brand-new | 4 | (2%) | 95 | (38%) |
| new-anchored | 114 | (45%) | 113 | (45%) |
| inferrable | 104 | (42%) | 19 | (8%) |
| textually given | 26 | (10%) | 22 | (9%) |
| situationally given | 2 | (1%) | 1 | (0%) |

**d. reversed specificational clauses with indefinite variable**

|  | value |  | indefinite variable |  |
|---|---|---|---|---|
| brand-new | 118 | (47%) | 1 | (0%) |
| new-anchored | 36 | (14%) | 115 | (46%) |
| inferrable | 9 | (4%) | 122 | (49%) |
| textually given | 83 | (33%) | 11 | (5%) |
| situationally given | 4 | (2%) | 1 | (0%) |

status of the subject in the two construction types ($\chi^2(4) = 341.9$, $p < .001$; Cramer's V: 0.828)[96] (cf. Table 24a,b, Figure 32).

---

[96] The chisquare test was based on the distribution of the data over five different levels of discourse-familiarity in Table 24 (viz. brand-new, new-anchored, inferrable, textually given, situationally given) for the indefinite variable subject (Table 24a) and the describee in predicative clauses (Table 24c).

7.3 Discourse-embedding of predicative and specificational clauses — **289**

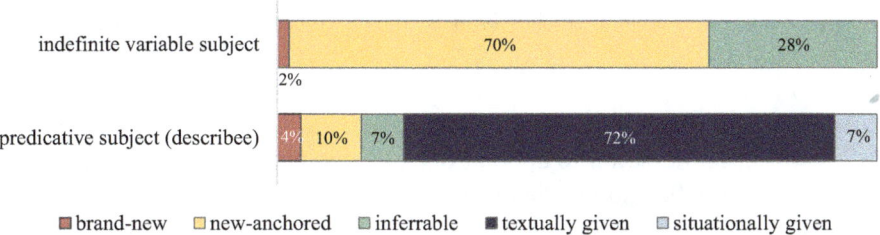

**Figure 32:** The discourse status of the subjects in predicative and non-reversed specificational clauses with indefinite variable.

More importantly, a comparison between the status of the subject and the complement in each clause type indicates that the hypothesised clause-internal contrast between 'given' vs 'new' information is only borne out for predicative clauses, not for specificational ones with indefinite variable.

In predicative clauses (Table 24a), the subject entity, with the role of 'describee', tends to convey familiar information, typically information that has already been textually evoked (72%). The complement, on the other hand, typically describes the subject entity in terms of new information, which is either brand-new (47%) or new-anchored (34%). In (43), for instance, the textually given *he* is characterised in terms of the brand-new description *a has-been*; in (44), the already evoked *neighbourhood committees* are described in terms of new information that is anchored to the prior discourse (e.g. via *crisis in Argentina*).

(43)    I know that bloke. It's Paul Daniels. I can't stand him. *He's a has-been.* (WB)

(44)    Argentina's neighbourhood committees are filling in the gaps left by a severe political and economic crisis. Argentines say that there was a 'vacuum of power', which led them to take matters into their own hands. The committees have been sustained by a political class that seems reluctant to take the reins and get the country back on track... To me, this suggests that *the neighbourhood committees are more <u>a sign of the perpetuation of crisis in Argentina</u>, than <u>the seed of some new movement pointing the way out of it</u>*. (WB)

These numbers corroborate previous observations (see Chapter 4) that predicative clauses typically display a 'direction of fit' in which a description is fitted to the describee. The low percentages of inferrable (10%) and textually given (9%) descriptions suggest that the alternative direction is nonetheless possible. In both (45) and (46), for instance, the description presents textually evoked information, to which a new describee is fitted in (45) and a situationally evoked one in (46).

(45) The Strategic Rail Authority's role appears to have been marginalised: it will have the power to appoint one just one non-executive director. [. . .] An unspecified number of members would play the role of shareholders in holding the board accountable, "but would have no additional powers." *Construction firms, train operators, passenger groups and employees were all possible members.* (WB)

(46) "Basically Dad recognised that I'm a good rhythm guitarist." – "I hate to burst your bubble, Jesse. But my dad probably thinks *I'm a good rhythm guitarist, too.*" (WB)

The typical patterns of discourse-embedding for predicative clauses can be contrasted with those for non-reversed specificational clauses with indefinite variable (Table 24b). In this second clause type, both the variable and the value typically convey unfamiliar information, predominantly new-anchored information, viz. 70% for the variable and 56% for the value. This is illustrated in (47), where the variable is anchored to the prior discourse via *this problem* and the value via *the need for high-quality training for skilled work*.

(47) Many vocational courses are highly weighted towards generic skills, like group work and communication skills, which used to be considered the kind of things that employees would pick up in the course of their jobs. In all of this, the training needed for skilled work is devalued. *One straightforward way of addressing this problem would be to focus on the need for high-quality training for skilled work, to be provided after-compulsory education.* (WB)

If we add to these numbers the percentage of brand-new information – which were much higher for the value (37%) than for the variable (2%) – then both the indefinite variable subject (72%) and its value (93%) are highly likely to express new information. The fact that the variable is unlikely to present *brand-new* information is consistent with the claim made in Chapter 3 that the variable has generalised reference, which is ad-hoc and text-bound. As Breban (2011: 530) argues, generalised instances are created on the spot by abstracting over spatio-temporal instances. Contrary to generic instances, which are retrieved from cultural knowledge, stored in long-term memory, generalised instances are invoked with reference to the local discourse context. The frequent use of secondary determiners (see Chapter 4) indicates that this is typically achieved via phoric links to the prior text (e.g. *another example is. . .*; *a further issue is. . .*; *a similar such word is. . .*).

The shared preference of indefinite variable subjects and the corresponding values for new-anchored information means that the two NPs often have the same level of discourse-familiarity, namely in 43% of the cases. This goes against Mikkelsen's (2005: 135) claim that the felicity of variable subjects depends on the requirement that they are more discourse-familiar than the value complement (see also Vallduví 1992: 21). Further evidence against this is found in a handful of specificational clauses (6%), in which the variable subject is even less discourse-familiar than the value. In (48), for instance, the textually evoked value *bullfighting* is specified for a variable that expresses non-evoked inferrable information.

(48)  **A.**  Tell me something. When you're over there, do you go to the bullfights?
      **B.**  No. No. . . I mean I mean. . . I mean people. . . they. . . they talk about, you know, banning them, but I suppose that if you ban bullfighting, it's like banning Spain's image to the world, because, I mean, *one of Spain's, you know, traditions is bullfighting.* (WB)

In sum, predicative clauses and non-reversed specificational clauses with indefinite variable are typically embedded in the discourse in different ways. Predicative clauses predominantly have textually evoked subject referents or describees, of which the complement gives a new description. Such a clear given-new contrast between subject and complement is rarely found in non-reversed specificational clauses, which instead normally introduce overall new information. This goes against the idea that the variable expresses a presupposition and therefore must be discourse-old (contra, for instance, Declerck 1988), or that it must be at least more familiar than the value complement (contra Mikkelsen 2005: 208).

## 7.3.2 The embedding of indefinite vs definite variable subjects

A second contrast that can be drawn is between the embedding of non-reversed specificational clauses with indefinite vs definite variable. This comparison brings to light subtle differences in how the (in)definiteness of the variable interacts with its discourse-status. These differences are visualised in Figure 33.

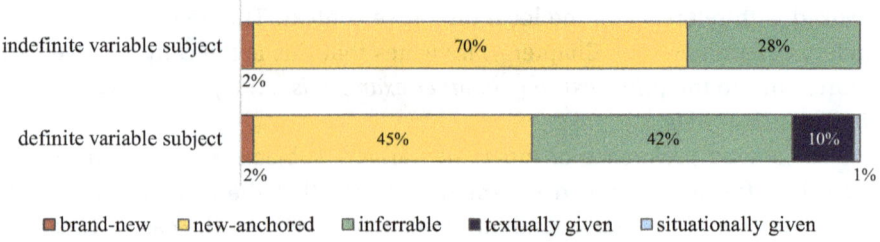

**Figure 33:** The frequencies of different discourse statuses of (in)definite variable subjects.

Like its indefinite counterpart, the definite variable subject has a preference for new-anchored information (45%), e.g. *the lesson for the West of Moscow's siege* in (49).

(49) The Daily Telegraph's Barbara Amiel responded to the Moscow siege by claiming that 'the fight to prevent the acquisition of weapons of mass destruction among truly evil people is the significant battle of our times' – even though the Moscow siege had nothing to do with the acquisition of weapons of mass destruction. For Amiel, 'if a state run by people with the same tactics and aims as those holding the hostages in Moscow were allowed to acquire such weapons, the consequences would be dire' – *and apparently the lesson for the West of Moscow's siege is 'the need to prevent the acquisition of weapons of mass destruction by evil people', everywhere from Iraq to North Korea*. How Amiel got from a Moscow theatre to North Korea is anyone's guess. (WB)

Nonetheless, the difference in discourse status between the two variables is significant ($p < .001$, Fisher's Exact Test[97]). This has to do with the fact that the preference for new-anchored information is much smaller with the definite variable (45%) than with the indefinite one (70%). Instead, definite variable subjects have a much higher percentage of inferrable (42%) and textually evoked (10%) information than the indefinite ones (i.e. 28% and 0% respectively). In (50), for instance, *the overall winner* can be inferred from the previously mentioned *Environmental Awards*. In (51), the variable *the emergency* reformulates the previously evoked *important but unforeseen engagement*.

---

[97] Because of the low numbers for brand-new information and situationally evoked information, the *p*-value was calculated by means of a Fisher's Exact Test. If we leave out the brand-new and situationally evoked categories, a chi-square test also points to a significant difference between indefinite and definite variable subjects ($\chi^2(2) = 45.144$, $p < .001$; Cramer's V: 0.304).

(50) During the reception the Lord Mayor presented the annual Environmental Awards: *the overall winner was Dr Kathy Lewis, of Hertfordshire University*. (WB)

(51) From the moment he arrived, [Taoiseach Bertie] Ahern seemed uncomfortable. After a while, he [...] explained that he would have to rush back to Dublin for an important but unforeseen engagement. On landing, the party officials who shared the return flight were taken aback to discover that *the emergency was, in fact, a pint-drinking session with a group of Ahern's constituency foot soldiers who had been canvassing*. (WB)

Together, the numbers for evoked and inferrable information demonstrate that definite variable subjects have an overall higher likelihood of expressing 'recoverable' information (53%) than indefinite ones (28%). The (in)definiteness of the variable therefore correlates with a binary contrast between discourse-new and -familiar information ($\chi^2(1)$ = 30.5, $p$ < .001; Cramer's V: 0.259). However, the distinction between the two variables is by no means clear-cut. Rather, as Figure 33 illustrates, indefinite and definite variable subjects merely have different preferences along a continuum from non-recoverable to recoverable information. The indefinite variable tends more strongly towards one end of the continuum, with a high concentration of new-anchored information; whereas the definite variable show more dispersion over different statuses, with a roughly equal frequency of 'new-anchored' and 'inferrable' information (resp. 45% and 42%).

Finally, the value complements that are specified for indefinite and definite variable subjects also show some (minor) variation in discourse status ($\chi^2(1)$ =12.532, $p$ = 0.005; Cramer's V: 0.158)[98] (see Figure 34). The value complements specified for the definite variable have a slightly higher percentage of inferrable (8%) and evoked (9%) information than the ones for the indefinite variable (respectively 3% and 4%). Overall, however, the value complement is most likely to be either new-anchored or brand-new in both clause types.

To conclude, no stark contrast appears for the typical discourse-embedding of specificational clauses with indefinite vs definite variable. Instead, the (in) definiteness of the variable NP interacts with its discourse status in more subtly different ways. The variable subjects in both clause types have the same preference, not for 'old' information (contra Declerck 1988: 14, 19) but for new-anchored information. Indefiniteness strengthens this preference, while definiteness makes it less pronounced. Therefore, it would seem that the semantic role of

---

**98** Because of the very low numbers for situationally evoked information, they were here taken together with textually evoked information as forming one 'evoked' category.

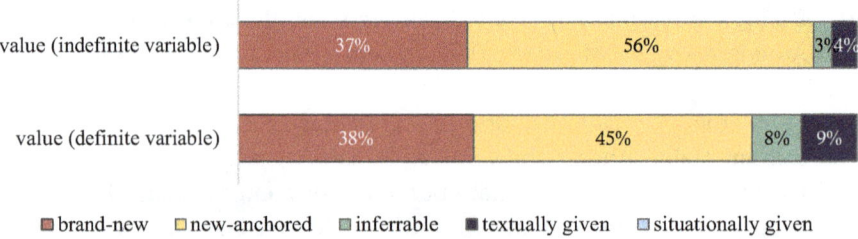

**Figure 34:** The discourse status of the value complement in non-reversed specificational clauses with indefinite vs definite variable.

the variable takes precedence in influencing the discourse status of the NP and that its (in)definiteness plays an additional mediating role. As a result, the distinction between indefinite and definite variables does not hinge (solely) on their discourse status, nor is it true that the variable must be discourse-old (contra Declerck 1988: 14, 19; Mikkelsen 2005: 135).

### 7.3.3 The embedding of non-reversed vs reversed specificationals with indefinite variable

The third and final comparison focuses only on specificational clauses with indefinite variable and examines the differences between the ones in which the variable is subject and those where it is complement. I will demonstrate that significant differences can be found for the discourse status of both the variable and the value in the two clause types. The results for the value in particular will be advanced as offering insights into what could motivate the speaker to construe the specificational clause in its reversed form rather than in its default non-reversed form.

The differences in discourse status between the variable subject vs complement are visualised in Figure 35. These differences are significant ($\chi^2(2)$=38.082, $p < 0.001$; Cramer's V: 0.278). Interestingly, they reject the hypothesis that the clause-initial position of indefinite variable subjects makes them more likely than variable complements to link up with the preceding text and, hence, to have an overall higher degree of discourse-familiarity.

Instead, when construed as complement, the indefinite variable does not show the unequivocal preference for new-anchored information (46%) that it does as subject (70%). Instead, its most likely discourse status is for the variable complement to express inferrable information (49%), e.g. *causative factors* in (52).

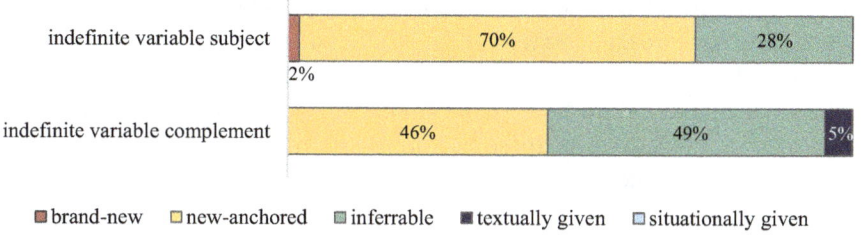

**Figure 35:** The discourse status of indefinite variable subjects vs indefinite variable complements.

(52) Repeated sports training and performance may lead to inflammation and stress fractures. *Poor technique such as running flat-footed or striking the heel hard are causative factors.* Care must be taken if you have taken up exercise to lose weight as being overweight causes increased loading. (WB)

In general, therefore, the indefinite variable complement has a slight preference for recoverable information (54%), while the indefinite variable subject favours new information (72%) ($\chi^2(1)=32.865$, p < .001; Cramer's V: 0.26).[99] These results go against the expectation, based on previous research (e.g. Birner 1994), that information that is presented more towards the end of the sentences tends to be newer than clause-initial information.

The discourse status of value complements vs value subjects further complicates the picture (Figure 36). Here too, significant differences can be found ($\chi^2(3)=125.86$, $p < 0.001$; Cramer's V: 0.502).

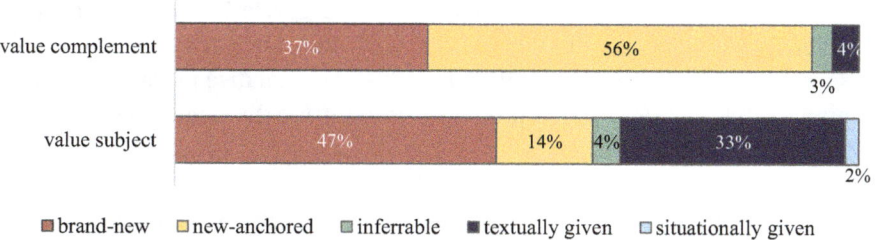

**Figure 36:** The discourse status of the value in non-reversed vs reversed specificational clauses with indefinite variable.

In non-reversed clauses, the expectation that the value is most likely non-recoverable from the prior context is confirmed (93%): the value complement

---

[99] These are the results of a chi-square test for a binary recoverable vs non-coverable contrast.

conveys either brand-new (37%) or new-anchored (56%) information. Reversed clauses, however, are split between two patterns of discourse-embedding, one where the value subject is textually evoked (33%) – e.g. *this* in (53) – and another in which it is brand-new (47%) – e.g. *Peter Roberts*, etc. in (54) . In the remainder of this section, I will describe these two patterns in terms of two different pragmatic purposes for which the reversed specificational clause can be used.

(53) What Shelley is in a sense trying to give us is not so much a tranquil reflection of experience as much as the experience itself white hot. Also, it is splendidly lyrical this opening, so that it is almost as if the words, the music of what Shelley is offering create the experience itself. *And this is one of the things that Shelley tries to do.* So we have the experience white hot and unsorted and it is created. (WB)

(54) Small companies are also feeling the pinch of rationalisation by service providers such as banks and post offices. They point to poor co-ordination between government departments, rural development agencies and local authorities. *Peter Roberts, a potter from Tywyn in Mid Wales, is one business owner who has felt the full force of rural decline.* Having built his business over two decades from its one-man band roots to employ a team of five, he finally shut up shop this summer. (WB)

Firstly, the fact that a large number of value subjects express textually evoked information (33%) corresponds to the unmarked presentation of information, whereby what has already been evoked precedes new information (Halliday 1967b: 205; Birner 1994). The positioning of recoverable information in initial position creates coherence in the text. The high frequency of evoked value subjects is related to the prevalence of demonstrative or relative pronouns as value subject (27%), e.g. (55). These pronouns account for the large majority of the evoked values in the dataset.

(55) The hair's looking more Rick Astley than ever because he's got the two little bits coming down. He's got the Superman curl. [. . .] He doesn't dance. *That's another one of his faults.* He doesn't dance. (WB)

One reason why especially demonstrative pronouns are so commonly used as value subject is the fact that they can establish anaphoric reference to information expressed by full sentences and even by larger stretches of discourse (Halliday & Hasan 1976: 52). Such 'extended text reference' provides a means for summarising a prior proposition or set of propositions as forming one single piece of information (Halliday & Hasan 1976: 52).

Secondly, in the other and more frequent pattern, the value subject conveys brand-new information (47%), so that the unmarked presentation of recoverable before non-recoverable information is overridden (Birner 1994). In (56), for instance, the normal 'flow of information' from given to new is turned around, with the brand-new value subject *French farmers* preceding the new-anchored variable *one main reason* etc. The presentation of new information in initial position – where normally coherence is signalled (e.g. Bolinger 1952; Halliday 1967) – results in a clause-initial 'peak' of information (i.e. so-called 'thematic' prominence). This is expected to require more 'processing effort' (Sperber & Wilson 2004), since the initial new information provides no direct clues as to how the clause relates to the prior discourse. The new value thereby grasps the hearer's attention, for instance to indicate a (sudden) shift towards a new (sub)topic.

(56) The single factor most likely to stop the talks [about rich countries helping poorer ones] dead is the European Union's stance that the "environment" must be on the table, too. This is code for wanting the right to ban imports, in advance of scientific evidence of any harm to people or the environment, a policy many countries think is no more than protectionism. *French farmers are one main reason why the EU has taken this stance.* Offering French forces to the coalition will no doubt continue to boost the French President in the polls ahead of elections. (WB)

The high frequency of this marked presentation of information suggests that givenness is not a decisive factor – or at least not the only deciding factor – for making the value the subject of the clause. In clauses where recoverable information is presented before non-recoverable information, other factors might be of influence, for instance the principle of 'end weight' (Leech 1983; Quirk et al. 1985; Kaltenböck 2000): long, heavy constituent are often placed at the end of a sentence to facilitate processing (Leech 1983: 83; Kaltenböck 2000: 166). In the dataset for this study, end weight does appear to affect the choice between a non-reversed and a reversed construal of the specificational clause at least to some extent: in non-reversed specificational clauses the value complement had an average length of 11.2 words (median: 9 words), whereas the value subject in reversed clauses had an average length of only 3.3 words (median: 2 words).[100]

---

**100** The high frequency of demonstrative values is one reason why the average and median length of value subjects is so low. But even if we leave these values out of the equation, the aver-

This is evidence that very long values tend to be placed in complement position. But what it does not explain is why speakers opt for a reversed construal when the variable and the value have roughly equal weight. In reversed specificational clauses, the variable complement has an average length of 4.4 words (median: 2.5), which makes it, on average, hardly longer than the value subject. What is more, the variable is, on average, actually shorter when it is complement than when it is construed as subject (average: 5.5 words; median: 4). This means that, unless the value is substantially longer than the variable, the influence of end weight is limited: it cannot explain, for instance, why the speaker would opt for the marked option of a reversed specificational construal over the unmarked non-reversed option, especially if the value subject is less recoverable than the variable complement.

Instead, as argued in Chapter 3, the difference between reversed and non-reversed specificationals is a meaningful modal choice, by which the responsibility for the validity of the assertion is vested in the participant that serves as subject (Halliday 1985: 76). Because the subject is the modally responsible element in the clause, the subject referent is likely to be a familiar entity. Therefore, the use of 'new' value subjects is marked not only because it (often) results in the presentation of new information in initial position, but also because new referents are normally not assigned modal responsibility.

An effect of this marked pattern – as proposed in Chapter 6 – is that the reversed specificational clause can acquire mirative overtones by making a brand-new value responsible for the validity of the assertion. Mirativity is commonly associated with the expression of 'surprise' or 'sudden realisation' (Delancey 1997: 33), but it has more recently been interpreted as also including meanings of 'unsurprisingness', 'self-explanatoriness', or 'obviousness' (Aikhenvald 2012: 432; Adelaar 2013). These meanings of 'sudden realisation' and, more importantly, of 'obviousness' and 'self-explanatoriness' seem to arise when reversed specificational clauses take new information as value subject. By vesting the validity of the proposition in a new value, the value is presented as information that can be readily accommodated by both speaker and hearer. In (57), for instance, the value subject *the conspicuous consumption of Donatella Versace* is discourse-new information, but the suggestion that it qualifies as something we can rely on 'pretty safely' is presented as plain and clear.

---

age length of the value subject is still considerably smaller (4 words; median: 2) than the value complement in non-reversed clauses.

(57) What can we rely on in these uncertain, straitened times? *The conspicuous consumption of Donatella Versace would be a pretty safe option.* Holed up in a suite at the Paris Ritz, Donatella window-dressed the place with huge bunches of white lilies and roses, Diptyque candles, iced buckets of Cristal and Melba toast piled high with caviar. She never touched any of it. (WB)

Mirative meanings, such as 'obviousness' or 'self-explanatoriness', need not be coded explicitly, but – as acknowledged in other studies (e.g. Beltrama & Hanink 2019) – they can also arise by implication via linguistic expressions that normally express other meanings than mirativity. That seems to be the case in the clauses discussed here: in reversed specificational clauses, it is the combination of the 'thematic prominence' of the initial new information and the modal responsibility of the subject that gives rise to the implication of mirativity.[101]

This mirative meaning is particularly common when the value is realised by what can be considered 'unused' information in Prince's (1981b) model (cf. Section 5.1). Unused information is brand-new to the discourse but assumed to be familiar to the hearer, e.g. *Saddam Hussein's Iraq* in (58) or *Harry Potter* in (59). These 'unused' discourse referents have homophoric reference: they are retrievable not from the prior discourse but from cultural knowledge that is assumed to be shared by interlocutors of the same community (Martin 1992: 121). Because these referents are assumed to be part of shared background knowledge, they are more likely to be given modal responsibility for the assertion, and their role in the specificational clause is more likely to be presented as 'self-explanatory' or 'obvious'. This is brought out explicitly by the use of the stance marker *obviously* in (58), but it can also be implied, for instance by the absence of further explanation about the specification relation between *Harry Potter* and *one* in (59) (after which a new paragraph begins in the original text).

(58) If the war on terrorism is to succeed, it must target not just terrorist groups but the states that support them and might equip them with the means to commit mass murder. *Saddam Hussein's Iraq was obviously one such state*, a rogue regime if there ever was one. (WB)

---

[101] A similar phenomenon has been observed for other languages, for instance Italian, in which fronting of a constituent expressing new information has been argued to trigger a mirative meaning of unexpectedness, i.e. so-called 'mirative fronting' (e.g. Brunetti 2009; Cruschina 2011), e.g. (i).

(i) Ma guarda te! **In bagno** ha messo le chiavi!
but look-imp.2sg you in bathroom have.3sg put the keys
"Look at that! He put the keys in the bathroom!"

(59)  There are children from dysfunctional families for whom removal from the family background gives them stability and continuity of care and other adult models to learn from. You could say that *Harry Potter is one*. (WB)

In total, 59 examples, or 24% of the value subjects, qualify as presenting 'unused' information. Other cases are more ambiguous. In (60), for instance, the value subject *the La Cage district of Marseille* is new to the discourse. The suggested 'obviousness' of the exemplification implies, however, that *the La Cage district of Marseille* is assumed to be shared knowledge. The writer, not knowing who their actual audience will be, seems to exploit the potential mirative effect of the reversed clause to present the 'La Cage' district *as if* it is an 'obvious' example. While the reader may or may not be familiar with 'La Cage', they are thereby informed that the reputation of the district makes it self-explanatory that 'La Cage' qualifies as a 'ghetto'.

(60)  There has been strong criticism of any European adoption of the reformulated American concept of the 'ghetto'. The word 'ghetto' has been commonly used in France in academic as well as popular literature [. . .] Certainly French cities [. . .] have witnessed the emergence of areas of very strong minority group concentration. <u>The La Cage district of Marseille is an obvious example</u>. (WB)

Of course, the examples in (58) and (60), and arguably (57), comment explicitly on the 'obviousness' of the value. The fact, however, that explicit expressions of 'obviousness' or 'self-explanatoriness' are found so easily in reversed specificational clauses indicates that the reversed specificational construction is conducive to these meanings. That is not to say that such meanings cannot occur in other constructions, for instance non-reversed specificationals. But the fact that reversed specificational clauses are likely to take values introducing 'unused' information, combined with the fact that the specificational relation is often not further explained or motivated in the following text, e.g. (52) or (56), is evidence that they often invite the implication that the value-variable relation is self-explanatory. They differ in that respect from non-reversed specificational clauses, where the following text typically motivates the variable-value relation, elaborating on the new (sub)topic introduced by the specificational clause.

In sum, the findings from the discourse-embedding of predicative and specificational clauses challenge existing assumptions that the two clause types can be described, or even defined, in terms of a given-new contrast (contra, for instance, Prince 1992: 301, 1978; Chomsky 1971; Wilson & Sperber 1979; Horn 1981; Delahunty 1982; Gundel 1985). Instead, while the semantic roles of describee and description and of variable and value set preferences for different discourse statuses in specific contexts of use, these two dimensions of linguistic structure are not determined by one another.

The case studies showed significant differences between the discourse-familiarity of the NPs in the four clause types. These differences were analysed in terms of three main contrasts. First, predicative and specificational clauses are integrated in the discourse in different typical ways. Predicative clauses often comment on a given subject, of which they give a new description. Non-reversed specificational clauses, by contrast, typically shift the discourse in a new direction by raising a new (or inferrable) (sub)topic with the variable/subject, on which the value elaborates.

Second, less substantial differences are found between non-reversed specificational clauses with indefinite vs definite variable. The first are typically new-anchored, while the second have a higher preference for inferrable information. However, no strong contrast in discourse embedding was found between these two clause types. This supports the point made in Chapter 3 that the choice between an indefinite or a definite variable is motivated primarily by the implicatures of (non-)exhaustive specification.

Finally, more important differences obtain between non-reversed and reversed specificational clauses. Reversed specificationals were split between two patterns of discourse embedding: one in which the value subject expressed brand-new information and another in which it picked up on textually given information. In the first pattern, the value subject often introduced 'unused' information, i.e. information that is new to the discourse but assumed to be familiar to the hearer. The use of such unused entities as subject was argued to trigger mirative meaning. In the second pattern, the value subject, often a demonstrative, was analysed in terms of the notion of 'extended text reference', i.e. the ability to summarise propositions and longer stretches of discourse and present them as one abstract discourse entity (Halliday & Hasan 1976). I proposed that, like non-reversed specificational clauses, this pattern of reversed clauses has a 'discourse-organising' function, not to shift the discourse to a new topic but to summarise the previous topic as answering the matter of current concern expressed by the variable.

## 7.4 Conclusion

This chapter dealt with the discourse embedding of predicative and specificational clauses, more specifically with the discourse-familiarity of the two NPs in the different clause types.

The findings from the corpus studies challenged existing assumptions about the discourse-familiarity of the two NPs in predicative and specificational clauses. Previous studies have claimed that while no specific discourse conditions apply to predicative clauses, specificational clauses are characterised by an intrinsic contrast between given 'presupposed' variables and new 'focal' values (e.g. Chomsky 1969; Akmajian 1979; Declerck 1988; Mikkelsen 2005). These pre-empirical assumptions were rejected by the evidence from the corpus studies, where both the variable and the value showed much more variation in their actual discourse-familiarity.

Against previous assumptions, I supported the view that the semantics of predicative and specificational clauses form a separate layer of coded meaning and cannot be conflated with the dimension of discourse structure. While the semantic roles of the describee and description and of the variable and value may set different preferences for specific discourse statuses, these semantics do not determine how the different roles are integrated in specific contexts of use, or vice versa.

Finally, by interpreting the discursive organisation as influenced by multiple factors, I showed that not only the semantics of predication and specification, but also the grammatical functions (i.e. subject vs complement) of the variable/value and the (in)definiteness of the variable have an influence on the typical patterns of discursive organisation. None of these factors, however, exclusively determines the actual discourse embedding of the copular clause. By looking in detail at the specific discourse patterns for the various clause types, this study has contributed to a better insight into the interaction between the clause types' semantic functions and the actual discursive functions they serve in specific contexts of use.

# Conclusion

The study of specificational copular clauses has, in the past, focused mainly on those with a definite variable. Taking these as the starting point for the descriptive analysis of specificational clauses often meant ignoring those with an indefinite variable altogether, or explaining them away by reducing them somehow to the former. The study in this book offered a comprehensive investigation of English specificational copulars with an indefinite variable as a distinct construction in its own right. By centring on these clauses as the main research topic, the book presented a positive description of their own characteristics. These were compared both to their specificational counterpart with a definite variable and to the predicative clause type with an indefinite predicate nominative, with which specificationals have typically been contrasted in the literature (e.g. Partee 1986a; Declerck 1988; Keizer 1992; Moro 1997; Mikkelsen 2005; den Dikken 2006; Heycock 2012; Patten 2012, 2016). The systematic data- and usage-based comparison of the different clause types ultimately led to a better understanding of how specificational clauses with an indefinite variable fit into the English copular clause system.

One of the main arguments in this book was that the contrast between specificational and predicative clauses is essentially a semantic one, coded by the lexicogrammatical structure of the two clause types. Following Halliday (1968: 190–191, 1985: 114), I explained, in Chapter 3, that specificational clauses code transitive processes between two participants, whose roles are those of variable and value, e.g. (1). Predicative clauses, by contrast, code intransitive processes with only one participant – the describee – while the other NP in the clause serves the non-participant role of description. The function of this NP – the predicate nominative – is therefore not to code a participant but to specify the content of the predicative process, e.g. *a delightful guide to the gardener's palette* in (2).

(1) If we're talking simple comforts in lovely settings, *another great wee place on the Whisky Trail is the Archiestown hotel.* (WB)

(2) 'Colour for Adventurous Gardeners' is a delightful guide to the gardener's palette. (WB)

The respective (in)transitivity of the two clause types was argued to be coded by their different clause structures. This was analysed in terms of the different orders in which the clause components are successively combined to form a composite structure. I followed Langacker (1991: 67–68) in interpreting predicative clauses as involving a composite relational predicate, derived from the integration of *be* + predicate nominative. The NP serving as predicate nominative is thereby reclassified as relational. This allows the NP to provide the specific content of the relation schematically profiled by *be*. In specificational clauses, by contrast, it was argued that no composite predicate is involved: only *be* is part of the relational predicate, which makes schematic reference to two participants, i.e. the variable and the value. Structurally, the two NPs integrate directly with the VP. The different structural relations in predicative and specificational clauses were shown to be reflected in their different formal behaviour (e.g. the coordination patterns they allow for, the possibility of a subject-complement switch).

As a result of their semantic role in the copular clause, the NPs serving as predicate nominative and as specificational variable were argued to have different referential statuses (contra the 'inverse' account, e.g. Partee 1986a; Moro 1997; Mikkelsen 2005; Patten 2012). The relational function of the predicate nominative leads to what is typically described as the 'non-referentiality' of the predicate nominative (e.g. Kuno 1970; Declerck 1988: 56–62; Keizer 1992: 39–40). Following Langacker (1991: 67–68), however, I stressed that the non-referentiality of the predicate nominative cannot be taken to mean that the NP designates a type, class or property (contra, for instance, Taylor 2002: 362; Patten 2012: 46). The full NP structure of the predicate nominative means that it designates an instance. It is because of its nominal structure and the fact that it designates an instance that the predicate nominative can attribute a fine-grained characterisation combining type specifications and qualitative features to the subject referent. Instead, the non-referentiality of the predicate nominative is more accurately explained in terms of the NP designating a virtual 'descriptional' instance that is conjured up solely for the purpose of providing a description. This virtual instance "has no status outside this predicate nominative construction" (Langacker 1991: 68). In specificational clauses, by contrast, the NPs that realise the functions of variable and value are both 'referential' (in the sense of establishing a discourse referent). I proposed that the referential status of the variable is best captured in terms of the notion of 'generalised reference' (Langacker 1999, 2005: 172; Breban 2011: 513). The variable, in other words, expresses a generalised instance. As Breban & Davidse (2003) and Breban (2011) observed, generalised instances imply 'dual reference' (a concept introduced by Ward & Birner [1995]): while the variable NP denotes a generalised entity at a higher level of abstraction, it simultaneously makes implicit reference to a more concrete instance it abstracts away from.

I further argued that the variable's generalised reference triggers the inference of two (contrasting) sets of more concrete entities that potentially meet the criteria set up by the generalisation (i.e. instances that potentially qualify as values for the variable). The first set is a set of actually qualifying entities; the second is a set of potential but failed entities. The choice between a definite or an indefinite variable NP indicates respectively whether the designated instance implies reference to all qualifying entities in the first set, or whether it singles out one qualifying instance from that set. This was further shown to trigger two pragmatic (and, hence, cancellable) implicatures. First, while the definite variable triggers the implicature that the instance specified by the value exhausts the set of qualifying entities (i.e. the specified value is the only instance corresponding to the variable), the indefinite variable was described as implying non-exhaustiveness (i.e. potentially multiple items correspond as values to the same variable). Second, as Declerck (1988: 24) points out, specificational clauses with definite variable also imply contrastiveness: because the specified value exhausts the set of qualifying entities, it thereby contrasts with all potential but failed entities. Since indefinite variables imply non-exhaustiveness, no such contrast between the specified value and potential others is triggered.

In Chapter 4, the different semantic roles of the predicate nominative and the indefinite specificational variable, and their corresponding referential statuses, were shown to be reflected in the distribution of different structural elements and their lexical realisation in the two NP types. A corpus-based analysis of the lexicogrammatical form of the predicate nominative and variable NP demonstrated that the selection of head nouns, the use of different pre- and postmodifier functions but also the choice of determiner correlated with the semantic role of the NP in the copular clause. Firstly, indefinite variable NPs select head nouns from more restricted lexicosemantic domains than the predicative nominative, often preferring more 'conceptual' nouns with a verb-like quality (e.g. *problem, question, option, possibility*). The type-specifications expressed by these more abstract head nouns are further restricted by content retrieved from the prior discourse or, more often, explicitly expressed in the form of post-head complements.

Secondly, indefinite variable NPs used premodifiers less frequently than predicate nominatives and were also more restrictive in their choice of specific adjectives. This smaller lexical set typically included adjectives that imply a qualitative comparison between instances (e.g. *notable, important*). I argued that these adjectives were used to stipulate extra qualitative criteria that the value that satisfies the variable has to meet.

Moreover, the determiners that were typically used in the indefinite variable NP allowed for a similar delineation of a more restrictive subset within the set of qualifying entities. While predicate nominatives mainly took an indefinite article or the 'zero-article' in the plural, indefinite variable NPs were highly likely to use either 'indefinite article + secondary determiner' or the quantifier *one*. Both determiner types are often used to comment on the non-uniqueness implicature that attaches to the indefinite NP. This was presented as evidence that the use of an indefinite variable is a meaningful choice that offers a contrastive option to the definite variable, motivated by the respective implicatures of non-exhaustiveness and exhaustiveness that they trigger.

The findings in Chapter 4 were adduced as evidence for the semantic contrast between predicative and specificational clauses posited in Chapter 3.

In Chapter 5, further evidence for this semantic contrast was presented by homing in on the construal of the VP, notably the use of aspect and modality, in the different clause types. By means of collostructional analyses (Stefanowitsch & Gries 2003), I showed that predicative and specificational clauses attracted, or repelled, different kinds of aspect and modality. Among specificational clauses, further differences were found between non-reversed and reversed clauses and between clauses with indefinite variable and the ones with definite variable. I analysed these results in terms of (i) the different perspectives on the specificational relation that are coded by non-reversed vs reversed clauses and (ii) the different implicatures of (non-)exhaustiveness triggered by the definite vs indefinite variable NP.

For aspect, I argued that only predicative clauses but not specificational ones can take progressive aspect. I suggested that, in predicative clauses, the composite predicate formed by *be* + NP can, under special circumstances, be construed as respectively bounded episodes of behaviour or perfective events (e.g. *he's being a bully*; *he's recently been a victim of robbery*). By contrast, in specificational clauses, the construal of a bounded episode of controllable behaviour is at odds with the inherently imperfective stative relation of specification. I further argued that indefinite perfect aspect can occur with both predicative and specificational clauses but only under very special circumstances. In both clause types, the use of the indefinite perfect appears to involve a shift of temporal focus: the speaker does not express that the copular relation no longer holds at the moment of encoding or decoding – as would normally be expected with an indefinite perfect – but s/he merely shifts the focus to a moment in the recent past when the process of predication or specification was particularly relevant.

The attraction, or repulsion, of modals was motivated by various factors. First, certain forms of dynamic modality – *viz*. ability, need and volition – are not possible with non-reversed specificational clauses, though they are (marginally) acceptable with predicative and reversed specificational clauses. This was explained in terms of the impossibility of ascribing participant-inherent force like ability, volition or need to the abstract criterial entity designated by the variable NP.

Secondly, predicative clauses attract epistemic and evidential modals. The descriptive function of these clause was argued to invite a subjective evaluation on the part of the speaker. The degree to which the speaker commits to the validity of this evaluation can be modulated by means of an epistemic modal. Alternatively, the speaker can use evidential markers to assign responsibility for the proposition to some external source.

Specificational clauses were also found to attract epistemic modals, especially when the variable NP was indefinite. The non-exhaustiveness implicature triggered by the indefinite variable tallies with contexts in which the speaker is not able or willing to specify all the values exhaustively or distinguish qualifying entities (real values) from potential, but failed candidates. The tentativity on the part of the speaker could then explain why epistemic modals are attracted to these clauses. A similar explanation was given for the repulsion of evidential markers by specificationals with indefinite variable: the non-exhaustiveness associated with indefinite variables implies a weaker commitment on the part of the speaker (Lyons 1999), so that evidential markers are less likely to be used to 'hedge' the assertion by citing 'external' evidence.

Chapter 6 then turned to the information structure of predicative and specificational clauses. It centred specifically on the assumption that specificational clauses can be recognised by the fixed assignment of focus to the value, which is contrasted with a presupposed variable. I demonstrated that such an interpretation of information focus hinges on a conflation of different layers of linguistic meaning, *viz.* (i) the lexicogrammatically coded specificational relation between a variable and a value, (ii) the pragmatic inferences triggered by the meanings at level (i) (notably the pragmatic presupposition of existence, as well as the logical direction of correspondence), and, finally, (iii) the information structure, including focus (and presupposition) marking and discourse-familiarity. I demonstrated that information focus, at level (iii), should be analysed independently of the other layers of meaning, even if interactions with the other layers can occur.

The analysis of spoken data demonstrated that only predicative clauses conform to the expected pattern with a non-prominent describee and a prominent description. Specificational clauses, by contrast, rarely exhibit the hypothesised contrast between a presupposed variable and a focal value. Non-reversed specificational are typically uttered on multiple tone units (TUs) so that both the variable and value are marked as focal within their own (sequence of) TUs. Reversed specificational clauses are often uttered one TU, but rather than assign focus to the value, they often mark the variable as focal. Therefore, the findings in Chapter 6 urge us to reconsider the analysis of specificational clauses as rooted in the assignment of information focus or other factors of prosodic prominence: specificational clauses are distinguished from predicative ones by their distinct semantic relations, which may set default preferences for a certain information structure, but by no means determine it.

Chapter 7, finally, looked at the discourse embedding of predicative and specificational clauses, more specifically the discourse-familiarity (Kaltenböck 2005) of the two NPs in these clauses. The findings challenged previous claims that, in specificational clauses, the variable expresses 'old' presupposed information and the value 'new' focal information (e.g. Chomsky 1969; Akmajian 1979; Declerck 1988; Mikkelsen 2005). Instead, while predicative clauses typically did exhibit such a contrast between 'given' describees and 'new' descriptions, specificational clauses showed much more variation, with both the variable and the value often expressing new information. Therefore, against previous assumptions, I argued that the semantic roles of the describee and description and of the variable and value may set different preferences for specific discourse statuses, but that these semantics do not determine how the different roles are integrated in specific contexts of use, or vice versa. Finally, by interpreting the discursive organisation as influenced by multiple factors, I showed that not only the semantics of predication and specification, but also the grammatical functions (i.e. subject vs complement) of the variable/value and the (in)definiteness of the variable have an influence on the typical patterns of discursive organisation.

To conclude, the studies in this book refuted a number of widespread assumptions about the meanings and the formal behaviour of specificational and predicative clauses. I have presented alternatives to these assumptions and thereby provided a better understanding of specificational clauses with indefinite variable, in particular, but also of the broader copular system and the place of these clauses in it.

The refutation of prior assumptions has opened up new avenues for future research. One such avenue is the information structure (IS) of copular clauses. Since this study provided counterevidence for the analysis of the IS of specificational copular clauses in terms of a presupposition-focus relation, the question arises if the IS of other specificational constructions, viz. clefts and pseudoclefts, may need to be revisited as well. Especially the cleft structure has commonly been interpreted as a grammaticalisation of the information-structural 'presupposition-focus' contrast (e.g. Lambrecht 2001; Lehmann 2008): here too, the semantic variable-value relation appears to be conflated with the focus marking, on the one hand, and discourse status, on the other.

Finally, I pointed out various interactions between the (im)possibility of (non-)unique identifiability (as coded by the (in)definiteness of the nominal) and interpersonal speaker-related meanings (e.g. tentativity). These observations raise the question whether such interactions can also be found in other related constructions, for instance between *it*-clefts (e.g. *It's John who doesn't eat meat*) and *there*-clefts (e.g. *There's John who doesn't eat meat, and I think Mary and Jane are vegetarians too*). These constructions reflect a similar distinction between (non-)exhaustiveness as specificational copular clauses with (in)definite variable. While clefts and copulars like the ones studied in this book differ on multiple counts, it would be worthwhile to examine to what extent correspondences between the prosodic realisations of these constructions can be found. If such correlations were found, it would further corroborate the interaction between (non-)exhaustive specification and the interpersonal speaker-related meanings found in this book. This would ultimately provide further support for the meaningfulness of the choice between exhaustive and non-exhaustive specification.

# References

Abbott, Barbara. 2010. *Reference* (Oxford Survey in Semantics and Pragmatics 2). Oxford: Oxford University Press.

Adamson, Sylvia M. 2000. A lovely little example: Word order options and category shift in the premodifying string. In Olga Fischer, Anette Rosenbach & Dieter Stein (eds.), *Pathways of Change: Grammaticalization in English* (Studies in Language Companion Series 53), 39–66. Amsterdam: John Benjamins.

Adelaar, Willem F.H. 2013. A Quechuan mirative? In Alexandra Aikhenvald & Anne Storch (eds.), *Perception and Cognition in Language and Culture*, 95–109. Leiden: Brill.

Adger, David & Gillian Ramchand. 2003. Predication and Equation. *Linguistic Inquiry* 34(3). 325–359.

Aikhenvald, Alexandra Y. 2004. *Evidentiality*. Oxford: Oxford University Press.

Aikhenvald, Alexandra Y. 2012. The essence of mirativity. *Linguistic Typology* 16(3). 435–485.

Akmajian, Adrian. 1970. Aspects of the grammar of focus in English. Cambridge, MA: MIT doctoral dissertation.

Akmajian, Adrian. 1973. The role of focus in the interpretation of anaphoric expressions. In Stephen R. Anderson & Paul Kiparsky (eds.), *A Festschrift for Morris Halle*, 215–226. New York: Holt, Rinehart and Winston.

Akmajian, Adrian. 1979. *Aspects of the grammar of focus in English*. Cambridge, MA: MIT doctoral dissertation.

Aktas, Rahime Nur. 2005. *Functions of "shell nouns" as cohesive devices in academic writing: A comparative corpus-based study*. Ames, IA: Iowa State University doctoral dissertation.

Ariel, Mira. 1990. *Accessing Noun-Phrase Antecedents*. London: Routledge.

Atlas, Jay David & Stephen C. Levinson. 1981. It-clefts, informativeness, and logical form: Radical pragmatics. In Peter Cole (ed.), *Radical Pragmatics*, 1–62. New York: Academic Press.

Austin, John L. 1953. How to talk: Some simple ways. *Proceedings of the Aristotelian Society* 53(1). 227–246.

Austin, John L. 1970. How to talk: Some simple ways. In James O. Urmson & Geoffrey J. Warnock (eds.), *J.L. Austin. Philosophical Papers*, 134–153. 2nd edn. Oxford: Oxford University Press.

Bache, Carl. 2000. *Essentials of Mastering English: A Concise Grammar*. Berlin/New York: Mouton de Gruyter.

Barth-Weingarten, Dagmar. 2016. *Intonation Units Revisited: Cesuras in Talk-in-Interaction*. Amsterdam: John Benjamins.

Beckman, Mary E. & Gayle Ayers Elam. 1993. Guidelines for ToBI Labelling. The Ohio State University Research Foundation.

Beltrama, Andrea & Emily A. Hanink. 2019. Marking imprecision, conveying surprise: *Like* between hedging and mirativity. *Journal of Linguistics* 55(1). 1–34.

Birner, Betty. 1996. *The Discourse Function of Inversion in English*. New York: Garland.

Birner, Betty J. 1994. Information status and word order: An analysis of English inversion. *Language* 70(2). 233–259.

Boersma, Paul & Vincent van Heuven. 2001. Speak and unSpeak with Praat. *Glot International* 5(9–10). 341–347.

Boersma, Paul & David Weenink. 2016. *Praat: doing phonetics by computer*. http://www.praat.org/.

Bolinger, Dwight. 1947. Review of K.L. Pike, Intonation of American English. *American Speech* 22. 134–136.
Bolinger, Dwight. 1952. Linear Modification. *PMLA* 67(7). 1117–1144.
Bolinger, Dwight. 1954. English Prosodic Stress and Spanish Sentence Order. *Hispania* 37(2). 152–156.
Bolinger, Dwight. 1967. Adjectives in English: Attribution and predication. *Lingua* 18. 1–34.
Bolinger, Dwight. 1968. Entailment and the meaning of structures. *Glossa* 2. 119–127.
Bolinger, Dwight. 1972a. *Degree Words*. The Hague: Mouton.
Bolinger, Dwight. 1972b. A look at equatives and cleft sentences. In Evelyn S. Firchow (ed.), *Studies for Einar Haugen. Presented on the Occasion of his 65th Birthday, April 19, 1971*. The Hague: Mouton.
Bolinger, Dwight. 1989. *Intonation and Its Uses: Melody in Grammar and Discourse*. Stanford: Stanford University Press.
Brazil, David. 1997. *The Communicative Value of Intonation in English*. Cambridge: Cambridge University Press.
Breban, Tine. 2011. Secondary determiners as markers of generalized instantiation in English noun phrases. *Cognitive Linguistics* 22(3). 511–533.
Breban, Tine & Kristin Davidse. 2003. Adjectives of comparison: The grammaticalization of their attribute uses into postdeterminer and classifier uses. *Folia Linguistica* 37(3). 269–317.
Brems, Lieselotte & Kristin Davidse. 2003. Absolute and relative quantification: beyond mutually exclusive word classes. *Belgian Journal of English Language and Literatures. New Series* 1. 49–60.
Brown, Gillian, Karen L. Currie & Joanne Kenworthy. 1980. *Questions of Intonation*. London: Croom Helm.
Brown, Gillian & George Yule. 1983. *Discourse Analysis*. Cambridge: Cambridge University Press.
Brunetti, Lisa. 2009. On the pragmatics of post-focal material in Italian (left peripheral focus looked from the other side). In Denis Apothéloz, Bernard Combettes & Franck Neveu (eds.), *Les linguistiques du détachement, Actes du Colloque de Nancy, Juin 7–9, 2006*, 151–162. Berne: Peter Lang.
Butler, Christopher S. 2013. Systemic Functional Linguistics, Cognitive Linguistics and psycholinguistics: Opportunities for dialogue. *Functions of Language* 20(2). 185–218.
Bybee, Joan. 1985. *Morphology: A Study of the Relation between Meaning and Form*. Amsterdam: John Benjamins.
Carlson, Gregory N. 1978. *Reference to Kinds in English*. Bloomington: Indiana University Linguistics club.
Chafe, Wallace. 1976. Giveness, contrastiveness, definiteness, subjects, topics, and point of view. In Charles N. Li (ed.), *Subject and Topic*, 25–55. New York: Academic Press.
Chen, Ping. 2009. Aspects of referentiality. *Journal of Pragmatics* (Childhood and Social Interaction in Everyday Life) 41(8). 1657–1674.
Chomsky, Noam. 1969. *Deep Structure, Surface Structure, and Semantic Interpretation*. Bloomington, IN: Indiana University Linguistics Club.
Chomsky, Noam. 1971. Deep structure, surface structure, and semantic interpretation. In Danny Steinberg & Leon Jakobovits (eds.), *Semantics: An Interdisciplinary Reader in Philosophy, Linguistics, and Philosophy*, 183–216. New York: Cambridge University Press.
Clark, Herbert H & Susan E Haviland. 1977. Comprehension and the given-new contract. In Roy O. Freedle (ed.), *Discourse Production and Comphrehension*, 1–40. Norwoord, NY: Ablex Publishing Corporation.

Coates, Jennifer. 1983. *The Semantics of the Modal Auxiliaries* (Croom Helm Linguistics Series). London: Croom Helm.
Comrie, Bernard. 1976. *Aspect: An Introduction to the Study of Verbal Aspect and Related Problems*. Cambridge: Cambridge University Press.
Cornillie, Bert. 2009. Evidentiality and epistemic modality: On the close relationship of two different categories. *Functions of Language* 16(1). 44–62.
Crain, Stephen & Henry Hamburger. 1992. Semantics, knowledge and NP modification. In Robert Levine (ed.), *Formal Grammar: Theory and Implementation. Vancouver Studies in Cognitive Science*, Vol. 2, 372–401. Vancouver: The University of British Columbia Press.
Croft, William. 1991. *Syntactic Categories and Grammatical Relations*. Chicago: Chicago University Press.
Cruschina, Silvio. 2011. Fronting, dislocation, and the syntactic role of discourse-related features. *Linguistic Variation* 11(1). 1–34.
Cruttenden, Alan. 1986. *Intonation* (Cambridge Textbooks in Linguistics). Cambridge: Cambridge University Press.
Cruttenden, Alan. 1997. *Intonation*. Cambridge: Cambridge University Press.
Crystal, David. 1969. *Prosodic Systems and Intonation in English*. Cambridge: Cambridge University Press.
Crystal, David. 1975. *The English Tone of Voice: Essays in Intonation, Prosody and Paralanguage*. London: Edward Arnold.
Davidse, Kristin. 1997. The subject–object versus the agent–patient asymmetry. *Leuven Contributions in Linguistics and Philology* 86. 413–431.
Davidse, Kristin. 1998a. Agnates, verb classes and the meaning of construals: The case of ditransitivity in English. *Leuvense Bijdragen* 87(3). 281–313.
Davidse, Kristin. 1998b. The Dative as participant role versus the Indirect Object: On the need to distinguish two layers of organization. In Willy Van Langendonck & William Van Belle (eds.), *The Dative. Vol 2. Theoretical and Constrastive Studies, Case and Grammatical Relations across Languages, 3*, 143–184. Amsterdam: Benjamins.
Davidse, Kristin. 1999. *Categories of Experiential Grammar* (Monographs in Systemic Linguistics 11). Nottingham: Nottingham Trent University.
Davidse, Kristin. 2000. A constructional approach to clefts. *Linguistics* 38(6). 1101–1131.
Davidse, Kristin. 2004. The interaction of identification and quantification in English determiners. In Michel Achard & Suzanne Kemmer (eds.), *Language, Culture and Mind*, 507–533. Stanford: CSLI Publications.
Davidse, Kristin. 2011. Alternations as a heuristic to verb meaning and the semantics of constructions. In Pilar Guerrero (ed.), *Morphosyntactic Alternations*, 11–37. London: Equinox.
Davidse, Kristin. 2018. Complex NPs with third-order entity clauses: Towards a grammatical description and semantic typology. In Alex Ho-Cheong Leung & Willem van der Wurff (eds.), *The Noun Phrase in English: Past and Present*, 11–46. Amsterdam: Benjamins.
Davidse, Kristin & Tine Breban. 2019. A cognitive-functional approach to the order of adjectives in the English noun phrase. *Linguistics* 57(2). 327–371.
Davidse, Kristin, Tine Breban & An Van linden. 2008. Deictification: The development of secondary deictic meanings by adjectives in the English NP. *English Language & Linguistics* 12(3). 475–503.
Davidse, Kristin & Lobke Ghesquière. 2016. Content-purport, content-substance and structure: focusing *mere* and *merely*. *Acta Linguistica Hafniensia* 48(1). 85–109.

Davidse, Kristin & Ditte Kimps. 2016. Specificational there-clefts: Functional structure and information structure. *English Text Construction* 9(1). 115–142.

Davidse, Kristin & Kathleen Rymen. 2008. Cognate and locative complements: Their effect on (a)telicity and their semantic relation to the verb. *Lingvisticae Investigationes* 31(2). 256–272.

Davidse, Kristin & Wout Van Praet. 2018. A cognitive-functional account of English specificational and predicative copular clauses. Unpublished working paper.

Davidse, Kristin & Wout Van Praet. 2019. Rethinking predicative clauses with indefinite predicate and specificational clauses with indefinite variable: A cognitive-functional account. *Leuven Working Papers in Linguistics* 38. 1–36.

Davidse, Kristin & Lieven Vandelanotte. 2011. Tense use in direct and indirect speech in English. *Journal of Pragmatics* 43(1). 236–250.

Davies, Eirian C. 2001. Propositional attitudes. *Functions of Language* 8(2). 217–250.

Declerck, Renaat. 1979. Aspect and the bounded/unbounded (telic/atelic) distinction. *Linguistics* 17(9–10). 761–794.

Declerck, Renaat. 1988. *Studies on Copular Sentences, Clefts, and Pseudo-Clefts*. Leuven: Leuven University Press.

Declerck, Renaat. 1991. *Tense in English: Its Structure and Use in Discourse* (Germanic Linguistics). London: Routledge.

Declerck, Renaat. 2006. *The Grammar of the English Tense System*. Berlin/New York: Mouton de Gruyter.

Delacruz, Enrique B. 1976. Factives and proposition level constructions in Montague grammar. In Barbara H. Partee (ed.), *Montague Grammar*, 177–199. New York: Academic Press.

Delahunty, Gerald Patrick. 1982. *Topics in the Syntax and Semantics of English Cleft Sentences*. Bloomington: Indiana University Linguistics club.

Delahunty, Gerald Patrick. 1984. The analysis of English cleft sentences. *Linguistic Analysis* 13(2). 63–113.

Delancey, Scott. 2003. Mirativity: The grammatical marking of unexpected information. *Linguistic Typology* 1(1). 33–52.

Denison, David. 2006. Category change and gradience in the determiner system. In Ans van Kemenade & Bettelou Los (eds.), *The Handbook of the History of English*, 279–304. Oxford: Blackwell.

Dik, Simon C. 1980. Cleft and pseudo-cleft in functional grammar. In Wim Zonneveld & Fred Weerman (eds.), *Linguistics in the Netherlands, 1977–1979*, 26–43. Dordrecht: Foris.

Dik, Simon C. 1983. Auxiliary and copular *be* in a Functional grammar of English. In Frank Heny & Barry Richards (eds.), *Linguistic Categories: Auxiliaries and Related Puzzles. Vol II: The Scope, Order, and Distribution of English Auxiliary Verbs*, 121–143. Dordrecht: D. Reidel Publishing Company.

Dik, Simon C. 1997. *The Theory of Functional Grammar. Part 1. The Structure of the Clause*. 2nd edn. Berlin/Boston: De Gruyter Mouton.

Dikken, Marcel den. 2006. Specificational copular sentences and pseudoclefts: A case study. In Martin Everaert & Hendrik van Riemsdijk (eds.), *The Blackwell Companion to Syntax*, vol. 3, 292–409. Oxford: Blackwell Publishing.

Dikken, Marcel den, André Meinunger & Chris Wilder. 2000. Pseudoclefts and ellipsis. *Studia Linguistica* 54. 41–89.

Donnellan, Keith. 1966. Reference and definite descriptions. *Philosophical Review* 75(3). 281–304.

Du Bois, John W. 1980. Beyond definiteness: The trace of identity in discourse. In Wallace Chafe (ed.), *The Pear Stories: Cognitive, Cultural, and Linguistic Aspects of Narrative Production*, 203–274. Norwoord, NJ: Ablex.

Fauconnier, Gilles. 1985. *Mental Spaces: Aspects of Meaning Construction in Natural Language*. Cambridge, MA: MIT Press.

Fauconnier, Gilles. 1994. *Mental Spaces: Aspects of Meaning Construction in Natural Language*. Cambridge: Cambridge University Press.

Firbas, Jan. 1992. *Functional Sentence Perspective in Written and Spoken Communication* (Studies in English Language). Cambridge: Cambridge University Press.

Flowerdew, J. 2003. Signalling nouns in discourse. *English for Specific Purposes* 22(4). 329–346.

Fonteyn, Lauren. 2016. From nominal to verbal gerunds: A referential typology. *Folia Linguistica* 23(1). 60–83.

Fox, Anthony. 1986. Dimensions of prosodic structure. *Working Papers in Linguistics and Phonetics (University of Leeds)* 4. 79–127.

Francis, Elaine J. 1999. A conceptual semantic analysis of thematic structure in predicate nominals. Paper presented at Texas Linguistics Society, Austin, Texas, 1999.

Francis, Elaine J & Laura E. Michaelis. 2003. Mismatch: A crucible for linguistic theory. In Elaine J. Francis & Laura E. Michaelis (eds.), *Mismatch: A Form-Function Incongruity and the Architecture of Grammar*, 1–27. Stanford, CA: CSLI Publications.

Francis, Gill. 1986. *Anaphoric Nouns*. Birmingham: Department of English, University of Birmingham.

Francis, Gill. 1994. Labelling discourse: An aspect of nominal-group lexical cohesion. In Malcolm Coulthard (ed.), *Advances in Written Text Analysis*, 83–101. New York.

Gazdar, Gerald. 1979a. *Pragmatics: Implicature, Presupposition, and Logical Form*. New York: Academic Press.

Gazdar, Gerald. 1979b. A solution to the projection problem. In Choon-Kyu Oh & David Dinneen (eds.), *Syntax and Semantics. Vol 11: Presupposition*. New York: Academic Press.

Geach, Peter T. 1962. *Reference and Generality. An Examination of Some Medieval and Modern Theories*. 1st edn. Ithaca, NY: Cornell University Press.

Geach, Peter T. 1968. *Reference and Generality: An Examination of Some Medieval and Modern Theories*. 2nd edn. Ithaca, NY: Cornell University Press.

Gentens, Caroline. 2016. The discursive status of extraposed object clauses. *Journal of Pragmatics* 96. 15–31.

Gimson, Alfred C. 1980. *An Introduction into the Pronunciation of English*. London: Edward Arnold.

Gisborne, Nikolas. 2007. Dynamic Modality. *SKASE Journal of Theoretical Linguistics* 4(2). 44–61.

Gonzálvez García, Francisco & Christopher Butler. 2006. Mapping functional-cognitive space. *Annual Review of Cognitive Linguistics* 4. 39–96.

Grabe, Esther, Greg Kochanski & John Coleman. 2007. Connecting intonation labels to mathematical descriptions of fundamental frequency. *Language and Speech* 50(3). 281–310.

Grice, H. Paul. 1975. Logic and Conversation. In Peter Cole & Jerry L. Morgan (eds.), *Syntax and Semantics, Vol. 3, Speech Acts*, 41–58. New York: Academic Press.

Gundel, Jeanette. 1988. Universals of topic-comment structure. In Michael Hammond, Edith Moravczik & Jessica Wirth (eds.), *Studies in Syntactic Typology*, 209–239. Amsterdam: John Benjamins.

Gundel, Jeanette K. 1977. Where do Cleft Sentences Come from? *Language* 53(3). 543–559.
Gundel, Jeanette K. 1985. 'Shared knowledge' and topicality. *Journal of Pragmatics* 9(1). 83–107.
Gundel, Jeanette K., Nancy Hedberg & Ron Zacharski. 1993. Cognitive status and the form of referring expressions in discourse. *Language* 69(2). 274–307.
Gussenhoven, Carlos. 2004. *The Phonology of Tone and Intonation*. Cambridge: Cambridge University Press.
Halliday, M.A.K. 1961. Categories of the theory of grammar. *Word* 17(3). 241–292.
Halliday, M.A.K. 1967a. Notes on transitivity and theme in English: Part 1. *Journal of Linguistics* 3(1). 37–81.
Halliday, M.A.K. 1967b. Notes on transitivity and theme in English: Part 2. *Journal of Linguistics* 3(2). 199–244.
Halliday, M.A.K. 1967c. *Intonation and Grammar in British English*. The Hague: Mouton.
Halliday, M.A.K. 1968. Notes on transitivity and theme in English: Part 3. *Journal of Linguistics* 4(2). 179–215.
Halliday, M.A.K. 1970a. Language structure and language function. In John Lyons (ed.), *New Horizons in Linguistics*, 140–165. Harmondsworth: Penguin.
Halliday, M.A.K. 1970b. Functional diversity in language as seen from a consideration of modality and mood in English. *Foundations of Language* 6(3). 322–361.
Halliday, M.A.K. 1970c. *A Course in Spoken English: Intonation*. London: Oxford University Press.
Halliday, M.A.K. 1978. *Language as Social Semiotic: The Social Interpretation of Language and Meaning*. London: Arnold.
Halliday, M.A.K. 1982. *A Short Introduction to Functional Grammar*. Sydney: Linguistic Department, University of Sydney.
Halliday, M.A.K. 1985. *An Introduction to Functional Grammar*. 1st edn. London: Edward Arnold.
Halliday, M.A.K. 1992. How do you mean? In Martin Davies & Louise Ravelli (eds.), *Advances in Systemic Linguistics: Recent Theory and Practice*, 20–35. London: Pinter.
Halliday, M.A.K. 1994. *An Introduction to Functional Grammar*. 2nd edn. London: Edward Arnold.
Halliday, M.A.K. & William S. Greaves. 2008. *Intonation in the Grammar of English*. London: Equinox.
Halliday, M.A.K. & Ruqaiya Hasan. 1976. *Cohesion in English*. London: Longman.
Halliday, M.A.K. & Christian Matthiessen. 1999. *Construing Experience through Meaning: A Language-Based Approach to Cognition*. London/New York: Cassell.
Halliday, M.A.K. & Christian Matthiessen. 2004. *Introduction to Functional Grammar*. 3rd edn. London: Hodder Arnold.
Halliday, M.A.K. & Christian Matthiessen. 2014. *An Introduction to Functional Grammar*. 3rd edn. London: Routledge.
Han, Chung-hye & Nancy Hedberg. 2008. Syntax and semantics of *it*-clefts: A tree-adjoining grammar analysis. *Journal of Semantics* 25. 345–380.
Hansen, Colin H. 2001. Fundamentals of acoustics. In Berenice Goelzer, Colin H. Hansen & Gustav A. Sehrndt (eds.), *Occupational Exposure to Noise: Evaluation, Prevention and Control*, 23–52. Geneva: World Health Organization.
Harries-Delisle, Helga. 1978. Contrastive emphasis and cleft sentences. In Joseph H. Greenberg (ed.), *Universals of Human Language. Vol. 4. Syntax.*, 419–486. Stanford: Stanford University Press.
Hawkins, John A. 1978. *Definiteness and Indefiniteness: A Study in Reference and Grammaticality Prediction*. London: Croom Helm.

Hawkins, John A. 1991. On (in)definite articles: Implicatures and (un)grammaticality prediction. *Journal of Linguistics* 27(2). 405–442.
Hedberg, Nancy & David Potter. 2010. Equative and Predicational Copulas in Thai. *Annual Meeting of the Berkeley Linguistics Society* 36(1). 144–157.
Heggie, Lorie. 1988. *The syntax of copular structures*. Los Angeles, CA: University of Southern California doctoral dissertation.
Heim, Irene. 1982. *The semantics of definite and indefinite noun phrases*. Amherst, MA: University of Massachusetts doctoral dissertation.
Hengeveld, Kees. 1988. Illocution, mood and modality in functional grammar. *Journal of Semantics* 6. 227–269.
Hengeveld, Kees. 1989. Layers and operators in functional grammar. *Journal of Linguistics* 25. 127–157.
Heringer, James A. 1969. Indefinite noun phrases and referential opacity. *CLS* 5. 89–97.
Heusinger, Klaus von. 2002. Specificity and definiteness in sentence and discourse structure. *Journal of Semantics* 19(3). 245–274.
Heycock, Caroline. 2012. Specification, equation, and agreement in copular sentences. *Canadian Journal of Linguistics/Revue canadienne de linguistique* 57(2). 209–240.
Heycock, Caroline & Anthony Kroch. 1999. Pseudocleft connectedness: Implications for the LF interface level. *Linguistic Inquiry* 30(3). 365–397.
Heycock, Caroline & Anthony Kroch. 2002. Topic, focus, and syntactic representations. In Line Mikkelsen & Christopher Potts (eds.), *Proceedings of West Coast Conference on Formal Linguistics (WCCFL) 21*. 101–125. Somerville: Cacadilla Press.
Heyvaert, Liesbet. 2003. *A Cognitive-Functional Approach to Nominalization in English*. Berlin/Boston: de Gruyter.
Higgins, Francis R. 1976. *The pseudo-cleft construction in English*. Cambridge, MA: MIT doctoral dissertation.
Higgins, Francis R. 1979. *The Pseudo-Cleft Construction in English*. London: Routledge.
Hinkel, Eli. 2001. Matters of cohesion in L2 academic texts. *Applied Language Learning* 12(2). 111–132.
Hirschberg, Julia & Gregory Ward. 1985. Fall-rise intonation and the place of intonational 'meaning' in linguistic theory. *Annual Meeting of the Berkeley Linguistics Society* 11. 447–458.
Hjelmslev, Louis. 1961. *Prolegomena to a Theory of Language*. (Trans.) Francis J. Whitfield. Madison: University of Wisconsin Press.
Horn, Laurence R. 1981. Exhaustiveness and the semantics of clefts. In V. Burke & J. Pustejovsky (eds.), *Papers from 11th Annual Meeting of the North Eastern Linguistic Society*, 125–142. Amherst: University of Massachusetts.
Huddleston, Rodney. 1971. *The Sentence in Written English*. Cambridge: Cambridge University Press.
Huddleston, Rodney. 1984. *Introduction to the Grammar of English*. Cambridge: Cambridge University Press.
Huddleston, Rodney & Geoffrey Pullum. 2002. *The Cambridge Grammar of the English language*. Cambridge: Cambridge University Press.
Kahn, Charles H. 1973. *The Verb "Be" In Ancient Greek*. Dordrecht: Reidel.
Kaltenböck, Gunther. 2000. It-extraposition and non-extraposition in English discourse. In Christian Mair & Marianne Hundt (eds.), *Corpus Linguistics and Linguistic Theory*, 157–175. Amsterdam: Rodopi.

Kaltenböck, Gunther. 2004. *It-extraposition and Non-extraposition in English. A Study of Syntax in Spoken and Written Texts*. Vienna: Braumüller.
Kaltenböck, Gunther. 2005. It-extraposition in English: A functional view. *International Journal of Corpus Linguistics* 10(2). 119–159.
Karttunen, Lauri. 1976. Discourse referents. In James D. McCawley (ed.), *Notes from the Linguistic Underground* (Syntax and Semantics 7), 363–386. New York: Academic Press.
Keizer, Evelien. 1990. A typology of copular clauses. *Linguistics* 28. 1047–1060.
Keizer, Evelien. 1992. *Reference, Predication and (In)definiteness in Functional Grammar: A Functional Approach to English Copular Clauses*. Utrecht: Drukkerij Elinkwijk Utrecht.
Keizer, Evelien. 2007. *The English Noun Phrase: The Nature of Linguistic Categorization* (Studies in English Language). Cambridge: Cambridge University Press.
Keizer, Evelien. 2016. The (the) fact is (that) construction in English and Dutch. In Gunther Kaltenböck, Evelien Keizer & Arne Lohmann (eds.), *Outside the Clause: Form and function of extra-clausal constituents*, 59–96. Amsterdam: John Benjamins.
Keizer, Evelien. 2017. English partitives in Functional Discourse Grammar: Types and constraints. *Glossa* 2(1). 1–40.
Kempson, Ruth M. 1975. *Presupposition and the Delimitation of Semantics*. Cambridge: Cambridge University Press.
Kimps, Ditte. 2016. *English variable tag questions: A typology of their interpersonal meanings*. Leuven: KU Leuven doctoral dissertation.
Kingdon, Roger. 1958. *The Groundwork of English Intonation*. London: Longmans.
Kirsner, Robert & Sandra A. Thompson. 1976. The role of inference in semantics: A study of sensory verb complements in English. *Glossa* 10(2). 200–240.
Kiss, Katalin É. 1998. Identificational focus versus information focus. *Language* 74(2). 245–273.
Klein, Ewan. 1980. Locating the articles (Review of Hawkings, 1978). *Linguistics* 18. 147–157.
Knowles, Gerald. 1984. Various strategies in intonation. In Dafydd Gibbon & Helmut Richter (eds.), *Intonation, Accent, and Rhythm: Studies in Discourse Phonology*, 226–242. Berlin/New York: de Gruyter.
Kochanski, Greg, Esther Grabe, John Coleman & Burton S. Rosner. 2005. Loudness predicts prominence: Fundamental frequency lends little. *The Journal of the Acoustical Society of America* 118(2). 1038–1054.
Kratzer, Angelika. 1978. *Semantik der Rede: Kontexttheorie, Modalwörter, Konditionalsätze* (Monographien Linguistik und Kommunikationswissenschaft 38). Königstein im Taunus: Scriptor.
Kripke, Saul A. 1971. Naming and necessity. In Donald Davidson & Gilbert Harman (eds.), *Semantics of Natural Language*, 253–355, 763–769. Dordrecht: Reidel.
Kuno, Susumu. 1970. Some properties of non-referential noun phrases. In Roman Jakobson & Shigeo Kawamoto (eds.), *Studies in General and Oriental Linguistics: Presented to Shirô Hattori on the Occasion of His Sixtieth Birthday*, 348–373. Tokyo: TEC.
Kuno, Susumu. 1972. Functional sentence perspective: A case study from Japanese and English. *Linguistic Inquiry* 3. 269–320.
Kuno, Susumu & Preya Wongkhomthong. 1981. Characterizational and identificational sentences in Thai. *Studies in Language* 5. 65–109.
Ladd, Robert. 1978. *The Structure of Intonational Meaning: Evidence from English*. Bloomington: Indiana University Press.
Ladd, Robert. 1980. *The Structure of Intonational Meaning: Evidence from English*. Bloomington: Indiana University Press.

Ladd, Robert. 2008. *Intonational Phonology* (Cambridge Studies in Linguistics 119). 2nd edn. Cambridge: Cambridge University Press.

Laeven, Thijs. 1983. Clivage dans la grammaire: La syntaxe de "ce+être+que." In Hans Bennis & W.U.S. van Lessen Kloeke (eds.), *Linguistics in the Netherlands 1983*, 139–148. Dordrecht: Foris.

Lahousse, Karen. 2009. Specificational sentences and the influence of information structure on (anti-)connectivity effects. *Journal of Linguistics* 45(1). 139–166.

Lambrecht, Knud. 1994. *Information Structure and Sentence Form: Topic, Focus, and the Mental Representations of Discourse Referents* (Cambridge Studies in Linguistics 71). Cambridge: Cambridge University Press.

Lambrecht, Knud. 2001. A framework for the analysis of cleft constructions. *Linguistics* 39(3). 463–516.

Langacker, Ronald W. 1986. An introduction to Cognitive Grammar. *Cognitive Science* 10(1). 1–40.

Langacker, Ronald W. 1987a. *Foundations of Cognitive Grammar: Theoretical Prerequisites*. Vol. 1. Stanford: Stanford University Press.

Langacker, Ronald W. 1987b. Nouns and verbs. *Language* 63(1). 53–94.

Langacker, Ronald W. 1991. *Foundations of Cognitive Grammar: Descriptive Application*. Vol. 2. Stanford: Stanford University Press.

Langacker, Ronald W. 1995. Raising and transparency. *Language* 71(1). 1–62.

Langacker, Ronald W. 1997. The contextual basis of cognitive semantics. In Jan Nuyts & Eric Pederson (eds.), *Language and Conceptualization*, 229–252. Cambridge: Cambridge University Press.

Langacker, Ronald W. 1999. *Grammar and Conceptualization*. Berlin/Boston: De Gruyter Mouton.

Langacker, Ronald W. 2002. Dynamicity, fictivity, and scanning: The imaginative basis of logic and linguistic meaning. Handout of a paper presented at the University of Leuven. Leuven.

Langacker, Ronald W. 2004. Remarks on nominal grounding. *Functions of Language* 11(1). 77–113.

Langacker, Ronald W. 2005. Dynamicity, fictivity, and scanning: The imaginative basis of logic and linguistic meaning. In Diane Pecher & Rolf A. Zwaan (eds.), *Grounding Cognition: The Role of Perception and Action in Memory, Language, and Thinking*, 164–197. Cambridge: Cambridge University Press.

Langacker, Ronald W. 2015. How to build an English clause. *Journal of Foreign Language Teaching and Applied Linguistics* 2(2). 1–45.

Langacker, Ronald W. 2017a. Grounding, semantic functions, and absolute quantifiers. *English Text Construction* 10(2). 233–248.

Langacker, Ronald W. 2017b. *Ten Lectures on the Basics of Cognitive Grammar*. Leiden/London: Brill.

Leech, Geoffrey. 1983. *Principles of Pragmatics*. London/New York: Longman

Leech, Geoffrey & Lu Li. 1995. Indeterminacy between noun phrases and adjective phrases as complements of the English verb. In Bas Aarts & Charles F. Meyer (eds.), *The Verb in Contemporary English*, 182–202. Cambridge: Cambridge University Press.

Lehmann, Christian. 2008. Information structure and grammaticalization. In Elena Seoane & María José López-Couso (eds.), *Theoretical and Empirical Issues in Grammaticalization* (Typological Studies in Language 77), 207–229. Amsterdam/Philadelphia: John Benjamins.

Levin, Beth. 1993. *English Verb Classes and Alternations: A Preliminary Investigation*. Chicago, IL: University of Chicago Press.

Lewis, David. 1979. Scorekeeping in a Language Game. *Journal of Philosophical Logic* 8(1). 339–359.
Löbner, Sebastian. 1985. Definites. *Journal of Semantics* 4(4). 279–326.
Los, Bettelou. 2009. The consequences of the loss of verb-second in English: Information structure and syntax in interaction. *English Language and Linguistics* 13(1). 97–125.
Lyons, Christopher. 1999. *Definiteness*. Cambridge: Cambridge University Press.
Lyons, John. 1968. *Introduction to Theoretical Linguistics*. Cambridge: Cambridge University Press.
Lyons, John. 1977. *Semantics*. Cambridge: Cambridge University Press.
Martin, James R. 1992. *English Text: System and Structure*. Amsterdam/Philadelphia: John Benjamins.
Mathesius, Vilém. 1975. *A Functional Analysis of Present Day English on a General Linguistic Basis*. The Hague: Mouton.
Matić, Dejan & Daniel Wedgwood. 2013. The meanings of focus: The significance of an interpretation-based category in cross-linguistic analysis. *Journal of Linguistics* 49(1). 127–163.
Matthews, Peter. 1997. *The Concise Oxford Dictionary of Linguistics*. Oxford: Oxford University Press.
McGregor, William B. 1990. *A Functional Grammar of Gooniyandi*. Amsterdam/Philadelphia: John Benjamins Publishing Company.
McGregor, William B. 1997. *Semiotic Grammar*. Oxford: Clarendon.
McGregor, William B. 2003. The nothing that is, the zero that isn't. *Studia Linguistica* 57, 75–119.
Mikkelsen, Line. 2004. Specificational subjects: A formal characterization and some consequences. *Acta Linguistica Hafniensia* 36(1). 79–112.
Mikkelsen, Line. 2005. *Copular Clauses: Specification, Predication and Equation*. Amsterdam/Philadelphia: John Benjamins.
Milsark, Gary. 1977. Toward an explanation of certain peculiarities of the existential construction in English. *Linguistic Analysis* 3. 1–29.
Moltmann, Friederike. 1997. Intensional verbs and quantifiers. *Natural Language Semantics* 5. 1–52.
Moro, Andrea. 1997. *The Raising of Predicates: Predicative Noun Phrases and the Theory of Clause Structure* (Cambridge Studies in Linguistics 80). Cambridge: Cambridge University Press.
Mosegaard Hansen, Maj-Britt. 2008. On the availability of 'literal' meaning: Evidence from courtroom interaction. *Journal of Pragmatics* 40(8). 1392–1410.
Narrog, Heiko. 2005a. On defining modality again. *Language Sciences* 27, 165–192.
Narrog, Heiko. 2005b. Modality, mood, and change of modal meanings: A new perspective. *Cognitive Linguistics* 16(4). 677–731.
Nuyts, Jan. 2001. Subjectivity as an evidential dimension in epistemic modal expressions. *Journal of Pragmatics* 33(3). 383–400.
Nuyts, Jan. 2005. Modal confusion: On terminology and the concepts behind it. In Alex Klinge & Henrik Høeg Müller (eds.), *Modality: Studies in Form and Function*, 5–38. London: Equinox.
Nuyts, Jan. 2006. Modality: Overview and linguistic issues. In William Frawley (ed.), *The Expression of Modality*, 1–26. Berlin/New York: Mouton de Gruyter.
Nuyts, Jan. 2008. Brothers in arms? On the relations between Cognitive and Functional Linguistics. In M. Sandra Peña Cervel and Francisco J. Ruiz de Mendoza Ibáñez (eds.), *Cognitive Linguistics*, 69–100. Berlin/New York: Mouton de Gruyter.

O'Connor, J. D. & G. F. Arnold. 1968. *Intonation of Colloquial English: A Practical Handbook.* London: Longmans.

O'Grady, Gerard. 2010. *A Grammar of Spoken English Discourse: The Intonation of Increments* (Continuum Studies in Theoretical Linguistics). London: Continuum International PubGroup.

O'Grady, Gerard. 2017. Intonation and systemic functional linguistics: The way forward. In Tom Bartlett & Gerard O'Grady (eds.), *The Routledge Handbook of Systemic Functional Linguistics*, 146–162. London: Routledge.

Palacas, Arthur L. 1977. Specificness in generative grammar. In Paul J. Hopper (ed.), *Studies in Descriptive and Historical Linguistics*, 188–208. Amsterdam: John Benjamins.

Palmer, Frank. 1986. *Mood and Modality.* 1st edn. Cambridge: Cambridge University Press.

Palmer, Frank. 1990. *Modality and the English Modals.* London: Longman.

Palmer, Frank. 2001. *Mood and Modality.* 2nd edn. London: Longman.

Palmer, Frank. 2003. Modality in English. In Roberta Facchinetti, Manfred Krug & Frank Palmer (eds.), *Modality in Contemporary English*, 1–17. Berlin: Mouton.

Paradis, Carita. 1997. *Degree Modifiers of Adjectives in Spoken British English* (Lund Studies in English 92). Lund: Lund University Press.

Paradis, Carita. 2000. Reinforcing adjectives: A cognitive semantic perspective on grammaticalization. In Ricardo Bermúdez-Otero, David Denison, Richard Hogg & C.B. Mccully (eds.), *Generative Theory and Corpus Linguistics: A Dialogue from 10 ICEHL*, 233–258. Berlin/
New York: Mouton de Gruyter.

Paradis, Carita. 2001. Adjectives and boundedness. *Cognitive Linguistics* 12(1). 47–65.

Partee, Barbara. 2010. Specificational copular sentences in Russian and English. *Oslo Studies in Language* (Oslo Studies in Language) 2(1). 25–49.

Partee, Barbara H. 1986a. Ambiguous pseudoclefts with unambiguous be. In Stephen Berman, Jae-Woong Choe & Joyce McDonough (eds.), *Proceedings of NELS*, Vol. 16. Amherst, MA: University of Massachusetts.

Partee, Barbara H. 1986b. Noun phrase interpretation and type-shifting principles. In Jeroen Groenendijck, Dick de Jongh & Martin Stokhof (eds.), *Studies in Discourse Representation Theory and the Theory of Generalized Quantifiers*, 115–143. Dordrecht: Foris.

Partee, Barbara H. 2000. Copula inversion puzzles in English and Russian. In Kijomi Kusumoto & Elisabeth Villalta (eds.), *Issues in Semantics and its Interface*, 198–208. University of Massachusetts, Amherst: GLSA.

Partee, Barbara H. 2004. *Compositionality in Formal Semantics: Selected Papers by Barbara H. Partee.* Oxford: Blackwell Publishers.

Patten, Amanda L. 2012. *The English It-Cleft: A Constructional Account and a Diachronic Investigation* (Topics in English Linguistics [TiEL] 79). Berlin/New York: De Gruyter Mouton.

Patten, Amanda L. 2016. Well-formed lists: Specificational copular sentences as predicative inversion constructions. *English Language and Linguistics* 22(1). 77–99.

Perek, Florent. 2012. Alternation-based generalizations are stored in the mental grammar: Evidence from a sorting task experiment. *cogl* 23(3). 601–635.

Perek, Florent. 2016. Using distributional semantics to study syntactic productivity in diachrony: A case study. *Linguistics* 54(1). 149–188.

Pierrehumbert, Janet & Julia Hirschberg. 1990. The meaning of intonational contours in the interpretation of discourse. In Philip R. Cohen, Jerry L. Morgan & Martha E. Pollack (eds.), *Intentions in Communication*, 271–311. Cambridge, MA: MIT Press.

Poutsma, Hendrik. 1928. *A Grammar of Late Modern English*. Vol. 1. Groningen: P. Noordhoff.
Prince, Ellen. 1978. A comparison of *wh*-clefts and *it*-clefts in discourse. *Language* 54(4). 883–906.
Prince, Ellen. 1981a. On the inferencing of indefinite-*this* NPs. In Aravind K. Joshi, Bonnie L. Weber & Ivan A. Sag (eds.), *Elements of Discourse Understanding*, 231–250. Cambridge: Cambridge University Press.
Prince, Ellen. 1981b. Towards a taxonomy of given-new information. In Peter Cole (ed.), *Radical Pragmatics*, 281–297. New York: Academic Press.
Prince, Ellen. 1986. On the syntactic marking of presupposed open propositions. In Anne M. Farley, Peter T. Farley & Karl-Erik McCullough (eds.), *Papers from the Parasession on Pragmatics and Grammatical Theory at the 22nd Regional Meetings of the Chicago Linguistic Society*, 208–222. Chicago: Chicago Linguistic Society.
Prince, Ellen. 1992. The ZPG letter: Subjects, definiteness and information status. In William C. Mann & Sandra A. Thompson (eds.), *Discourse Description: Diverse Linguistic Analyses of a Fund-Raising Text*, 295–325. Amsterdam: John Benjamins.
Quirk, Randolph, Sidney Greenbaum, Geoffrey Leech & Jan Svartvik. 1972. *A Grammar of Contemporary English*. London: Longman.
Quirk, Randolph, Sidney Greenbaum, Geoffrey Leech & Jan Svartvik. 1985. *A Comprehensive Grammar of the English Language*. London: Longman.
Rigter, Bob. 1982. Intensional domains and the use of tense, perfect and modals in English. *Journal of Semantics* 1(2). 95–145.
Rivero, Maria-Luisa. 1975. Referential properties of Spanish noun phrases. *Language* 51. 32–48.
Romero, Maribel. 2005. Concealed questions and specificational subjects. *Linguistics and Philosophy* 28(6). 687–737.
Ross, John R. 2000. The frozenness of pseudoclefts: Towards an inequality-based syntax. In John L. Boyle & Arika Okrent, *Proceedings of the 36th Regional Meeting of the Chicago Linguistic Society*, 385–426. Chicago: Chicago Linguistic Society.
Rothstein, Susan. 1999. Fine-grained structure in the eventuality domain: The semantics of predicative adjective phrases and *be*. *Natural Language Semantics* 7(4). 347–420.
Rothstein, Susan. 2001. *Predicates and their Subjects*. Dordrecht: Kluwer.
Schlenker, Philippe. 2003. Clausal equation: A note on the connectivity problem. *Natural Language and Linguistic Theory* 21. 157–214.
Schmid, Hans-Jörg. 2000. *English Abstract Nouns as Conceptual Shells: From Corpus to Cognition*. Berlin/New York: Mouton de Gruyter.
Schmid, Hans-Jörg. 2001. 'Presupposition can be a bluff': How abstract nouns can be used as presupposition triggers. *Journal of Pragmatics* 33(10). 1529–1552.
Schmid, Hans-Jörg & Helmut Küchenhoff. 2013. Collostructional analysis and other ways of measuring lexicogrammatical attraction: Theoretical premises, practical problems and cognitive underpinnings. *Cognitive Linguistics* 24(3). 531–577.
Sharp, Alan E. 1953. Falling-rising intonation patterns in English. *Phonetica* 2(3–4). 127–152.
Silverman, Kim, Mary E. Beckman, John Pitrelli, Mari Ostendorf, Colin Wightman, Patti Price, Janet Pierrehumbert & Julia Hirschberg. 1992. TOBI: A standard for labeling English prosody. *2nd International Conference on Spoken Language Processing (ICSLP 92)*, 867–870. Banff, Alberta.
Stalnaker, Robert. 1973. Presuppositions. *Journal of Philosophical Logic* 2(4). 447–457.

Stalnaker, Robert. 1974. Pragmatic presuppositions. In Milton K. Munitz & Peter K. Unger (eds.), *Semantics and Philosophy*, 197–214. New York: NYU Press.
Stefanowitsch, Anatol & Stefan Th. Gries. 2003. Collostructions: Investigating the interaction of words and constructions. *International Journal of Corpus Linguistics* 8(2). 209–243.
Stefanowitsch, Anatol & Stefan Th. Gries. 2005. Covarying collexemes. *Corpus Linguistics and Linguistic Theory* 1(1). 1–43.
Strawson, Peter Frederick. 1959. *Individuals*. London: Methuen.
Svartvik, Jan (ed.). 1990. *The London Corpus of Spoken English: Description and Research* (Lund Studies in English 82). Lund: Lund University Press.
Tadros, Angele. 1994. Predictive categories in expository text. In Malcolm Coulthard (ed.), *Advances in Written Text Analysis*, 69–82. New York: Routledge.
Taglicht, Joseph. 1972. A new look at the English predicative construction. *Lingua* 29. 1–22.
Taverniers, Miriam. 2005. Subjecthood and the notion of instantiation. *Language Sciences* 27(6). 651–678.
Taverniers, Miriam. 2008. Hjelmslev's semiotic model of language: An exegesis. *Semiotica* 2008(171). 367–394.
Taylor, John R. 2002. *Cognitive grammar*. Oxford: Oxford University Press.
Tench, Paul. 1988. *The Roles of Intonation in English Discourse*. New York: Peter Lang.
Tench, Paul. 1990. *The Roles of Intonation in English Discourse* (Forum Linguisticum 31). Frankfurt am Main: Peter Lang.
Tench, Paul. 1996. *The Intonation Systems of English*. London: Cassell.
Tench, Paul. 2003. Processes of semiogenesis in English intonation. *Functions of Language* 10(2). 209–234.
Vallduví, Enric. 1990. The role of plasticity in the association of focus and prominence. *Proceedings – Eastern States Conference on Linguistics (ESCOL)* 7. 295–306.
Vallduví, Enric. 1992. *The Informational Component*. New York/London: Garland.
Van linden, An. 2012. *Modal Adjectives: English Deontic and Evaluative Constructions in Diachrony and Synchrony*. Berlin/Boston: Walter de Gruyter.
Van Praet, Wout. 2019a. Focus assignment in English specificational and predicative clauses: intonation as a cue to information structure? *Acta Linguistica Hafniensia* 51(2). 222–241.
Van Praet, Wout. 2019b. Aspect and modality in English predicative and specificational copular clauses. *English Text Construction* 12(2). 196–234.
Van Praet, Wout & Kristin Davidse. 2015. Revisiting the typology of English copular clauses: Ascription and specification in categorizing and identifying clauses. *Leuven Working Papers in Linguistics* 4(19). 1–32.
Van Praet, Wout & Gerard O'Grady. 2018. The prosody of specification: Discourse intonational cues to setting up a variable. *Journal of Pragmatics* 135, 87–100.
Verplaetse, Heidi. 2003. What you and I want: A functional approach to verb complementation of the modal "want to." In Roberta Facchinetti, Manfred Krug & Frank Palmer (eds.), *Modality in Contemporary English*, 151–190. Berlin: Mouton.
Verstraete, Jean-Christophe. 2001. Subjective and objective modality: Interpersonal and ideational functions in the English modal auxiliary system. *Journal of Pragmatics* 33(10). 1505–1528.
Verstraete, Jean-Christophe. 2005. Scalar quantity implicatures and the interpretation of modality. *Journal of Pragmatics* 37(9). 1401–1418.

Verstraete, Jean-Christophe. 2007. *Rethinking the Coordinate-Subordinate Dichotomy: Interpersonal Grammar and the Analysis of Adverbial Clauses in English* (Topics in English Linguistics [TiEL] 55). Berlin/New York: Mouton de Gruyter.
Wall, Larry, Tom Christiansen & Jon Orwant. 2000. *Programming Perl*. 3rd edn. Sebastopol, CA: O'Reilly Media.
Ward, Gregory & Betty Birner. 1995. Definiteness and the English existential. *Language* 71(4). 722–742.
Wardhaugh, Ronald. 1997. Understanding English grammar: A linguistic approach. Oxford: Blackwell.
Watt, David L.E. 1992. An instrumental analysis of English nuclear tones. In Paul Tench (ed.), *Studies in Systemic Phonology*, 135–160. London/New York: Pinter Publishers.
Wells, John C. 2006. *English Intonation: An Introduction*. Cambridge: Cambridge University Press.
Wichmann, Anne. 2000. *Intonation in Text and Discourse: Beginnings, Middles and Ends*. (Studies in Language and Linguistics). Harlow: Longman.
Wierzbicka, Anna. 1987. *English Speech Act Verbs: A Semantic Dictionary*. New York: Academic Press.
Wierzbicka, Anna. 1988. *The Semantics of Grammar* (Studies in Language Companion Series 18). Amsterdam: Benjamins.
Wiggins, David. 1965. Identity statements. In R.J. Butler (ed.), *Analytic Philosophy. Second Series*, 40–71. Oxford: Blackwell.
Willemse, Peter. 2005. *Nominal reference-point constructions: Possessive and esphoric NPs in English*. Leuven: KU Leuven doctoral dissertation.
Willemse, Peter. 2007. Indefinite possessive NPs and the distinction between determining and nondetermining genitives in English. *English Language & Linguistics* 11(3). 537–568.
Williams, Edwin. 1983. Semantic vs. syntactic categories. *Linguistics and Philosophy* 6(3). 423–446.
Wilson, Deirdre & Dan Sperber. 1979. Ordered entailment: An alternative to presuppositional theories. In Choon-Kyu Oh & David Dinneen (eds.), *Syntax and Semantics*, vol. XI: Presupposition, 299–323. New York: Academic Press.
Zaring, Laurie. 1996. Two "be" or not two "be": Identity, predication and the Welsh copula. *Linguistics and Philosophy* 19. 103–142.

# Index

absolute quantifier. *See* quantification
adjective  2, 26, 43–48, 50–54, 60, 82, 93, 112, 121, 123–127, 130–131, 133–136, 148–149, 153, 155–156, 168–169, 171, 268, 305
adjective-intensifier. *See* premodification
anaphoric  43, 66, 115, 147, 215, 228, 241, 248, 259–262, 264, 273–274, 296
argument-focus. *See* focus
aspect  20, 57, 146, 173–204, 277, 306
– imperfectivity  177–178, 188–189, 203, 277, 306
– perfect  175, 177–179, 185–191, 203, 306
– progressive  57, 175–177, 179, 183, 185–191, 203, 306
– simple  175–177, 179, 183, 185–188, 306

bare noun  26, 44, 46, 48, 50, 52, 136, 153
brand-new information  155, 263, 279–281, 286, 288–299, 301

classifier. *See* premodification
class-inclusion  19, 42–43, 53, 67, 70, 85, 87
class-membership  42–43, 50, 53, 67, 70, 128, 174
cataphoric  260–262, 273
cleft  12, 26, 28–29, 79–80, 86, 90, 94, 107, 308
Cognitive Grammar (CG)  3, 14–17, 44, 50, 54, 56, 66
complement, adjectival  26, 50, 53–54, 112, 153
composite predicate  44, 46–50, 67–68, 82–83, 116, 188–89, 203, 304, 306
constituent order. *See* word order
contrastiveness. *See* implicature
coordination  27–29, 48–49, 82–83, 104–105, 304
criterial entity  86, 98, 100, 103, 105, 120, 155, 203, 306

definiteness  2–4, 6, 8, 12, 18–21, 25–26, 28–31, 33–36, 54, 64, 66, 72–73, 75–77, 79–81, 86–92, 94, 98–100, 104, 108, 117, 120, 123, 128, 130, 132, 172, 174–175, 182–186, 192, 194–195, 198–203, 213, 218, 222–226, 229–233, 238, 240–242, 247, 249, 252–254, 258–260, 268–271, 274, 276, 278, 282–285, 287–288, 291–294, 301, 303, 305–306, 308
definite variable  2–4, 18–19, 26, 28–31, 33–36, 73, 76, 79–81, 87–88, 90, 92, 94, 172, 175, 182–185, 192, 194–195, 198–201, 218, 222–226, 229–233, 238, 240–242, 247, 252–254, 258–260, 291–294, 301, 303, 305–306
degree modifier. *See* intensifier
demonstrative  11, 64, 129, 152, 215, 228, 252, 259–265, 296–297, 301
deontic modality. *See* modality
describee  1, 6, 20, 28, 32, 41, 47–48, 50, 57–60, 95, 111, 115–117, 142–144, 175, 183, 205, 209, 219, 223–224, 226, 230, 233–236, 240–241, 244–244, 248, 250, 252–253, 264, 266–267, 270, 287–291, 300, 302–303, 307–308
description  1–3, 6–9, 11–13, 17–18, 20, 23, 28–29, 32–34, 37–38, 47–48, 54, 58–59, 66–68, 76–77, 95, 108, 111, 115–117, 121, 124, 126–128, 142–144, 154, 157, 168, 182–183, 188, 195, 199, 202–203, 205, 209, 219, 224–226, 230, 232–234, 236, 240–241, 244–245, 248, 250, 252–253, 256, 264, 266–267, 269–271, 279–280, 284, 287–289, 291, 301–304, 307–308
descriptionally-identifying clauses  11–12, 54, 76
determiner  89, 90–91, 93, 99–100, 102–103, 118, 120–124, 127–133, 135–136, 155, 158, 160–171, 173, 275, 277–278, 291, 305
– primary  99, 124, 127–130, 136, 160, 162
– secondary  99–100, 103, 124, 128–131, 133, 136, 155, 162–171, 291, 305
direction of fit  112–13, 116, 142–43, 209, 248, 250, 289

discourse-embedding 19–20, 42, 116, 159, 225, 247–248, 252, 266–302, 307
discourse-familiarity 12, 18–20, 101, 109, 113, 118, 214, 225, 228–229, 241–243, 248, 252, 259, 261, 263–264, 267–268, 270–294, 298–302, 307
dual reference 98, 100, 102, 105, 117, 168, 208, 304
dynamic modality. *See* modality

ellipsis 49, 120, 124, 128, 146
endophoric 273–274
epistemic modality. *See* modality
epithet. *See* premodification
esphoric 274
equative 7–10, 26, 39, 40, 69, 73–76, 84
evidentiality 182–183, 185, 191–195, 200–204, 306–307
evoked information 64, 113, 142, 164, 241–243, 248, 260, 279–284, 286, 289–293, 296
exclusiveness 27, 73, 88, 91–92, 102, 104–105, 121, 158, 167, 169, 171, 256, 259–260, 271
exemplification 97, 104, 139, 146–147, 190, 255, 274, 300
exhaustiveness. *See* implicature
existential clause 100, 129, 178, 284
exophoric reference 11, 273

first-order entitites 135, 137
focus markers 128, 131, 136, 162–163, 165, 167
fronting 59, 299

generalised instance. *See* instance
generalised reference. *See* reference
generic reference. *See* reference
gerund 184–85, 271, 276–78
given-newness 58, 100–101, 103, 106–109, 113–114, 133, 143, 145–147, 157, 164, 168–169, 206–208, 210, 214, 217, 241, 243–244, 247–249, 252, 254, 257, 260–261, 263–265, 266–270, 274, 278–302, 308
grounding 55–56, 160, 162, 166–167, 169, 172

Halliday 1–9, 13–18, 42–43, 47–50, 54–60, 76–79, 81–84, 96–97, 113–14, 120, 179, 206–8, 210–18, 227–28, 243–44, 259–61, 264–65, 273–77, 296–98, 316
head noun 50–51, 53, 61, 64, 118–119, 122, 124, 126–128, 132, 135–144, 146–147, 158, 170–171, 173, 305

identification 6–8, 10–11, 26, 53–54, 78–79, 83–84, 87, 128, 130–131, 155, 160, 174, 270–271, 276, 284–285
identificational clauses 10–11, 26
identity statement 8–9, 26, 84
imperfectivity. *See* aspect
implicature 6, 8, 15, 20, 28, 36, 64, 72–73, 80, 86, 88, 90–95, 102, 104–105, 107, 109–110, 115–117, 119–121, 132, 134, 146, 152, 155, 157–158, 165, 167, 169, 171–172, 174–175, 178, 183, 186, 195, 199–200, 202–204, 207, 211–212, 214–216, 227–228, 240, 243, 245, 253, 255–256, 258–261, 264–265, 271, 273, 301, 305–309
– contrastiveness 6, 94–95, 107, 109, 175, 186, 195, 200, 207, 211–212, 214–216, 227–228, 243, 260–261, 306
– exhaustiveness 28, 72, 80, 86, 88, 90–94, 117, 119–121, 132, 146, 169, 174–175, 186, 200, 203–204, 253, 258, 260, 301, 306–309
– non-contrastiveness 105, 115, 211–212, 215–216, 228, 243, 245, 256, 259–260, 264–265
– non-exhaustiveness 36, 80, 88, 90–93, 117, 120–121, 132, 134, 146, 155, 157, 167, 169, 171–172, 183, 195, 199–200, 202, 204, 240, 255, 260, 305–307, 309
inclusiveness 73, 90–92, 102, 119, 121, 152, 158, 167, 171–172, 200, 255, 269
inferrable information 249, 279–283, 286–295, 301
information focus 1, 5–6, 20, 22, 29, 39, 41–42, 46, 69, 71–72, 78, 83, 94, 97, 106–110, 113–116, 118, 173, 205–219, 222, 224–228, 234, 238–245, 247–249, 252–253, 256–257, 259–261, 264–267, 307

Index — 327

- argument  107, 110, 211
- broad  110, 212, 243, 245
- contrastive  6, 211–212, 215–216, 227, 243
- marked  71, 97, 206–207, 211–212, 216, 227, 243, 260–261
- narrow  83, 212, 215–216, 227, 243, 245, 264
- non-contrastive  211–212, 216, 243, 245
- predicate  107, 211
- sentence  107, 110, 211
- unmarked  206–207, 211, 216, 243, 264

information structure  2, 6, 19, 20, 22, 29, 39, 42, 46, 69, 71–72, 76, 78, 105–116, 118, 173, 205–265, 266, 307–308
- marked  207, 211–212, 215–216, 227
- unmarked  206–207, 211–212, 216

information unit  106, 113–114, 118, 206–208, 210, 212, 215–218, 222, 225, 239–240, 242–244, 247, 249, 258, 265

instance  1, 6, 8, 10, 42, 44–46, 48, 50–54, 56, 60–68, 70, 73, 80, 86–87, 89–93, 98–105, 116–117, 119–120, 123, 125, 127–130, 142–143, 145–146, 152–153, 155, 157–160, 162–165, 168–171, 177, 241, 249, 256, 271–276, 278, 282, 284–285, 304–305
- actual  66–68, 99, 102, 145
- arbitrary  63, 66, 68, 272
- descriptional  67–68, 117, 304
- generalised  80, 98–103, 117, 119–120, 145,162, 164–165, 168–171, 208, 290, 304
- generic  42, 101, 105, 290
- intensional  65, 68
- non-specific  63, 66, 68, 87, 103
- random. *See* arbitrary
- representative  62, 64, 68, 272–273, 275, 285
- specific  10, 61, 65, 68, 100–101, 168
- virtual  61, 65–68, 117, 119, 165, 284–285, 304

instantiation  14, 46, 64–65, 98–99, 102, 105, 169, 312, 323

intensifier. *See* premodification
intensity  30, 219–222, 229–230, 233–236, 240, 242, 244–251, 265
intensionality  65–68, 74–75

interrogative  28–29, 31–34, 36, 54–55, 111, 142, 179–180, 207–209, 211–212, 215, 227
intonation  19–20, 21, 29–30, 106–109, 116, 205–265
intonation unit. *See* tone unit
inversion  4–5, 19, 39–40, 70–74, 119, 167, 214, 268

Langacker  3–4, 13–17, 40–41, 44–56, 59–63, 65–68, 82, 98–99, 101–2, 116–17, 119, 122–23, 128–30, 158, 160, 174–77, 271–73, 275–76, 304, 319

mirativity  263, 298–301
modality  20, 51, 55–57, 59, 66, 103, 118, 126, 128, 173–204, 255, 306–307
- deontic  179–183, 185, 191–195, 197–198
- dynamic  175–176, 181–183, 185, 191–195, 197–198, 202–203, 304, 306
- epistemic  51, 128, 179, 182–183, 185, 191–195, 1981, –200, 202–204, 255, 306–307
mood  29, 41, 47, 54–57, 59–60, 81, 84, 95, 98, 173, 263, 298–299

narrow focus. *See* focus
new-anchored information  249, 254, 281–282, 284–285, 288–297, 301
nominalisation  49, 184–185, 271, 276, 278, 285–286
non-contrastiveness. *See* implicature
non-exhaustiveness. *See* implicature
non-referentiality  2, 4–6, 33–34, 38–42, 44, 50–51, 54, 60, 66, 68–74, 76, 98, 105, 109, 117, 119, 142, 152, 165, 170, 174, 208, 248, 284–285, 304
non-uniqueness  8, 20, 73, 88, 158, 169, 172, 255, 275
noun-intensifier. *See* premodification
nuclear accent. *See* tonicity

partitive  128, 134, 136, 150–152, 155, 157–159, 166, 169–170, 282
pitch  23, 30, 94, 106, 113, 205–206, 210–212, 216–217, 219–222, 229–234, 236, 239, 240, 242–251, 253, 265

polarity 32, 55–56, 59, 184, 186, 212, 265
postdeterminer 129
post-head dependent 20, 118, 122, 126–128, 135–136, 148–152, 154, 157–159, 274, 279, 305
– post-head complement 127–28, 136, 148, 150, 152, 154–155, 158–159, 171, 305
– post-head modifier (or postmodifier) 20, 118, 127, 151, 158–159, 274, 279
  – categorising 127, 136, 150–151
  – determining 127, 136, 150–151
  – qualifying (or qualitative) 127, 136, 150–151, 154–155, 159
predeterminer 129
predicate-focus. *See* focus
predicate nominative 2–3, 12, 19–20, 21, 38, 40–46, 48, 50–52, 54–55, 57–58, 60–61, 66–69, 82, 96, 98, 111–112, 116–117, 119–121, 132–137, 139–144, 147–155, 157–163, 165–166, 170–172, 173, 184, 188, 191, 203, 207–208, 225, 248, 270, 285, 303–305
premodification 1, 51–54 121–127, 130–131, 133, 135–136, 141, 143, 148–151, 154–155, 159, 165, 169, 171, 203, 269, 305
– classifier 51–54, 122–127, 133, 135–136, 141, 155
– epithet 51, 121–122, 125–127, 130–131, 133, 135, 149, 154–159, 169 , 171, 203
– intensifier 122, 125–126, 131, 133, 135–136, 148–150
  – adjective-intensifier 125, 135–136, 148–149
  – noun-intensifier 125–126, 131, 135–136, 149–150
– metadesignative 122, 125–126, 130, 136, 149, 150, 153
– submodifier 51–52, 122, 125, 136, 148, 302
presupposition, information-structural 38, 78, 87, 106–110, 120, 205–208, 211, 214–216, 227–228, 236, 243, 247, 261, 264, 266–269, 291, 307–308
presupposition of existence 64–66, 68, 75, 77, 86–87, 98–99, 102–105, 117, 162, 165, 208, 264, 307
process-participant configuration 17–20, 41, 5845, 47, 80–81, 88, 95, 116, 132, 173–174

prominence 22, 30, 56, 58–59, 71, 78, 106, 108, 206, 219–220, 222, 229–230, 232–234, 236, 244–245, 247–248, 250, 252, 256, 258, 265
– prosodic 106, 108, 116, 206, 219–220, 222, 229, 233, 236, 244, 247–248, 250, 252, 265, 307
pseudoclefts 26, 90, 308, 314, 322

quantification 8, 20, 124, 126, 128, 130, 136, 146–147, 160, 162, 166, 169, 244, 273, 278, 305
– absolute 129–30, 136, 166, 170
– relative 129

recoverability 114, 152, 164, 206, 225, 229, 241, 243, 274, 281–282, 293, 295–298
reference (or referentiality) 4–5, 8–9, 33–34, 39–40, 51, 54, 56, 60–62, 64–65, 67–70, 73, 76–77, 86, 90–91, 98–99, 101, 104–105, 110, 117, 145, 168, 207–208, 272
– generalised 41, 98–103, 105, 145, 147, 164–165, 168, 208, 290, 304
– generic 62, 64, 67–68, 101, 103, 272–273, 275, 278, 285
– strong 75, 170
– weak 40, 69, 77, 105
referential status 41–42, 46, 60–61, 69, 73, 77, 80, 98, 100, 117, 119, 165, 168
relative clause 28, 51, 73, 86, 92, 127, 158, 257
representative instance. *See* instance
retrievability 43, 86, 120, 123, 128, 133–134, 142–143, 147, 155, 163– 164, 168, 171, 206, 261, 271–275, 278–283, 285, 290, 299, 305
reversibility (or subject-complement switch) 5, 7–8, 10–12, 27, 29, 60, 76, 81, 95, 112, 304

secondary determiner. *See* determiner
second-order entities 135, 137
sentence-focus. *See* focus
set-membership. *See* class-membership
SFG (Systemic Functional Grammar) 14–17, 56,

shell noun  145, 147
submodifier. *See* premodification

temporal focus, shift of  190–191, 203, 306
tense  55–57, 176–178, 181, 187
third-order entities  135–137, 140, 144, 147
ToBI, 221, 241
tonality  30, 114, 210, 212, 218, 222–225, 236, 242, 247, 251, 261
tone  23, 30, 94, 113, 210, 212–213, 217–219, 221–222, 236–238, 240, 243, 253–259
– compound  217–218
tone unit (TU)  23, 94, 113–115, 208, 210–212, 216, 218–219, 222–224, 229, 236–237, 243, 252–254, 257–258, 265, 307
tonic accent. *See* tonicity
tonicity  23, 30, 78, 113, 116, 210–212, 214–219, 221–222, 224–229, 236–237, 239–245, 247–249, 253, 257, 259–261, 264–265
topic  107, 145, 214, 251, 265, 268, 297, 300–301

type specification (TS)  8, 44, 46, 50, 52–54, 56, 60, 64–65, 67–68, 86, 90–92, 100–101, 116, 119–120, 122–125, 134–135, 143–147, 152–153, 155, 158–160, 165–168, 171, 209, 252, 270, 276, 278, 304–305

uniqueness  6, 8, 61, 84, 90–91, 93, 119, 128, 158–159, 167, 200, 252, 269–272, 274–276, 278, 282, 284–285, 308

value  4–5, 7–10, 38–43, 78–87, 94–97, 104–105, 114–118, 155–157, 199–200, 202–205, 214–217, 219–222, 224–230, 232–243, 253–255, 257–261, 263–268, 294–295, 297–305, 307–308
variable  1–10, 76–81, 83–87, 95–98, 103–105, 117–121, 154–158, 186–187, 190–194, 207–209, 218–222, 224–229, 232–240, 242–245, 249–251, 253–262, 264–270, 290–294, 301–305, 307–308

word order  7, 58, 81, 95, 311

www.ingramcontent.com/pod-product-compliance
Lightning Source LLC
Chambersburg PA
CBHW050514170426
43201CB00013B/1950